THE WORLD REIMAGINED

Americans and Human Rights in the Twentieth Century

Concerns about rights in the United States have a long history, but the articulation of global human rights in the twentieth century was something altogether different. Global human rights offered individuals unprecedented guarantees beyond the nation for the protection of political, economic, social, and cultural freedoms. *The World Reimagined* explores how these revolutionary developments first became believable to Americans in the 1940s and the 1970s through everyday vernaculars as they emerged in political and legal thought, photography, film, novels, memoirs and soundscapes. Together they offered fundamentally novel ways for Americans to understand what it means to feel free, culminating in today's ubiquitous moral language of human rights. Set against a sweeping transnational canvas, the book presents a new history of how Americans thought and acted in the twentieth-century world.

Mark Philip Bradley is the Bernadotte E. Schmitt Professor of History at the University of Chicago, where he also serves as the Faculty Director of the Pozen Family Center for Human Rights and Chair of the Committee on International Relations. He is the author of *Imagining Vietnam and America: The Making of Postcolonial Vietnam* (2000), which won the Harry J. Benda Prize from the Association for Asian Studies, and *Vietnam at War* (2009). He is the co-editor of *Familiar Made Strange: American Icons and Artifacts after the Transnational Turn* (2015), *Making Sense of the Vietnam Wars* (2008), and *Truth Claims: Representation and Human Rights* (2001). Bradley is the former president of the Society for Historians of American Foreign Relations. His work has been supported by the American Council of Learned Societies and the National Endowment for the Humanities.

HUMAN RIGHTS IN HISTORY

Edited by
Stefan-Ludwig Hoffmann, University of California, Berkeley
Samuel Moyn, Harvard University, Massachusetts

This series showcases new scholarship exploring the backgrounds of human rights today. With an open-ended chronology and international perspective, the series seeks works attentive to the surprises and contingencies in the historical origins and legacies of human rights ideals and interventions. Books in the series will focus not only on the intellectual antecedents and foundations of human rights, but also on the incorporation of the concept by movements, nation-states, international governance, and transnational law.

Also in the series:

THE WORLD REIMAGINED

Americans and Human Rights in
the Twentieth Century

Mark Philip Bradley

University of Chicago

CAMBRIDGE
UNIVERSITY PRESS

CAMBRIDGE
UNIVERSITY PRESS

One Liberty Plaza, 20th Floor, New York, NY 10006, USA

Cambridge University Press is part of the University of Cambridge.

It furthers the University's mission by disseminating knowledge in the pursuit of education, learning, and research at the highest international levels of excellence.

www.cambridge.org
Information on this title: www.cambridge.org/9780521829755

© Cambridge University Press 2016

First published 2016

Printed in the United States of America by Sheridan Books

A catalogue record for this publication is available from the British Library.

Library of Congress Cataloguing in Publication Data
Bradley, Mark, 1961– author.
The world reimagined : Americans and human rights in the twentieth century / Mark Philip Bradley (The University of Chicago).
New York, NY : Cambridge University Press, 2016.
Human rights in history   Includes bibliographical references and index.
LCCN 2016008587   ISBN 9780521829755 (hardback : alkaline paper)
LCSH: Human rights – United States – History – 20th century.
United States – Foreign relations – 1945-1989.   Human rights –
Language – History – 20th century.   Social change – History – 20th century.
War – Moral and ethical aspects – History – 20th century.
Decolonization – History – 20th century.   Globalization – Political aspects –
History – 20th century.   Transnationalism – Political aspects – History –
20th century.   World politics – 1945–1989.
LCC JC599.U5 B63   2016   DDC 323.0973/0904 – dc23
LC record available at https://lccn.loc.gov/2016008587

ISBN 978-0-521-82975-5 Hardback

To Ilsa Lillian and Peter Johan

Contents

Figures

Acknowledgments

If historians were slow to discover human rights as a subject of study, as this book suggests we were, much of the intellectual excitement for me as I worked on this project has come from knowing and learning from the remarkable community of senior and younger historians engaged in writing the new human rights history. Because other disciplines found human rights long before most historians did, my work has also been a welcome opportunity to draw on the methods and conceptual frames of anthropologists, political scientists, sociologists, and scholars of literature, visual culture, and the law who have written some of the most engaging studies of human rights thought and practice. Being part of the construction of a new field is simultaneously liberating and challenging, and it is a great pleasure to acknowledge my considerable debts to these multiple influences.

In the earliest stages of this project, I got to know the amazing Ken Cmiel. His untimely death meant that his own work on American human rights history would never be fully realized, but through our intense conversations I came to better understand where I should take my own work. Ken, as all his friends and colleagues know, was never shy in voicing his opinions, and it is not clear to me that where this book has ultimately gone would necessarily please him entirely. But his presence was always palpable for me as I wrote. I have known Sam Moyn now for the better part of a decade, first as an appreciative reader for Harvard University Press of his field-defining *Last Utopia*, but over time as a colleague and friend. Sam invited me to a terrific conference on 1970s human rights history at Freiburg that he co-organized with Jan Echols and that helped me fully understand the global scope of that decade; more recently he was kind enough to co-convene with me a conference at the University of Chicago on the history of humanitarianism. Sam has seldom agreed with anything I have written about human rights, but in another sign of his remarkable intellectual generosity he has included this book in the series he co-edits at Cambridge University Press. It is an honor to be a part of the series.

As I have struggled to understand the histories of the 1940s and 1970s, both their human rights dimensions and their larger transformative place in the international history of the twentieth century, my thinking has been informed by my conversations with Melani McAlister, Helle Porsdam, Robert Brier, Sarah Snyder, Carol Anderson, Barbara Keys, Andrew Preston, Fredrik Logevall, Brooke Blower, Odd Arne Westad, Heide Fehrenbach, Linda Kerber, Elizabeth Borgwardt, Akira Iriye, Petra Goode, Naoko Shibusawa, David Minto, Melvyn Leffler, Alice Conklin, Christian Ostermann, John Lewis Gaddis, William Hitchcock, Jay Winter, Vanessa Ogle, Heonik Kwon, Daniel Rodgers, Thomas Bender, Marilyn Lake, Paul Kramer, David Engelman, Linda Gordon, Mark Lawrence, Hang Nguyen, Allen Hunter, Susie Linfield, Eric Stover, Michael Allen, Steven Jensen, James Loeffler, Marco Duranti, Mary Dudziak, Penny Von Eschen, Daniel Cohen, Atina Grossman, Geoffrey Robinson, Monica McWilliams, Aryeh Neier, Michael Salman, Tim Borstelmann, J. Timothy Lovelace, Daniel Sargent, Kenton Clymer, Michael Cullinane, Benjamin Nathans, Brian Simpson, Emily Rosenberg, Devin Pendas, Didier Fassin, Peter Redfield, Jan Eckel, Carl Bon Tempo, Stephen Hopgood, Brad Simpson, Lou Roberts, and Al McCoy. Carol Anderson and Barbara Keys offered very helpful comments on portions of the manuscript. Melani McAlister read it all and provided the kind of feedback authors dream about.

I am also grateful for the commentary I have received at public lectures and presentations of work in progress at the University of Melbourne, University of California, Irvine, the Miller Center at the University of Virginia, the School of History and the Social Sciences at the Fundação Getulio Vargas in Rio de Janeiro, the Annenberg Seminar in History at the University of Pennsylvania, University of Copenhagen, University College Dublin, Claire College at University of Cambridge, Nuffield College at Oxford University, the Mershon Center for International

Security Studies at Ohio State University, Northern Illinois University, University of Illinois at Chicago, Temple University, Rice University, University of Utah, Indiana University, University of California, Los Angeles, University of Connecticut, Vassar College, University of Michigan, and the University of Wisconsin-Madison. I also appreciate the insights gained from commentators and the audiences for conference papers I presented at the annual meetings of the American Historical Association, Organization of American Historians, the American Studies Association, the Law and Society Association, and the Society for Historians of American Foreign Relations.

This book has had several institutional homes. My work on it began when I was a faculty member at the University of Wisconsin-Milwaukee. There I was fortunate enough to co-organize a conference on cultural representations of human rights with Patrice Petro, which also gave me the opportunity to come to know Leon Golub. His paintings became central to my analysis of American human rights vernaculars in the 1970s. I also profited from a fellowship with the Center for Twenty-First Century Studies under the direction of Daniel Sherman, who, along with my Milwaukee colleagues in the History Department, was so supportive of my work. I am especially grateful for conversations with Dan, Merry Wiesner-Hanks, Margo Anderson, Aims McGuiness, and Jasmine Alinder. When I moved to the History Department at Northwestern University, Michael Sherry both welcomed me and helped me become a better historian as I watched him in action as we co-taught and served on various thesis committees together. Mike has been kind to me in so many ways personally and professionally in the years since. Among other things he has helped me see how LGBTQ rights needed to become part of the story I told. My conversations with colleagues Laura Hein, Nancy MacLean, Peter Carroll, Susan Pearson, Ji-Yeon Yuh, Joseph Barton, Sara Maza, Tessie Liu, Karen Alter, and Brian Edwards at Northwestern were also instrumental in setting the broad analytical scope of this project into motion.

I completed the book at the University of Chicago, although as I think about it now, the project really did start there too. Michael Geyer organized what remains the single best academic conference I have ever attended – an interdisciplinary conference on torture in 1999. It was there that Michael convinced me to turn my focus to human rights history. Jim Hevia, Bruce Cumings, Jim Ketelaar, Jim Sparrow, Leora Auslander, Chris Stansell, and Jane Dailey have been my intellectual and professional anchors at Chicago. For helping me make this a better book through the inspiration of their own work and their engagement in mine, my thanks also to Tara Zahra, Tom Holt, Jan Goldstein, Adam Green, Amy Dru Stanley, Matthew Briones, Brodie Fischer, Mauricio Tenorio, Kathleen Belew, Ken Pomeranz, Julie Saville, Michael Rossi, Emily Osborn, Johanna Ransmeier, and Moishe Postone. Teaching about human rights at Chicago has been essential to my figuring out how to think its history. I learned much from a wonderful graduate seminar on writing human rights history, co-teaching Human Rights 2 with Patrick William Kelly, teaching a group of marvelous Chicago undergraduates in a human rights study abroad program in Vienna, and co-teaching the International History Seminar with Jim Hevia. Jim is a total skeptic on the very idea that human rights could have a history. That has been good for me.

I have also learned so much from the graduate students I have worked with at Chicago while writing this book, including Patrick William Kelly, Sarah Miller-Davenport, Shaul Mitelpunkt, C. J. Alverz, Hadji Bakara, Ingu Hwang, Jaewoong Jeon, Samuel Lebovic, Emma MacKinnon, John McCullum, Savi Sedlacek, Erica Tschinkel, and Lael Weinberger. All have or are writing spectacular dissertations. Patrick's and Ingu's recently completed theses on human rights history are already transforming the field, and I am especially grateful to Patrick for his acute reading of my manuscript just before it went to press. I also want to thank Michael Reese and Matthias Staisch, my colleagues in Chicago's Committee on International Relations, for their support. In my work with the Pozen Family Center for Human Rights at Chicago, I have been lucky to be a part of its lively interdisciplinary community. Getting to know the work of Sonali Thakkar, John Kelly, Justin Richland, Jennifer Pitts, Eric Slauter, Kimberly Nugyen, and Ben Laurence has been especially important to me, as has been our graduate student Human Rights Workshop so ably led by Lael Weinberger and Emma Mackinnon. I am also grateful for the support I have received from Susan Gzesh, who has helped me better understand what it means to do human rights practice. In all this, however, Michael Geyer looms very large. He was not only there at the beginning of the project but he also pushed and shaped it over its long gestation; perhaps most importantly for me, he always had confidence that it would come together in the end.

Marilyn Young has been key in what is one of those impossible to ever fully describe how important a person is in your life kind of relationship. She has been there for me since I was a graduate student – always full of encouragement but also reading critically and not at all shy about telling me what she thought was working and what, in her view, was quite definitely not working. Over the years, whether hanging out in the Family Circle at the Met, talking over meals, or just walking around the streets of New York together, it has been marvelous to become her friend. As Marilyn knows, this book could never have been written without her.

I am grateful for the financial support I have received for this project, including a Frederick Burkhardt Residential Fellowship for Recently Tenured Scholars from the American Council of Learned Societies and a National Endowment for the Humanities University Faculty Fellowship. I also want to acknowledge the support I received through the Weinberg College of Arts and Sciences at Northwestern University from Dean Daniel Linzer, and from the Division of the Social Sciences at the University of Chicago from Deans Mark Hansen, Mario Small, and David Nirenberg. I was lucky enough to have excellent research assistants at Chicago and offer deep thanks to Sarah Miller-Davenport, Andrew Miller, and Matthew Fouracre for their many efforts to track down key sources, and to Joy Lin for putting together the complex permissions needed for a book dealing in part with visual culture.

Portions of several chapters originally appeared in somewhat different form as follows: "After War: Making Peace as a Project of Moral Reconstruction," *Cambridge History of World War II*, volume 3, edited by Michael Geyer and Adam Tooze (Cambridge University Press, 2015): 528–51; "President Jimmy Carter's Inaugural Address," in *The Familiar Made Strange: American Icons after the Transnational Turn*, edited by Brooke L. Blower and Mark Philip Bradley (Ithaca: Cornell University Press, 2015): 141–54; "American Vernaculars: The United States and the Global Human Rights Imagination (Presidential Address)," *Diplomatic History* 38.1 (January 2014): 1–21; "The United States and Global Human Rights Politics in the 1940s," in *Civil Religion, Human Rights and International Relations*, edited by Helle Porsdam (London: Edward Elgar, 2012): 118–35;

"The Origins of the 1970s Global Human Rights Imagination," *The 'Long 1970s': Human Rights, East-West Détente and Transnational Relations,* edited by Poul Villaume, Rasmus Mariager and Helle Porsdam (Abingdon: Ashgate, 2016): 15–32; and "Approaching the Universal Declaration of Human Rights," in *The Human Rights Revolution: An International History,* edited by Akira Iriye, Petra Goode, and William Hitchcock (New York: Oxford University Press, 2011): 327–43.

It has been such a pleasure to work with Cambridge University Press on this book. Lew Bateman signed the project (I know, Lew, that was some time ago now and you have the patience of Job), and it has come into being under the watchful eye of Debbie Gershenowitz. Her close reading of the entire manuscript at two critical moments has helped clarify its broader architecture. Working with Debbie is a true delight. My thanks too to her assistant Kristina Deusch for her considerable help with a number of production issues along with Marielle Poss for moving the book through production so splendidly and to Gail Naron Chalew for her excellent copy editing.

My mom and dad did not live to see the book completed, but they are always with me in all that I do. My wife Anne Hansen's patience and good cheer allowed the book to be written, and her careful reading of parts of the manuscript at key points was essential to its completion. My children, Ilsa and Peter, because of who they are and their own political commitments, made this a way better book than it might have been otherwise. This one is for you, with love!

How It Feels to be Free

A T THE DAWN OF THE TWENTY-FIRST CENTURY, human
rights became enshrined as the dominant moral language of our
time. Nobel Peace Prize winner Elie Wiesel described human rights as
"a world-wide secular religion." Former Secretary General of the United
Nations Kofi Annan termed human rights "the yardstick by which we
measure human progress."[1] Faith in the moral authority accorded to
invocations of human rights crosses the present-day political landscape
from the corridors of state power to the streets of oppositional grassroots
politics. U.S. president George W. Bush and British prime minister Tony
Blair turned to human rights to defend the wars in Afghanistan and Iraq.
So too did the Russian feminist punk rockers Pussy Riot to protest their
imprisonment after they performed "Mother of God, Drive Putin Out"
in a Moscow cathedral. The contemporary presence of human rights has
become almost prosaic. Some American fifth graders now spend as much
time studying the Universal Declaration of Human Rights as they do
Mark Twain's *Tom Sawyer*. Even the fiercest critics of the global scope and
uneven enforcement of human rights, who rue that "the age of human
rights is upon us," acknowledge the ubiquity of its moral power.[2] It was
not always so.

On October 1, 1949, at the Musée Galliéra in Paris, the United Nations
Educational, Social, and Cultural Organization (UNESCO) opened a
massive public exhibition to celebrate "mankind's age-old fight for freedom" in honor of the adoption of the Universal Declaration by the
United Nations just one year earlier. A document that has become almost
commonplace in the twenty-first century was unfamiliar if not downright
strange in the late 1940s. In fact, human rights had been virtually absent

1

from the world stage before the mid-twentieth century. Most striking in retrospect about the UNESCO exhibition was the apparent need by its organizers to teach visitors what human rights actually were and to inculcate in them a shared obligation to bring human rights to life. The exhibition's primary purpose was a didactic one, making visible what the organizers termed "the universal nature of the responsibility for achieving and defending human rights."

Visitors to the UNESCO exhibition first encountered a small planetarium in a darkened room. Through its windows they saw the Earth turning in space – its political divisions symbolically left unmarked – while listening to a recorded voice that read from the first three articles of the Universal Declaration with its promises that "everyone has the right to life, liberty, and the security of person." Adjacent to Earth, the exhibitors had placed a small drawing of Adam and Eve frolicking under the apple tree to lay down a marker for their vision of human rights as rooted in an almost timeless past. Exiting the planetarium, visitors strolled through a hallway of illustrated panels and panoramas that depicted "man's slow emancipation" from prehistoric times to the present to "illustrate the contribution of all peoples, nations and civilizations to the sum total of Human Rights." Panels depicting the *Rights of Man through the Ages* presented the Magna Carta, the U.S. Declaration of Independence, and the French Declaration of the Rights of Man while *Fighters for Freedom* featured such figures as Montesquieu, Abraham Lincoln, and Mahatma Gandhi.

Visitors next entered several rooms that offered a pictorial "history book" of the 1930s to demonstrate "how rights were abused and violated by totalitarian states." This state of affairs, the exhibit argued, led to the outbreak of World War II and to "democratic states" working "to re-assert rights" through the establishment of the United Nations. Passing into a hall in which a dozen pillars devoted to the thirty articles of the 1948 Universal Declaration illustrated past examples of their protections and violations, viewers were reminded of the centrality of the Declaration in the "struggle for human rights." The final room of the exhibition was "devoted to the duties each person must fulfill if Human Rights are to become and remain a reality for all." That pressing task, organizers told visitors as they were leaving the exhibition, "will only be complete when the Universal Declaration of Human Rights has been converted into fact."[3]

The pedagogic narrative of human rights history in the UNESCO exhibition was largely a fiction. Even beyond the imagined reach of the human rights past to the biblical times of Adam and Eve, its insistence on a linear and progressive history across time and space elided the astonishing singularity of the turn to global human rights in the 1940s. Without question, concerns about rights have a long history that can be traced to the early modern world, if not before. Rights talk was central to the French, American, and Haitian revolutions.[4] The antislavery movement and the rise of nineteenth-century humanitarian practices opened up new forms of transnational empathy.[5] So too did appeals in the early twentieth century that drew public awareness to humanitarian suffering in the imperial Congo and the Armenian genocide.[6] At the same time, the collective rights of minority peoples also began to attract international attention.[7] But the articulation of *global* human rights in the 1940s was something altogether different. The unprecedented guarantees they offered extending beyond the confines of the nation-state to universal political, civil, economic, and social rights for everyone fundamentally challenged dominant understandings of the relationships between individuals, states, and the world community. Over the second half of the century, the growing global presence of human rights would point toward new ways of feeling what it meant to be free. But for visitors to the UNESCO exhibition in 1949, human rights remained a historical novelty.

This book examines how and why human rights went from an exotic aspirational language to an everyday vernacular. It does so by exploring the entanglements of the United States in the rise of what I call the twentieth-century global human rights imagination. The book asks three central questions: What set global human rights in motion and made them believable for Americans after 1940? How did human rights simultaneously come to reflect and shape transformations in broader American sensibilities of being in the world? Why have human rights become a ubiquitous moral language today, and what are its limits?

To have posed such questions about human rights as a historian even a decade ago might have seemed quixotic at best. The history of twentieth-century human rights has only recently begun to be told. The most enduringly influential accounts of the place of the United States in the post-1945 world order left human rights to the side, as did most traditional accounts of American diplomatic history. Except for a brief and seemingly obligatory nod to Jimmy Carter's "discovery" of human rights in the 1970s, most international historians saw human rights as no more than a sideshow that rightly remained in the shadows of the more important Cold War struggle between the United States and the Soviet Union.[8] Nor did historians of social movements in postwar America devote sustained attention to human rights as such. Civil rights, not human rights, were more commonly the object of study.[9] The flagship *American Historical Review* did not publish an article with the phrase "human rights" in its title until 1998, and eight years would pass before an article dealing with modern human rights history appeared in the journal.

The first decade of this century, however, brought a dramatic upsurge of historical interest in human rights. As one former president of the American Historical Association put it, "we are all historians of human rights." The decade of the 1940s first became the subject of the new human rights history, most notably in studies that focused on the making of a UN-based human rights order. More recently, scholars have begun to excavate the global explosion of human rights concerns in the 1970s. Once at the margins, human rights and its history are now at the intellectual vanguard of the historical profession.[10] But if we have a growing and sophisticated body of global human rights history that was almost unimaginable a decade ago, what we should make of human rights for the larger narratives we tell about U.S. engagement in the twentieth-century world is considerably less clear.

Much of this new work has pivoted around a contested debate over when global human rights politics and its American iterations really began to matter. On one side are historians who view the 1940s as the magic decade, claiming that the normative heft of the Universal Declaration of Human Rights still hovers powerfully over contemporary practices. Another group of historians is less sure, arguing that the alleged human rights revolution of the 1940s was little more than "death in birth"[11] and dismissing the Universal Declaration as a Great Power feint that most contemporaries were certain would never disturb the smooth operation of realist power politics. For them, the 1970s was when the real business of human rights politics got started as a global moral vocabulary that trumped once-prevailing ideologies of the Cold War and Third World revolutionary nationalism. It is, they argue, the indispensable decade that set today's global human rights landscape in motion.[12]

In this take-no-prisoners competitive sweepstakes for the origins of the contemporary preoccupation with human rights, both parties bring a similar conception of time and narrative to their arguments that needlessly hamper efforts to make sense of a transnational human rights past. The literary scholar Frank Kermode asks us to think about the ticking of a clock. "We agree," he writes, "that it says *tick-tock*," but in doing so "it is we who provide the fictional difference between the two sounds: *tick* is our word for physical beginning, and *tock* our word for end." But such commonsensical perspectives, he argues, ignore the critical interval between "*tock*" and "*tick*." By inventing narratives to order the world that favor "the closed to the open," Kermode tellingly suggests, we can ignore fortuitous moments – most famously, he notes, the enigmatic appearances of the Man in the Mackintosh in Joyce's *Ulysses* – that defy more sweeping narratives, but are nonetheless constitutive of them.[13] Much of the new human rights history is keen to tell what Kermode would call a conventional *tick-tock* narrative. It searches for a point of origin, a take-off moment, in which human rights gain the traction that makes them a central presence today. Tick is the 1940s or the 1970s. Tock is now.

What human rights were understood to be by the historical actors who gave them shape and form in the mid-twentieth century and beyond is a considerably messier and more complex process than the linear narratives of the new human rights history would allow. Human rights history can read quite differently if we think about the second half of the twentieth century through the prism of the interval between *tock* and *tick*, attentive to the potential men (and women) in mackintoshes. This book returns to the 1940s and 1970s as its central focus. But it approaches the two decades as contrapuntal moments to offer both an alternative narrative of the place of the United States in twentieth-century human rights history and a new approach to the writing of global human rights history itself. The book is not so much concerned with the state and Great Power politics or with the diplomatic negotiations through which the international human rights legal regime came to be formed, the subjects of much of the new human rights history. The central protagonists of this book are what we now call nonstate actors, although they often did not identify themselves in that way in the historical moment. Diplomats and policy makers are not entirely absent in the pages that follow. But the focus is on what we might in retrospect call human rights amateurs who collectively brought into being a distinctly twentieth-century global human rights imagination; they include photographers, lawyers, film-makers, doctors, musicians, physicists, statisticians, writers, clergy, grass-roots activists, students, and senior citizens. Quite simply, it was these "amateurs" who made human rights after mid-century believable to a variety of American publics. Critically they did so on a transnational canvas.

This book situates their efforts against the epochal global ruptures that defined the 1940s and the 1970s and the very different ways in which these two decades shaped the place of the United States in the twentieth-century world. Importantly, both decades were liminal moments in which the very structures and meanings of international order were up for grabs. In neither was it clear at the outset what was to come. The Cold War of the late 1940s was an almost unimagined possibility for most Americans as World War II came to a close. Similarly few would have anticipated that the superpower confrontation between the United States and the Soviet Union that underlay the high Cold War international order after the 1940s would begin to come undone in the 1970s. This contrapuntal history is especially attentive to the critical place of contingency in how the 1940s and 1970s were understood and felt by the Americans who lived through them. It recovers the interpretatively rich points of friction between the global and the local in these two threshold eras that made possible the capacious and often revolutionary lenses through which Americans began to reimagine the world around them, among them newly formed conceptions of human rights.[14]

Global human rights emerged for the first time on the international stage and in the United States in the 1940s as part of a larger transnational conversation about the meanings of the postwar peace. A constellation of sometimes inchoate but always interlocking internationalist sentiments – among them calls for multilateralism, global justice, international policing, and humanitarian intervention, along with human rights – lay in tension with territorially bounded conceptions of unilateral state sovereignty as the prime mover of relations between nations. In this postwar moment when prevailing notions of sovereignty and the international were in flux, a variety of transnational and local actors pushed against what were seen as the era's elastic conditions of possibility. Some operated in the elite sphere of the United Nations. Others emerged in more quotidian local spaces. Together they created the imaginative terrain of what might transform the postwar world. The 1940s moment proved fleeting, engulfed and largely pushed to the side by the political and social force of the Cold War and, in what was just as unanticipated, the rapid-fire pace of decolonization. But before it passed, human rights became believable in the United States not just at the level of writing international declarations and covenants but also as a powerful weapon to advance domestic campaigns for racial justice at home. America was both in the world, and the world was in America.

A similarly open-ended and transformative global moment marked the 1970s, though ultimately with very different implications for what human rights would come to mean in an American context. In that decade an intensification of global capitalism and the emergence of neoliberalism, shifting patterns of international migration, the end of empire, and the transnational diffusion of new technology and media all pushed against the nation-state–based international order that structured the high Cold War era. These fragmentations in world order enabled novel forms of transnational humanitarian, environmental, and human rights politics to come into being. A growing belief in the authenticity of the interior world for making sense of individual suffering was at the heart of this new politics. Lived experience, moral witness, and testimonial truth became keywords of the era, reshaping the contours of global politics and morality and remaking global human rights thought and practice. But unlike the 1940s when Americans were present at the creation, human rights in the 1970s got almost everywhere else first before coming to the United States. Nor did human rights come home again as a primary means for addressing domestic social suffering and injustice. Without question the world shaped the thought and practice of human rights in 1970s America, but human rights became a resonant vernacular largely for problems beyond the United States.

The ways in which the global transformations that propelled human rights were experienced in 1940s and 1970s America form one of the central concerns of this book. How it felt to have rights or to lose them was critical to the growing believability of the global human rights imagination and its American vernaculars. So too were new ways of apprehending how the suffering of strangers could come to matter as much as one's own. In foregrounding shifts in global affect and feeling for the making of human rights history, this analysis marks a sharp departure from the more common practices of writing international and human rights history. Historians seemingly more easily articulate the imagined physicality of geopolitics than structures of feeling, and yet the historical present is often understood affectively before it is perceived in other ways. Recent work in literary theory helps us see what has generally remained invisible to historians. "The present is not an object but a mediated affect," writes Lauren Berlant. It is "a thing that is sensed and under constant revision ... a genre of social time and practice in which a relation of person or worlds is sensed to be changing but the rules of habitation and the genres of storytelling about it are unstable."[15] Human rights and its believability emerged in just such volatile and unstable moments.

To uncover the pivotal place of affect in the rise of global human rights during the 1940s and the 1970s requires the use of a broader range of sources that get at these more allusive historical forces. This book draws on traditional, political, diplomatic, and legal texts, but it also turns to such imaginative and visual sources as photographs of Depression-era social suffering, newsreel footage of atrocities in Nazi death camps, and memoirs, folk art, and soundscapes depicting torture and other human rights abuses in 1970s Latin America and the Soviet Union to make sense of how transformations in affect shaped the more visceral ways in which American began to understand human rights. It is, for instance, far more concerned with exploring how an encounter with Dorothea Lange's *Migrant Mother* or Alexandr Solzhenitsyn's epic three-volume *Gulag Archipelago* might have shaped American understandings of what human rights mean and how their absence can feel than the ins and outs of the drafting of the Universal Declaration of Human Rights or 1970s-era U.S. human rights diplomacy with the Soviet Union.

That these American sensibilities had global roots is also critical to the arguments made here. To focus on the place of the United States in the making of a global human rights imagination might initially strike readers as a return to the exceptionalist narratives that have too often informed the writing of American history.[16] The approach here is quite the opposite, seeking to provincialize how Americans operated on the world stage by lifting up the critical role of processes initially set in motion far beyond U.S. shores. In doing so, it contributes to ongoing efforts to situate American history in frames both smaller and larger than the nation.[17] Decentering the United States in the history of human rights normalizes American actors. They did not, as some U.S. historians have suggested, bring human rights to the world. Instead like local actors in a variety of geographical places in and after the mid-twentieth century, Americans struggled to find a vernacular language to articulate the meanings of what for them too was an entirely novel turn to global human rights talk.

Provincializing America also helps us rethink how to write the history of the engagement of other states and peoples in the making of the twentieth-century global human rights order. Much of the existing history of human rights often feels closed in on itself, so intent on recovering what has been a lost history that it fails to consider how human rights shaped and were shaped by the larger historical processes of empire, decolonization, the Cold War, and globalization after 1945. Frictions between the global and the local that created an American vernacular of human rights operated in other geographical spaces as well. The multiple human rights vernaculars that such frictions helped produce were always inflected by local particularities, and yet we know too little about them. What a displaced person in the DP camps established in the immediate aftermath of World War II or a Soviet, Chilean, or South Korean dissident in the 1970s understood human rights to be is only just beginning to come into view. In writing about American understandings of human rights from the bottom and the middle up, rather than from the top down, while being attentive to the wider global processes through which they emerged, this book seeks to advance what might be considered a second generation of human rights history.

Finally, viewing the place of Americans in the making of the global human rights imagination through a transnational lens challenges how historians have explained the broader patterns of U.S. engagement in the world after 1940. In more conventional accounts of U.S. foreign relations, the preponderance of American power in the second half of the twentieth century invariably puts the United States at the center of the world. "The present world system sprung from the United States more than other actors in the global theatre," writes Walter LaFeber, capturing what remains a virtual consensus among American diplomatic historians. "The influence of that system on the United States" was never "as great as the American influence on the system." More recently Fredrik Logevall has argued that decentering the United States is "to risk being ahistorical, by assigning greater influence to some actors than they may in fact deserve. The United States is not merely one power among many and has not been for a very long time."[18] Daniel Rodgers, whose work has been at the center of the recent transnational turn in the writing of American history, offers an intriguing twist on these more traditional formulations. He agrees that Americans "were everywhere after 1945," but argues that their collective self-perceptions that the United States "saved the world" through its intervention in World War II meant "it would not thereafter be easy to imagine that there was still much to learn from it." Americans were always "in the world" during the second half of the twentieth century, Rodgers suggests, but they were almost never "of it."[19] Yet, the interplay between the global and the local in the making of human rights vernaculars in the United States brings into question assertions of both the unilateral exercise of American power and the hermetic terms of its global engagement. Here, power and influence were more often relational and multidirectional. In the realm of human rights, Americans could be both in and of the world.

The World Reimagined has two parts. The first examines the surprising prominence of human rights language in 1940s America during and after World War II in a broad cosmopolitan frame. The chapters explore the visual, textual, and legal dimensions of the wartime human rights imagination. Visual forms of rights consciousness emerged alongside sustained wartime conversations that produced remarkably detailed proposals for an international bill of rights, anticipating the claims made in the 1948 Universal Declaration. The chapters in Part One also consider the ways in which the believability of this new language prompted sustained efforts in the immediate postwar period to introduce human rights into African American, Asian American, and Native America struggles against racial discrimination at home, as well as the forces that pushed human rights to the side for most Americans after the 1940s.

Part Two takes up the rediscovery and remaking of the global human rights imagination and its American vernaculars in the 1970s. It begins far outside the United States, suggesting that the fragmentation of the Cold War international order and the new affective forms of transnational politics it produced offered the starting point for what human rights would come to mean for Americans. Receptivity to this new global human rights imaginary – one that lifted up individual victims of human rights and privileged political and civil rights to bodily integrity over economic and social rights – was conditioned by a fracturing of the collective bonds that had shaped the American Cold War state. These chapters explore the transnationally inflected making of popular American conceptions of human rights over the decade and chart the explosion of a nonstate grassroots and professional movement that ultimately embedded human rights in everyday thought and practice in the United States.

The visions of human rights in 1940s and 1970s America were always partial and uneven. Some human rights in some places came to matter to Americans. Human rights in other modes and locales did not. And far from all Americans embraced human rights in these decades. The array of true believers was remarkably diverse in the 1940s; they were somewhat less so in the 1970s. A coda draws on these complex and sometimes contradictory legacies for our contemporary age of human rights. After September 11, another liminal moment in how American saw their place in the world, the disjuncture between how Americans have imagined what human rights can do and everyday practice is stark. Torture and drone warfare as weapons of choice in the war against terror, mass incarceration, racial profiling, and enormous and rising imbalances of wealth and income put new pressures on the believability of human rights.

The singer and activist Nina Simone, in a contralto voice that rang with fierce honesty, captured the incongruities between American rights talk and practice when she sang,

> I wish I knew how it would feel to be free …
> I wish I could share all the love that's in my heart,
> Remove all the bonds that keep us apart,
> And I wish you could know what it means to be me,
> Then you'd see and agree that every man should be free.[20]

Human rights since the mid-twentieth century came to offer Americans one way of understanding what it means to be free. But no matter how deeply felt, the modes and forms of transnational empathy that enabled the growing belief in human rights did not necessarily bring freedom in its wake. Many Americans today still wish they knew how it would feel to be free. The reach and the limits of the global human rights imagination and its American vernaculars can help us understand why.

PART ONE

THE 1940S

O N SATURDAY EVENING, December 10, 1949, more than three thousand people packed into Carnegie Hall in New York City. They did so to celebrate the first anniversary of the adoption of the Universal Declaration of Human Rights by the United Nations at a concert performed by the Boston Symphony Orchestra with Leonard Bernstein at the podium. The crowd in the hall was largely made up of delegates to the United Nations General Assembly, which hours before had just brought its fourth regular session to a close, as well as many of those figures like Eleanor Roosevelt who were seen as playing central roles in drafting the Declaration. A larger listening public heard the event as it was broadcast on radio and televised live by the National Broadcasting Company.[1]

The program opened with a new work that had been commissioned specially for the event, Aaron Copland's *Preamble for a Solemn Occasion*, a short six-minute piece for orchestra and narrator. Copland took as his text for the composition this portion of the Preamble to the 1945 UN Charter:

> We the peoples of the United Nations, determined to save succeeding generations from the scourge of war, which twice in our lifetime has brought untold sorrow to mankind, and to reaffirm faith in fundamental human rights, in the dignity and worth of the human person, in the equal rights of men and women of all nations large and small, and ... to promote social progress and better standards of life in larger freedom, ... have resolved to combine our efforts to accomplish these aims.[2]

When Sir Lawrence Olivier, the preeminent actor of the day, came onto the stage at Carnegie Hall, the audience stood in silence as he read the full preamble to the Universal Declaration of Human Rights and its more specific calls for the respect and observance of individual human rights as the common standard of achievement for all peoples and nations. Copland's *Preamble* began in a dissonant vein aimed to evoke the scourge and sorrows of war. The mood shifted in its second section toward a more triumphant sensibility supported by the liberal use of brass and percussion. Olivier read from the United Nations Charter, his voice quietly underlined by an orchestral reprise of the opening segment of the piece, after which the triumphal valences of the second section returned to bring the composition to an affirmative and ringing climax.[3]

The musical language of Copland's *Preamble for a Solemn Occasion* and its reception in Carnegie Hall capture a moment in the making of the twentieth century global human imagination that was extraordinary, if still imperfectly, understood. Upon adoption in 1948 by the UN General Assembly, the Universal Declaration of Human Rights was the first international instrument to articulate global human rights norms and duties. Its thirty articles were hammered out over a period of two years in committees that brought together such leading international figures as Eleanor Roosevelt, René Cassin of France, Charles Malik of Lebanon, and P.C. Chang of China along with the active participation of representatives from a variety of Latin American states, the Soviet Union and India. The Declaration's catalog of rights was as expansive as its sweeping guarantees of their protections. "Everyone is entitled to all the rights and freedoms set forth in the Declaration," its authors promised, "without distinction of any kind."[4] Nothing, seemingly not even state sovereignty, was to trump the individual, political, civil, economic, and social rights enumerated in the document. In its concern with the individual, its expansive sensibility about what constituted human rights, and its global aspirations for their protection, there had simply never before been anything quite like the Universal Declaration.

Along with the Declaration, regional and international bodies produced an unparalleled series of declarations, covenants, and conventions in what became the human rights moment of the 1940s. Among with them were the Nuremberg Principles (1946), the American

Declaration of the Rights and Duties of Man (1948), the Convention on the Prevention and Punishment of the Crime of Genocide (1948), the Fourth Geneva Convention Relative to the Protection of Civilian Persons in Time of War (1949), the European Convention on Human Rights (1950), and the United Nations Conventions Relating to the Status of Refugees (1951) and Stateless Persons (1954); also drafted during this period were the documents that would become the International Covenants on Political and Civil Rights (1966) and Economic, Social, and Cultural Rights (1966).

Setting all of this in motion, as it did the Copland *Preamble,* was the United Nations Charter. Along with the "affirmation" of human rights in its Preamble, the Charter's purposes and principles called on member states of the United Nations to promote "universal respect for … human rights and fundamental freedoms for all without distinction as to race, sex, language or religion." The kind of work human rights might do in the global sphere emerged most clearly in Articles 55 and 56, with pledges by all member states "to take joint and separate action in cooperation with the organization" to promote the observance of human rights. The Charter also called into being a Human Rights Commission that contemporaries rightly anticipated would draft the Universal Declaration. From the Charter's preamble to its more specialized provisions, human rights infused the aims of the proposed United Nations.[5]

That human rights were all over the UN Charter and the 1940s is more of a puzzle than it might seen today when human rights have become an omnipresent and naturalized global language. In the summer of 1945, however, the claim that the promotion of individual human rights was a fundamental purpose of global community was unparalleled, if not revolutionary. Just a quarter-century earlier, the League of Nations Covenant, which established the precursor of the United Nations, made no mention of human rights. Its preamble focused on the more familiar relationships among states, international law, and war. The Covenant did give brief attention to promoting "humane labor conditions" and addressed the problem of "traffic in women and children,"[6] but human rights were nowhere present. What were they doing in the Charter? How did they get there? And what meanings did contemporaries begin to accord to human rights?

Human rights historians of the 1940s have answered those questions in quite different ways, none of them fully satisfying. For some the apparent centrality of human rights in the decade emerged in tandem with a global populism in which wartime sacrifices and suffering demanded a rights-based "people's peace." For others, the wartime rhetoric of the Atlantic Charter and Franklin Roosevelt's Four Freedoms address was so powerful that these documents acted as the "star" that guided the drafters of the human rights language in the Charter and the Universal Declaration.[7] Without question, the language of human rights was circulating among global and American publics in ways that it had not before. But in leaping as these historians often do from the 1941 Atlantic Charter to the 1945 UN Charter and the 1948 UN Universal Declaration of Human Rights, they leave largely unexamined the intricate processes through which human rights came to be understood by American publics and the transnational forces that shaped them.[8]

More skeptical voices have argued that the presence of human rights in the UN Charter was little more than oratorical "ornamentalism," a kind of sop to pesky if well-intentioned internationalist do-gooders. Moreover, they question whether much came of the Charter's human rights promises, noting that the aspirational quality of the Universal Declaration lacked any kind of legal grounding.[9] Skeptics do make clear the sometimes unsavory realities behind the lofty rhetoric of human rights. It was Field Marshal Jan Smuts, among the architects of the South African's postwar regime of apartheid, who drafted the human rights language in the Charter's Preamble. They also usefully throw up cautionary flags against seeing the moment of the 1940s as what Winston Churchill famously termed "the enthronement of human rights."[10] It was not. In the years after the celebration of human rights at Carnegie Hall in December 1949, human rights could sometimes seem to occupy the margins of an international order shaped by the Cold War and decolonization. Indeed the front-page headlines of the *New York Times* the day following the Carnegie Hall concert did not mention human rights, but instead trumpeted imminent Indonesian independence, the introduction of Chinese military advisors into the French war in Vietnam, and the negotiations that would lead to the establishment of the North Atlantic Treaty Organization.[11]

Yet if human rights were simply a throwaway line in 1940s, it is difficult to make out why American policy makers and the nonstate actors pushing them along wanted to use that language at all. In drafting the UN Charter they could have turned to more familiar and established idealistic rhetoric about promoting "international co-operation ... to achieve international peace and security" that had framed the League of Nations Covenant and been the default mode for most American internationalists in the 1920s and 1930s. Indeed this more traditional, and familiar, internationalist language is present in the Charter. Its drafters could have left well enough alone. Even from the most cynical point of view that sees the employment of human rights as mere window dressing, the choice of that particular vocabulary and not another is striking.

In fact, the prominence of human rights language in the 1940s marks a critical moment in which an emergent global human rights imagination began to manifest itself in world and American cultural politics. Dismissing it entirely obscures how the global human rights imagination came to be in the first place and why Americans, for whom rights talk had been a generative if usually contested part of domestic political culture for centuries, turned to what at the onset of World War II was still an unfamiliar language of human rights. Human rights in the 1940s were clearly present for American wartime rights advocates who worked to put them into the Charter of the United Nations and for those who helped draft the Universal Declaration. A focus on the top-down elite sphere of human rights norm making at the United Nations, which has been held by so much of the history of human rights in the 1940s, can obscure an understudied but perhaps even more prevalent constellation of everyday on-the-ground efforts to harness the fluidities of the immediate postwar moment for the making of a new global human rights politics. Human rights were just as present in the 1940s for an African American couple in Detroit about to lose their home because of a restrictive racial housing covenant and for the Iowa widow of a decorated Native American soldier when a cemetery reminded her of its "Caucasian Only" burial policy as his body was about to be placed into the grave.

There was sometimes more than a trace of American exceptionalism in the embrace of human rights in the United States. And the moment of the 1940s proved to be a fleeting one. There are few direct causal lines between it and the resurgence of human rights in 1970s America. The deeply felt and transnationally inflected American place in the making of the 1940 global human rights imagination is more diffuse. But in the moment it was revolutionary, especially in the breadth and depth of its cosmopolitan engagement. The imaginative, political, ethical, and legal sensibilities that gave the wartime global human rights imagination shape and form began quite modestly. One place to track its origins is a Southern California pea-picker camp in February 1936.

CHAPTER 1

At Home in the World

ATE ON A COLD AND RAINY DAY in February 1936, while driving north on U.S. Highway 101, the photographer Dorothea Lange passed a crude hand-lettered sign near Nipomo, California, that read "PEA-PICKER CAMP." She drove past, eager to get home to her family after a month of taking pictures in the field. But as she did, Lange asked herself: "Dorothea, how about that camp back there? What is the situation back there?" She turned around. Lange later wrote,

> I saw and approached a hungry and desperate mother. ... I do not remem-
> ber how I explained my presence or my camera to her, but I do remem-
> ber she asked me no questions. I made five exposures, working closer and
> closer from the same direction. I did not ask her name or her history. She
> told me her age, that she was thirty-two. She said that they had been living
> on frozen vegetables from the surrounding fields, and birds that the chil-
> dren killed. She had just sold the tires from her car to buy food. There she
> sat in that lean-to tent with her children huddled around her, and seemed
> to know that my pictures might help her, and so she helped me. There was
> a sort of equality about it.[1]

One of the photographs Lange made on that bleak afternoon became known as *Migrant Mother* (Figure 1.1): it has become perhaps the most familiar image of Depression-era America. It was part of an explosion of mass-circulated images in the 1930s that depicted what in today's par-lance would almost inevitably be called violations of individual human rights. As many as 250,000 similarly themed photographs were made over the decade under the auspices of the Farm Security Administra-tion (FSA), a New Deal agency created to address the problems of rural

1.1. Dorothea Lange. *Migrant Mother.* 1936. LC-DIG-fsa-8b29516. FSA/OWI Collection, Prints & Photographs Division, Library of Congress.

poverty. Others were commissioned for use in the newly burgeoning photojournalism of the period or were the individual projects of the photographers themselves. The work of Lange and such photographers as Walker Evans, Margaret Bourke-White, Ben Shahn, Tina Modotti, and Carl Mydans in this era collectively captured moments in the lives of the disadvantaged and oppressed, making their situations legible for those who viewed their work and implicitly, and sometimes explicitly, urging viewers to make these problems their own. As Lange said, the photographers might help their subjects, but the images might also expand the moral horizons of those who encountered them.

Seven years after Dorothea Lange made *Migrant Mother*, the Office of War Information (OWI) organized an outdoor exhibition titled "This Is

Our War" in February 1943 at Rockefeller Center in New York City. It put human rights at its center. In the fifteen months since the United States officially entered World War II, Franklin Roosevelt's Four Freedoms address, the Atlantic Charter, and the United Nations Declaration had emerged for wartime policy makers as an almost sacred trinity that expressed the purposes of the United States and its allies in the war against Germany, Italy, and Japan. All three were couched in what for many Americans was the still unfamiliar language of human rights. In his January 1941 Four Freedoms address, President Franklin Roosevelt told Congress that "freedom means the supremacy of human rights everywhere." The August 1941 Atlantic Charter promised the "right of all peoples to choose the government under which they will live" and in victory offered "the assurance that the men in all lands may live out their lives in freedom from fear and want." If the words "human rights" were absent from this document, American officials made clear that their sensibilities were a palpable presence. "There must be no swerving," Undersecretary of State Sumner Welles told one audience, "from the great human rights and liberties established by the Atlantic Charter." The United Nations Declaration, a joint statement of war aims by the United States and its allies issued in January 1942, proclaimed, "Complete victory over their enemies is essential to defend life, liberty, independence and religious freedom and to preserve human rights and justice in their own lands as well as in other lands." In speech after speech in the early years of the war, American diplomats pointed to the realization of what they termed the "concepts and spirit of human rights and human freedom" as a primary aim of the war.[2]

At the center of "This Is Our War" was an altar-like structure that displayed copies of the Atlantic Charter and the United Nations Declaration (Figure 1.2). Surrounding it were four large allegorical sculptures, with soaring golden plinths arising out of each of them to illustrate how victory in war would bring with it the attainment of the Four Freedoms. A dead and coiled serpent illustrated the return of freedom of speech. Two unbound hands, with open palms, stretched upward to nearly reach severed ropes that had once restrained them, symbolizing the restoration of freedom of religion. A slain dragon represented the conquering of freedom from fear. And a dog released from his tether, the vanquishing of

1.2. The Atlantic Charter and the United Nations Declaration, surrounded by sculptures illustrating the Four Freedoms, are at the center of the Office of War Information's "This Is Our War" exhibition at Rockefeller Center in 1943. LC-DIG-fsac-1a34588. FSA/OWI Collection, Prints & Photographs Division, Library of Congress.

freedom from want. If the symbolism could at times be a bit opaque, the intended message was carefully calibrated – Liberty. Freedom. The Four Freedoms. Human Rights. For the exhibition organizers, the terms were synonymous and interchangeable, one building on the other to provide an essential lexicon for understanding the purposes of war.[3]

The mounting of the exhibition itself pointed toward anxieties over whether this new language of human rights had resonated with the American public. There was more than a little official worry that it had not. A January 1942 poll revealed that only 21 percent of Americans had heard of the Atlantic Charter. Six months later a July 1942 poll reported that only 35 percent had heard of the Four Freedoms. Even more distressing, only 5 percent had heard of the freedom from fear or want. Pollsters never directly asked Americans whether they knew the term "human rights," but if they had, the results would likely have been similar.[4] Most lexical measures of the printed usage of "human rights" suggest it was virtually absent from the vocabulary of U.S. cultural politics in the first half of the twentieth century. With the coming of World War II, its presence spiked upward, in part reflecting the increasing employment of a human rights frame to articulate the purposes of the war.[5] But frequency of use tells little about whether and how human rights concerns might have resonated with their intended audiences.

What did spectators make of the human rights on display at Rockefeller Center? Or put more broadly, how might American publics have made the unfamiliar language of human rights that drove so much of wartime rhetoric their own? *Migrant Mother* offers the beginning of an answer. Evoking human rights as such was never among the ways photographers like Dorothea Lange and those who encountered their work in the 1930s consciously glossed these Depression-era photographs. There was no bright line that seamlessly joined them to wartime evocations of human rights in the Four Freedoms, the Atlantic Charter, or the United Nations Declaration.

The connections are at once more tenuous and scattered. To understand the affective appeals and new convictions that drove the growing believability of human rights in wartime America requires a willingness to put works of the imagination in conversation with political and legal texts. The philosopher Richard Rorty insists that societies hold together because of the shared vocabularies that emerge from telling stories about desired futures. Drawing on David Hume's notion that corrected sympathy is preferable to Kantian imperatives of reason, Rorty argues that expressions of human rights are less a question of law than what Hume called a progress of sentiments.[6] Rorty's focus on the importance of telling and hearing stories – whether they be sad, sentimental, or emancipatory – about the rights of others and ourselves resonates with moral philosopher Martha Nussbaum's claims that imaginative work

is not separable from philosophical content, but is, itself, part of content – an integral part then of the search for and the statement of truth. ... This suggests ... that there may be some views of the world and how one should live in it – views, especially, that emphasize the world's surprising variety, its complexity and mysteriousness, its flawed and imperfect beauty – that cannot be fully and adequately stated in the language of conventional philosophical prose ... but only in a language and in forms themselves more complex, more allusive, more attentive to particulars.[7]

The historian Lynn Hunt's pioneering exploration of how human rights came to occupy a central place in early modern Europe grounds these more abstract claims in an examination of the changing nature of eighteenth-century print culture and its impact on thought and behavior. Hunt suggests that the rise of epistolary novels such as Rousseau's *Julie* (1747–48) and Richardson's *Clarissa* (1770) tied communities of readers together in ways that produced a new subjective sentimentality, transcending older boundaries of social distinction and ultimately producing a moralization of politics. "For human rights to become self-evident," Hunt argues, "ordinary people had to have new understandings that came from new kinds of freedom."[8]

The mass-circulated documentary photographs of the 1930s and the broader visual culture that surrounded them – as revolutionary a set of aesthetic experiences as the rise of the epistolary novel in the eighteenth century – opened up new ways of seeing the world that narrowed the distance between artist, subject, and audience. In seeking to make the suffering of strangers as visible and deeply felt as one's own, photographers like Lange were simultaneously engaged in imaginative, moral, and political interventions. Importantly, they did so in a transnational space that shaped both their own practice and the forms through which their images circulated. Like the work of other *reportage* artists around the world in the 1930s, the photographs they made spoke to the possibility of forging empathetic connections between themselves, their subjects, and those who encountered their work in newspapers, magazines, books, and popular exhibitions. As a 1935 *Nation* editorial put it, they allowed "the average man ... to look at things from points of view he has never taken and to see them in arrangements he has never made."[9]

In all these senses it is perhaps no surprise that the Office of War Information chose visual forms to make legible the human rights aims of World War II. If the sculptures at Rockefeller Center are now largely forgotten, and perhaps on aesthetic grounds deservedly so, the more enduring presence of works like *Migrant Mother* provide visual flashpoints to understand a growing American concern with and consciousness of what in wartime came to be called human rights.

TRANSNATIONAL CIRCULATIONS OF *REPORTAGE*

Depression-era photography was not the first time that concerns about social suffering in the United States had been displayed in visual form. Lithographs had often accompanied reformist tracts and imaginative texts in the mid- to late nineteenth century that sought to raise awareness of urban poverty; they were also part of turn-of-the century campaigns against sex trafficking. American documentary photography itself emerged in the Progressive era, most notably Jacob Riis's photographs of immigrant tenement lives published in his 1890 *How The Other Half Lives* and later Lewis Hine's images of factory and child labor.[10] But what was quite different by the 1930s was the ubiquity, and intensity, through which photographs of all sorts came to circulate and the wider transnational frame that shaped their production and reception.

The period after World War I saw the increasing popularity of illustrated Sunday supplements to newspapers and the rise of picture magazines, developments driven by technological changes that enabled newspaper and magazine publishers to inexpensively reproduce high-quality photographs. These new pictorially driven forms first enjoyed significant popularity in Europe, where photographic magazines, such as the French *Vu* and the German *Berliner Illustrierte Zeitung,* came to enjoy circulations of more than two million after 1919. Such a large readership and its implications for advertising revenue prompted American publisher Henry Luce to experiment with photographs in *Time* and *Fortune* in the late 1920s and early 1930s and encouraged the publishers of the *Des Moines Register* to launch what would become a nationally syndicated Sunday photograph supplement. A 1932 Gallup poll suggested that these supplements were the most widely read section of the Sunday paper, with readers three times more likely to encounter their contents than other sections. The debut of the pictorial weekly *Life* in November 1936 and the monthly *Look* in February 1937, whose circulations quickly reached several million, brought an even wider forum for the display of photographic images.[11]

The American embrace of these visual cultural forms in the 1930s also rested on changing technology within photography itself. New smaller cameras such as the German-made Leica, the use of long strips of 35 mm film, and improvements in flash photography transformed the processes of making photographs. Although treated with disdain by some documentary photographers, these "miniature" cameras not only enabled professional photographers to more easily take multiple exposures of single scenes but also began to foster an increasing coterie of amateur photographers who became especially attuned to the changing styles and subjects of work done by professionals.[12]

A broader transnational engagement not only provided some of the impetus for the growing visibility of photography in 1930s America; it also was central to bringing into being the form and subject of documentary photography itself. The cosmopolitan sensibilities that drove this work were a part of the larger genre of *reportage* through which photographers, along with writers, filmmakers, and other visual artists, sought to foster a critical awareness of social reality. Too often seen as a distinctly American idiom that gave voice to unique domestic political, economic, and social problems, 1930s visual and textual *reportage* in the United States was in fact both a local and a global phenomenon. It was influenced in part by the sensibilities of Weimar Germany's *Neue Sachlichkeit* or "New Objectivity," the desire to promote a critical awareness of social reality through sober and objective realism that informed the work of Bertolt Brecht, Otto Dix, and Heinrich Mann. *Reportage* emerged in a variety of local contexts in the Americas, Europe, and Asia in the 1930s and took a number of expressive forms, including investigative studies, fiction, photography, documentary film, and public murals. In this sense, works like Lange's *Migrant Mother* or John Steinbeck's 1938 *Grapes of Wrath* were joined in form, content, and purpose to similar works by British, Indian, Chinese, Vietnamese, Mexican, and French writers and artists such as George Orwell, Mulk Raj Anand, Ding Ling, Vu Truong Phung, Diego Rivera, David Alfaro Siqueiros, and Maryse Choisy.[13]

Not only did the concerns of *reportage* transcend national borders but the works of American photographers, writers, and artists were also mutually constituted, sometimes indirectly and at other times directly, in transnational space. This was especially so for photography. The modernist aesthetics of the Weimar New Objectivity heightened interest in using photography to consciously and critically draw attention to social reality, prompting new forms of documentary photography to emerge in interwar Germany and central Europe. Variously termed worker photography (*Arbeiterfotographie*) in Germany and social photography (*szociofotó* or *sociálna fotographia*) in Hungary and Czechoslovakia, these were often consciously left-wing political projects that gave attention to urban and rural poverty. They produced an expansive network of amateur photographers and shaped the perspectives of professional photojournalists whose work increasingly appeared in more specialized and popular pictorial magazines in the 1930s. What gave these new photographic forms their greatest visibility were the *Film und Foto* exhibitions that traveled to major European cities in 1929 and 1930. Europeans took the vast majority of the photographs on display, but a few American documentary photographers were also invited to exhibit their work. In 1931, a version of the exhibition came to Japan where it helped spark a new appreciation of the social character of photography and jumpstarted development of 1930s Japanese photojournalism.[14]

The global processes through which documentary photography in the Americas emerged and the dialogical processes that shaped it are most fully reflected in the work of the photographers Margaret Bourke-White, Tina Modotti, and Walker Evans, whose images were among those most prominent in 1930s American visual culture. Before it took a documentary turn in the 1930s, Margaret Bourke-White's work was primarily concerned with the machines, factories, and commodities of industry and commerce; it was largely produced for corporate patrons and later for Henry Luce's *Fortune*. Her usually nonfigurative visual canvas favored tightly framed repetitions of identical objects, sharp upward angles, and often quite dramatic lighting that conveyed a kind of industrial monumentalism (Figure 1.3). In 1930, Bourke-White traveled to the Soviet Union for a *Fortune* assignment to photograph the Soviet industrial and agricultural landscape at the time of the Soviet Union's first five-year plan. But in several subsequent trips on her own she increasingly turned her attention from Soviet dams, cement plants, and agricultural collectives to workers and peasants, ultimately publishing forty of those images in her 1931 book *Eyes on Russia* and as a series of photo essays in 1932 on

1.3. Margaret Bourke-White. *The Towering Smokestacks of the Otis Steel Company, Cleveland.* 1925. Gelatin silver print, 13 1/8 × 7 5/16 in. (33.4 × 18.6 cm). ©Estate of Margaret Bourke-White/Licensed by VAGA, New York, NY.

the impact of Soviet communism on the ordinary citizen that appeared in the *New York Times Magazine*.[15]

As she later wrote in her autobiography, her work in the Soviet Union and a subsequent 1934 assignment for *Fortune* to photograph struggling farmers in the Dust Bowl prompted a political awakening that caused her "to see everything in a new light." She told her art director at *Fortune* in 1935 of "her growing interest in the lives of workmen. It seems to me that while it is very important to get a striking picture of a line of smoke stacks or a row of dynamos, it is becoming more and more important to reflect the life that goes on behind these photographs."[16] Her politics moved to the left, and her photography exhibited a new social consciousness, most dramatically in the images of Southern poverty she produced for her best-selling 1937 collaboration with the novelist (and her soon-to-be husband) Erskine Caldwell, *You Have Seen Their Faces*. The visual language of these photographs, like that in her 1936 *Clinton, Louisiana*, was not so different from that in Bourke-White's earlier industrial and commercial works (Figure 1.4). As one scholar notes, her images of the rural poor have the "same exaggerated scale, strong diagonals, repetition of visual motifs and dramatic lighting." But the shift in subject from industry to the rural poor betrays the transformative effects of Bourke-White's experiences in the Soviet Union.

Tina Modotti's documentary photographs of Mexican poverty from the late 1920s operated in a different visual register, but their intent of drawing public attention to the inequities among the lives of the disadvantaged and to promote a collective societal responsibility for their amelioration bore significant transnational influences as well. Among her most arresting images are *Two Children* and *Elegance and Poverty*. *Two Children* comes from a series of images Modotti made of the impoverished children in one of the poorest barrios of Mexico City, the Colonia de la Bolsa. Severely cropped and thus eliminating all distractions, the photograph's composition brings the children to the forefront and intensifies the viewer's reaction to their poverty. In *Elegance and Poverty* (Figure 1.5), Modotti more directly confronts the contrasts of class and wealth in Mexican society. The photo depicts an apparently dejected and impoverished worker sitting on a curb beneath a billboard for a clothier that reads, "From head to foot we have everything a gentlemen needs to dress

1.4. Margaret Bourke-White. *Clinton, Louisiana.* 1936. Gelatin silver print, 13 ¼ × 10 in. (33.7 × 25.4 cm). The Museum of Modern Art. © Estate of Margaret Bourke-White/Licensed by VAGA, New York, NY. Digital Image © The Museum of Modern Art/Licensed by SCALA/Art Resource, NY.

elegantly." The "head to foot division" of the photograph, the dual focus on the hands of the worker in the foreground and on the man in the tuxedo on the billboard behind him, and the placement of the worker in front of a stone wall all literally and figuratively suggest the deep and seemingly ineradicable divisions in Mexican society.

Both Modotti and the influences on her work were perhaps quintessentially transnational. Born in Italy in 1896, she immigrated to

1.5. Tina Modotti, *Elegance and Poverty*. 1927. Gelatin silver print (photomontage), 9 ¾ × 6 ½ in. (24.8 × 16.5 cm). © Getty Images (US), Inc.

the United States when she was seventeen years old and settled with her husband, the American photographer Edward Weston, in Mexico in the early 1920s. There she became closely associated with a variety of leftist political and intellectual circles, including the Mexican branch of International Red Aid and the Mexican Communist Party. Her documentary photographs were initially produced for *El Machete*, the primary organ of the party, but they circulated more broadly in magazines and exhibitions in the late 1920s and early 1930s in the United States and

Western Europe. The composition and subject matter of Modotti's images of social poverty were in part shaped by the Mexican muralists Diego Rivera and David Álfaro Siqueiros, whose work reflected their radical politics (both were founders of *El Machete*) and their efforts to create a visual language that raised public consciousness of Mexican social conditions. But Modotti's *photography* was also deeply influenced by the German *Arbeiterfotograf* movement and its efforts to employ the camera as "the eye of the working class." As Modotti observed in the late 1920s, "I look upon people now not in terms of race [or] types but in terms of classes. I look upon social changes and phenomena not in terms of human nature or of spiritual factors but in terms of economics."[17] In turn Modotti and this larger transnational intellectual milieu shaped a persistent concern with poverty and social justice that informed *reportage* texts, images, and films in 1930s Mexico and Latin America.[18]

The movement of influences on form, content, and meaning in global space, however, was not one whose vectors necessarily flowed one way from Europe to the Americas. In the case of Walker Evans, and the photos of poor Southern sharecroppers he is best known for, the circulatory patterns were anchored in the Global South. In subject matter, composition, and social bite, the photographs Evans made in the American South bear powerful traces of his globally inflected experiences on the streets of New York and Havana earlier in the 1930s. In 1933 Evans was asked to travel to Cuba to take photographs for the radical journalist Carleton Beals's indictment of the regime of President Gerardo Machado, what became *The Crime of Cuba*. Before he embarked on his trip, Evans encountered an intellectual scene in New York City shaken by the controversy that had erupted over the mural painted by Diego Rivera at Rockefeller Center, *Man at the Crossroads*. Rivera, who had hired Evans to photograph the artwork while it was in progress, anchored the giant mural with images of peasants, workers, and soldiers, as well as one of Lenin. In May 1933, as Evans was preparing to leave for Cuba, the massive, partially finished mural was boarded up at the insistence of the Rockefeller family (the image of Lenin was a bit too much for them) and was soon destroyed. The resulting controversy, in which Evans played a part, led to protests, demonstrations, and petitions. As Evans sailed for Havana, the battle over

1.6. Walker Evans. *Havana: Country Family.* 1933. Gelatin silver print. 17.8 × 22.5 cm (7 × 8 ⅞ in.). The J. Paul Getty Museum, Los Angeles. © Walker Evans Archive, The Metropolitan Museum of Art.

Rivera's work and its visual images of social justice were very much on his mind.[19]

Evans's experiences in Cuba and the photographs he made there, which marked a sharp departure from his previous largely nonfigurative work, brought into being the qualities that distinguished his later photographs of the American South: subjects at a middle distance viewed straight on, the camera held at eye level, no special lighting effects, and a quietness that despite its artifice conveyed to viewers a mutual regard and respect between photographer and subject. *Havana Country Family* (Figure 1.6) comes from his work in Cuba in the early 1930s. It depicts a homeless and destitute family that had migrated from the Cuban countryside to the capital. It predates by more than two years his better known and often reproduced photograph of the Southern sharecropper Bud Fields and his family (Figure 1.7). The Cuban photographs foreshadow in

Bud Fields and his family at their home in Alabama. 1935.
US DEPT.AGRIC. FARM SECURITY ADM   LC-USF 342-   8147-A   PHOTO BY   Walker Evans
Negative No.

1.7. Walker Evans. *Bud Fields and His Family at Home, Hale County, Alabama.* c. 1935. LC-USF-342–8147A. FSA/OWI Collection, Prints & Photographs Division, Library of Congress.

composition and subject matter Evans's simultaneously empathetic and damning portrait of poverty and social injustice in 1930s America.

The circulation of Evans's Cuban photographs in *The Crime of Cuba* also anticipated one of the ways in which his American-centered work and those of other 1930s-era photographers found their intended audiences. The genre of phototextual books, in which image and word were equal and built on one another, provided a major vehicle for the dissemination of documentary photography in the 1930s. Among them were Margaret Bourke-White's and Erskine Caldwell's 1937 *You Have Seen Their Faces*, Archibald MacLeish's 1938 *Land of the Free*, Dorothea Lange's and Paul Taylor's 1939 *American Exodus*, James Agee's and Walker Evans's 1941 *Let Us Now Praise Famous Men*, and Richard Wright's 1941 *12 Million Black Voices*.[20] *You Have Seen Their Faces* and *Land of the Free* enjoyed especially wide circulation, with the best-selling *You Have Seen* appearing not only in more expensive hardcover editions but also in what was a new, and inexpensive, paperback form.

Many 1930s-era documentary photos also circulated through traveling exhibitions at museums, libraries, schools, universities, and department stores. Most notable were the Museum of Modern Art's 1939–40 road show *Documents of America: The Rural Scene*, which traveled to twelve U.S. cities, and the Photographic Society of America's 1941 touring show *In the Image of America*. The images also appeared in specialist publications such as *U.S. Camera* and *Popular Photography* and in the socially progressive *Survey Graphic*, whose editor Paul Kellogg would later become an advocate for social and economic rights provisions in wartime planning efforts for an international bill of human rights. But the documentary photographs of the 1930s became most commonly known in more quotidian ways, appearing in hundreds of local newspapers and their Sunday supplement sections, as well as in popular weekly and monthly magazines such as *McCall's, Collier's, Fortune, Time, Literary Digest, Life*, and *Look*. Farm Security Administration records suggest that by 1940 more than 1,400 of its photographs were distributed to the popular press each month. The broader visual power of these images was reinforced by complementary forms of textual and visual *reportage*, such as John Steinbeck's best-selling *Grapes of Wrath*, Pare Lorentz's 1938 film *The River*, and the 1940 John Ford film of *Grapes of Wrath*.[21]

WAYS OF SEEING

How were the widely circulated American *reportage* photographs of the 1930s seen by those who encountered them? Much recent critical scholarship has in fact called into question their imaginative power, arguing that their provenance and modes of composition ultimately compromised their visual integrity. Some scholars claim that, because so many of the most commonly circulated photographs were made under the auspices of the FSA, they were excessively shaped by the ideological imprint of New Deal politics and liberal reformism, an orientation only intensified by the shooting scripts and directives that FSA chief Roy Stryker gave to his staff.[22] Critics have also drawn attention to the artifice involved in the making of the photos themselves, whether it was the unintentional

or deliberate arrangement of their subjects and settings or the obscuring of their subject's identities. The "realism" of documentary photography "was not the result of clinical, photographic field work," one argues,
"but deliberate, calculated and highly stylized." When subjects became
objects, potentially used and exploited in the very act that purported
to help them, these critics argue, 1930s-era photographers risked reinscribing the patterns of power they sought to unmask in making legible
concrete instantiations of social injustice.[23]

Without question manipulation was part of the aesthetic practice of
reportage. A close look at Tina Modotti's *Elegance and Poverty*, for instance,
reveals a seam joining two images, one of the billboard and one of a
worker, between the wall and the advertisement (it is more visible on
the right). The image of the billboard that appears to conveniently rise
above the man sitting dejectedly on the curb was a photograph Modotti
took in another location and inserted above the worker. Moreover, the
image of the worker is not a candid street photograph, but is carefully
posed by Modotti, with the worker's face cast in deep shadow to suggest
an everyman quality to this unemployed working-class individual. Similarly Bourke-White's *At the Time of the Louisville Flood*, which first appeared
in *Life* in 1937, more brashly juxtaposes a segregated relief line of African
American victims of the flood with a billboard sponsored by the National
Association of Manufacturers, a vocal opponent of the New Deal, depicting an almost satanically happy white middle-class family as part of its
"There's No Way like the American Way" campaign (Figure 1.8). In fact
the African American men and women in the photo were not in front
of the billboard when Bourke-White arrived on the scene: she deliberately moved them there to frame the photograph.[24] The conscious
manipulation of both images heightens their social power, but nonetheless surrenders the agency of their human subjects to Modotti's and
Bourke-White's larger artistic and political purposes.

Some critics have also dismissed the photographs Bourke-White col-
lected in *You Have Seen Their Faces* for sentimentalizing and overdramatiz-
ing her subjects. Bourke-White makes clear in the epilogue to *You Have
Seen* that she brought her own very definite top-down preconceptions
of how to convey poverty: "Sometimes I would set up the camera in a
corner of the room, sit some distance away … and watch people while

1.8. Margaret Bourke-White. *At the Time of the Louisville Flood.* 1937. Gelatin silver print, 9 ¾ × 3 ⅛ in. (24.7 × 33.4 cm). The Museum of Modern Art © Estate of Margaret Bourke-White/Licensed by VAGA, New York, NY. Digital Image © The Museum of Modern Art/Licensed by SCALA/Art Resource, NY.

Mr. Caldwell talked with them. It might be an hour before their faces or gestures gave us what we were trying to express." Those preconceived expressions, critics argue, were reinforced by the invented quotations that accompanied the photographs, such as "I got more children now than I know what to do with, but they keep coming along like watermelons in summertime," that exaggerated a patronizing sense of cultural backwardness and foregrounded stereotypes about race and class.[25]

Late twentieth- and early twenty-first-century concerns about the ethical politics of representation, however, can elide the ways of seeing through which viewers in the 1930s first encountered these photographs. John Raeburn in his cultural history of 1930s photography usefully warns against a Whiggish privileging of present-day aesthetic concerns; he notes the prevailing cultural beliefs of the period that a photograph inevitably captured the reality of its subject and that abstract typifying of individuals was considered an appropriate and respectful means of conveying social categories. *You Have Seen Their Faces* was in fact a huge commercial and critical success. Contemporary critics called Bourke-White's photographs "superb," "almost beyond praise," "beautiful," and "mature."[26] Moreover, their responses suggested that the social issues Bourke-White wanted to foreground resonated with her audience. As one critic wrote in 1937, "If all the talk of the sharecropper's plight is ever translated into action it will be largely because of this book. One may be indifferent to the sufferings of others when running across stray articles in the newspapers, but is impossible not be deeply moved by what is shown here."[27]

Whether encountered in books, exhibitions, or the popular press, 1930s-era *reportage* photographs invited viewers into an unfamiliar world in which an encounter with the visual potentially offered new forms of social and cultural intelligence about the self and society. As the art historian Sarah Miller has perceptively argued, intelligence "is not knowledge about facts, situations, problems, and causes; it does not carry an implication of truth to be wielded. Intelligence, a skill to be cultivated, is the *ability* to create, acquire, or apply knowledge, or to inspect anew what is already agreed to be knowledge." In the 1930s, "learning to think with photographs" was "a distinctively new, contentious, highly variable, and always politically fraught process."[28]

The preserved public comments from one of the precursor exhibits to the Museum of Modern Art's *Documents of America* exhibition that featured documentary photography of the era suggest the deep engagement of viewers with the photographs they saw and the range of political and emotive responses they elicited. Nearly five hundred visitors deposited comments in the exhibit's comment box. Among them were the following:

You exhibited only the ugly pictures – the exhibit is meant to be one sided / Perfect picturization of American life as it is not shown in newspapers / First real pictures have ever seen on American families / Popularizing the worst is bad policy /Pictures which give social and economic situations at a glance rather than a bunch of trick angle shots. This makes photography worthwhile / Subject very sordid and dull for exhibition / Sensational and enlightening. Important educational feature that should reach thousands of people who don't believe such conditions can possibly exist in the U.S. / Poor peoples plight should not be exhibited, but help rendered instead /

They tell a story that should be repeated many times over / True to life / Interesting and thought-provoking / Human / These pictures force your mind to ponder a great social problem which must be solved before we can really be proud of our so-called "American Standard of Living" / They surely aren't flattering to a progressive land like ours. / Horrible pictures of conditions that are a blot on American civilization / Very terrible, something should be done about it. Foreign countries aren't the only ones – we have it right here. / Your pictures clearly demonstrate that one half the people do not know how the other half live /Anything to be able to help themselves should be done, but not thru direct relief / Teach the underprivileged to have fewer children and less misery / Wake up smug America! / We should be ashamed. Charity begins at home /Did or didn't you know slavery was abolished? / We need a Hitler.[29]

The comments provide rare, unmediated traces of the meanings accorded to 1930s documentary photographs by contemporary viewers. The range of political responses does not neatly map onto New Deal liberalism, as calls for an American Hitler suggest. Some clearly chose to pull away from what they had seen, expressing skepticism about the seeming ubiquity of economic and social distress on display. But the overwhelming sensibility that emerges from these comments is an emphatic apprehension of social suffering at home, illustrating how encounters with documentary photographs in the 1930s could produce the often intangible structures of feeling that were one critical element of an emergent wartime human rights consciousness.

In a world at war in which human rights in part drove the United States and its allies forward, the potency of these 1930s photographs provided one ready visual frame through which freedom from fear and freedom from want could not only begin to be understood but also felt. Lange's *Migrant Mother*, which has taken on an iconic status in the years since it was made, has been subjected to some of the same criticisms as those that drew attention to the artifice and ideology in other 1930s documentary photography. Indeed Lange arranged the positions of the mother and children in the photograph, and she later airbrushed away a distracting hand.[30] *Migrant Mother*'s visual power has variously been seen as conveying anxiety, victimhood, survival, determination, and selflessness. These emotions are sometimes rooted in place and time, but just as often are more universalizing and, as Lange's leading biographer argues, ideologically charged constructions through which the photo came to be seen as connoting the resilience of the American character, self-sacrificing motherhood, or the Christian iconography of the Madonna.[31]

And yet in a less deterministic register *Migrant Mother* also worked on its 1930s viewers to convey a remarkable empathy between photographer and subject. "Understanding," Hannah Arendt wrote, "is a complicated process that never produces equivocal results. It is an unending activity by which, in constant change and variation, we come to terms with and reconcile ourselves to reality." This urge, in Arendt's words, "to try to be at home in the world" hovered over the 1930s project of *reportage*.[32] As Lange herself believed, "my pictures might help her, and so she helped me." When a San Francisco newspaper first published *Migrant Mother* in March 1936, hundreds of individuals sent contributions totaling more than $200,000 to help the impoverished pea-pickers in Nipomo. Like Lange, the contributors too yearned to be at home in the world.

CHAPTER 2

The Wartime Rights Imagination

"I DON'T THINK A WORLD ORGANIZATION CAN COMMAND loyalty anywhere," Quincy Wright told a conference organized by the
World Citizens Association in Chicago in April 1941, "unless people feel
that it is based upon a fundamental concern for human rights." This
self-styled "conference of experts" with the ambitious title of *World's Destiny and the United States* brought together thirty distinguished diplomats,
jurists, journalists, academics, and policy makers from Europe, Latin
America, Asia, and the United States to "examine the most important
problems" confronting a world at war. Eight topics were on the table.
Human rights was one of them.[1]

Wright, a University of Chicago professor of international relations,
had been invited to introduce the subject. He presented his case that
"effective international organization is not possible unless it protects
basic human rights against encroachments by national States" in especially bold terms. Wright offered up six human rights for international
protection: freedom of opinion and religion, freedom of information,
freedom of trade, freedom from economic exploitation, equality before
the law, and respect for rights without regard to race, religion, or nationality. Protection of these basic rights of the individual, Wright argued,
was "not a domestic question." It must be part of an "international document, which should receive universal ratification," "be considered as fundamental" as the League of Nations Covenant, and be "legally superior to
the municipal law" of individual states. Wright concluded by proposing
what he termed a "revolutionary procedure," one that allowed individuals to directly petition an international tribunal if their human rights
were violated. "[W]hat I am suggesting is that the individual should be

competent to appeal above the highest court of his State," Wright told the conference, if "he feels that some of the rights which have been guaranteed him by the world bill of rights have been denied him by national legislation or by a national court."[2]

Wright's presentation met with great enthusiasm. Even Hans Kelsen, a towering figure in twentieth-century international law whose hard-edged scholarship was sometimes invoked by skeptics of a global rights order in the postwar period, weighed in favorably. Kelsen in fact singled out the most radical of Wright's proposals, the right of individual petition to an international court, for praise and elaboration. He pointed out to the conference that the "[r]ights of individuals are not excluded by the nature of international law, as many professors of international law teach who say that international law is incompatible with a direct obligation or authorization of individuals." Rather, international law, Kelsen claimed, "can immediately obligate and authorize individuals" if they "have direct access to an international court." To which Edvard Hambro, a noted Norwegian internationalist who would later serve as a delegate to the San Francisco conference that adopted the United Nations Charter, added approvingly, the right to individual petition "would lead the development of international law away from national law ... which is definitely the right tendency in favor of which we all ought to work."[3] At the end of the conference, Wright remarked that he "felt there was a general approval of the idea of certain human rights being assured."[4]

If a visual language of rights consciousness began to emerge in the United States by the eve of the United States' entry into World War II, so too did a searching and unprecedented set of conversations about international legal guarantees of rights and their protections. The Chicago conference was the setting for the earliest of those conversations.[5] Like the forms and circulations of prewar *reportage*, rights talk in wartime America was also embedded in a broader transnational frame. The central actors in these wartime conversations were just as often lawyers and scholars from Europe and Latin America who had taken wartime refuge in the United States as they were American citizens. Together they were intent on the creation of an international bill of rights that would begin to concretize what official pledges "to preserve human rights and justice" at home and abroad might actually mean in practice. Long before the drafters of the 1948 Universal Declaration of Human Rights sought to make protections for human rights part of international law, the deliberations of wartime rights advocates were the first sustained international effort to identify rights of individuals that transcended the nation-state and how those rights might be protected and enforced in a transnational space beyond the nation.

Vigorous debate rather than easy consensus over the scope of what could be considered global human rights and their means of protection frequently marked these conversations. But at their center was a shared certainty that a viable postwar order demanded unprecedented attention be given to human rights. These discussions displayed both a willingness to entertain a vastly expanded catalog of protected rights and an inclination to radically rethink the relationships between individuals and the state through a new international order in which more traditional notions of inviolable state sovereignty might become considerably diminished. Wartime rights advocates believed, in the words of one, "that some form of an International Bill of Rights is a major purpose of the war" and "an essential condition of international peace and international progress."[6] Together their conversations and debates constituted the expansive bounds, and the confines, of mid-century American and global human rights imaginations.

WARTIME HUMAN RIGHTS TALK

Wartime rights talk emerged in a variety of nonstate and state spaces. The American Law Institute began constructing an international bill of rights in 1942 in a project supported by the Carnegie Endowment and the American Philosophical Association. Headed by the institute's director William Draper Lewis, it drew on experts from Canada, China, France, pre-Nazi Germany, India, Italy, Panama, Poland, the Soviet Union, Spain, Syria, Great Britain, and the United States who after two years of deliberation would eventually produce the "Statement of Essential Human Rights by Representatives of the Principal Cultures of the World."[7] The American Jewish Committee invited the renowned British international legal scholar Hersch Lauterpacht to compile an "International Bill of Rights of Man," which when completed offered the most rigorous and thoughtful account of the potentialities of international human rights law in this period.[8] U.S. State Department planners also began drafting an international bill of rights in 1942, as well as the outlines of what would become the United Nations Charter that envisioned including such a bill in it.[9] In the Americas, Mexico and Cuba began to prepare human rights declarations for presentation at a pan-American conference in Mexico City in early 1945 that helped produce the Inter-American Juridical Committee's *Draft Declaration of the International Rights and Duties of Man* later that year with substantial participation by U.S. state and nonstate actors.[10]

These efforts were joined by the newly founded Commission to Study the Organization of the Peace led by James T. Shotwell, a Columbia University professor of international relations who had served as a member of President Woodrow Wilson's policy advisory group at the 1919 Paris Peace Conference. Although the commission did not undertake the formal design of an international bill of rights, it engaged in vigorous public advocacy for the centrality of human rights to the postwar international order, with Quincy Wright often serving as its primary human rights spokesperson.[11] So too did the American Jewish Committee, which formed a series of study groups to consider international protections of individual rights and the problems of minority rights and statelessness.[12] In these broader advocacy efforts, the two groups were joined by such organizations as the Council on Foreign Relations, the Commission to Study the Bases of a Just and Durable Peace, the American Bar Association, the National Catholic Welfare Conference, the Federal Council of the Churches of Christ in America, the American Jewish Conference, the World Jewish Congress, and the National Association for the Advancement of Colored Persons – all of which advocated for the international protection of individual human rights as an essential component of the postwar peace.

Although these various nonstate projects were independent of one another, there was considerable interchange among those leading them and with State Department efforts to develop a draft international bill of rights. The central figures in the efforts of the Commission to Study the Organization of the Peace, American Law Institute, and the American Jewish Committee to frame postwar understandings of human rights were in regular contact with one another, with key individuals often serving on various human rights committees of more than one organization and sharing planning documents back and forth. The ultimate contours of the State Department's bill bore the influence of James Shotwell, who chaired the Commission to Study the Organization of the Peace and was a vocal member of the State Department Subcommittee on Postwar Legal Problems. Diplomats at the State Department also closely followed the deliberations of the American Law Institute and the Inter-American Juridical Committee. Similarly, the human rights work of the American Jewish Committee was intertwined with that of the Commission to Study the Organization of the Peace, and members of the Inter-American Juridical Committee were in dialogue with participants in the American Law Institute project.[13]

Strong transnational forces influenced these deliberations. If American constitutionalism and its bill of rights tradition was a starting point for many conversations, interest in economic and social rights and in past models for enforcement drew on what advocates came to learn about social welfare provisions in Europe and Latin America and about earlier international mechanisms aimed at protecting minority rights.[14] The cosmopolitan quality of wartime rights talk also reflected the geographic diversity of those engaged in it. The American Law Institute and Inter-American Juridical Committee projects were most self-consciously global, but Canadian, European, and Latin American jurists were a part of almost all of these discussions.

American wartime rights talk was also enmeshed in broader state and nonstate efforts to act on the perceived lessons of the United States' unwillingness to join the League of Nations and the subsequent failure of the League itself. In part these efforts were concerned with articulating a structure of international organization that could more effectively promote international peace and cooperation than the League had done. But they were just as concerned with suasion, convincing American publics that maintaining engagement in world affairs through participation in international organizations, as the United States had not done after World War I, was absolutely essential for the postwar peace. These efforts were motivated not so much by a fear of isolationism, but rather by the sense that neutrality no longer offered a credible path forward for the conduct of international relations. Public support was seen as critical not only for moving a treaty committing the United States to membership in a future United Nations through the U.S. Senate but also for building an engaged world public, which was increasingly viewed as essential to the success of any international organization. At times it was nonstate actors who were pushing the Roosevelt administration toward a firmer commitment to a postwar United Nations. As the war progressed, however, increasingly the State Department's public diplomacy sought to cultivate the engagement of domestic groups in support of these initiatives.[15] Advocates of a postwar global human rights order, many of whom were also involved in this larger internationalist project, saw human rights as offering a potentially transformative path toward international peace.

Three central concerns were threaded through wartime conversations about human rights: Why rights in a time of war? Which rights deserved international protection? And how best to enforce these guarantees beyond the nation-state? Discussions among participants often began by trying to flesh out for themselves and a broader public why human rights ought to be central to a world at war. Unsurprisingly their starting point was usually the promises of the Four Freedoms, the Atlantic Charter, and the United Nations Declaration, which they sometimes wielded like legitimating clubs in support of how various international guarantees of rights mapped onto this or that clause from the Atlantic Charter or one of the Four Freedoms; for example, "Freedom of Religion = Four Freedoms 4" or "Social Security = Four Freedoms 3; Atlantic Charter 5, 6," as one author put it in the mechanistic style that characterized some wartime writing on human rights.[16]

Although these declarations remained foundational, there was a more general recognition that their porous and self-reinforcing, if not tautological, qualities required a fuller articulation of why human rights were essential to the peace. The rise of Hitler and Mussolini in the 1930s had been increasingly seen through the prism of "totalitarianism" and "fascism," themselves new and sometimes opaque conceptual terms that loosely conveyed a sense of powerful states whose policies collapsed distinctions between the public and the private and imposed radical state-defined projects of collective action hostile to individual identities, liberties, and freedom of action. By the late 1930s there was a growing sense among Americans of a wider world confronted by a stark choice between

2.1. "Abolition of Justice" tableau at the Office of War Information's "Nature of the Enemy" exhibition, Rockefeller Center, New York City. May 1943. LC-USW3–028788-D, FSA/OWI Collection, Prints & Photographs Division, Library of Congress.

the antithetical demands of democracy and a militant dictatorial totalitarianism.[17] Throughout the early years of the war, the totalitarian dangers that Nazi fascism posed at home and abroad were a common part of official and unofficial efforts to build American support for the war.[18]

Among the most visually dramatic efforts was the Office of War Information's "Nature of the Enemy" exhibition that opened in May 1943 in New York City's Rockefeller Plaza. Beneath banners asserting "The Enemy Plans This For You" and surrounded by twenty-two foot tall photomurals of Nazi and Japanese war victims were larger-than-life three-dimensional tableaus that represented methods of political control under the Axis powers. One titled "Abolition of Justice" showed an American citizen with hands bound and back lacerated by a whip, standing before a judge whose parted robes reveal a Nazi uniform (Figure 2.1). Others graphically drew attention to violations of religious freedom and freedom of thought. The provocative tableau illustrating "Desecration of Religion" (Figure 2.2) brought home the Nazi religious threat by

2.2. "Desecration of Religion" tableau at the Office of War Information's "Nature of the Enemy" exhibition, Rockefeller Center, New York City. May 1943. LC-USW3–028786-D, FSA/OWI Collection, Prints & Photographs Division, Library of Congress.

juxtaposing a large-scale model of a simple New England town square clapboard church with the blasphemous caption, "Adolph Hitler Is the True Holy Ghost," a quotation the Office of War Information attributed to Hans Kerrl, whom it called the Nazi Minister of Church Affairs. "Suppression of Thought" depicted a model of the New York Public Library on the steps of which books were being burned. Attracting tens of thousands of spectators, this massive outdoor exhibition sought to viscerally convey "America's fate if the Allies did not win the war."[19]

If concerns about fascism and totalitarianism were often popularly expressed in the looser rhetoric of freedom and democracy, wartime rights talk went further. The assertion that the "relationship between human rights and a just peace is close and interlocking," made in a 1944 report of the Commission to Study the Organization of the Peace, was widely shared by many wartime rights advocates. They drew attention to the evisceration of rights in Nazi Germany, and to a lesser extent in Japan and Italy, to make the case for the necessity of a peace that protected individual human rights. The "present reliance upon brute force" by the Germany military regime and its "totalitarian empire of coercion," a 1941 report of the Commission argued, meant that the "threat to liberties in any part of the world" caused "political fear in every other part of the world." It continued, "The destruction of civil liberties anywhere creates the danger of war. The peace is not secure if any … population is permanently subject to a control which can create a fanatical national sentiment impervious to external opinion."[20]

Securing the "rights of man," wrote Hersh Lauterpacht, "is an essential condition and requirement of international peace." It must now, he argued, "be regarded as axiomatic that tyranny and dictatorship are in themselves a danger to international peace. Their essence is a denial of law … not only within their borders, but also outside the confines of their States." In its 1944 report on international human rights, the Commission to Study the Organization of the Peace noted "how easily" we have seen "the step … from internal oppression to external aggression, from the burning of books and of houses of worship to the burning of cities." We have it maintained, "seen the diseased nation engage in propaganda campaigns which spread the infection abroad and weaken the victim nation by germs of religious and racial hatred." For that reason, the Commission argued, "international concern for individual human rights goes to the heart of realistic measures for wiping out aggressive war."[21]

Similarly the Mexican Ministry of Foreign Affairs called for an international bill of rights because "our generation has been brought face to face with the truth of the fact that oppression and violence practiced by a State over individuals give cause for concern to all other States and constitute a threat to world peace." Or as a 1944 report on human rights by the American Jewish Committee put it,

> It has become increasingly evident that one important cause of war has been the existence of large-scale persecutions within the borders of a given country with other nations unable to intervene. With the development of modern science and technology, a sinister group that seizes power in one country can poison the beliefs and morals of the rest of the world through cunning propaganda and use of our perfected systems of communication. … Domestic policy, in a world as closely linked as ours,

can only arbitrarily be separated from matters of direct international concern. A threat to civilization in one country is a threat to civilization through the world.[22]

The metaphor of disease – and the language of germs, poison, and infection – shaped wartime conversations about the urgent need for human rights. Quincy Wright offered an armchair psychological analysis of the lessons of the Nazi system to buttress his belief in an international bill of rights. He argued the troubled state was like the troubled individual:

> The psychologists tell us that an individual in isolation becomes somewhat insane. It is only through social contacts that sanity is preserved. I believe it is the same with the state. A population which is shut off from contact with other populations of the world becomes insane. It gets an ingrowing tendency which makes it eventually aggressive. That, I believe, is one of the fundamental reasons why the world community must protect human rights in every state.[23]

For Wright and others, the very notion of human rights provided the opportunity to cultivate an enlightened world public opinion. In doing so, they consciously built on Woodrow Wilson's claims that no lasting peace could succeed that did "not satisfy the opinion of mankind" and must provide "an eye that is everywhere watchful and attentive" to the concerns "where the heart to humanity beats."[24] The individual, Wright wrote, "can scarcely be loyal to an international organization unless" it "does something for him. ... I think of nothing that could increase the individual's interest more than to feel that the world organization is the protector of his fundamental rights and liberties."[25]

Discussions of the groundings for the international protection of human rights could also move beyond the exigencies of war and unbridled German state power. Some rights advocates pointed toward new universalizing sociological conceptions of human nature in the work of Robert E. Park and others that argued that "sentiments and impulses that are human ... belong to mankind at large, and not to any particular race or time. ... The desire for new experience, the desire for security, the desire for recognition, the desire for response."[26] In perhaps the most capacious wartime accounting of "the more permanent and pervasive" foundations of international recognition and the protection of human rights, Hersch Lauterpacht explored what he termed the "reciprocal relations" between natural law, international law, and the rights of man. Where other commentators made perfunctory bows to John Locke and the laws of nature, Lauterpacht was concerned with demonstrating how natural law provided the "hidden springs and enduring core" for a global regime of human rights. "It might seem clear," he wrote, "that the protagonists of an International Bill of the Rights of Man would do well to steer clear of any elusive and illusory conceptions of the law of nature and natural rights." After all, he noted, realist legal philosophers such as Hans Kelsen "have treated the law of nature with little respect."

But to do so, Lauterpacht believed, misjudged "historical experience and the essential requisites of a durable and effective protection of the human rights." Indeed he devoted as much attention in his *International Bill of the Rights of Man* to a careful philosophical exegesis of the Greek Stoics, Cicero, Grotius, and Vattel in support of his claims that the notion that "all rights come from the States and that there are no rights unless they are recognized by it ... is as utterly inadequate as a general jurisprudential proposition as it is inacceptable to the spheres of morals and politics." It reduced law to a "mere instrumentality" without moral force. He wrote,

> [I]t is the very purpose of the Bill of Rights to translate the natural rights of man into positive law of a high degree of effectiveness. The law of the State is not a purpose unto itself, but an instrument for realizing the welfare of the individual as the ultimate unit of all law. It is proper that international law, in embodying the rights of man in the form of a positive international enactment, should give recognition to that ultimate source and justification of legal autonomy. ... A law of nations effectively realizing that purpose would acquire a substance and dignity which would go far towards assuring its ascendancy as an instrument of progress.[27]

For Lauterpacht, neither natural law nor positive law alone but rather their overlapping and intertwined character ultimately produced the conditions of possibility for a global rights order.

TOWARD AN INTERNATIONAL BILL OF RIGHTS

These more philosophical wartime considerations of the groundings for the protection of individual rights beyond the nation were accompanied by sustained attention to what the substance of an international bill of rights might look like, especially, as one author put it, to "[h]ow far the bill should go." The November 1942 planning documents for the American Law Institute's project to draft an international bill of rights put the basic issues on the table. In framing an agenda for these initial discussions, the institute's director William Draper Lewis asked, "Should the Bill of Rights be confined exclusively to negative rights such as those of the first ten amendments to the constitution of the United States?" And if drafters preferred a wider scope, should "positive rights" be included requiring governments to take on responsibility for a "program of social planning to protect and further the welfare of the individual in the social and economic spheres?" He might also have added this question: What are the rights of minorities and the stateless?[28]

For the drafters of wartime bills of rights, guarantees of civil rights were largely uncontroversial. All four of the major wartime bills of rights offered substantial protections for civil rights, a position that also met with the full support of the Commission to Study the Organization of the Peace. Freedom of religion and speech, in particular, were often lifted up as occupying a "foremost place," because their violations by the "fascist-ruled countries" were viewed as "in part responsible for the recent war."[29] Freedom of information, distinct from if sometimes linked to freedom of speech, was also put forward in reaction to what was widely seen as the "most pernicious" wartime practices of "totalitarian governments" to isolate their own peoples. Relating his encounters with Germans in a 1937 visit, Quincy Wright told the Commission that "if they had continuous access to the press from outside, there would have been a much larger body of opinion in Germany skeptical" of Nazi "propaganda and their doubt might have been an effective deterrent to the aggressive policies of that government." Wright's widely shared conclusion that "protection of the basic human right to speak and to listen is one of the protections which the world community needs against potential aggressive governments" would provoke some controversy in the postwar period, especially

among newly decolonizing states for which protection of their own frag-
ile postcolonial independence felt more pressing than concerns about
the Nazi legacies of the war. But freedom of information was generally
viewed as an essential component of the postwar international order
by most American state and nonstate actors.[30] As with civil rights more
broadly, this consensus rested on how closely these provisions mirrored
the U.S. Bill of Rights and defined the Allied war aims against the Nazi
regime.

Guarantees of economic and social rights provoked sharper wartime
debates. Most acknowledged that in the wake of the international depres-
sion of the 1930s these concerns were coming to play a central role in an
emergent global rights consciousness. Indeed the transnational circulation of *reportage* that made poverty visible was one popular instantiation
of such a growing awareness. New Deal social welfare legislation began
to concretize economic rights claims in an American context, with Roosevelt's Four Freedoms address one early manifestation of their salience
in wartime America. The release in Great Britain of what was popularly
known as the Beveridge Report, which would form the basis of the postwar British welfare state, was another wartime manifestation of these
increasingly palpable concerns. In part the product of transatlantic dialogue among American and British social reformers in the 1920s and
1930s, the 1942 report was widely circulated in the United States. Its lead
author William Beveridge, the noted progressive British economist and
social reformer, toured the country on a Rockefeller Foundation-funded
visit, giving as many as one hundred lectures to appreciative crowds.[31]
What contemporaries christened the "American Beveridge Plan" soon
emerged in the form of a bill of economic rights from the National
Resources Planning Board that called for the right to work and fair pay,
to social security, to education, and to rest and leisure.[32] This bill of rights
was widely disseminated in poster form as "Our Freedoms and Rights,"
and some contemporary observers approvingly termed its focus on economic and social rights as "a revolutionary answer to the needs of a revolutionary age" that "epitomizes ... the contrast between the way of life of
free men and way of life in dictatorships." One called it a "natural supplement to the Atlantic Charter, but ... far more inspiring to the average
man."[33]

Most dramatically President Roosevelt took up economic and social rights in his 1944 State of the Union Address. Political rights, Roosevelt argued, "proved inadequate to assure us equality in the pursuit of happiness." He said, "We have come to a clear realization of the fact that true individual freedom cannot exist without economic security and independence. ... People who are hungry and out of a job are the stuff of which dictatorships are made. In our day these economic truths have become accepted as self-evident." Roosevelt proposed what he termed a second bill of rights, one that guaranteed work and earnings "to provide adequate food and clothing and recreation" and the rights to medical care and good health; protection from the "economic fears of old age, sickness, accident, and unemployment"; and to a "good education." All of these rights "spell security," Roosevelt contended, and "after this war is won we must be prepared to move forward, in the implementation of these rights, to new goals of human happiness and well-being." He also insisted on the link between them and a new international order after World War II. "America's own rightful place in the world," Roosevelt concluded, "depends in large part upon how fully these and similar rights have been carried into practice for all our citizens. For unless there is security here at home there cannot be lasting peace in the world."[34]

Several months later, 131 delegates representing forty-one states came together in Philadelphia at an International Labor Organization conference to discuss the place of economic and social rights in the postwar period. To considerable fanfare, they produced what contemporaries dubbed the "Philadelphia Charter" that offered a catalog of rights very similar to those Roosevelt included in his second bill of rights. The Charter also insisted that such rights were a matter of both domestic and global concern. Roosevelt himself likened the Philadelphia Charter to the U.S. Declaration of Independence, claiming that "poverty anywhere constitutes a danger to prosperity everywhere."[35]

Against this broader transnational turn toward a more capacious rights language, those who insisted on including economic and social rights guarantees in any international bill of rights often engaged in exercises in comparative constitutionalism to make their case. They painstakingly cataloged the increasing number of national constitutions that, unlike that of the United States, made reference to these guarantees.[36]

"The constitutions of more than thirty-five states," reported the Ameri-can Law Institute subcommittee that oversaw questions of economic and social rights, "contained guarantees concerning such matters as social security, education, employment, fair pay and right of labor to organize." The Soviet, Weimar German, and interwar Polish constitutions were fre-quent points of reference, as were economic and social provisions in the constitutions of various Central and South American states, among them Mexico, Cuba, Costa Rica, El Salvador, Brazil, Bolivia, Venezuela, and Uruguay. "It is striking," the subcommittee argued, "the extent to which it has become customary during the last twenty years ... to formulate certain principles of social and economic policy in close relationship with declarations of fundamental individual rights." While acknowledg-ing that the range of protected rights varied geographically, the subcom-mittee forcefully called for incorporating protections for economic and social rights into an international bill of rights. So too did the Inter-American Commission, Hersch Lauterpacht, and, to a muted extent, postwar planners in the U.S. State Department.[37]

The pressing urgency to include economic and social rights prompted wartime debate over the proper scope of an international bill of rights. Discussions at the 1941 World Citizens Association conference in Chicago presaged these fault lines. On one side were proponents of the inclusion of economic and social rights. Several delegates registered their surprise that economic and social rights were not playing an even larger role in their discussions. "I am not at all certain," Percy Corbett, McGill Uni-versity professor of international law, said, "that the whole structure of supranational community won't disintegrate if you don't go a long way toward eliminating want." Individual economic rights would be objectives to give "hope to the world," added Paul Kellogg, editor of *Survey Graphic* that had often featured photographic *reportage* of American poverty in the 1930s. The French diplomat Henri Bonnet concurred, arguing that "to show the will to establish real security in the economic life" is "the only way to enlarge confidence ... after the war is over."[38]

But other participants expressed considerable skepticism about inter-national guarantees of economic and social rights. "If we try to pro-vide social security for everyone in the world," the conference chair and Stanford University president Ray Wilbur interjected, "we will lead any organization we have down a path that isn't worked out in any nation yet, let alone any particular world arrangement." Hans Kelsen was especially exercised about the utopian implications of guaranteeing rights like social security, prompting this vigorous exchange of views around the table:

KELSEN: "[I]f we go too far in this catalog of internationally recognized legal rights ... then we shall have to establish a federal world State. ... [I]f we do not wish to suggest an Utopian scheme, we must accept a minimum and not a maximum program of human rights. A maximum program of human rights is Utopia. Imagine ... the situation of an international court, when an individual says, 'My right of social security is violated by my own State, because I have no job. I have a right to work, and now I am without a job.'"

CORBETT: "He has a claim against his State for compensation as an individual."

KELSEN: "Imagine a State where there are millions of unemployed ... "

WILBUR: "Perhaps there has been a crop failure. You have to work things out more from a definitely biological standpoint."

WRIGHT: "I agree with Mr. Kelsen. There is a difference between saying there are certain freedoms of which the State cannot deprive the individual no matter how poor a State is, and saying you must give this person a certain degree of comfort, a radio, and so on. If you attempt to guarantee social security, the court will continually be running up against an impossibility: Conditions may have arisen so that the State cannot give economic security it would like to give all its citizens."

CORBETT: "I believe it would be just as easy to provide reasonable protection for such a right as for any other fundamental right."[39]

Similar debates persisted throughout the wartime period. Percy Corbett, active in the American Law Institute project, continued to be a forceful advocate for the inclusion of economic and social rights. His claim that "there was too much demand, too much movement and sentiment for positive action ... to ignore this matter" at American Law Institute meetings paralleled those of international lawyer and former Panamanian president Ricardo Alfaro, who argued that "the Bill should recognize that man may be oppressed not only by political power but also by

economic power." An international bill of rights with protections for economic and social rights, Alfaro continued, would "serve as an expression of conscience of civilization." Hersch Lauterpacht made a similar
if more pragmatic argument that in "a world of economic interdependence and free exchange of goods – a condition which must be assumed
as part of an orderly and progressive development of international relations – improvements in social conditions cannot be fully achieved by the
efforts of one State or group of States." Some State Department planners
praised the economic bill of rights proposed by the National Resources
Planning Board, urging that the "style and phraseology" of its articles be
included in the department's draft bill. More generally the International
Labor Organization's 1944 Philadelphia Charter suggested the continuing wartime concern for international protections of economic and social
rights.[40]

But others remained unconvinced about the efficacy of such international guarantees. Manley O. Hudson, a leading American scholar of
international law and active in the American Law Institute's drafting of
an international bill of rights, followed Hans Kelsen in asserting that
categories of protected rights depended on the nature of international
enforcement. If the Institute's final bill was simply aspirational, Hudson
argued, he could "easily envision the inclusion of economic and social
rights." But "they seem to me not workable as standards of binding commitments," and "I cannot possibly imagine the United States going in
for any such program." A State Department summary of the plenary sessions devoted to the report of the Institute's subcommittee on economic
and social rights conveyed real "skepticism" on the part of many Institute
members "as to the desirability and feasibility of including human rights
in the elaborate form suggested in the subcommittee report."[41] The cautionary assessments offered by Hudson and some in the State Department reflected an increasingly unsettled domestic political landscape on
questions of economic and social rights, with vocal conservative critics in
Congress and the business world expressing escalating concerns about
the dangers that a European-style welfare state posed to American free
enterprise. For them, a little comparative constitutionalism was a dangerous thing.[42] In the end the American Law Institute did include articles
dealing with economic and social rights in the final draft of the bill, as did

the other wartime bills of rights. But to sidestep what its director termed "political controversy," it tabled discussion of enforcement mechanisms. Hersch Lauterpacht, recognizing the potential enforcement problems for the protection of economic and social rights, advocated a considerably looser enforcement regime for them than for civil and political rights.[43]

THE LIMITS OF WARTIME RIGHTS TALK

Throughout their wartime deliberations, American rights advocates expressed hesitations about what to do about the issues of statelessness and the rights of minorities. Most recognized that the rapid growth of statelessness was an increasingly "acute" international problem, one they linked to Soviet, Italian, and especially Nazi policies of collective and individual denationalization. Nazi policies – first applied to "denaturalize" German Jews and, as the war progressed, to Jews in occupied territories as well – along with the denationalization of other religious, ethnic, political, and sexual groups targeted by the Axis powers, meant that as many as two million persons were stateless at the end of the war. Some, including those engaged in the American Law Institute's draft bill of rights, argued that because any international bill of rights was universal the question of citizenship did not matter.

Many, however, thought it did and so supported guarantees for the right of nationality. The provisions of the State Department bill – that "no state shall deny to a person born within its territory the citizenship of the states unless he acquires at birth citizenship in another state" – provided a minimal protection. Lauterpacht and the Inter-American Juridical Committee offered stronger language more sensitive to the wartime explosion of state-induced statelessness, coupling the State Department's language with specific prohibitions on states against depriving their citizens of nationality. The American Jewish Committee, which understandably held that the problem of Jewish statelessness was particularly severe, supported nationality provisions in international bills of rights, but believed that the elimination of statelessness also depended on the adoption of a binding international convention on statelessness and the establishment of an international commission to oversee compliance. In this it not only anticipated the difficulties of bringing the problems of wartime statelessness to an end, but also postwar efforts through the 1949 Fourth Geneva Convention, the 1951 Refugee Convention, and the 1954 Convention Relating to the Status of Stateless Persons that began to construct an international legal regime to protect the stateless.[44]

The question of minority rights prompted even more extended discussion. Minority rather than individual rights had been the focus of international concern in the wake of World War I, producing a set of minority treaties that required some but far from all postwar European nation-states to provide linguistic, educational, and religious autonomy to the more than twenty-five million minority peoples who lived in their borders. The treaties provided mechanisms for minorities to petition bodies within the League of Nations if these guarantees were violated and for some international juridical and administrative supervision of state policy. With the Nazi rise to power in Germany and that country's withdrawal from the League, the system fell apart in the 1930s.[45] Growing awareness of Hitler's escalating use of population transfers and mass murder to remake the racial map of Europe inflected wartime rights discussions, though seldom with a particular focus on the fate of European Jews, except for those within the American Jewish community. But the minority treaty system itself was viewed with ambiguity. The "potentialities" were "tremendous," Hersch Lauterpacht succinctly put it, "but the system came to grief almost from its inception" and "acquired a reputation for impotence."[46]

In looking beyond the nation to the League of Nations as the ultimate guarantor of rights, many wartime human rights advocates believed that the minority rights treaties marked a revolutionary departure from past practices. But like Lauterpacht these advocates generally viewed the implementation of these treaties with considerable skepticism. Oscar I. Janowsky, a leading scholar of minority populations in Europe, told the Commission to Study the Organization of the Peace as early as 1941 that the "treaties had been a qualified failure." They were not entirely an "empty gesture," he claimed, pointing to interwar Czech policies of minority cultural freedoms. "Even Poland, Rumania and Hungary dare not assume the high-handed manner in which Mussolini and Hitler have employed to minorities," Janowsky suggested, with "the threat of public condemnation by the League Council ... sufficient to hold in check most offenders." But the treaty regime, Janowsky argued, was fundamentally flawed. The failure of the League to establish a commission on minorities, as it had done with colonial mandated territories, to empower independent observers to visit minorities and the "cumbersome and dilatory process" of investigating violations of minority rights were severe "defects" – so much so that Janowsky claimed the "section of the League dealing with minorities came to be called derisively the 'Hush-Hush' section."[47] These critiques were widely shared. The most frequently cited work in American wartime discussion of minority rights, the 1943 *Were the Minority Treaties a Failure?* commissioned by the New York-based Institute for Jewish Affairs, acknowledged some advances in international protections during the interwar period and the continuing need for them in the postwar period, but was sharply critical of League efforts.[48]

Most wartime advocates of international bills of rights argued that the patchwork system of the minority rights treaties – in which some states but not others were required to uphold minority rights – and an exclusive focus on minorities themselves could not provide the kinds of protections as those offered by a universalizing individual human rights regime in which all states were required to protect the ethnic, religious, or linguistic minorities within their borders. Others were less sure. Raphael Lemkin, who was at the margins of these discussions but would emerge as the leading proponent of the Genocide Convention in the postwar period, called for the development of "adequate machinery for the international protection of national and ethnic groups against extermination attempts and oppression in time of peace" in his 1944 study, *Axis Rule in Occupied Europe.* Hersch Lauterpacht, in a rare public wartime reference to the plight of the Jews under the Nazis as a people who had suffered more "cruelly from a denial of elementary human rights" than any other, was especially concerned that the "abandonment of the minority treaties without" the adoption of an international bill of rights "would mean disservice to minorities, to the cause of international protection of human rights, and to international peace and progress."[49] Lauterpacht and most other observers, however, embraced an emergent genealogy for the international protection of the rights of individuals rather than collective rights, in which the minority treaty regime, shorn of its particularities and defects, was put forward as a legitimating precedent on which to build a more effective international system of rights enforcement. Even the American Jewish Committee, which viewed the minority treaties as "half-hearted" failures, argued that the "best protection for Jews" and other minorities is "the security of all human beings" in the form of an international bill of rights.[50]

There remained an inclination, when confronted with particular violations of minority rights, to push them to the margins of discussions about an international bill of rights. Discussions of violations of the rights of African Americans were particularly fraught, and ultimately most wartime rights advocates were willing to push that issue to the side. Hersch Lauterpacht asked to "what extent can" we "be indifferent to situations such as the disfranchisement ... of large sections of the Negro population in the United States?" His answer in large measure was that "we" could, arguing that "[n]o Bill of Rights is likely to prove acceptable which in an inelastic or uncompromising fashion makes ... the matter of direct and immediate international concern."[51]

Lauterpacht was not alone in his unwillingness to address the question of race in the American context. State Department drafters were skittish each time talk of rights emerged that potentially touched on the "exclusion of negroes," in every case preferring language that did not fundamentally disturb the Jim Crow status quo.[52] In its final report, "International Safeguard of Human Rights" in May 1944, the Commission to Study the Organization of the Peace argued, "The cancerous Negro situation in our country gives fodder to enemy propaganda and makes our ideals stick like dry bread in the throat. In anti-Semitism we are a mirror of Nazi grimaces. These motes in our own eye are not to be passed over." But the report nonetheless advocated a distancing from "the Negro situation," contending,

> There is ... a vast difference between a governmental policy of persecution, as in Germany, and laggard customs which have not yet been broken on the wheel of a legal policy which forbids them. We cannot postpone international leadership until our own house is completely in order. Nor can we expect nations to agree that their own houses should be brought into order by the direct intervention of international agencies. We have only

to consider the difficulties which any such course would encounter in our own or other countries. Through revulsion against Nazi doctrines, we may, however, hope to speed up the process of bringing our own practices in each nation more in conformity with our professed ideals.[53]

Deeply critical of the kind of gradualism that drove these timid approaches to African American rights, the National Association for the Advancement of Colored Persons (NAACP) saw the issue quite differently. As Walter White, the head of the NAACP, bluntly put it in a wartime speech, "Every lynching, every coldblooded shooting of a Negro soldier ... every filibuster against an anti-poll tax or anti-lynching bill, every snarling, sneering reference ... to 'burr headed niggers' ... builds up a debit balance of hatred against America." Southern whites, he continued, "utilized hatred of the Negro precisely as Hitler used prejudice against Jews, Catholics and Christians." But African Americans who took "literally the shibboleths of the Four Freedoms," White argued, "intended to secure and enjoy those freedoms ... to put an end to the old order."[54] Within the broader context of the African American Double V campaign to win the war and postwar rights, the NAACP came to play an active wartime role in putting stronger human rights language in the United Nations Charter, but remained at odds with its largely white allies on international guarantees of African American rights at home.[55]

Women's rights also occupied a marginal place in discussion of wartime bills of rights. The American Law Institute's bill was the only one to explicitly offer equal protection against discrimination because of sex. The others were silent on questions of gender. Lauterpacht offered a defense similar to one he employed to elide questions of discrimination against African Americans, arguing that "it was not a problem which can be solved within the framework of a general international instrument," given differing national social conditions and public opinion. Again practicality or, as Lauterpacht put it, "the necessity of not impeding the acceptance of the Bill" trumped an expansion of the rights lexicon. Within the State Department, the issue was removed from the table almost as soon as conversations about an international bill of rights began. In an early November 1942 meeting of the State Department's Subcommittee on Postwar Legal Problems, one member asked if "it was desired to retain the reference to sex" in the draft bill's antidiscrimination article. The query prompted a terse conversation about this "difficult question" and a unanimous agreement "to remove the reference."[56]

These omissions were telling and foreshadowed postwar American debates about the place of economic and social rights and African American rights in the making of a new global rights order. But taken together what is most striking about the international bills of rights drafted in the wartime period is the expansive catalog of civil, economic, social, and political rights they put on the table. Without hyperbole, it is fair to say that provisions of these international bills of individual rights were unprecedented. There had in fact been one effort in the 1920s to draft this sort of declaration, the International Law Institute's 1929 Declaration of the International Rights of Man. Though occasionally referenced in wartime rights conversations, it was a minimalist document (making reference to only a limited number of civil rights) and was virtually ignored in its day.[57] More significantly, the wartime international bills of rights largely anticipated the 1948 United Nations Universal Declaration of Human Rights (see Figure 2.3 for a comparison of the provisions of the four major wartime bills of rights with those in the Universal Declaration of Human Rights). Except for the Universal Declaration's guarantee of the right to asylum, one or more of the wartime bills contained all of its other substantive provisions.

THE BOUNDS OF SOVEREIGNTY

Perhaps even more significant than the range of rights articulated in the wartime period was the expansiveness of discussions about enforcement that offered strong challenges to traditional notions of state sovereignty. Almost without exception, those engaged in wartime global rights talk advocated an elastic notion of sovereignty in which states would no longer be the sole arbiter for the protection of individual human rights. An international bill of rights, most of its proponents acknowledged, was a "radical innovation" that required a "revolutionary" rethinking of the place of international law in the relationship between the individual and the nation. As Hersch Lauterpacht pointed out, international protection of human rights "implies a more drastic interference with the sovereignty

	Universal Declaration of Human Rights	State Department Bill	American Law Institute Bill	Lauterpacht Bill	Inter-American Commission Bill
Life & Liberty	X	X	X	X	X
Slavery	X			X	
Torture	X	X		X	
Recognition Before Law	X	X	X	X	X
Trial	X	X	X	X	X
Arbitrary Arrest		X	X	X	X
Innocence	X	X		X	
Privacy	X	X	X	X	
Movement	X			X	
Asylum	X				
Nationality	X (strong)	X (weak)		X (strong)	X (strong)
Marriage & Family	X				X
Property	X	X	X		X
Religion	X	X	X	X	X
Speech	X	X	X	X	X
Association	X	X	X	X	X
Political Participation	X	X	X		X
Social Security	X		X	X	X (expansive)
Employment, equal pay, unions	X	x (minimal)	x (not unions)	X	x (expansive)
Health and wellbeing	X	x (not health care)	X	x (not health care)	X (not health care)
Education	X	X	X	X	X
Cultural Life	X	X	X	X	X
Non-discrimination: race, origin, belief, sex, religion	X	x (not sex)	X	x (not sex)	x (not sex)

2.3. International guarantees of human rights in the 1948 United Nations Universal Declaration of Human Rights and the four major wartime international bills of rights. *Sources:* United Nations Universal Declaration of Human Rights (http://www.un.org/en/ documents/udhr/); U.S. Department of State Special Subcommittee on Legal Problems, "Bill of Rights," 3 December 1942 in Harley Notter, *Postwar Foreign Policy Preparation, 1939– 1945* (Washington, DC: US Government Printing Office, 1949: 483–85; American Law Institute, "Statement of the Essential Human Rights" in *Annals of the American Academy of Political and Social Sciences*, 243 (January 1946): 18–26; Hersch Lauterpacht, *An International Bill of the Rights of Man* (New York: Columbia University Press, 1945): 69–74; and, Inter-American Juridical Committee, *Draft Declaration of the International Rights and Duties of Man* (Washington DC: Pan American Union, 1945): 1–12.

of the State than the renunciation of war ... touching as it does intimately upon the relations of the State and the individual." International recognition of protected human rights, he argued, "cannot be accepted without a substantial sacrifice by States of their freedom of action."[58]

At issue in legal terms was the question of whether the individual could be the subject rather than the object of international law. "It has been suggested," Quincy Wright claimed, "that international law cannot directly concern itself with human rights, because if it did so it would compromise its fundamental premise that only states are its subjects." This argument, he said, "appears to beg the question. ... [T]here is nothing to prevent international jurists from searching for new procedures to accomplish the end sought, that of assuring basic freedoms to everyone." Similarly, the American Jewish Committee argued that "the theory of the total sovereignty of the state, with its corollary doctrine that only the state, and not the individual, may be the subject of international law" was dangerous and outmoded:

> The consequence is that no true international order can exist. If a state is completely sovereign it can determine as it pleased when it will and when it will not accept the discipline of the community of states. This is anarchy. Sovereignty has become all the more dangerous as the development of close economic, transportation and migration ties has bought in its train closer and more critical international relations than existed when international affairs were more largely a matter of dynastic rivalries and diplomatic procedure. Even then, the most clear-sighted students of affairs realized the inviability of total sovereignty.[59]

The assertions of Wright and the American Jewish Committee met with support not only by advocates of international bills of rights but also within the larger community of international legal scholars. "We have taught the layman," Philip Jessup suggested, "to worship the arch-fiction of the sovereign state." His critique was echoed by Hans Kelsen, who suggested that only those who mistakenly believed in the "theology of the state" refused to recognize a more expansive role of international law. "We can derive from the concept of sovereignty nothing else than what we have purposely put into its definition."[60] In fact as early as the 1920s international jurists began to make claims for the individual as a proper

subject of international law. According to one influential 1928 accounting, "Formerly the sovereign State was an iron cage for its citizens from
which they were obliged to communicate with the outside world, in a
legal sense, through very close-set bars. Yielding to the logic of events,
the bars are beginning to open. The cage is becoming shaky and will
finally collapse."[61]

Wartime legal observers believed the cage was almost fully open,
prompting the American and Canadian Bar Associations to undertake
a joint project focused on the "international law of the future." Involving a veritable who's who of international lawyers in a two-year study, the
project sought to articulate how law could lay "the bases of a just and
enduring world peace." Among its recommendations was the principle
that "[e]ach state has a legal duty to see that conditions prevail within its
own population in a way which will not violate the dictates of humanity
and justice or shock the conscience of mankind." In a supporting commentary, the report suggested that the "precept of State freedom cannot
be absolute if conditions prevailing in one part of the world have been
so ... shocking ... that peoples generally have been unwilling to tolerate
them." This principle was "particularly important at the present time,"
the report argued, when "efforts are being made in more than one part
of the world to exterminate whole groups of human beings."[62]

If a more supple conception of sovereignty was widely shared, wartime
rights advocates offered a range of mechanisms through which international guarantees of individual human rights might be structured. At
one end of the spectrum were minimalist calls for an aspirational bill
of rights without any specific internationalist enforcement procedures
beyond urging that its provisions be incorporated into the domestic law
of individual states. The State Department's bill took this approach. Its
drafters argued that this "would represent the simplest and least complicated method of putting an international bill of rights into effect." It
was an argument of expediency. "Such a procedure has the advantage
of provoking a minimum of opposition, which is important in a step
as radical in character as giving universal legal recognition to individual
human rights."[63] At the other end of the spectrum were expansive proposals for individual petition to an international court of human rights.
"After an individual has sought to get protection through the courts of his

state and still finds his rights denied," Quincy Wright argued, "he should have an opportunity to bring his case before a world tribunal which can declare that the legislation ... of a national state that has transgressed the bill of rights is null and void and can award appropriate remedies."[64]

Most wartime rights advocates, including the Commission to Study the Organization of the Peace, the Inter-American Judicial Committee, Hersch Lauterpacht, and the American Jewish Committee, took a middle ground, though one it should be emphasized that embodied a potentially transformative departure from past practices. This consensus incorporated the idea that there was a place for national enforcement and included provisions for making the international bill of rights a part of municipal law. At the same time, it embraced the idea that an international bill should contain language making it part of international law and emphasizing that its protections of the individual were now a matter of world concern. But the wartime consensus went further, calling for the establishment of an international human rights commission that would have educative, supervisory, and investigative powers and to which individuals and nonstate actors along with states would have the right to petition. In doing so, proponents pointed to a set of international precedents to legitimate and normalize the intrusions their proposals necessarily required into questions that had once seemed to be entirely bounded by the domestic space of the nation.

Some harkened back to early nineteenth-century international conventions abolishing the slave trade and the gradual emergence of a global antislavery regime. Others pointed to the mandate system through which some colonized territories were put under international supervision and to the establishment of international labor conventions that emerged after World War I. Acknowledging that these initiatives were "limited to particular areas," many believed they were "susceptible to generalization." It was the minority treaties, however, that were most frequently referenced as a way of consciously learning from the perceived internationalist mistakes of the past to craft an effective regime for the international protection of individual rights. The insistence on a permanent human rights commission with broad investigative powers to which individuals and nonstate groups could petition was articulated in explicit contrast to the perceived toothlessness of the minority treaty regime, as well as the restrictions it imposed on how and who could raise questions about violated rights.[65]

Wartime rights advocates were wary about what a simple declaration of rights without any enforcement powers might mean in practice. Lauterpacht in particular was suspicious of a statement limited to principles, suggesting that such a "grandiloquent incantation ... would betray a lack both of faith and candor" and "would be rudimentary to the point of being academic." But others were less sure. The American Jewish Committed argued,

> Even if an international bill of human rights is at first little more than a pious expression of noble sentiments, something will be gained by putting the nations solemnly on record. In the short run it will lead to the observance of a less ambitious but more concrete informal minimal stand of human rights, since states would tend to avoid any gross violation of the formal bill of rights. This would be an important practical gain. ... In the long run the degree of its observance may increase with time until the document is very widely held in respect and there is a close obedience to its provisions.[66]

Indeed most recognized the pragmatic need for a more gradualist path to the international articulation and protection of individual rights. "We are still dealing with a world of nation-states," the Commission to Study the Organization of the Peace wrote in its final 1944 report titled *International Safeguards on Human Rights,* and "not with individual citizenship in world government. World citizenship for the foreseeable future is not a working conception."[67] Its own summary of the critical elements of the postwar global rights order captured the prevailing wartime consensus that combined means of overlapping national and international enforcement: the immediate need for the promulgation of an international bill of rights, the establishment of a United Nations Commission on Human Rights to determine methods for its international enforcement, the incorporation of the protections of the bill into national constitutions, and the right of individuals and groups after exhausting local remedies to petition the UN commission. The right to individual petition aside, this wartime consensus first articulated the conceptual building blocks that came to shape the enforcement architecture of the postwar global human rights order.

Wartime rights talk had a scale and scope that went far beyond the promises of the Four Freedoms, the Atlantic Charter, and the UN Declaration, which had first situated the language of human rights at the center of World War II's aims and purposes for the United States and its allies. American driven but transnationally inflected, it provided the critical connective tissue that linked, and grounded, the lofty rhetoric of the early war years with the presence of human rights language in the United Nations Charter at war's end. But if these remarkable conversations provided the scaffolding for contemporary understandings of individual human rights and their international protections, getting human rights language into the UN Charter was still no sure thing. The Dumbarton Oaks conference in the summer and fall of 1944, which aimed to draft a provisional charter for the United Nations, made only passing reference to the need to "promote respect for human rights and fundamental freedom" in a clause buried toward the end of its final October 1944 *Proposals for the Establishment of a General International Organization*.[68] Putting human rights at the center of the postwar international order remained a work in progress.

CHAPTER 3

Beyond Belief

O N THE MORNING of April 10, 1945, readers of the *Los Angles Times* and *Washington Post* encountered a photograph of a U.S. army major, John Scotti of Brooklyn, kneeling in a woodshed next to a stack of nude corpses. It was taken at Ohrdruf, a subcamp of the Nazi Buchenwald concentration camp system with a prison population numbering more than ten thousand men and women who supplied forced labor for railroad construction. The camp's larger eliminationist purpose was to kill Jews and others the Nazi regime saw as threats to the Third Reich. Nazi SS troops began to evacuate Ohrdruf's prisoners by rail to the main camp complex in late March 1945. Those too ill to walk to the railcars were murdered. On April 9 Major Scotti was among the soldiers of the U.S. Armored Division who entered the camp to discover piles of bodies, some covered with lime and others partially incinerated (Figure 3.1). Ohrdruf was the first Nazi death camp liberated by American troops as World War II in Europe came to a close. Sixteen days later, on April 25, the San Francisco conference opened to draft the final language of the United Nations Charter. In the meantime, as more and more Nazi camps were liberated by American troops, horrific photographs of what was found in them filled newspapers and magazines in the United States and around the world. To many contemporaries who encountered the images, the photos were beyond belief.[1]

The photographs of the Nazi camps did not put human rights in the United Nations Charter, just as *Migrant Mother* did not directly set in motion wartime human rights talk in the United States. But in the late spring and early summer of 1945 the atrocity photographs loomed over the deliberations at San Francisco. Their impact was heighted by a

3.1. Major John R. Scotti, of Brooklyn, New York, surrounded by corpses found in a wood-shed of the liberated Nazi concentration camp in Ohrdruf, Germany, on April 9, 1945. AP Photo/Byron H. Rollins.

public campaign for human rights led by secular and religious wartime rights advocates. Deeply disappointed by the marginal place of human rights in the Dumbarton Oaks proposals, these advocates sought to mobilize popular opinion beginning in the fall of 1944 in support of more deeply infusing the protection of individual rights into the founding document of the new international organization. Their efforts gained more urgency with the demands made in early 1945 by Latin American states at a major regional conference in Mexico City for tougher rights language in the UN Charter. The intersection of this public campaign and the widespread circulation of the atrocity photographs was, of course, entirely accidental. Indeed the campaign had begun long before the liberation of the camps and the atrocity photographs had entered popular consciousness in April and May. And yet together the photographs and the campaign profoundly shaped the cultural politics through which Americans at the San Francisco conference undertook their work and the meanings they accorded to it. They simultaneously offered the still novel concept of human rights as one vocabulary for apprehending photographs for which most contemporaries "had no words" and hauntingly reinforced claims for the necessity of the protection of human rights in the making of the postwar international order.

MOBILIZING FOR HUMAN RIGHTS

The public campaign to draw attention to human rights brought American Protestant, Catholic, and Jewish leaders together with secular wartime advocates for an international bill of rights. On December 14, 1944, timed to coincide with the 153rd anniversary of the U.S. Bill of Rights, the American Jewish Committee and the Commission to Study the Organization of the Peace made public a "Declaration of Human Rights," insisting that the postwar peace "must be based on the recognition that the individual human being is the cornerstone of our culture and civilization." Arguing that "Hitlerism has demonstrated that bigotry and persecution by a barbarous nation" make "it a matter of international concern to stamp out infractions of human rights," the declaration insisted "[n]o plea of sovereignty shall ever again be allowed to permit any nation to deprive those within its borders of these fundamental rights on the claim that these are matters of internal concern." The declaration called for the promulgation of an international bill of rights as "a vital step forward on the long road at the end of which civilization seeks to create a world based on the common fatherhood of God, and the common brotherhood of man." Among its 1,326 signers were Vice-President Henry Wallace, Supreme Court Justice Frank Murphy, and former Under Secretary of State Sumner Wells. President Roosevelt conveyed his sympathies through his personal secretary: "While it is not the practice of the President to sign documents of this nature, I can assure you he fully sympathizes with all popular movements in support of this which he himself has affirmed on so many occasions."[2]

In a reflection of the growing wartime engagement by religious groups in human rights, the Declaration of Human Rights was also signed by 348 Christian and Jewish religious figures. Along with the American Jewish Committee, Catholic and Protestant organizations issued major statements on human rights in late 1944 and early 1945. The Federal Council of the Churches in Christ in America opened a broad educational campaign in the fall of 1944 that equated the defense of religious liberty with the international protection of human rights. It was led by Lutheran theologian Frederick Nolde, who would later play a role in drafting the human rights provisions of the UN Charter at the San Francisco conference. Just a year earlier American diplomat John Foster Dulles, who would also participate in the San Francisco conference, had chaired the Federal Council of Churches in Christ's Commission to Study a Just and Durable Peace. Its final report, *Six Pillars of Peace*, which included as its sixth pillar the international protections of "religion and intellectual liberty," was widely circulated in the media and among Protestant churches. Dulles and other commission members traveled to more than one hundred cities in the fall of 1943 to meet with local congregations and service organizations to discuss the *Six Pillars*.[3]

American Catholics and Jews were similarly engaged in human rights issues. As early as 1941, the Catholic Association for International Peace called for the protections of the "rights of man" to be "secured" through "world union" and prepared a brief ten-point international bill of rights. The French Catholic theologian Jacques Maritain spent much of the war in the United States where he articulated influential claims that aimed to ground protection of human rights in Catholic traditions of natural rights. In April 1945, in part to express their displeasure with the marginal place of human rights in the Dumbarton Oaks proposals, American Catholic bishops issued a major statement in support of the adoption of an International Bill of Rights, arguing that the "dangers to world peace have come from the unjust treatment of minorities, the denial of civil and religious liberties and other infringements on the inborn rights of men."[4] The American Jewish Committee's role in the Declaration of Human Rights and its wider efforts to promote international human rights emerged in part out of immediate concerns about the murder of European Jews by the Nazis and its traditional advocacy for the international protection of minorities. But as the historian James Loeffler has argued, it also flowed from "a rancorous intra-Jewish battle between Zionists and non-Zionists for control of the American Jewish community" in which international human rights appeared to offer the American Jewish Committee a political and ideational bulwark against its more Zionist-leaning organizational competitors.[5] At the same time engagement in human rights by Jews, Protestants, and Catholics alike mapped onto broader wartime interfaith efforts to self-consciously set Nazi German's visceral hostility to religion against American cultural pluralism.[6]

Along with the strong presence of human rights in American wartime domestic and ethnic politics, foreign ministers from the American republics at the Inter-American Conference on the Problems of War and Peace held at Chapultepec Castle in the center of Mexico City in late February and early March 1945 were calling for more specific human rights language in the United Nations Charter. Discussions in part focused on the establishment of a regional bill of rights, what later became the 1948 American Declaration of the Rights and Duties of Man. But the final resolutions of the conference also endorsed a twelve-point international bill of rights for the United Nations Charter, arguing that in the making of the postwar peace "it is important to extend to the whole world the international recognition of the rights of man." These developments were closely followed by the official U.S. delegation, headed by Secretary of State Stettinius, to the conference.[7]

American religious and secular groups further pressed their views about human rights in official Washington in the spring of 1945. The Commission to Study the Organization of the Peace met repeatedly with State Department officials to present its recommendations for the Charter's human rights provisions, issuing another statement signed by 150 lawyers and activists calling for more vigorous charter human rights language. On behalf of the Federal Council of Churches in Christ, Reverend Frederick Nolde also lobbied State Department officials for a stronger official commitment to human rights. The Federal Council's Commission on a Just and Durable Peace held a national conference in Cleveland at which thirty-nine Protestant denominations agreed to lobby for a binding bill of human rights and a United Nations human rights commission. The director of the American Law Institute sent its international bill of rights directly to both the State Department and the White House. President Roosevelt and leaders of the American Jewish Committee met on March 20, 1945, when Roosevelt apparently indicated he was "profoundly interested in an international bill of rights."[8]

MASS WITNESS

The first reports of atrocities at the Ohrdruf concentration camp began to circulate in the popular press just a few weeks after the White House meeting with the American Jewish Committee leadership. Then came the liberation by American and British forces of Buchenwald on April 11, Nordhausen on April 12, Bergen-Belsen on April 15, and finally Dachau on April 29. Newspaper coverage first began inside the papers; the initial brief wire service dispatches were followed by more extended blow-by-blow descriptions of what journalists encountered, as their stories gradually moved toward the front page. At Buchenwald, "tens of thousands were systematically starved, tortured, hanged, poisoned, shot and incinerated in specially built plants. ... Behind one building was the most gruesome sight of all – bodies piled up on each other like logs ready for mass burial." In Nordhausen "[b]odies littered the dirt floors. It was hard to distinguish between the dead and the dying except that sometimes the dying moved a hand and tried to whisper a plea for food. Hundreds of shrunken bodies, stripped naked by Nazi guards, had been stacked nearly like cordwood." Belsen "contained typhus, typhoid, tuberculosis, nakedness, starvation, heaps of unburied corpses, mounds covering great burial heaps, and one cavernous pit half filled with blackened bodies."[9]

A front-page *Chicago Tribune* report on April 25 sought to survey the "full horror of the Germany atrocities." It began as follows: "Piles of corpses, stacked in high tiers like cordwood, still were in the camps. Crematoriums still contained charred skeletons. Piles of bone ash lay about. Over all hung the stench of the dead and dying. As gruesome as the corpses were the thousands of emaciated living prisoners, stark hatred flaming in their eyes." *Tribune* correspondents saw "the gallows hooks where victims hung like sides of beef for hours until they died ... great ovens where thousands were exterminated ... a courtyard where mass hangings took place ... virtual pig styies where more thousands were deliberately starved to death ... scenes of wholesale death by gas."[10]

With words also came images. Photographers accompanied journalists as the camps were liberated; among them was Margaret Bourke-White whose photographic *reportage* of poverty in Depression-era America had helped make social suffering visible. Their images quickly became a primary means through which the shock of the German camps was communicated to readers. Within a three-week period in April and May 1945 Americans were exposed to a barrage of horrific images, which appeared with considerable frequency in daily and Sunday newspapers. By the end of April, what came to be called the atrocity photos accompanied feature stories about the camps in weekly news and pictorial magazines.[11] A number of images appeared, but a few became omnipresent in the coverage of the camps. One was the photo of Major Scotti at Ohrdurf crouched in front of a pile of human bodies. Another was a long view of the courtyard at the Nordhausen camp that portrayed thousands of victims' bodies awaiting burial, laid one against another in what looked to be an almost endless horizon (Figure 3.2). Photographs of corpses at Buchenwald and Dachau piled in wagons or open railcars also frequently appeared in the press, as did those of mass burial sites and crematoria filled with the ash of human remains.

Americans encountered the atrocity images in other ways too. Film footage taken by the U.S. Army Signal Corps during the liberation of the camps was shown in newsreel form at movie theaters throughout the country beginning in early May 1945.[12] An exhibition of twenty-five "life size atrocity photographs," many of which had already been circulated in newspapers and magazines, titled "Lest We Forget," was organized in St. Louis under the auspices of Joseph Pulitzer, editor of the *St. Louis Post-Dispatch*, in cooperation with the federal government. Opening in early May, the photomural exhibition attracted more than 80,000 spectators before it moved to the Library of Congress in June (Figures 3.3 and 3.4).[13] Atrocity photographs circulated in more quotidian ways as well. Amateur photographers among those who liberated the camps – foot soldiers, chaplains, and individuals in other military roles – took snapshots of what they found. One soldier said later, "We weren't taking pictures of each other. We were taking pictures of conditions." Their atrocity photographs were sometimes reprinted in hometown newspapers and circulated among their families and friends.[14]

If the almost unimaginable horrors depicted in the photographs were clear, their meanings were far from stable in the spring and summer

3.2. A widely circulating image of victims at a Nazi concentration camp in Nordhausen, Germany, in spring 1945. Copyright Bettmann/Corbis/AP Images.

of 1945. They are not, as some historians mistakenly believe, evidence that the Holocaust was the driving force of wartime human rights concerns.[15] The atrocity photographs were presented as images of unprecedented suffering without specific contextualization. They seldom appeared in such a way that viewers would know that vast numbers of victims were Jewish, murdered by the Nazis because they were Jews. In the commentary that accompanied the photographs, their subjects were "political prisoners," "military prisoners," "slave laborers," or "civilians of many nationalities" and only occasionally "Jews."[16] As Barbie Zelizer,

3.3. Crowds of visitors view a photomural of corpses piled on the ground at Bergen-Belsen concentration camp at the "Lest We Forget" exhibition at the Library of Congress in June 1945. Photograph 10619. United States Holocaust Memorial Museum courtesy of the Martin Luther King Memorial Library and *Washington Star.*

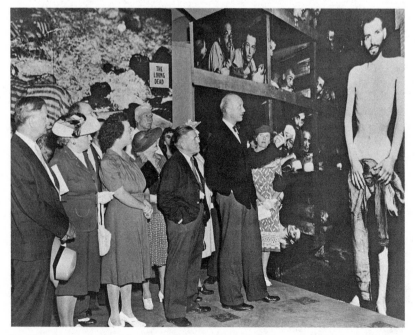

3.4. Visitors encounter a photomural of survivors in their barracks in Buchenwald at the "Lest We Forget" exhibition at the Library of Congress in June 1945. Photography 10621. United States Holocaust Memorial Museum courtesy of the Martin Luther King Memorial Library and *Washington Star.*

the leading interpreter of the atrocity photographs suggests, individual photographs were usually employed to illustrate the broader "Nazi horror" with little attention to specific place and circumstances: a Buchenwald photo might illustrate a story about Belsen and a Belsen photograph a story about Dachau. The major concern of journalists covering the liberation of the camps, she argues, was fear that the enormity of the barbarism they were encountering would simply not be believed.[17] Many journalists reported that the shock of what they were seeing was often difficult to fully capture in words. A *Baltimore Sun* correspondent wrote, "You had heard of such things in Nazi Germany. ... But now that you were actually confronted with the horror of mass murder, you stared at the bodies and almost doubted your own eyes." Harold Denny told readers of the *New York Times*, "What I saw was so horrible I would not have believed it if I had not seen it myself." CBS radio correspondent Edward R. Murrow explained to a global audience in one of the most widely received accounts of the liberation of Buchenwald, "I have reported what I saw and heard. But only part of it. For most of it I have no words."[18]

American military officials shared these anxieties. In a press conference held at Ohrdurf shortly after its liberation, General Dwight Eisenhower said, "[T]he things I saw beggar description." He immediately called for what Zelizer terms "a mass witnessing of the atrocities," relaxing some of the constraints on the wartime press to enable journalists and photographers to more easily enter the camps and disseminate their work. Eisenhower organized delegations of U.S. congressional representatives, newspaper publishers, and clergy to tour the camps.[19] The circulation of visual images of the Nazi camps in newspapers, magazines, newsreels, and exhibitions also became a powerful form of mass witnessing. Those who saw the supersized versions of the atrocity photographs at the *St. Louis Post-Dispatch* exhibition commented as follows:

These photographs show what madmen can impress on youthful minds. I urge as many parents as possible to see these pictures. The stern lessons of intolerance and the futility of war are well worth passing along to future citizens / Stories of these horrors cannot be bought forcibly enough to the attention of the people. We pray that our children's children will never have to view photographs such as are displayed here today / Such pictures as these must become relics of a barbaric age / I urge everyone to see these pictures as a reminder that we must be united / We must let the people know the truth about what happened – the German people too / I'm going to send my two daughters down here. They're only so-so when they read stories about German atrocities / It's unbelievable, but true. It's not just the piles of dead prisoners. Look at the expressions on the faces of those living people! / These pictures show terrible things, but I find not a single picture objectionable. The pictures should be exhibited. I came in from the country to see them, and I am not sorry. I feel the trip was worth while / If boys our age are going to have to help run this country, we ought to know about these things / These pictures should teach people to love democracy more / I am shocked by these photographs. But I feel they should be exhibited. Even if many more people come to see them out of morbid curiosity, I am sure they go away in a serious, thoughtful frame of mind, having learned something /Realizing what these atrocities mean is our only hope for a better life and the end of wars / These pictures show that, if anything so horrible can happen in one country, it soon can spread to the rest. The world is a family of nations, and every country is an integral part. We are responsible for the acts of all / The atrocity picture is most effective. I don't think we'll have any more atrocities like this.[20]

The last week of April and the first week of May marked the densest concentration of atrocity pictures in the media. The liberation of Dachau on April 29 unleashed a new round of stories and photographs in daily newspapers. So too did the horrified reports of a delegation of American newspaper and magazine editors who were visiting the camps. Newsreels showing conditions in the camps were first shown beginning on May 1 in first-run and neighborhood movie theatres. Perhaps most dramatically magazines with huge circulations like *Time* and *Life* undertook their first photo spreads on the liberation of the Nazi camps. *Time*'s illustrated five-page story was titled "Horror," whereas *Life*'s similarly sized photo spread on May 7 was titled "Atrocities: Capture of the German Concentration Camps Piles up Evidence of Barbarism that Reaches Low Point of Human Degradation." Both included some of the most graphic images of mass death.[21]

AT SAN FRANCISCO

As it happened the overwhelming presence of the atrocity photographs in the public mind coincided with the most intensive discussions of the place of human rights in the making of the United Nations Charter at the San Francisco conference. In an unprecedented move for a diplomatic conference, some forty-seven "consultants" representing a variety of prominent American nonstate organizations had been invited to join the official U.S. delegation in San Francisco. Their inclusion reflected the State Department's deep concern with garnering public support for the United Nations after the failure of the United States to join the League of Nations.[22] Among these consultants were many wartime human rights advocates, including representatives from the Commission to Study the Organization of the Peace and the American Jewish Committee. On May 1, 1945, the consultants were told that the official American delegation was about to announce the changes that it sought to the United Nations Charter, but had not yet decided if it would recommend expanding on the limited human rights language in the Dumbarton Oaks proposals. The consultants' reaction was swift, drafting a round-robin letter of protest that was read to Secretary of State Stettinius by Frederick Nolde of the Federal Council of Churches at a meeting the following afternoon. Although the letter never referenced the atrocity photographs explicitly, it is difficult to imagine they did not lend new urgency to a case for human rights driven by concerns with Nazi barbarism and popular opinion.

"The conscience of the world," the letter argued, "demands an end to persecution and Hitlerism has demonstrated that persecution by a barbarous nation throws upon the peace-loving nations the burden of relief and freedom." The letter asked the U.S. delegation to "take a position of leadership" by sponsoring amendments to the language of the Charter that added human rights to the purposes and principles of the United Nations and established a commission for the protection of human rights. It "would come as a grievous shock," the letter continued, "if the constitutional framework of the organization would fail to make adequate provision for the ultimate achievement of human rights and fundamental freedom. The Atlantic Charter, the Four Freedoms, the Declaration of the United Nations and subsequent declarations have given mankind the right to expect that the area of international law would be expanded to meet this advance toward freedom and peace." The letter concluded that sponsorship "of this project by the American delegation would win the enthusiastic support of the American people, and … would command their hearty approval."[23]

Judge Joseph Proskauer, head of the American Jewish Committee, followed up with a passionate speech, which further grounded the imperative of human rights language for the Charter in the demands of public opinion. "If there is to be freedom in the this world, and peace, human rights must be safeguarded and there must be machinery within the United Nations to promote such freedom, to make fundamental human rights a living reality," Proskauer told the secretary of state. "I am here to tell you that the voice of America is speaking in this room … [a]nd this is what it is saying to you: 'If you make a fight for these proposals and win, the band will play and flags will fly. If you make a fight for it and lose, we are still with you. If you lie down on it, there is not a man or woman within the sound of my voice that will have a world to say for your charter! You will have lost the support of American public opinion and I submit to you that you will never get a charter ratified.'" Proskauer's concerns were echoed by a representative of the Congress of Industrial Organizations who was present in the room, and said, "I am not just speaking for the CIO. I believe I am speaking for … all labor when I tell you Judge Proskauer is 100% right. Mr. Secretary, don't lie down on your job."[24]

Stettinius met with the U.S. delegation later that evening, remarking that he had been "deeply impressed" by his discussions with the consultants and planned to report to President Truman on the "sincerity" of their concerns about the "expansion of the reference to human rights and fundamental freedoms."[25] In the end, the U.S. delegation did propose much of the language the consultants had requested, as the text of the final draft of the Charter reflects. Historians have treated the meeting between Stettinius and the consultants in radically different ways.[26] For some, in a historiography that can verge on hagiography, the intervention of the consultants was the critical moment in which human rights language entered the Charter. Without their intervention, it simply would not have happened. Others are dismissive of the impact of the consultants, suggesting that what was in fact a short half-hour meeting with the secretary of state could not have had such significance. It is true that some of the language the consultants proposed was already circulating among members of the official delegation, although the explicit call for a human rights commission was not.[27] And there is a good deal of self-aggrandizement in the retrospective accounts of the delegates.

But in their focus on this singular encounter, celebratory and dismissive accounts alike fail to acknowledge the wider domestic and transnational forces that were shaping human rights talk at the San Francisco conference and the iterative processes through which these forces joined advocates and policy makers together. In part these accounts too easily dismiss the strong presence of ethnic politics at San Francisco, most notably the ways in which the moderate forms of human rights protections that Judge Proskauer recommended in his speech sought to advance a broader agenda of encouraging the U.S. government to see the political utility of the American Jewish community as a partner in postwar foreign policy.[28] These accounts also elide the transnational frame shaping the Charter's human rights language, including proposals by various Latin American delegations at San Francisco that drew on the concerns they had expressed at the Mexico City Inter-American conference held earlier in March.[29] In truth the letter prepared by the consultants was no more than a distillation of the public campaign waged by secular and religious advocates of human rights since the winter of 1944 and of the wartime conversations about an international bill of rights beginning in 1941.

Nor was the insistence on public opinion new. Both wartime advocates and policy makers frequently asserted that public opinion required special attention to be given to human rights in the Charter, with policy makers especially attentive to these claims given their concerns about ratification of the Charter by the U.S. Senate. Among those in the official U.S. delegation at the San Francisco conference was former isolationist and Republican senator Arthur Vandenberg, who proposed adding language to the purposes of the Charter that read "to establish justice

and to promote respect for human rights and fundamental freedoms."
Vandenberg's support for the consultants' position at the May 2 meeting
of the official U.S. delegation – the meeting notes suggest "he approved
of taking a public stand on this issue" because "it would make for better public relations all around"[30] – was just one example of many in
which human rights, public opinion, and the postwar international order
became intertwined.

Into this mix the circulation of atrocity photographs heightened
instrumental and more principled concerns about public attitudes
toward the place of human rights in the Charter. In his May 15 statement at San Francisco introducing the human rights proposals, Secretary
of State Stettinius said, "Never before have the destruction, the turmoil
and the hatreds of war affected lives of so many people in all part of the
world. ... The people of the world will not be satisfied simply to return to
an order which offers them only worn-out answers to their hopes. They
rightly demand the active defense and promotion of basic human rights
and fundamental freedoms. It is a matter of elementary justice that this
demand to be answered affirmatively."[31] One U.S. diplomat, comment-
ing on the "enormous significance" of a "clear cut and articulate recognition of the fundamental freedoms of human rights" in the Charter,
offered an even closer connection to the photographs of the Nazi camps:
"When you look at the atrocity pictures and read the story of what happened under Nazi and Fascist rule, you begin to see in concrete form
that not only did you have the barbaric destruction of human life, but
also the very deprivation of the most fundamental freedom."[32]

Some wartime rights advocates were almost giddy at the conclusion
of the San Francisco conference. James Shotwell who had overseen the
human rights efforts of the Commission to Study the Organization of
the Peace wrote in its immediate aftermath, "Human rights and fundamental freedoms have now been proclaimed to the world as fundamental
purposes for the organization of civilization in the future. In the course
of this war, taught by the horrors of persecution and savagery which
were almost before our eyes, the structure of the new society must get
beyond the old barriers of international law which recognize the limits
of sovereignty to the point of almost never interfering with regard to the
rights of the individual in another country." Rights advocates appeared

to have a new ally in President Harry S. Truman, who told the delegates in an address at the closing session of the conference that under the Charter "we have good reason to expect the framing of an international bill of rights, acceptable to all the nations involved. That bill of rights will be as much a part of international life as our own Bill of Rights is a part of our Constitution. The Charter is dedicated to the achievement and observance of human rights and fundamental freedoms. Unless we can attain those objectives for all men and women everywhere – without regard to race, language or religion – we cannot have permanent peace and security."[33]

By war's end Americans from across the political spectrum expressed considerable satisfaction that human rights occupied a central place in the United Nations Charter. At the close of the conference, Republican senator Vandenberg publicly "endorsed" human rights "1000 percent" and later confided to his diary with delight: "Everything I want in respect to 'justice' and 'human rights' and 'fundamental freedoms' is in."[34] Perennial Republican presidential candidate Harold Stassen, also a member of the official delegation at San Francisco, had pushed for the creation of a commission for the promotion of human rights. He later wrote in the monthly magazine of Rotary International, itself a new champion of human rights, that a "fundamental code of human rights is direly needed." The "new level of government must emphasize human rights rather than national rights. The United Nations organization will be foredoomed to tragic failure if it is not founded on a deep respect for the fundamental dignity of man of whatever race or color or creed."[35] At Senate hearings on the Charter in July 1945, dozens of religious groups, labor and farmer leaders, and civic, professional, and women's organizations gave testimony that lauded its attention to human rights as a "historical milestone," "a world Conscience in favor of justice and human rights," and "a new era in the history of freedom," and "rejoice[d]" in the "creation of the commission on human rights and that these rights are referred to in its preamble."[36] Standard Oil Company's first postwar annual report referred to the Charter's human rights provisions in an early articulation of what today is referred to as global corporate social responsibility. The report argued that if "we are to have a world at peace, we must make substantial and steady progress toward elimination of the underlying causes of war – chief among them poverty and want, preju-dice, fear, and the suppression of the rights of man."[37]

Others were considerably less sanguine about the meanings of the Charter's human rights language – none more so than Hans Kelsen, the international legal authority who had joined in early wartime rights dis-cussions. "No other subject matter is so often referred to in the Charter as human rights and freedom," Kelsen noted in early 1946. And yet the pres-ence of the Charter's domestic jurisdiction clause and its prohibitions on the ability of the United Nations to act in cases within the domestic juris-diction of any one state, he argued, meant "it was hardly possible" for the organization to fulfill its human rights functions "effectively." Philip Jes-sup, who also played a role in wartime rights conversations, was a bit more hopeful, writing in the late fall of 1945 that the "Charter marks not one milestone but several upon what most international lawyers would have considered a few years ago a very long road to the international recogni-tion and protection of the rights of man." If, Jessup wrote, "one must be on one's guard against millennial relaxation, one can be inspired by the anticipation of revolutionary developments."[38]

HUMAN RIGHTS COMES HOME

American international lawyers and human rights advocates in the imme-diate postwar period vigorously debated the relationship between domes-tic law and the Charter. As Hans Kelsen noted, the Charter's domestic jurisdiction clause promised that "nothing in the Charter should autho-rize ... intervention in matters that are essentially within the domestic jurisdiction of any state." But what would "essentially" come to mean? Some rights activists argued that one of the Charter's human rights provisions, Article 56, requiring "[a]ll members pledge themselves to take joint and separate action" to promote respect for human rights, offered an elasticity that opened up the possibility of challenging tra-ditional notions of state sovereignty.[39] Emergent international human rights norms, they claimed, could trump sovereignty.

If the meanings of the Charter's legal status were far from stable in the fall of 1945, and they would be hotly contested in the years to come, the growing believability of human rights and the kind of political work

3.5. Lynching of Thomas Shipp and Abraham Smith in the public square in Marion, Indiana on August 7, 1930. The photograph was one of many that circulated to a white audience as souvenir postcards of lynchings. Photograph by Lawrence Beitler. © Bettmann/ Corbis /AP Images.

they might do were among the most important immediate inheritances of the wartime period. In this, African Americans and Japanese Americans became central players. Here the atrocity photographs of the Nazi camps that were so present in American visual culture in the waning days of World War II indirectly set the stage for where and how the domestic politics of human rights in postwar America initially played out.

Although almost never acknowledged at the time, there was an alternative tradition in the United States of circulating images of atrocity. It was one quite different from the very public moral witness of the Nazi camp photographs. Between 1882 and 1945, an estimated 4,717 African Americans met their deaths by lynch mobs. Their deaths and the carnival-like atmosphere surrounding them were often photographed, reappearing later for white audiences as popular picture postcards and trading cards (Figure 3.5). These lynching postcards displayed a kind of cruelty

3.6. Oliver W. Harrington. *Germany and Sikeston, Missouri.* February 1942. Courtesy of Helma Harrington.

that today remains as difficult to look at as the World War II–era images of mass death in the German camps, a cruelty magnified by their status as prized souvenirs by those who originally acquired them.[40]

In strictly numerical terms, lynchings began to diminish in the mid-1930s, but they persisted, with well-publicized incidents in Mississippi, Florida, and Missouri in 1941 and 1942, and dozens of other cases were under investigation during the war years. More generally racial tensions ran high during the war, with serious rioting in Detroit over housing and in New York City over police brutality in 1943.[41] The uneasy connections that some African American contemporaries made between Nazi policies and Jim Crow emerged most strongly in a February 1942 cartoon by Oliver W. Harrington, art director and political cartoonist for the Harlem-based African American newsweekly, *The People's Voice*. In the first panel, Harrington depicted the Nazi slaughter of a German civilian. The second panel juxtaposed a drawing of a black man with a rope around his neck resting against a sign pointing toward "Sikeston, MO, U.S.A." in a reference to the recent lynching there of Cleo Wright (Figure 3.6).[42] The contradictions between young black men being sent to fight against Nazi Germany while experiencing extreme forms of discrimination at home were deeply felt by many African Americans. Hiding in plain view during World War II were also the camps holding Japanese Americans. In the wake of the attack on Pearl Harbor, President

Franklin Roosevelt ordered the incarceration of 120,000 Japanese Americans in a network of sixteen remote and often desolate camps in the western and southern United States. Dorothea Lange was among those who photographed the camps. But the War Relocation Authority, which oversaw the operation of the camps, closely monitored her work as it did other photographers who were commissioned to record them. Unlike the mass-circulating *Migrant Mother*, Lange's photographs of camp life and others were impounded during the war if they threatened to depict anything but the most anodyne representation of the camps. Officially sanctioned photos invariably showed the interned Japanese American as cheerful and smiling. Those that did not circulate told a more disturbing story of rights violations, one largely absent from wartime rights talk about international protections of minority groups. Certainly the imprisonment of Japanese Americans did not bring the barbarous practices of torture and death so commonplace in Nazi camps to the United States. But as the leading scholar of these images argues, official "photographs of Japanese American incarceration ... naturalize the state of exception with the false assurance of the smile." Clem Albers's April 1942 photograph (Figure 3.7) illustrates how the Japanese internment was often presented to American publics during the war. Such images elided what Lange's suppressed photographs (Figure 3.8) of desolate barracks and divided families bring into view: the deprivation of rights, the forced abandonment of homes and businesses, segregated internment based on racial difference.[43]

These were stark realities for African Americans and Japanese Americans as the war came to a close. The UN Charter offered the possibility of new ways to understand and demand their rights as American citizens. It proclaimed that the promotion of respect for human rights without distinction to "race, sex, language or religions" was among the central purposes of the United Nations. These novel international claims were ones they immediately seized.[44] But as African Americans and Japanese Americans did so in the immediate postwar period, they also faced the ambiguities of the Charter's domestic jurisdiction clause, which did not make clear how much weight UN human rights promises might have in an American domestic context. And they would bear the burden of the private transcript of wartime rights discussions that made clear American

3.7. Clem Albers. Three Japanese-American women headed to War Relocation Authority camps for wartime internment. April 1, 1942. Courtesy of U.S. National Archives (Photo #210-G-B18).

3.8. Dorothea Lange. *Tanforan Assembly Center. San Bruno, California.* April 29, 1942. Courtesy of U.S. National Archives (Photo #210-G-C334).

racial inequalities were not intended to be the proper subject of international attention. Ultimately the legacies of the wartime human rights moment in the United States would unfold on the segregated streets of Detroit and the agricultural fields of California, rather than in the distant transnational hallways of the United Nations.

CHAPTER 4

Conditions of Possibility

I N THE SPRING OF 1946, Orsel and Minnie McGhee turned to the Detroit branch of the National Association for the Advancement of Colored Persons (NAACP) for some help. A group of white property owners in northwestern Detroit had gone to the circuit court for Wayne County to oust the McGhees, who were African American, from the home that they had purchased some ten years earlier. The case rested on a racially restrictive covenant adopted by white homeowners that held that no property in the neighborhood "shall be used or occupied by any persons except those of the Caucasian race." Among the signatures on the covenant were those of the white couple who had sold their home to the McGhees. Two Detroit-based African American attorneys, both members of the NAACP's National Legal Committee, took the case. The circuit court ruled against the McGhees.[1]

The McGhee's attorneys then appealed their case to the Supreme Court of Michigan. In *Sipes v. McGhee*, their appellant brief emphasized the ways in which the lower court ruling was contrary to what it termed "sound public policy." To support this argument, the brief gave sustained attention to a decision by the neighboring Ontario High Court, *In re Drummond Wren*, that refused to enforce a restrictive covenant against Jews because it transgressed the human rights provisions of the United Nations Charter that Canada had recently ratified. The relevance of the opinion in the *Wren* case, the brief continued, was reinforced "by the wide official acceptance of the international policies and declarations frowning on the type of discrimination which the covenant would seem to perpetuate." Amicus curiae briefs filed by the national office of the NAACP and the Wolverine Law Association, a Michigan-based African American legal group, lent further support for these transnational claims.[2]

Around the same time that the McGhees were battling Detroit's racially restrictive covenants for the right to remain in their home, Kajiro Oyama was challenging the State of California's appropriation of property he had bought for his son. Oyama was a Japanese national who had lived in the United States for more than thirty years, but by federal naturalization law was ineligible for American citizenship. Oyama purchased the property in question in the mid-1930s under his son's name, Fred, who was six at the time and an American citizen. At issue in the case was the California Alien Land Law that prohibited resident aliens from owning agricultural land in the state; in its real effect the law was directed at persons of Japanese descent. Although it was possible for resident aliens to arrange for gifts of land to their citizen children, the California state government made it as difficult as possible to do so. As it happened, the state had enacted a new reporting requirement during World War II with which Oyama had failed to comply in large measure because he and his family were among the Japanese Americans incarcerated by the U.S. government during the war.[3]

In *Oyama* v. *California*, the Oyamas' attorneys argued before the California Supreme Court that the Alien Land Law was a "discriminatory law denying Japanese aliens, solely because of their race, the rights vouchsafed to all others, aliens and citizens." To support these claims, the brief argued that the California law "flaunts, for all the world to see, a conflict with the Charter" of the United Nations. Like the McGhee case in Michigan, the Oyamas' brief underscored its claims that the human rights provisions of the UN Charter provided grounds to strike down the Alien Land Law with reference to the Ontario High Court's decision in *Wren* to refuse to enforce a restrictive covenant against Jews.[4] Both the Japanese American Citizens League and the California chapter of the American Civil Liberties Union (ACLU) filed amicus curiae briefs in the case that made similar UN Charter claims.[5]

Sipes v. *McGhee* and *Oyama* v. *California* were the first of an escalating series of cases that made their way through American courts in the late 1940s and employed the novel legal argument that the controlling authority of international human rights norms trumped existing federal and state laws. Most often they pointed to the language of the UN charter itself and its promises of protections for individual human rights across national borders. Brought by Japanese American, African American, and Native American plaintiffs, these cases used a transnational frame to approach a variety of instances of domestic racial discrimination in housing, in land and fishing rights, in public accommodations, in education, and in one case where a dead body could come to rest.[6] Yet in none of these cases did the plaintiffs ground their arguments solely in the international sphere. Reflecting their expansive legal strategies and uncertainty over the kinds of claims that might be most persuasive to judges, their briefs included extended arguments rooted in U.S. constitutional law as well as sociological discussions of the deleterious social consequences of racial discrimination. But they also put forward strong UN Charter human rights arguments to underscore how these covenants and laws undermined sound public policy. Human rights had come home in what was the first instance after 1945 of international human rights norms entering directly into the landscape of U.S. legal and cultural politics.

These global rights cases of the 1940s emerged against an extremely fluid political moment following World War II at home and abroad. In this liminal postwar moment when articulations of both rights and sovereignty were in play at the intersection of the domestic and the transnational, efforts to interweave civil rights and human rights in the United States pushed on what were seen as the era's elastic conditions of possibility. Petitioners, their lawyers, a host of nonstate actors, and at times even some agents of the U.S. government came to look outside the nation to international human rights norms as a powerful moral language to combat domestic racial discrimination. They believed that U.S. judges might be receptive to such transnational legal claims. To an extent, they were correct.

As the global rights cases made their way through the American judiciary, the terms of engagement for the United States in the postwar world remained in the process of becoming. What some contemporary observers began to call the "Cold War" had yet to become the dominant prism for understanding the place of the United States in the world. For most Americans the escalating pace of decolonization in the

Global South was also an unanticipated contingency. Global protections for human rights too remained a historical novelty. In fact few contemporaries saw human rights in isolation, instead viewing them as part of a constellation of sometimes inchoate but always interlocking projects of multilateralism, global justice, international policing, and humanitarian intervention that lay in tension with more nationally bounded and traditional conceptions of unilateral state sovereignty.[7] It was this bundle of internationalist sentiments that helped drive the global rights cases forward.

Many international historians have described the immediate postwar period as a kind of prelude to what they see as the full-blown Cold War between the Soviet Union and United States that shaped international relations for much of the second half of the twentieth century. For them the unilateralist policies of American muscular realism slowly gaining strength in the late 1940s, such as the Truman Doctrine, the massive airlift in response to the Soviet blockade of Berlin, and the broader enshrinement of the doctrine of containment, are the critical building blocks of the postwar international order and so are far more important than emergent postwar expressions of internationalist multilateralism like the United Nations and its human rights machinery, the International Monetary Fund, and the World Bank. In this view, human rights in the 1940s are at best a sideshow.[8] But what is more striking in that moment was the interpenetration of internationalism and Cold War realism in postwar elite and popular American discourse. Neither human rights and the larger internationalist commitments they were embedded in, nor the Cold War alone, fully animated how most Americans viewed the immediate postwar period. Both conceptions of being in the world were in play.[9]

In these spaces that are too often rendered as simply Cold War history, there was until the coming of the Korean War in 1950 considerable room for human rights talk and a willingness to rethink the bounds of sovereignty. The meanings accorded to the human rights provisions of the UN Charter were central to the conversation. By decade's end the growing believability of the Cold War and the rapid pace of decolonization put pressure on human rights, so much so that by the mid-1950s American state and nonstate actors began to distance themselves from the emergent international human rights order. But before they did, human rights became a critical lens for understanding what a new international order might mean at home and abroad. Viewed within the larger transnational frame of which they were a part, the rights cases that came before American courts help us see the contested moral and political terrain that made up the conditions of possibility for the 1940s global human rights imagination.

THE POSTWAR HUMAN RIGHTS LANDSCAPE

The global rights cases of the 1940s in the United States unfolded against the drafting of an unprecedented series of transnational human rights declarations, covenants, and conventions immediately following World War II that sought to remake the moral contours of the world order. As the Lebanese diplomat Charles Malik announced when he put the Universal Declaration of Human Rights before the General Assembly for a vote in 1948, it had "the moral authority of the world." Malik's invocation of morality was largely aspirational. But the Declaration and the UN Charter itself were part of a far wider postwar phenomenon that sought to articulate a global vocabulary for the protection of individual civil and political rights and the promotion of collective economic and social welfare that transcended the nation-state.[10] In Latin America, wartime discussions about human rights culminated in the adoption of the 1948 American Declaration of the Rights and Duties of Man. At the same time Western European states began to draft their own rights lexicon, producing the European Convention on Human Rights in 1950.[11] Discussions at the United Nations centered on a convention to outlaw genocide, a global freedom of information covenant, protective rights of asylum for refugees, a convention on statelessness, and the drafting of legally binding guarantees of the political, economic, and social rights promised in the Universal Declaration.[12]

Postwar efforts at revising the Geneva Conventions and the International Military Tribunals at Nuremberg and Tokyo illustrate how deeply human rights, morality, and the law became intertwined in the immediate postwar period. In Geneva member societies of the International Committee of the Red Cross (ICRC) began discussions in 1946 to craft new protections for soldiers and civilians in wartime. A series of Geneva Conventions from 1859 to 1929 had gradually expanded the rights of soldiers to medical treatment and the rights of prisoners of war. The pattern in each successive agreement had been reactive, meeting the deficiencies that had become apparent in the convention after a just-concluded war. In 1946, however, the corrective was seen as potentially more expansive, given the impact of total war on civilian populations, whether through forced transfers of population, extrajudicial killings, death camps, or genocide. The ICRC, drawing on the moral vocabularies of the immediate postwar era, hoped to "guarantee in all circumstances the essential rights of the individual, as well as the respect of the human dignity for all persons who, for any reason whatever, are in the hands of the enemy." ICRC-led negotiations between 1946 and 1949 produced not only expanded protections for prisoners of war but also the Fourth Geneva Convention that outlined protections for civilians in times of war and the obligations of all parties to protect their well-being. In another innovation that pushed hard against traditions of national sovereignty, the new Common Article 3 asserted that some principles of the Geneva Conventions that had originally been designed to regulate war between states should now also apply in cases of internal conflict or civil war. As one ICRC official noted, "It was an almost un-hoped for extension" of human rights protections into the legal charter of the laws of war.[13]

Meanwhile the Nuremberg and Tokyo trials drew on emergent connections between human rights and morality to develop new concepts of universal justice. The International Military Tribunal at Nuremberg that operated between November 1945 and October 1946 brought twenty-four individual defendants, mainly high-level figures in the Nazi regime, before British, American, and Soviet judges. Former U.S. Supreme Court Justice Robert Jackson, who became the chief prosecutor at Nuremberg, put the defendants up on three major charges, all of which involved novel departures from past international practices: crimes against the peace, war crimes, and crimes against humanity. Charges of crimes against the peace accused the Nazis of waging an illegal aggressive war and looked back to the Kellogg-Briand Pact of 1928 and efforts to outlaw war in the interwar period to stake their claims. War crimes were parsed as violations of laws of war codified in the existing Hague and Geneva Conventions, because the 1949 Fourth Convention on the rights of noncombatants was not yet a part of international law. In what was the most innovative charge at Nuremberg, crimes against humanity were defined as "murder, extermination, enslavement, deportation, and other inhumane acts against any civilian population, before or during the war, or persecutions on political, racial or religious grounds ... in connection with any crime within the jurisdiction of the tribunal, whether or not in violation of domestic law of the country where perpetrated."[14] Its sensibility would become embedded in the language of the 1948 Genocide Convention.

More immediately the insistence on holding individuals responsible for violations of international norms contributed to what in 1947 came to be called the Nuremberg Principles. It was no longer, as it had been in the past, acceptable to say, "I was just following orders." In what was perhaps the most substantial push against national sovereignty and for the individual as the rightful subject of international law in the immediate postwar period, the judgments at Nuremberg argued that "individuals have international duties that transcend the national obligations of obedience imposed by the individual state."[15] There were differences around whether international law could retrospectively be applied in these cases. Justices at Nuremberg largely believed the Nazis could not be tried for crimes committed before the war began, but they did affirm that defendants could be charged for war crimes even if Nazi Germany was not a signatory to the full array of Hague and Geneva Conventions.[16]

The cases that came before the Tokyo-based International Military Tribunal for the Far East between April 1946 and November 1948 largely followed the precedents set by Nuremberg in their focus on crimes against the peace, war crimes, and individual accountability. War crimes charges focused on mass atrocities committed by Japanese troops in Nanking in 1937 and the gross mistreatment of prisoners of war, most notably in what was termed the Burma-Siam Death Railway and the Bataan Death March. The Tokyo trials were later criticized for giving almost no attention to the operation of the Japanese wartime "comfort woman" system, the human medical experimentation in bacteriological warfare that was part of the notorious Japanese Unit 731 in Manchuria, or, more generally, gross violations of civilian human rights. In fact, recent studies of the trials suggest that a wider array of war crimes and crimes against humanity did come before the Tokyo tribunal, including charges of sexual slavery and medical experimentation, and note that the final judgments referenced not only war crimes against prisoners of war but also massacres, rape, and torture of civilians.[17]

GLOBAL RIGHTS LITIGATION IN 1940S AMERICA

In this transnational moment when the 1940s global human rights imagination was in the process of construction, African American, Japanese American, and Native American plaintiffs turned to the language of human rights in the cases they brought before U.S. courts. It was also a moment when civil rights litigation was ascendant on the domestic political stage in postwar America. The kinds of claims advanced by the civil rights movement in this era were far more complex and contingent than previous scholarship has acknowledged. As Jacquelyn Dowd Hall and Risa Goluboff have argued, a scholarly and popular fixation on *Brown* v. *Board of Education* as the foundational genealogy for the civil rights movement obscures the varied scope and significance of the human rights discourse and practices in the 1940s in which calls for workplace democracy, union wages, fair and full employment, universal health care, and affordable housing were just as common as, and seen as complementary to, demands for political enfranchisement and educational equity.[18] In this emergent and more capacious conception of the domestic politics of civil rights, invocations of UN Charter provisions on human rights in the global rights cases of the 1940s were part of a diverse repertoire of rights claims that Americans advanced in the postwar period.

Among the first mentions of employing the Charter to combat instances of domestic discrimination were found in deliberations at an NAACP conference on racial covenants in July 1945, just a month after the Charter was signed in San Francisco. As part of far-reaching conversations about legal strategies for attacking racial covenants, participants discussed the relevance of the Charter's human rights articles both for domestic public policy and for exploiting public opinion to their advantage.[19] At the same time domestic activists and engaged legal scholars began to discuss the utility of its human rights provisions for legal efforts to combat restrictive covenants, the California Alien Land Law, and other forms of domestic racial discrimination.[20] Critical to these discussions was what contemporaries termed the "landmark" precedent of the October 1945 judgment by the Ontario High Court in the case, *In Re Drummond Wren*, that cited the human rights language in the Preamble and Articles 1 and 55 of the UN Charter to strike down a restrictive covenant against Jews.[21]

The Canadian decision and the domestic human rights imperatives that it suggested flowed from the Charter framed the views of a variety of nongovernmental advocacy groups – including the NAACP, the American Jewish Congress, the National Lawyer's Guild, the ACLU, the Japanese American Citizen's League, and the American Association for the United Nations – that lent vocal support to the global rights cases in amicus briefs when they came before state and federal courts on appeal.[22] Typical of their approach was an amicus brief in *Bob-Lo Excursion Company* v. *Michigan*, a case concerning discrimination against African Americans in public accommodations, which drew attention both to the precedent of *In Re Drummond Wren* and to Articles 55 and 56 of the Charter that pledged member states, including the United States, to take joint and separate action to promote human rights in making its argument.

These groups came to embrace the use of Charter language over time, and there was considerable discussion and coordination between them about using it in their legal strategies. Draft briefs for the *Oyama* case written by ACLU lawyers in mid-1946 initially made no reference to the Charter, with one lawyer suggesting "the UN Charter point" added little more than "a flourish."[23] Still the reference was there. By early 1947 the ACLU's final amicus brief to the U.S. Supreme Court in the *Oyama* case devoted sustained discussion to the relevance of Charter arguments, claiming "[n]ot only is [the] Court's review of the instant case important from the standpoint of the development of law in the United States, but it is also important from an international point of view." Citing the Charter's human rights language, the ACLU argued that the Supreme Court should review the Oyama case "not only to determine whether the

United States Constitution has been correctly interpreted, but also to determine whether our treaty obligation has been observed." To drive home the urgency of viewing the case through the lens of the Charter, the brief drew attention to the incarceration of Japanese Americans during World War II and its impact of American civil rights practices abroad:

> The international effect of the assertion in the Charter will depend in part upon the determinations of the courts of the United States on matters of race; for such determinations will serve as examples and precedents in other Nations and before international tribunals with respect to the interpretation and effectuation of the Charter provision. The fact that the ethnic group here involved consists of aliens would tend to make the instant proceeding particularly noteworthy internationally.[24]

Elements of the U.S. government itself adopted these arguments about the potential of the UN Charter for the domestic rights claims. They surfaced in the deliberations of President Truman's Committee on Civil Rights. Its celebrated 1947 report, *To Secure These Rights*, put forward what it termed a "strong argument" that U.S. ratification of the UN Charter and its human rights provisions gave to Congress treaty power to protect domestic civil rights.[25] The Department of Justice made a similar argument. Along with claims rooted in domestic practice and constitutional law, the amicus brief prepared by Attorney General Tom C. Clark and Solicitor General Philip B. Perlman in the restrictive covenants case *Shelley* v. *Kraemer* drew attention to American support of international human rights agreements to argue that racially restrictive covenants were inconsistent with the public policy of the United States. The brief highlighted the Preamble and Articles 55 and 56 of the UN Charter that dealt with human rights protections, reminding readers of the U.S. Senate's approval of the Charter as a treaty in 1945. It also pointed toward American support for the Act of Chapultepec at the Inter-American Conference on Problems of War and Peace held in Mexico City in 1945, which included provisions for the protection of human rights, as well as to the Ontario High Court decision in *In re Drummond Wren*, to support their public policy arguments.[26]

In preparing the brief, Attorney General Clark sought out the views of the State Department's legal advisor Ernest A. Gross on the efficacy of making these claims. Goss argued that the Charter did not impose "a legal obligation to guarantee observance of specific human rights and fundamental freedoms without distinction as to race, sex, language or religion." But at the same time, he suggested that "the various Charter references to human rights … do indicate the general public policy of the United States. The same may be said generally of the Act of Chapultepec." Moreover, Gross pointed out that "the United States has been embarrassed in the conduct of foreign relations by acts of discrimination taking place in this country." Reflecting broader concerns about how racial issues in the United States were playing out internationally in the immediate postwar period, he added, "These matters assume greater importance to our foreign policy by virtue of the fact that human rights now constitute an important field of activity in the United Nations."[27] Perhaps the most embarrassing of these episodes for the U.S. government was the decision of the NAACP, spearheaded by W. E. B. Du Bois, in the summer of 1946 to submit a petition to the UN exposing racist practices in the United States and its violations of Charter norms. In what became *An Appeal to the World!* the NAACP acknowledged such matters had been seen as "a domestic question which is purely a matter of internal concern." But under the UN Charter, the *Appeal* claimed that it "becomes inevitably an international question and will in the future become more and more international, as the nations draw together." Discrimination against African Americans infringed on "the rights of the peoples of the world and especially upon the ideals and work of the United Nations."[28]

Human rights as a marker for the civil rights struggle resonated more broadly in the American domestic political culture of the late 1940s. At the 1948 Democratic National Convention in Philadelphia, the party platform marginalized protections of civil rights in an effort to keep Southern Democrats in the fold during what was perceived to be a tough presidential election year. A minority plank, the work largely of then-mayor of Minneapolis Hubert Humphrey, adopted the recommendations of *To Secure These Rights* in which President Truman's Committee on Civil Rights had foregrounded how Charter human rights provisions necessitated vigorous domestic action to ensure fair employment practices and the right to vote, to outlaw lynching, and to open military service to all. Humphrey was told by many in the hall to let it go, warning he would not get the needed floor votes in support and that speaking for the minority plank could permanently damage his political career. Humphrey pushed these concerns aside. On the final night of the convention, he spoke to the hot and bored delegates, transforming them into a cheering audience by a ringing speech heard by a radio audience of sixty million. "People!," Humphrey cried, "People! Human beings! – this is the issue of the twentieth century. ... To those who say this bill is an infringement on states' rights, I say this – the time has arrived in America. The time has arrived for the Democratic party to get out of the shadow of states' rights and walk forthrightly into the bright sunshine of human rights." Minutes later came the platform vote, producing an unprecedented rejection of the compromise civil rights platform language in favor of Humphrey's expansive human rights alternative.[29]

Ultimately no single American legal opinion brought a full resolution to the proper place of the Charter's human rights provision for U.S. rights practices. But a substantial number of state and federal courts, and in one case several Supreme Court justices, proved receptive to Charter claims. These juridical responses reveal the horizons of possibility in the late 1940s and early 1950s for articulating looser constructions of state sovereignty in cases of domestic racial discrimination. They ranged from a willingness to grant moral if not legal authority to transnational rights guarantees to a full embrace of the controlling power of the UN Charter's human rights provisions for U.S. state and federal law.[30] The softest interpretation of the relationship between global rights norms and sovereignty emerged in the Michigan Supreme Court's May 1948 decision in *Sipes* v. *McGhee*. The majority opinion was particularly concerned with sorting out the efficacy of the various "public policy" arguments, including those based on the UN Charter, against private racial covenants made by the McGhees' lawyers and in amicus briefs. In the end the court was willing to acknowledge no more than their suasive powers:

It is suggested that the intervention of a World War and the declarations of statesmen and international deliberative bodies now makes the device of restrictive covenants against minority racial groups a matter of concern and public policy rather than that of private contract. ... Some of the briefs go so far as to insist that the declarations of the Atlantic Charter and the United Nations' conference at San Francisco are international treaties and have the effect of law. ... We do not understand it to be a principle of law that a treaty between sovereign nations is applicable to the contractual rights between citizens of the United States when a determination of these rights is sought in State courts.

For the Michigan court, "these pronouncements are merely indicative of a desirable social trend and an objective devoutly to be desired by all well-thinking peoples. These arguments are predicated upon a plea for justice rather than the application of the settled principles of established law."[31] In the end the court let the racial covenant stand, rejecting both domestic and transnational public policy arguments.

In several other cases, however, judges were willing to grant more binding authority to UN Charter human rights provisions. In his May 1947 dissent in *Hurd* v. *Hodge* from a majority opinion that refused to strike down racial covenants in Washington, DC, U.S. Circuit Judge Henry W. Edgerton devoted sustained attention to the symbolic significance of international human rights norms for U.S. public policy on domestic racial discrimination. Noting the Charter human rights provisions and the decision of the Canadian court in *In Re Drummond Wren*, Edgerton argued, "America's adherence to this Charter, the adherence of other countries to it, and our American desire for international good will and cooperation cannot be neglected in any consideration of the policy preventing men from buying homes because they are Negroes." In many countries, he continued, "the color of a man's skin is little more important than the color of his hair and in many others the favored color is not white. In Western Europe, to say nothing of other parts of the world, the position of Negroes in America is widely advertised and widely resented." Edgerton reminded readers that President Truman had recently said the following in a speech at the National Press Club:

We see colonial peoples moving toward their independence. It is a process that we, as Americans, can understand and sympathize with, since it parallels our own struggle for independence. ... One way in which we can help is to set an example of a nation in which people of different backgrounds and different origins work peacefully and successfully alongside one another. ... We are learning what loud echoes both our successes and our failures have in every corner of the world. That is one of the pressing reasons why we cannot afford failures. When we fail to live together in peace, the failure touches not us, as Americans, alone, but the cause of democracy itself.

Cases like *Hurd* v. *Hodge*, Edgerton concluded, "and the ghetto system they enforce, are among our conspicuous failures to live together in peace."[32] A Harvard-trained lawyer and former professor at Cornell Law School who was appointed to the U.S. Court of Appeals by Franklin Roosevelt in 1937, Judge Edgerton was held in especially high regard in legal circles. His dissent was hailed by proponents of the American global rights cases as "excellent" and immediately regarded as potentially influential for the Supreme Court's own approach to racial covenants.[33]

One state court went further than Edgerton. In the Japanese land rights case *Namba* v. *McCourt*, the March 1949 majority opinion of the Oregon Supreme Court to strike down the state's Alien Land Law directly articulated how UN Charter human rights provisions were relevant for what the court called "our understanding of constitutional law." In its review of five previous decisions by the U.S. Supreme Court upholding alien land laws, the Oregon court argued that in the quarter-century that had passed since their announcement,

> significant changes took place in our understanding of constitutional law, in our governmental structure, in our relationship with other nations and their people, in the number of ineligible aliens within our borders, and in the attitude of the American citizen toward others who do not have his individual color, creed or racial background. ... When our nation signed the Charter of the United Nations we thereby became bound to the following principles ... "Universal respect for, and observance, of human rights and fundamental freedoms for all without distinction as to race, sex, language, or religion."

In an extended analysis that combined discussion of domestic and international precedents, UN Charter human rights provisions directly informed the court's conclusion that the Oregon law "infringes upon the equal protection clause of the Fourteenth Amendment" and its holding that the Alien Land Law was "invalid."[34]

Three other opinions brought even more forceful articulations of the controlling authority of global human rights norms for domestic practices. In the Japanese land rights case *Oyama v. California*, the majority opinion of the U.S. Supreme Court in 1948 did not make reference to Charter arguments, but two concurrences strongly supported striking down the Alien Land Law in part because it violated Charter human rights obligations. In his concurrence Justice Hugo Black specifically referred to Article 55 of the UN Charter, asking "how can this nation be faithful to this international pledge if state laws which bar land ownership and occupancy by aliens on account of race are permitted to be enforced?"[35] Justice Frank Murphy, who had signed the Declaration of Human Rights in 1944 that was part of the domestic campaign to get human rights into the center of the UN Charter, put the case even more strongly in his concurrence, arguing,

> [T]his nation has recently pledged itself, through the United Nations Charter, to promote respect for, and observance of, human rights. ... The Alien Land Law stands as a barrier to the fulfillment of that national pledge. Its inconsistency with the Charter, which has been duly ratified and adopted by the United States, is but one more reason why the statute must be condemned. ... It is an unhappy facsimile, a disheartening reminder, of the racial policy pursued by those forces of evil whose destruction recently necessitated a devastating war.[36]

In its claim that a higher law trumped American federal and state law in cases of domestic racial discrimination, the opinion in another Japanese land rights case, *Sei Fujii v. California*, was the most muscular assertion in this period of the controlling power of international norms. In an April 1950 opinion, California's District Court of Appeal explicitly rejected the claims of Fujii and his lawyers that U.S. constitutional law invalidated the racially discriminatory nature of the Alien Land Law. Instead the court looked to what it termed "a more potent authority" to provide redress for Sei Fujii. Justice Emmet H. Wilson wrote in a unanimous opinion:

In the period of thirty years since the Alien Land Law was adopted we have revised our opinions concerning the rights of other peoples. Out of the travail of World War II came the concept of "respect for human rights and for fundamental freedoms of all without distinction as to race, sex, language or religion" as expressed in the Charter of the United Nations. ... The integrity and vitality of the Charter and the confidence it inspires would wane and eventually be brought to naught by failure to act according to its announced purposes. ... This nation can be true to its pledges to the other signatories of the Charter only by cooperating in the purposes that are so plainly expressed in it and by removing every obstacle to the fulfillment of such purposes. ... A perusal of the Charter renders it manifest that restrictions contained in the Alien Land Law are in direct conflict with the plain terms of the Charter.

Wilson concluded that "discrimination against a people of one race is contrary to both the letter and to the spirit of the Charter which, as a treaty, is paramount to every law of every state in conflict with it. The Alien Land Law must therefore yield to the treaty as the superior authority. The restrictions of the statute based on eligibility to citizenship, but which ultimately and actually are referable to race or color, must be and are therefore declared untenable and unenforceable."[37]

California's District Court of Appeal was even more emphatic in its curt rejection in May 1950 of the California attorney general's petition for a rehearing of the *Sei Fujii* case. In defending its opinion, the judges explicitly took on the implications of the UN human rights norms for the meaning of sovereignty in an American context. On the one hand they argued that the opinion made "no suggestion that sovereign rights of the Government have been surrendered or that the United Nations can impose its will upon any member nation. The sovereignty of the member states is expressly recognized in the portion of the Charter quoted in our opinion." But they also pointed to the ways in which the Charter's emphasis on both rights and duties required a redefinition of more fixed notions of state sovereignty: "Section 2 of Article 2 of the United Nations Charter recognizes that there are rights and benefits on one side of the ledger and obligations on the other. The Members of the Organization are pledged to fulfill in good faith the 'obligations' in order to ensure the 'rights and benefits' resulting from membership."[38]

If none of these opinions brought a full resolution to relationships between international human rights norms and domestic rights practices, they nonetheless suggest that the efforts of the plaintiffs and their lawyers to link the efflorescence of civil rights and transnational rights in the immediate postwar period to a more relaxed notion of national sovereignty did find political and legal traction in the late 1940s. Intriguingly, as one commentator has argued, in the absence of the *Sei Fujii* decision, the "creative use of the Charter to inform constitutional analysis" in the *Namba* opinion might have ushered in a more tolerant view of the efficacy of UN human rights norms in American jurisprudence and domestic political culture.[39] The outcry to *Sei Fujii*, however, foreclosed that possibility.

PERFORMANCES OF SOVEREIGNTY

The *Sei Fujii* opinion brought with it an immediate storm of controversy. Within days of the announcement of the California court's decision, it was denounced on the floors of the U.S. House and Senate. "Our sovereignty," the Minnesota Republican representative Paul Shafer told his colleagues in one typical response, "is too sacred to be tossed away for a mess of international pottage." In the Senate, several members deplored the decision for opening up to Congress the right to legislate issues that they believed the Constitution reserved to the states, among them "suffrage, schools, segregation, [the] poll tax, [and] freedom from seizure."[40] Frank Holman, president of the American Bar Association (ABA), attached almost apocalyptic significance to the opinion. He argued that *Sei Fujii* essentially allowed a foreigner, the United Nations, to become president and that it threatened to turn the U.S. government "from a republic to a socialistic and centralized state." The decision "opens a Pandora's box of possibilities. It leaves Russia or communist China free to furnish their nationals with funds to buy strategic property up and down our Pacific Coast whenever they can find a willing seller."[41]

Adding legitimacy to these alarmist claims were the responses of some influential legal scholars and practitioners. Manley O. Hudson, widely acknowledged as one of the leading American experts on international law, cabled the California attorney general as soon as he learned of the *Sei Fujii* opinion to register his "astonishment" over the court's claims that state law "must yield to the Charter of the United Nations as the superior authority."[42] Hans Kelsen did not specifically refer to *Sei Fujii* in his influential 1951 *Law of the United Nations*, but he made clear his belief that the Charter's domestic jurisdiction clause rendered its human rights articles "meaningless and redundant." The *Sei Fujii* decision was also taken up in the popular press. In his syndicated *New York Times* column, Arthur Krock noted the broader implications of the opinion for state and national sovereignties. He suggested the "ruling has raised questions as grave as they are interesting which must somehow be resolved by the highest authority."[43]

The American Bar Association's simultaneously hysterical and dismissive response to *Sei Fujii* reflected the growing disquiet of its top leadership about U.S. participation in global human rights politics. Beginning in 1948, the ABA began to wage a very public campaign against United Nations human rights norm making as "revolutionary and dangerous," targeting the Universal Declaration of Human Rights and the Genocide Convention as offering a "blank check" to undermine "our whole concept and theory of government." In an article titled "Human Rights on Pink Paper," in which he deployed the Red-baiting common to these efforts, ABA president Frank Holman warned that "by a few pages of treaty language" the economic and social rights provisions of the Universal Declaration "have transformed the government of the United States into a socialist state." The ABA's newly formed Committee on Peace and Law organized a series of sixteen regional seminars around the country in late 1948 and 1949 at which Holman and others raised questions about international human rights law. In September 1949 its annual House of Delegates meeting approved the group's formal opposition to the Genocide Convention.[44]

The ABA position was something of an outlier until the *Sei Fujii* decision. It was the only major civic and professional organization to give testimony against U.S. ratification of the Genocide Convention in hearings before the Senate in January and early February 1950. Yet the organization was divided on human rights questions. The ABA's Section of International and Comparative Law favored ratification of the Genocide Convention with some minor reservations and, more generally, supported UN human rights efforts, as did the International Law Committee of the New York Bar Association.[45] The legal advisory committee to the major coalition of nonstate actors working in support of the Genocide Convention, among them such distinguished lawyers as Adolf Berle and Allen Dulles, suggested that "even a cursory glance at the Convention confutes" any constitutional objections. Other legal experts also offered considerably less alarmist analyses of the impact of UN human rights norms on the United States, suggesting that their suasive rather than legal powers were likely over time to favorably "alter the course of domestic law" without making the United States hostage to subversive external forces. Holman, one moderate legal scholar suggested, "stated his views with more vehemence than legal reasoning." Others, although critical of dimensions of UN human rights treaty making, emphasized the need of "repelling as baseless the attacks" made by the ABA. Quincy Wright, who had been at the center of wartime rights talk, mounted a full-throttled defense of the Charter arguments made in the global rights cases.[46]

The decision in *Sei Fujii* ultimately shifted that balance, emerging as a powerful symbolic vehicle through which proponents of what became known as the Bricker Amendment sought to severely limit U.S. participation in the global human rights order. In 1951 Ohio Senator John Bricker introduced a resolution opposing the draft UN International Covenant on Human Rights, which was an effort to give international legal teeth to the largely aspirational Universal Declaration on Human Rights. The Covenant, Bricker argued, "would be more appropriately entitled as a Covenant on Human Slavery or subservience to government. ... [T]hose who drafted the Covenant on Human Rights repudiated the underlying theory of the Bill of Rights – freedom to be let alone." At the same time, Bricker cited *Sei Fujii* as evidence of the ominous potential of the UN to effect unwanted changes in American domestic policy.[47]

In early 1952 Bricker decided the grave peril that these cases and the Covenant presented to American sovereignty and values required recourse to a constitutional amendment that severely constrained the treaty-making power of the president. The voluminous hearings held on the Bricker Amendment in 1952 and 1953 are a particularly rich site for capturing the nature of American opposition to transnational intrusions on domestic policy and rights questions. Laced throughout these discussions and debates, Senator Bricker – along with his allies in the Republican Party, the ABA, and a host of conservative organizations – made frequent reference to *Fujii* and other global rights cases as emblematic of the transnational assault on "existing laws which are in our Bill of Rights and our Constitution, thereby forcing unacceptable theories and practices upon the citizens of the United States of America." The draft UN Covenant on Human Rights was also denounced in testimony as "utter nonsense," "a blueprint for tyranny," and the "greatest threat to American sovereignty."[48] In these hearings, the global rights cases and free-floating fears of UN human rights law emerged as markers and accelerators of more deeply rooted conservative suspicions of the international sphere and "big government statism," and were invoked as part of efforts to preserve the sensibilities and practices of Jim Crow segregation in the postwar period.[49]

The unfolding of opposition to the assertion of global rights norms in an American context as it emerged in the very public hearings in the U.S. Senate on the Bricker Amendment is best viewed as a performance of sovereignty, particularly of what some scholars of the state have called the necessity of "repeated performances of sovereignty" to mask its inherent instability.[50] In their shrill insistence on an exceptional American state set apart from the global processes that surround it, the Bricker Amendment hearings betrayed the essential brittleness of such imagined constructions of sovereignty.[51] It is hard to imagine a person better suited to the performance of sovereignty than John Bricker, the junior Republican senator from Ohio. A bombastic orator who recalled the Midwest of Sinclair Lewis's *Babbitt*, Bricker was one of the most outspokenly conservative members of the Senate.[52] "Our forefathers sparked the American revolution by dumping tea in Boston's harbor," Bricker told his Senate colleagues in one typically windy pronouncement on the evils of global human rights norms. "Does anyone seriously believe that a people whose ancestors rebelled at paying a trifling stamp tax will permit every aspect of their daily lives to be regulated by the United Nations?" The operation of world organization, he continued, "would destroy the sovereignty of the United States."[53]

In stage-managing the hearings surrounding his amendment, Bricker sought testimony from such reliable conservative allies as the Chamber of Commerce, the American Flag Committee, and the Daughters of the American Revolution, along with the ABA. He also invited a variety of notionally plain-spoken Americans from the heartland to testify who voiced their shared outrage at the threats to U.S. sovereignty posed by global rights norms. Illustrative is the testimony of Walter McGrath, who ran a heating company in Cincinnati and was a member of the U.S. employer delegation to the International Labor Organization in Geneva. As McGrath told the Senate subcommittee,

> The thing that has mystified me for a long time is where do all of these
> ideas originate from that are so incompatible with our way of thinking over
> here. And the resentment that I feel about what is being proposed here is
> that we import these ideologies and ideas from other places of the world,
> apparently to improve our way of life. I don't think it improves our way of
> life from what I have seen. ... [I]t is quite clearly ... a plan of government
> of the world to plan the way of life for the people of the world on the
> theory that the people of the world are so dumb that they can't promote
> their own interest under our system of government.[54]

Although ultimately if narrowly defeated, the Bricker Amendment prompted a public pledge by the Eisenhower administration in the spring of 1953 that the United States would opt out of further participation in human rights treaty making in the United Nations. It also brought the administration's promise to withdraw the Genocide Convention and other pending international human rights instruments from consideration for ratification by the U.S. Senate. President Dwight Eisenhower and Secretary of State John Foster Dulles both viewed Senator Bricker with some distaste, and the administration vigorously opposed the Bricker Amendment in large measure because of its broader challenge to the authority of the executive branch in making foreign policy. In doing so, however, the Eisenhower administration fully embraced the performative dimensions of the Bricker hearings to undercut the potential political potency of the human rights and sovereignty arguments made by Bricker and his supporters. In his testimony to the Senate subcommittee that indicated that President Eisenhower would not sign any additional international human rights treaties, Dulles said, "We do not ourselves look upon a treaty as a means which we would now select as the proper and most effective way to spread throughout the world the goals of human liberty." The administration, he continued in a reference to the global rights cases of the 1940s, welcomed "a reversal of the trend toward trying to use the treaty-making power to effect internal social changes."[55]

Bricker's and the Eisenhower administration's performances of sovereignty marked a shutting down of the liminal space in which the 1940s global human rights imagination had flourished in the United States. Bricker and his allies were successful in forcing what would become an almost two-decade-long official U.S. aversion to human rights politics. Many nonstate American actors, especially those civil liberties and civil rights groups so closely involved in the global rights cases of the 1940s, also retreated from efforts to link domestic rights claims with human rights. Along with the Bricker Amendment controversy, the rise of McCarthyism in the 1950s and the specious insistence on connections between Soviet communism and UN human rights treaties helped make human rights toxic in American politics. In advancing rights claims at home, the civil rights movement increasingly turned to a domestic language of rights almost entirely decoupled from reference to international human rights norms.[56] Indeed when human rights concerns did reemerge in 1970s America, they were largely oriented outward toward human rights violations in other places in the world rather than at home.

THE 1940S GLOBAL HUMAN RIGHTS MOMENT

The litigants in the American rights cases were not alone in their insistence that the Charter offered the possibility of remaking the bounds of sovereignty to protect individual human rights nor in their assessment of the limits they would encounter to what political and moral work human rights could do in the world. Viewed against a larger transnational canvas, the American cases can help us rethink the global history of the 1940s human rights moment. The elastic conditions of postwar possibility were first tested outside the United States in a 1946 campaign for Indian rights in South Africa led by the Indian delegation to the United Nations. The delegation sought to win majority support in the General Assembly for a resolution that criticized the South African government's passage of the Asiatic Land Tenure and Indian Representation Act, which legalized discriminatory treatment of the country's Indian population. The ironies here ran especially deep. The South African premier, Field Marshal Jan Smuts, who had helped draft the human rights language in the Preamble to the UN charter, apparently never dreaming it would have any substantive implications for South Africa's own apartheid government, insisted that the domestic jurisdiction clause prevented UN discussion of or action on the treatment of Indians in South Africa. But after tense and sustained debate, India's argument that the General Assembly could hear and rule on cases like this one that violated Charter human rights language won the day by a two-thirds majority of Assembly members. "The treatment of Indians in South Africa," the Assembly ruled, "shall be in conformity with international obligations under the agreements concluded between the two Governments and the relevant provisions of the Charter."[57]

For some observers, the South African case suggested that the Charter provided considerably more than a statement of principles and spoke not only to the promotion but also the protection of individual human rights. Wartime rights advocate Hersch Lauterpacht's 1948 report to the International Law Association conference in Brussels argued that UN member states were "under a legal" and "not merely a moral obligation" to "respect human rights and fundamental freedoms as repeatedly reaffirmed in the Charter." Lauterpacht believed that "the tendency to question or ignore" its "binding character" was rooted in a "somewhat alarmist interpretation given" to the Charter's domestic jurisdiction clause, which claimed that a nation's treatment of its citizens was "essentially within the domestic jurisdiction of the State." Quite the opposite, Lauterpacht argued. Individual human rights were "essentially of international concern." This was not only the case in situations of "systemic and flagrant violation of human rights on a scale likely to affect international peace and security" such as those of Nazi Germany, he added. Lauterpacht drew attention to the General Assembly debates in the South African case and the "view, repeatedly given expression in the debate, that questions relating to human rights are not among those covered" by the domestic jurisdiction clause. Not only did the Charter bind member states to the protection of human rights at home, he believed, but it also implicated private contracts like those of the restrictive covenants. Pointing to *In Re Drummond Wren* and discussions within President Truman's Committee on Civil Rights, Lauterpacht emphasized that the Charter imposed on its members "the legal duty" to "prevent a denial of human rights and freedoms resulting from discrimination on account of race, color, creed or national origin in cases in which such conduct emanates from bodies other than the State member of the United Nations."[58]

Efforts to push outward on the conditions of human rights possibility in the early postwar period emerged in a variety of local spaces. What would become postwar West Germany was deeply influenced by the human rights postwar moral imagination, one that saw Germany during the war as a rights-abusing totalitarian state in sometimes very contradictory ways. Emergent global rights norms often framed conceptions of domestic civil liberties along with more critical examinations of the crimes of the Nazi past. West Germany was the first state to introduce phrases from the Universal Declaration of Human Rights directly into its constitution and was a vigorous proponent of the right to individual petition in the European Convention on Human Rights. But as Lora Wildenthal and Pertti Ahonen have shown, the language of human rights could also inform appeals on behalf of Germans who were not Jewish or targeted by the Nazis, but who saw themselves as victims of the Allies and had fled or were expelled from their homes in Czechoslovakia, Poland, and elsewhere in Europe during the war. Conservative German legal experts and expellee organizations sought international redress in the immediate postwar period, arguing that their forced expulsions were violations of emerging international human rights norms. So too, some argued, were Allied policies of aerial bombardment during the war and the forced retention of prisoners of war during occupation. If these claims produced little political traction as the enormity of Nazi crimes became apparent, they nonetheless built on the larger wartime and postwar sensibilities about the individual as the subject of international law and the relaxation of national sovereignty to adjudicate rights disputes.[59]

European conservative political and religious figures too put the moral language of human rights to their own purposes in postwar state-led projects of European reconstruction. During the war the itinerant French Catholic publicist Jacques Maritain praised the "concept of, and devotion to, the rights of the human person" as "the most significant political improvement of modern times," employing rights talk in a deliberately communitarian vein to lift up the moral "human person" against what he saw as the dangers of the atomistic individual of liberal capitalism. When European conservatives found their way to human rights in the postwar period, they came to articulate a third way between liberal atomism and materialist communism in what was an avowedly anti-secularist agenda. For these figures, human rights were "the essential hallmark of Western civilization in contrast to 'totalitarian' state slavery." Among the main advocates for the European Convention on Human Rights, Samuel Moyn and Marco Duranti have argued, were Christian personalists whose interest in defining European civilization in terms of human rights and claims for a "spiritual union" of Western European states "consecrated the basic values of the Western side in Cold War politics."[60]

New histories of displaced persons (DPs) in 1940s Europe point to the ways in which the practices of postwar moral reconstruction and the quotidian experiences of rights were mutually constituted. As Daniel Cohen has argued, the crisis posed by the presence of 1.4 million DPs in postwar Europe transformed definitions of statelessness from negative constructions of the prewar stateless as individuals deprived of citizenship to the postwar "political refugee" who was "positively branded as a victim of human rights violations entitled to international protection." Cohen also suggests that local representatives of the vast machinery established by the United Nations to manage displacement in Europe decisively contributed to the making of human rights law, most notably the 1949 Fourth Geneva Convention and the 1951 Refugee Convention.[61]

If the moral vocabularies of human rights held a range of local meanings in the postwar era, they contained their own contradictions and fragilities. The tensions were perhaps clearest in the postwar war crimes trials. Hovering over the Tokyo tribunal, as they did over Nuremberg, were accusations of victor's justice. It was the Allied powers that sat in judgment over their now vanquished enemies, and there was little question of putting the United States on trial for firebombing Tokyo or dropping atomic weapons on Hiroshima and Nagasaki or the British for their sustained wartime bombing of Dresden. The problem of victor's justice was more acute in Tokyo given the remarkable dissent of Justice Rahabinod Pal, the Indian justice on the tribunal. In what was almost a book-length dissent, Pal disagreed with virtually the entire majority opinion of the tribunal. Much of Pal's argument went to his opposition to retroactive applications of international law, but he also launched a broader attack on the assumption that international law promoted peace and human well-being. In reality, Pal argued, the Great Powers like the United States used law to advance their own expansionist aims against weaker powers in the international system. The exclusion of Western colonialism and the use of the atomic bomb from the formal counts of war crimes, along with the absence of judges from the defeated powers on the tribunal, made clear "the one thing the victor cannot give to the vanquished is justice."[62]

Official Allied rebuttals to Pal's charges of victor's justice and the tribunals' careful parsing of war crimes never fully resolved the universalizing contradictions in the trials themselves. Telford Taylor, one of the chief prosecutors at Nuremberg, argued that German attacks on Allied cities were not a war crime because both Allied and Axis powers shared an understanding that "aerial bombardment of cities and factories has become a recognized part of modern warfare as carried out by all nations." In another instance at the Nuremberg trials, justices normalized the use of atomic weapons under the practices of aerial bombardment, arguing there "is no doubt that the invention of the atomic bomb, when used, was not aimed at non-combatants ... but dropped to

overcome military resistance." The judges at Nuremberg did acknowledge the partiality of immunities granted to Allied war criminals, but
noted that the "enforcement of international law has traditionally
been subject to practical limitations" and excused the one-sidedness
of the tribunals as the result of "the extraordinary…situation in
Germany."[63]

Similarly the universalizing inclination of 1940s human rights morality tended to erase the particularities of the Nazi genocide against European Jews. Drained of its specificities, a particular Jewish fate came to be
represented as universal human suffering. Not only was this so at the
Nuremberg trials where the murder of Jews was subsumed under the
label of "crimes against humanity"; the universalizing impulse resonated
even more broadly at the level of popular culture. As several scholars
have recently noted, the presentation and reception of Anne Frank's
diary published in 1947 as it became an international best-seller and later
a popular stage play and film downplayed the centrality of the Jewish
dimension of the story and the vividness of Anne's multifaceted personality. In their place, the lives of the Franks were rendered as an uplifting
symbol of humanity and Anne a clichéd figure "who possessed a seemingly never-ending optimism and hope for mankind."[64]

The problems of human rights universalism did not go unnoticed by
some contemporary observers. The American Anthropological Association's 1947 "Statement on Human Rights," prepared at the invitation of
those drafting the Universal Declaration, rejected the notion of universal
human rights altogether, emphasizing the plurality of cultural references
and authorities for conceptions of rights.[65] Similarly UNESCO director
Julian Huxley's efforts in 1947 to find a common philosophical basis for
human rights floundered, with some interlocutors questioning the whole
enterprise of universal rights making. Gandhi, for instance, declined an
invitation to be a part of the project, writing Huxley to say he was more
concerned with duties than rights: "the very right to live accrues to us
only when we do the duty of citizenship of the world. From this one fundamental statement, perhaps it is easy enough to define the duties of
Man and Woman and correlate every right to some corresponding duty
to be first performed."[66] The more general tendency toward absolutism
in defining a universal human rights order, as well as the reluctance to

consider political, social, and cultural particularities, would continue to inflect human rights politics long after the 1940s.[67]

The conditions of possibility that produced the human rights moment of the 1940s, and the broader internationalist sensibilities of which it was a part, collapsed in the decade that followed. In their abandonment of the language of human rights, American state and nonstate actors were not alone. Human rights were increasingly in a minor key in Western Europe and much of the Global South as well. The intensification of Soviet–American hostility and the emergence of the Cold War as the dominant framework for international relations after 1950 contributed to the waning of the human rights moment, pushing human rights talk to the edges of international politics in the 1950s and 1960s except as an extension of the superpower ideological polemics.[68] In far messier and more complex ways, the Cold War also functioned locally as an agent of social repression. The historian Hajimu Masuda has drawn attention to the pattern of "social purges" that "appeared in many parts of the world almost simultaneously" in the early 1950s, among them not only McCarthyism in the United States but also antilabor drives in Great Britain, a Red Purge in Japan, the suppression of "un-Filipino" activities in the Philippines, and a White Terror in Taiwan. Central to this "global phenomena of purges," he argues, was the deployment of anticommunist rhetoric to put into place more conservative visions of state and society around questions of race, labor, gender, and the family.[69] In this broader climate, it is easy to see how global human rights could come to dangerously represent the forces of disorder at home as they did in the Bricker hearings in the United States.

Decolonization too played a role in the decline of the 1940s global human rights imagination. The imperial powers in Western Europe, most notably Great Britain and France, remained wary of advancing a transnational human rights agenda that potentially undermined their efforts to maintain control over colonial territories. They were especially concerned about provisions in the European Convention that promised the establishment of a transnational European Court of Human Rights whose decisions could trump domestic courts, because it raised the possibility that colonized subjects might bring claims to the new court for the right of self-determination.[70] At the same time, the attention of most states and peoples in the Global South was increasingly focused on collective self-determination in the decolonization struggles of the 1950s and 1960s, rather than on the individual rights claims central to the Charter-inspired human rights discourse that drove much of the human rights politics of the 1940s.[71]

If the postwar effort to put human rights at the center of the international order in the 1940s had reached its end times, a final American legal case from this period illuminates how the fluid complexities of the era's global rights imagination operated in the United States, as well as its diffuse legacies. *Rice* v. *Sioux City Memorial Cemetery, Inc.*, emerged in 1953 in the wake of the death of Sergeant John Rice in the Korean War and on the eve of the Bricker-inspired Eisenhower administration's rejection of international human rights norms. Rice's widow, Evelyn, had entered into a contract with the Sioux City cemetery for her husband's burial. Evelyn Rice was white; John Rice was Native American, a member of the Winnebago tribe. At the graveside services, several cemetery officials noticed what they took to be a number of Native American mourners and suspected Rice himself might have been Native American. They later visited his widow, who told them their suspicions were correct. The cemetery, with a "Caucasians only" burial policy, ordered her husband's body be dug up and removed.

The action drew immediate and national attention, prompting President Truman to intervene and arrange for Sergeant Rice to be buried at Arlington National Cemetery. Not fully placated by Truman's symbolic gesture, Evelyn Rice sued in Iowa courts in part on UN Charter grounds. When the Iowa Supreme Court dismissed the case, ruling that the Charter's human rights provisions "had no application to the private conduct of individual citizens of the United States,"[72] Rice took her case to the U.S. Supreme Court. In their brief for the Supreme Court, Rice's lawyers dwelt at some length on Charter-inspired claims, arguing the

> purposes of the United Nations Charter cannot be fulfilled if the racially restrictive covenant in question can be used as a defense to the conduct of the cemetery. If the cemetery is to prevail, it is because petitioner married an American Indian rather than a member of the Caucasian Race. It logically must follow that, while the cemetery could not avoid the payment

of damages if it had acted in a similar fashion against one whose husband was a member of the Caucasian Race, yet, nonetheless, it can avoid the payment of damages to this petitioner because of an interracial marriage. The Iowa Court is tolerating this discrimination and, at least indirectly is punishing this petitioner because she married a non-Caucasian.

The Iowa court, the brief concluded, had "violated the basic and very fundamental concepts of equality not only announced but also pledged by the United Nations Charter and all of the member nations of which the United States is one."[73]

The persisting use of UN Charter human rights provisions in the Rice case echoes other American global rights cases of the period. And its appearance after the Bricker Amendment controversy suggests that the Eisenhower administration's official hostility to international human rights guarantees was not completely acknowledged in the realm of domestic civil society. But while Evelyn White and the Native American community shared the indignities of Sergeant White's death and burial, the individualist renderings of human rights so common the 1940s did not inform her legal brief. Native American activists in the 1950s increasingly saw efforts by the American state to contest tribal sovereignty, self-government, and cultural autonomy as their most pressing challenge. For them it was not the individual rights claims that underlay the UN Charter and 1940s human rights imagination, but struggles for collective self-determination in the decolonizing Global South, and increasingly by other indigenous groups elsewhere in the world, that resonated more deeply.[74]

The 1940s American global rights cases operated at the interstices of the transnational and the local in what was part of a growing postwar moral belief that human rights ought to shape world order and local practices. When those sensibilities began to recede, it was never clear in the moment that they might one day be recovered.

PART TWO

THE 1970S

"**T**HE WORLD IS NOW DOMINATED BY A NEW SPIRIT," President Jimmy Carter told the American people in his inaugural address on January 20, 1977. "Peoples more numerous and more politically aware are craving, and now demanding, their place in the sun – not just for the benefit of their own physical condition, but for basic human rights." Four months later in an address at the University of Notre Dame that would for the first time put human rights at the heart of U.S. foreign relations, Carter said, "Throughout the world today, in free nations and in totalitarian countries as well, there is a preoccupation with the subject of human freedom, human rights." In this new embrace of human rights diplomacy, as one Carter political operative put it, the United States became "the one nation where human rights is center stage for the world."[1] Jimmy Carter was right to suggest there had been a global explosion of interest in human rights in the 1970s. But Americans did not get there first, and one might argue that they got there last. Indeed it is curious that they got there at all.

If the United States had been fully present at the creation of a global human rights imagination in the 1940s, the language of human rights had largely vanished from American political discourse by the mid-1950s. Human rights were almost invisible in the foreign policies of Presidents Dwight D. Eisenhower, John F. Kennedy, and Lyndon B. Johnson. They were completely dismissed by President Richard M. Nixon and his National Security Advisor Henry Kissinger as "sentimental nonsense" and "malarkey."[2] American social movements of the 1960s only infrequently invoked human rights. In a domestic political climate in the wake of the Bricker Amendment hearings in which the United Nations and human rights were increasingly linked to what McCarthyism helped frame as a sinister project of world government and potential Soviet subversion, mainstream civil rights actors like the NAACP no longer saw the utility of the language of global human rights for advancing their cause. Indeed they consciously pulled away from human rights, concerned it might offer yet another impediment to the realization of their domestic rights agenda.[3] Malcolm X did famously draw on human rights in a 1964 speech that unfavorably contrasted civil rights or what he called "asking Uncle Sam to treat you right" with what he saw as the more capacious notion of human rights "that are recognized by all nations of this earth." The vocabularies of human rights also took a more prominent place in Martin Luther King Jr.'s campaigns against poverty and economic injustice toward the end of his life. But more commonly the struggle for African American rights was framed as a matter of civil rather than human rights.[4]

Nor did the leaders of the growing opposition to the American war in Vietnam in the 1960s, and the burgeoning social protest movements that accompanied it, use the language of human rights. Even commentators responding to the most widely publicized incidents of what we would now almost reflexively term "human rights violations," such as the massacre of Vietnamese civilians by U.S. troops at My Lai, almost never used the language of human rights.[5] More broadly the *New York Times Index* reveals only a handful of references to human rights in the 1960s; the same was true of leading journals of opinion and more popular weekly newsmagazines. Even Jimmy Carter came to human rights very late in the day. They played a marginal role in his 1976 presidential campaign, and except for a brief nod in one of the presidential debates, Carter made little public mention of human rights until his inaugural address.[6] As one American human rights activist writes about the early 1970s, "I did not use the words 'human rights' to describe our cause. It was not part of my everyday vocabulary and would have meant little to most people at that time."[7]

What made human rights suddenly visible to Americans again? Most American diplomatic historians are certain that Jimmy Carter's pioneering if not always successful human rights diplomacy, along with growing congressional interest, were the motors that drove the turn to human rights in the 1970s. In this view human rights were largely a top-down affair firmly rooted in Washington politics; and their rediscovery was a quest to recover lost virtue at home and reclaim the exceptionalist position of the United States in world affairs after the traumatic failed war in Vietnam upended comfortable Cold War verities. Critical too was the Watergate scandal – revelations about former president Richard Nixon's abuses of executive power and then his ignoble resignation – in unleashing what American historians have termed a crisis of confidence in the American state. Shame, embarrassment, and anger over Vietnam pulled American liberals toward human rights as a reassertion of moralism in the projection of U.S. power throughout the world, while a conservative embrace of human rights acted as a banner to revive the flagging Cold War consensus. "At its core the human rights revolution of the 1970s was an emotional response to the trauma of the Vietnam War," writes historian Barbara Keys. "The human rights idea became popular because it offered a sense of purity and transcendence."[8]

But in fact human rights became an everyday vernacular in 1970s America in far more expansive, worldly, and interior ways that fundamentally decentered the place of the United States in the making of the decade's global human rights imagination. The human rights moment of the 1970s is less the story of American virtue recovered and exported out into the world than the importation of transnational ideas and practices into domestic space from the bottom up rather than the top down. Human rights in this era is best approached in the United States as a guest language,[9] one that returned to American cultural politics through what Americans came to know about dissidents in the Soviet Union, political activists in Latin America and Asia, and such transnational rights advocates as Amnesty International. Human rights became a central optic through which a variety of states and peoples saw the world around them almost everywhere else long before they came to American shores. Not only was Amnesty International, the leading global human rights nongovernmental organization in the 1970s, a European importation into American politics but there was also a broader and diverse network of translocal actors in the Soviet Union, Latin America, Western Europe, and Asia whose protean conceptions of human rights would deeply shape the contours of human rights thought and politics in the United States.

Soviet dissidents came to the language of human rights in the early 1970s. So too did anti-torture activists in Uruguay, Brazil, Chile, and South Korea, as did states and peoples in Western Europe. In all this American actors were, initially, bit players.

For Americans in the 1970s, the rediscovery human rights did not mean a simple borrowing of the human rights vocabularies forged in the 1940s. The language was there for the taking, and indeed it is almost impossible to imagine the florescence of human rights in the decade without those lexical building blocks already in place. But when Americans found human rights again, they did so in a world that was being transformed. A global rupture in the structures and sensibilities that had shaped the Cold War international order since the 1950s enabled novel forms of transnational politics in which the rising power of moral witness and testimonial truths began to remake the thought and practice of global human rights. American receptivity to this new global human rights imagination – one that lifted up individual victims of human rights and privileged political and civil rights over economic and social rights – was conditioned by the fracturing of the collective bonds that had shaped the American Cold War state. A new faith in the self-regulated market and the primacy of the self, the remaking of ethnic identities, and a rising Holocaust consciousness all contributed to making human rights believable again in 1970s America.[10] But unlike in other places in the world, human rights never fully came home in the United States as they did in the 1940s. As human rights became the prevailing language to understand social suffering outside the United States, Americans only infrequently turned to them to make their own claims for rights at home in the 1970s. In this, the United States was indeed exceptional.

These chapters are not concerned with the ways in which the American state came to employ human rights in its diplomacy during the 1970s, an effort that as other scholars have begun to ably document was fraught with tensions and contradictions.[11] Rather they recover the complex interplay of the global and local in shaping efforts by American publics to craft their own often partial and uneven human rights vernacular. By the end of the 1970s human rights were everywhere on the American scene. It became increasingly difficult to pick up a newspaper and or magazine that did *not* talk about human rights violations somewhere in the world.

At the same time a flood of journalistic accounts, memoirs, photographs, paintings, music, and films began to put global human rights front and center in the American consciousness. A virtual avalanche of grassroots and professional organizations in the United States started to turn their attention to making human rights and their violations more visible. Long before Jimmy Carter raised the banner of human rights, they were well on their way to becoming institutionalized American public and private norms. Viewed from the bottom up rather than the top down, the making of the 1970s American human rights moment helps us understand how human rights have become the dominant moral language of our time.

To get there we need to start not in Washington, DC at Jimmy Carter's inauguration in January 1977 but at St. Martin-in-the-Fields in London more than a decade and a half earlier.

CHAPTER 5

Circulations

DECEMBER 10, 1961. Actress Julie Christie and calypso singer Cy Grant are standing on the porch of the Anglican church, St. Martin-in-the-Fields, in central London. On what is the thirteenth anniversary of the United Nations' adoption of the Universal Declaration of Human Rights, the two popular British celebrities are bound together by a cord. Joining them is Odette Churchill, a national heroine celebrated for working with the French resistance during World War II, withstanding Gestapo torture, and enduring internment in the Nazi Ravensbrück concentration camp. Six months earlier, a full-page "Appeal to Amnesty" had appeared in the British press, launching what would become Amnesty International. It began as follows:

> Open your newspaper any day of the week and you will find a report from somewhere in the world of someone being imprisoned, tortured or executed because his opinions or religion are unacceptable to his government. There are several million such people in prison – by no means all of them behind the Iron and Bamboo Curtains – and their numbers are growing. The newspaper reader feels a sickening sense of impotence. Yet if these feelings of disgust all over the world could be united into common action, something effective could be done.

At the very center of St. Martin's towering Corinthian columns, looking out over Trafalgar Square, Odette Churchill lights the Amnesty candle whose flame slowly burns through the cord to liberate Christie and Grant. Appearing on the steps around them, a group of former political prisoners begin a vigil for those whom Amnesty terms "prisoners of conscience."[1]

DECEMBER 5, 1965. At six o'clock in the evening a crowd gathers in Moscow's Pushkin Square, just a mile from the Kremlin, to protest the recent arrest of the writers Andrei Sinyavsky and Yuli Daniel for the charge of spreading anti-Soviet propaganda. During the cultural thaw under Khrushchev, Sinyavsky, a prominent member of the Union of Soviet Writers, had begun to write novellas depicting a menacing and surreal Stalinist state. Although Daniel had a more muted public reputation before his arrest, he had also published several satirical novels about contemporary Soviet society. The mathematician and nonconformist poet Alexsandr Volpin, twice confined to psychiatric hospitals for writing "anti-Soviet poems" in the Stalinist era, organized the protest. He did so very deliberately on Soviet Constitution Day, the state holiday honoring what was known as the Stalin constitution of 1936, arguing that obedience to "Soviet legality" legitimated the protest and required a public trial. A crowd of 250 protestors and approving bystanders carry banners that read, "We demand an open trial for Sinyavsky and Daniel" and "Respect the Soviet Constitution." The KGB quickly disperses the crowd, confiscates the placards, and detains some of the participants, including Volpin, for questioning.[2]

MARCH 15, 1973. In São Paulo the General Assembly of the National Council of Brazilian Bishops commemorates the upcoming twenty-fifth anniversary of the Universal Declaration of Human Rights by committing the church to "honor the exigencies of Human Rights vis-à-vis all those who collaborate with her." Since a military regime took power in 1964 the Catholic Church in Brazil had been among the only institutions in civil society to speak out against the dictatorship's growing abuses of power. With the passage of draconian laws in 1968 that undid legal protections for civil and political rights and unleashed a reign of terror and rights abuses, the church itself became a victim of the junta's repression. Many came to agree with the sentiments of the archbishop of Fortaleza in northeastern Brazil, who had closed the city's churches one Sunday in 1969 after the arrest and imprisonment of a priest for giving a sermon critical of the regime. "If the Church were to remain silent when it witnesses the violation of human rights," he said, "it would be a deplorable omission or a flagrant confession of its lack of confidence in Christ." In

March 1973 at the General Assembly the Brazilian bishops go even further, calling for the establishment of "a world tribunal on Human Dignity, whose function would be to judge from an ethical point of view, the
regimes which violate the basic rights of the human person."[3]

In London, Moscow, and São Paulo the universal languages of conscience, socialism, dignity, faith, and human rights were becoming entangled. These episodes point toward what became a global eruption of
human rights talk and practice in the 1970s. Amnesty International
reported only 32,000 members worldwide in 1973. By 1980, however, the
organization counted hundreds of thousands of members in 134 countries and a Nobel Peace Prize among its accomplishments. In addition,
the number of international nongovernmental organizations (NGOs)
working on human rights almost doubled over the decade. At the local
level, the increase in numbers was even more dramatic. Hundreds of local
groups around the globe took up the banner of human rights, increasingly enmeshed in a transnational network of advocacy and information
politics. In one accounting, domestic groups founded in the 1970s that
put human rights at the center of their work numbered 1,401 in Western Europe, 220 in Latin America, 168 in Asia and the Pacific, and 88 in
Africa and the Middle East.[4] Together they set the 1970s global human
rights imagination in motion.

The surge of transnational nonstate human rights politics was part
of a broader growth in global social mobilization. Human rights advocacy emerged simultaneously with new concerns about the environment,
humanitarianism, global feminism, and apartheid. Along with Amnesty,
the formation of the Friends of the Earth (1969), Greenpeace (1971),
and Médecins sans frontières (1971) helped launch this new nonstate
transnational advocacy. The establishment of the Anti-Apartheid Movement (1959) in Great Britain initiated what would become a growing global campaign against apartheid in South Africa. Major UN-
sponsored international conferences on the environment (1972) and
women (1975), both the first of their kind, accelerated the growth and
development of NGOs, in part because parallel if more decentralized
meetings of activists variously termed "people's forums" or "people's
tribunals" were organized alongside the official sessions.[5] In aggregate

numbers, international NGOs grew more than tenfold in number between 1960 and 1984, from 1,268 to 12,686, with the bulk of the growth occurring in the 1970s. The increase in number of their local branches over the same period – from 24,136 to 79,786 – meant that the diffusion and presence of nonstate actors in the international system were even more dramatic.[6]

The novel presence of transnational human rights politics and global social mobilizations in the 1970s simultaneously reflected and contributed to a profound shift in the world order. On one level, the state-based political and economic structures that had formed the Cold War international order had begun to come undone. But just as importantly the rise of new affective bonds between the individual, the state, and the world community – ones fashioned by the growing authority of moral witness in framing conceptions of suffering and injustice – began to reshape the kinds of political claims made in the international sphere. These transformations in world structure and affect deeply shaped transnational human rights thought and practice in the 1970s. And yet, they remained unstable concepts. The growing global engagement with human rights in the 1970s was initially scattered, episodic, and improvisational. Rights talk in London, Moscow, São Paulo, and elsewhere in the world was not necessarily human rights talk. Rather these human rights origins stories of the seventies speak to the contingent, provisional, and often contested formations of what human rights came to mean by the end of the decade. Just as it would in the United States, human rights operated as a guest language that produced a variety of local vernaculars that were sometimes in tension with other competing moral and political visions. The circulations and plural vocabularies of the global human rights imagination profoundly affected how Americans later in the 1970s came to fashion their own human rights vernaculars.

STRUCTURAL TRANSFORMATIONS

The conditions of possibility that enabled the global social mobilizations of the 1970s were in part rooted in epochal changes in the very structures of the political and economic world order. In most traditional international histories of the decade, the 1970s has commonly been rendered as another chapter in the history of the superpower-driven Cold War.[7] But although Soviet–American Cold War tensions endured in the 1970s, helping launch a new round of deadly proxy wars in such places as Angola, Afghanistan, and Nicaragua,[8] the forces of neoliberal globalization began to transform the contours and dynamics of world politics. An intensification of global capitalism, new patterns of international migration, the end of empire, and the transnational diffusion of new technology and media all pushed against the nation-state–based international order that structured the high Cold War era.

These new global economic, social, and cultural ruptures began to decenter the place of the state, even of superpowers like the United States and the Soviet Union, in the making of international relations. As the sociologist Saskia Sassen argues, the seventies were a "tipping point" that initiated the move "from an era marked by the nation-state and its capture of all major components of social, economic, political, and subjective life to one marked by a proliferation of orders."[9] Shifts in the global political economy were especially profound. The rise of global finance capital in the 1970s began to upend prevailing statist economic planning and the public provision of social welfare, which were among the central building blocks of the political order shaping the conditions of global political life in the Cold War era. Offshore financial holdings leapt from 1.2 percent of world GDP in 1964 to 16.2 percent in 1980, with a tripling of world trade in the same period, in what marked the rapid growth of new forms of borderless capitalism and an individualistic market-oriented turn from the more collective and social ethos of state and world politics in the 1940s and 1950s. Empowering markets at the expense of government, 1970s globalization brought about significant erosion in the capacity of nation-states to manage their own economies and halted the continued construction of the postwar welfare state in its various American, European, and Japanese iterations. Complex interdependence between a variety of state and nonstate actors, rather than Cold War superpower politics, increasingly shaped the contours of the international system.[10]

State power did not so much disappear in this new era of neoliberal globalization as begin to reinvent itself. In part, the state became an agent of a prevailing ethos of "privatization, deregulation, and marketization" in managing what had earlier been seen as public goods. But the state was also less and less a unitary actor on the world stage. Political scientist Anne-Marie Slaughter draws attention to the coming of the "disaggregated state" in which its component parts – most particularly legislators, judges, and regulatory agents – began to form cross-national horizontal networks and supranational vertical linkages around common concerns with trade and finance, the environment, and human rights. The formation of pan-European legal associations, for instance, produced a burgeoning nonstate jurist advocacy movement in Western Europe that underlay the move over the decade toward a regional European human rights legal regime. This more fluid global order opened up a wider space for transnational activists increasingly engaged in a variety of local, regional, and global struggles.[11]

The subjects at the center of global social mobilization in the 1970s were shaped too by the movement of peoples, most notably changes in both where migrants and refugees were coming from and where they were going. The rise of an intensified cross-border labor market beginning in the 1970s accelerated the intensity of shifting patterns in international migration. This cross-border market was especially important in the uptick of contract labor migration after 1973 from India, Pakistan, Sri Lanka, and the Philippines to the Middle East, where the massive rise in oil prices produced an unprecedented demand for workers in the oil-rich though sparsely populated states of the region. At the same time labor migration to Japan, Singapore, and Taiwan from elsewhere in East and Southeast Asia also dramatically increased over the decade, as did the number of economic migrants from Mexico, Central America, and Latin America to the United States and Canada. The massive movements of economic migrants produced unease about labor rights and human trafficking, while the intensified levels of resource extraction in oil, minerals, fishing, and timber that the work of these migrants facilitated heightened environmental anxieties about the protection of land, water, and the biosphere. As broader global migration flows began to shift from Western Europe, which had been the primary destination before the 1970s, to North America and Australia, the new presence of migrants in these regions would raise concerns about racial discrimination, the nature of citizenship, and cultural rights.[12]

Migration patterns and the numbers of refugees also shifted quite dramatically with the end of empire in the 1970s. Here the decade served as another tipping point, bringing the post–World War II era of decolonization to a close. By the mid-1970s, almost all of the colonized world had become independent, territorially based nation-states.[13] With this change the migratory patterns that had characterized the first decades of the postwar period, which had been largely around and within Europe, began to give way to flows of people with Asian and African origins. Decolonizing wars of independence and heightened ethnic conflict accounted for much of this movement. In Asia, the breakup of Pakistan in 1971 and the bloody war that accompanied the creation of Bangladesh produced as many as a million refugees.[14] The end of the Vietnam War in 1975 would ultimately put some three million people on the move. In postcolonial Africa, armed ethnic conflict pushed the region's refugee population from 300,000 in 1960 to more than one million in 1970 and 3.5 million in 1981. The number of migrants from Latin and Central America also increased in the 1970s. The rise of repressive military regimes in Latin America produced increasing numbers of refugees and exiles, some of whom would become key actors in the making of global human rights politics in the 1970s. Civil wars in Central America, especially in El Salvador and Guatemala, displaced another several million people by the early 1980s. Between 1960 and 1980, the number of refugees, or forced migrants, shot up from two million, or 2.9 percent of the total migrant population, to nine million, or 9.1 percent of the nearly 100 million people crossing national borders as the seventies came to a close. In all these cases, questions of humanitarian relief and asylum gained new urgency for a variety of nonstate actors.[15]

If the end of empire in the 1970s contributed to reshaping the global movement of peoples, it also helped bring into operation the first transnational human rights court. The European Court of Human Rights, although a part of the 1950 European Convention on Human Rights (ECHR), had largely been moribund in the period after World War II. Among the most radical provisions of the European Convention, the court gave individuals the right to petition it if they were unable to redress violations of rights guaranteed by the ECHR in national courts. States were to be bound by the court's decisions, which trumped domestic law. For the European colonial powers, those provisions were troubling, given the continuing mechanisms of repression that accompanied efforts to retain imperial control of much of Africa and Southeast Asia in the 1940s and the 1950s. The very idea that colonized peoples could make a rights-based case to a supranational court provoked fear in the colonial offices of Great Britain and France. These concerns, however, waned in the 1960s as the imperial order finally began to pass into history. Britain recognized the right to individual petition and the jurisdiction of the court in 1966, whereas France waited until 1974 to ratify the ECHR altogether (it did not recognize the right of individual petition until 1981). In doing so, empire's end brought the European Court for Human Rights to life, and with it its gradually expanding caseload and its revolutionary ability to provide transnational adjudication of local rights claims that was a legacy of the wartime rights imagination of the 1940s.[16]

Along with new global flows of capital and people, technological changes and their diffusion contributed to the emergent linkages and networks that informed the global social mobilizations of the seventies. The first communications satellite was launched in the early 1960s, quickly followed by the establishment of a global infrastructure for satellite broadcasting that marked a quantum leap in the speed and range of transnational communication. Television ownership worldwide increased from 251 million sets in 1969 to 558 million in 1980, significantly widening the instantaneous circulation of mass images. At the same time, the advent of jet travel more than halved the cost of passenger air travel. Two measures of its impact were the sharp rise in international travel, with the number of international tourists growing from 69.3 million in 1960 to 284.8 million in 1980, and air travel's increasingly middle-class rather than luxury clientele. Another was the dramatic expansion of educational exchange, with 144,708 international students and scholars studying in American colleges and university in 1970 and 311,882 in 1980. These direct transnational encounters – the meeting of peoples across national borders – undergirded the decade's acceleration of global networks of thought and practice.[17]

More broadly, commodities and information were moving faster in the 1970s than they had in the past. The increasing ubiquity of the shipping container reduced the expense and increased the speed of international trade, contributing to a 320 percent rise in world trade in the early 1970s. Similarly, the first commercialized fax machines, which could transmit a letter-sized document in six minutes, were in mass circulation by the mid-1970s. UPS began delivering in the forty-eight contiguous United States in the mid-1970s, launching its international services in 1979. Federal Express installed its first overnight drop box in 1975 and expanded its overnight services internationally in the early 1980s. Although the speed and technological sophistication of the personal computer, the Internet, and social media can now seem to dwarf these developments, what Marshall McLuhan famously called the "global village" was coming into being in the 1970s.[18] If the global social mobilizations in the decade did not necessarily constitute McLuhan's dream of a technologically mediated world that thought and acted in unison, their growing influence rested on the increasingly sophisticated uses of these new forms of more rapid communication.

To argue that the processes of globalization in the 1970s transformed the structures of the Cold War international order is not to suggest that globalization itself is without a history or that elements of these dramatic changes were not present in the past. The telegraph, the steamship, and the telephone reshaped key dimensions of the state, society, and world order in the late nineteenth century. International trade, investment, and business grew substantially in the same period, reworking the nature of the international economy. Indeed, statistical evidence of global flows of trade, investment, and labor in the nineteenth century suggests that the growing economic interdependence of the 1970s was not unprecedented.[19] Moreover, international NGOs were a presence in the world system before the seventies. And of course technological change helped drive the transnational circulation of images of social suffering in the 1930s that contributed to the growing believability of human rights in the mid-twentieth century. But to overly stress these historical continuities risks obscuring the singularities of the world of the 1970s and later in which the intensity and velocity of global networks began to remake the nation-state and unbundle the relationships among sovereignty, territoriality, and state power.

Still, celebratory talk of 1970s globalization can elide how the neoliberal order and its faith in the power of the individual and the self-regulating market produced new structures of inequality within and among states. As the economist Thomas Piketty has demonstrated, inequalities in income and wealth diminished in Western Europe and the United States during much of the twentieth century, but began to rise very sharply beginning in the seventies not just in the West but also in emerging economies in the Global South. Leading economic and social measures of the era show a growing inequality between the economies of the United States, Western Europe, and Japan and those of new postcolonial states in what the geographer David Harvey calls "accumulation by dispossession."[20] Ironically the turn to the individual if not the market paralleled the sensibilities of the era's social movements. Individual political, and civil rights were often at these movements' center; claims for collective economic and social rights, especially in the West, were generally in a minor key. The structural transformations of the world order in the 1970s did not have a single trajectory, being neither inexorably oppressive nor inevitably emancipatory. But their particularities both shaped and constrained the engagement of local actors in the wider world.

A NEW GLOBAL AFFECT

Although these structural transformations provided the undergirding for the rise of novel forms of transnational social mobilization, a new global affect toward power and territoriality came to almost entirely reshape the kinds of political claims made by nonstate actors in the 1970s. A growing belief in the authenticity of the interior world of individual suffering, rather than the external structures that produced it, was at the heart of this new politics. Individual consciousness, lived experience, moral witness, and a testimonial turn became the keywords for activists of this era and began to reshape the contours of global politics and morality. Some contemporaries began to call the seventies the "Earthrise era" in reference to the now iconic photograph of the Earth taken from the American Apollo 17 space mission in December 1972 (Figure 5.1) that contributed to the decade's fundamental recasting of sensibilities toward being in

5.1. The Earth seen from Apollo 17, December 7, 1972. Courtesy of NASA.

the world. Most commonly associated with the rise of the environmental movement, the photograph in part reflected the decade's shifting imagined spatial geographies. But it also symbolically captured for contemporaries a larger and ongoing reworking of political, moral, scientific, and commercial imaginations into novel forms of what the sociologist Sidney Tarrow calls "rooted cosmopolitanism." As one historian notes, "The word 'globalization' and the phrases 'global environment,' 'global economy' and 'global humanity' did not exist before the Earthrise era."[21] Transnational social activism offered one locale in which their diverse meanings and political possibilities were worked out.

The global student protest movements of the late 1960s contributed to the inclination of human rights and other transnational social activists to speak in these new languages. Sparked in part by opposition to the U.S. war in Vietnam, global student protest unleashed fundamental challenges to existing political and social institutions, opening up the potentialities of political and moral activism in a transnational space untethered by national identities. Whether in New York, Berlin, Paris, Tokyo, or Mexico City, massive demonstrations and strikes across the world in 1968 captured a prevailing anti-establishment mood by a younger generation that questioned the very premises of a Cold War order and the nation-based political systems that sustained it. These critiques often reached beyond politics as it was conventionally defined toward a revolutionary redefinition of the self. As the historian Akira Iriye notes about these transformations, "to search for one's identity apart from that defined by the nation's political elites was ... destined to reshape national and international affairs." Forms of consciousness raising were critical to what became an entanglement of the personal with the political. For some, it was the means through which to challenge racial and gender inequalities or to reorient sensibilities about stewardship of the land and the environment. Still others reexamined their own sexual identities to question prevailing heteronormative social attitudes toward marriage and the family. But whatever the target, an insistence on the centrality of individual autonomy and choice became a primary lens through which many of these young activists saw the world.[22]

Even more critical to the new structures of feeling that infused the politics of global social mobilization in the 1970s was the rise of an emergent Holocaust consciousness and its insistence on the power of individual witness and testimony. The historian Annette Wieviorka speaks of "the era of the witness," referring to the ways which testimony about the Holocaust multiplied beginning in the 1960s. It was at the trial of Adolf Eichmann in 1962 that the global testimonial turn first emerged. Eichmann, a former SS officer living under a false identity in Argentina, had been captured by Israeli agents two years earlier and was brought to Israel to stand trial for his role in organizing the mass deportations of European Jews to the Nazi extermination camps such as Auschwitz during World War II. Coverage of the fifty-six-day trial not only put the Holocaust on the front page of world newspapers but also the decision of the Israeli prosecutor to call more than one hundred survivors as witnesses was unprecedented. At the Nuremberg trials in the late 1940s perpetrators and written documentation had been the focal points, with the voices of victims off to the side. Now the Eichmann trial put victims and lived experience at the center.[23]

The testimony of the first witness, Ada Lichtman, at the Eichmann trial marked a rupture in the trial itself and in the broader public understanding of the Holocaust. Lichtman asked permission to speak in Yiddish rather than Hebrew as she gave her testimony. "Suddenly, the language of the exterminated Jewish population of Europe filled the courtroom," writes the legal scholar Lawrence Douglas. "As one observer commented, 'You shivered on hearing the words of the language of the slaughtered and the burned.'"[24] Lichtman and the other witnesses were present not just to implicate Eichmann but also to serve as key players in a larger pedagogical project designed to publicly remember their own survival and the murder of their Jewish compatriots. In her opening testimony, Lichtman told the court that in 1941,

> They drove together some twenty religious Jews, clad in the clothes of the religious, long caftans, with prayer shawls and prayers books in their hands. They ordered all of them to sing religious songs and to pray, to raise their hands to God, and then some German officers came up and poured kerosene or petroleum over them and set them on fire with prayer shawls and everything.

"This you saw yourself?" the prosecutor asked. "Yes," Lichtman replied, "I saw it with my own eyes." Lichtman was not alone. "The testimony of Lichtman and more than a hundred other survivors at the Eichmann trial," Annette Wieviorka writes, "freed victims to speak" and simultaneously "created a social demand for testimonies."[25]

As survivor testimony resonated beyond the Israeli courtroom, it brought into being a heightened Holocaust consciousness in the 1970s that directly informed the testimonial practices through which advocates of humanitarianism, environmental protection, and human rights began to remake the form and content of transnational political and moral interventions. Moral witness shaped this new affectually driven politics. Central to it was an insistence on forms of public testimonial in which a regard for the authenticity of experience and concerns with the psyche, the therapeutic, and the emotions became as important as detached analytical research and statistical measures in making truth claims. As the sociologist Didier Fassin points out, the contrast with earlier political and moral interventions was sharp:

[U]ntil the 1960s, volunteers went off to fight alongside peoples in their liberation struggles. ... [N]ow humanitarian workers go to take care of victims of conflict. Where previously the language evoked in defending oppressed peoples was that of revolution, current usage favors the vocabulary of psychology to sensitize the world to their misfortune; today we reveal its psychic traces. Not so long ago we glorified the resistance of populations; we henceforth scrutinize the resilience of individuals.[26]

The self-conscious act of witnessing by members of Médecins sans frontières (MSF) in the early 1970s helped set in motion this radical shift in nonstate engagement in the global politics of the era. MSF was founded in the midst of the Biafran War (1967–70), waged over the secession of Biafra from Nigeria and the result of long-standing ethnic, political, and economic tensions. A famine that followed in the wake of a blockade around Biafra imposed by Nigerian military forces claimed the lives of more two million civilians. Photographs of starving and emaciated Biafran children circulated around the world. They were often rendered as examples of an "African Auschwitz" that drew on the era's new Holocaust consciousness in what has been called the first postcolonial transnational surge of humanitarian sentiment.[27] MSF challenged prevailing humanitarian practices by the International Red Cross of promising confidentiality and discretion to governments and parties at war. Instead, it pioneered a form of public witnessing, what the group called *témoignage*, that outspokenly used the global media to raise awareness of humanitarian suffering and the need for intervention.[28] In this, the personal was also the political. The physicians who made up the membership of the initially French-based MSF were in part responding to what they unfavorably viewed as an increasingly statist bureaucratic and technocratic approach to medicine in France itself. As a personal act, *témoignage* by French doctors sent on MSF relief missions to the Global South offered them the opportunity for what one scholar, in a reference to Max Weber's notion of progressive disenchantment in the bureaucratized and secular modern world, calls a "re-enchantment of their profession."[29]

The MSF use of the power of witness marked a broader transformation during the 1970s of the nature of global advocacy and of those who were engaged in it. Witnessing and testimonial truths shaped the

new politics of the environment and human rights in ways that sometimes combined the secular language of the self with more religious
vocabularies and sentiments. The Quaker notion of "bearing witness,"
the historian Frank Zelko writes of Greenpeace, helped forge a transnational environmental activism that ultimately combined "holistic eco-
logy, McLuhanism, and counterculture idealism." Greenpeace's early
founders were deeply influenced by Quaker expressions of nonviolence
and their willingness to speak truth to power. Witnessing lay at the heart
of highly visible Greenpeace campaigns in the mid-1970s, in which its
members literally acted as human shields against sperm whalers' har-
poons and club-wielding hunters of baby Harp seals (Figure 5.2). Exem-
plifying the era's melding of the political and the personal through
witness, Greenpeace co-founder Paul Watson, wrote of the moment he
threw himself on top of a baby seal: "I look down in its ebony eyes which
look back quizzically with such innocence that I burst into tears ... Now I
was personally involved, not simply making a protest of principle. I had
saved that particular pup's life, held it in my arms, felt its warm body
against mine."[30]

Amnesty International too called on Quaker notions of witness, coming to offer to its members a kind of secular religion of human rights
that drew on the Quaker and Catholic beliefs of its founders. Amnesty
coined the term "prisoner of conscience" to reflect its primary concern
with "any person who is physically restrained (by imprisonment or otherwise) from expressing (in any form of words or symbols) any opinion
which he honestly holds and which does not advocate or condone personal violence." Amnesty members bore witness to these violations of
individual conscience. The organization formed small groups, initially
called Groups of Three, which each adopted three individual prisoners
of conscience – one in the Western world, one in the communist bloc,
and one in what was then called the Third World – in order to cross
existing Cold War divisions. What Amnesty called "threes" were critical
to broader organizational efforts to self-present as an impartial force in
civil society. So too were Amnesty rules that local groups could not work
on adoption cases or rights issues in their own states.[31]

Members of local Amnesty groups worked to gain the immediate and
unconditional release of their prisoners through letter-writing and other

5.2. Greenpeace co-founders Paul Watson and Robert Hunter sit down with a Harp seal pup to blockade a Norwegian ship on the Labrador ice flows during the 1976 Canadian seal hunt. © Greenpeace/Patrick Moore.

publicity campaigns with the help of information and guidelines provided by the London-based International Secretariat. As the organization grew, most notably through its worldwide Campaign against Torture beginning in 1973, witnessing and conscience continued to drive Amnesty's efforts to make visible and help those it said were "suffering unjustly and cannot help themselves." Amnesty founder Peter Berenson termed these foundational organizational concepts an extension of "Christian witness." The "world was then divided into three," Berenson recalled in an interview, "and should really be one, in that suffering in one part of the world is equally important as suffering in another part of the world." For Berenson, a Jewish convert to Roman Catholicism, overcoming the Cold War geopolitics of three worlds through witness was akin to a spiritual quest to realize the Christian trinity. *The Appeal to Amnesty* that launched the organization in 1961, for instance, was intentionally timed to coincide with Trinity Sunday.[32]

If moral witness and testimony increasingly served as the mechanism for staking claims in the global sphere in the 1970s, a sweeping rupture in how expert knowledge was constituted informed its practice. In what anthropologist Peter Redfield calls a turn to "motivated truth," the authority of MSF and other nonstate transnational actors increasingly rested on the grounds of experience. Sentiment and reason were blended in ethically motivated empirical inquiries that combined personal testimony, statistics, and independent research. In part, such key epistemological qualities as quantification, empiricism, and objectivity that had made up what came to be considered professional expertise in the mid-twentieth century remained an essential part of the practices of witnessing in the 1970s. But as Redfield notes, these qualities were increasingly refracted through a "distinctly moral framing vision" in which the knowledge produced and circulated by transnational advocacy groups was "always undeniably motivated and built out of facts assembled directly in the service of humanity."[33]

In these new forms of the cultural production of knowledge, the political authority of mid-century individual experts in the public sphere – one thinks, for instance, of the scientist Robert Oppenheimer or the economist John Kenneth Galbraith – began to give way to the growing influence of the collective actors who made up NGOs. As they gathered and disseminated specific facts and on-the-ground stories from those they saw as authentic voices, nonstate actors simultaneously reshaped expressions of moral truth and the contours of political action for an international audience. "What counts," in these new formulations, as Didier Fassin suggests, "is not that the facts be stated, but that they be experienced." The event itself no longer "constitutes truth, but the trace it leaves in the psyche or the mark it makes in the telling. In the testimony brought to the world's consciousness, affect is present both as that which testifies (the suffering of the people) and that which is produced by testimony (the public's compassion)."[34]

Amnesty International's pioneering development of what it called "country reports" during the seventies reveals the central place of motivated truth in the transformation of global structure and affect that shaped the era's human rights advocacy. Designed to make credible Amnesty's claims of human rights violations to a variety of global audiences, the reports relied on painstaking fact-finding missions and the work of the organization's increasingly professionalized research staff in London. But they also combined these more traditional forms of expertise with direct testimonials by victims of human rights abuses. The forms of motivated truth that structured Amnesty's country reports became the template for what grew into a flood of similar efforts by the growing global human rights community in the 1970s.

The country report, *1974 Chile: An Amnesty International Report*, illustrates how this genre worked in practice. After the military overthrow of the government of Salvador Allende in September 1973 and amid reports of arrests, torture, executions, and threatened deportations, Amnesty sent an official mission to Chile made up of three lawyers: Frank Newman, a professor of law at the University of California–Berkeley, who led the delegation; Bruce Sumner, a former California Superior Court justice; and Roger Plant, a researcher in Amnesty's International Secretariat in London and the only member of the delegation who was fluent in Spanish. Newman later recalled the ride from the airport and the delegation's first days in Santiago: "As we approached the city we began to see all kinds of military equipment and guards, who stopped us from time to time. It seemed to get tighter and tighter as we got closer to the city center. We would stop at each block. And when we were quite close to the center of the city, a guy stuck his rifle in at us. It was an automatic."[35]

The eight-day mission was intended to be one of inquiry and reporting. Conditions were difficult. The delegation's hotel phones were tapped, and gunfire filled the night air. But they operated under Amnesty-imposed constraints as well. As Newman notes, "At that point Amnesty had a very limited mandate, as they call it, as to what were their concerns. ... Our major instruction was to investigate 'arbitrary killing or killings by torture or treatment that was torturous'" and report on "the condition of detainees." Tellingly, Newman continues, "we were instructed to follow the mandate very carefully. ... The revolutionary cause, either before or after the revolution, was none of our business. Dissent wasn't part of our business. Military forces were not our concern. Relations with other nations? None of that was supposed to be our business."[36]

The final eighty-page report issued from London was spare in its discussion of the political, economic, and social tensions in Chile. It offered only a few pages of background history along with the disclaimer that "this report does not describe the overall conditions that have prevailed in Chile since the coup" nor does it "evaluate the validity of the evidence for or against" political claims made by supporters of the former Allende government or the military regime. Instead most of the report was "limited to a description of the situation of political prisoners, their identity, their legal situation, their treatment and conditions." The fundamental premise of the report, its authors argued, "is that prisoners cannot hope to receive adequate treatment and safeguards when the independence of the judiciary has been threatened or destroyed." The "major concerns of Amnesty International," they reminded readers, "are to seek the release of prisoners of conscience, to work for adequate treatment of all prisoners, and to fight for the protection of rule of law."[37]

This was Amnesty's motivated truth. It infused the Chile report that combined careful and collectively compiled accountings of numbers and overall conditions with experiential first-person accounts of detention and torture. In part the report offered the kind of material evidence that would establish the veracity of legal claims about rights violations, including the numbers of prisoners detained; their places of detention; the overall nature of prison conditions; incidents of torture, execution, and disappearance; and violations of the rule of law and due process. The evidence offered in support of these claims relied on a sober exposition of traditional forms of expertise: the firsthand observations of the delegation itself, supplemented by conversations with Chilean government officials, local diplomats, UN officials, members of the press, religious figures, and lawyers representing detainees and their families. Amnesty researcher Roger Plant also made several clandestine visits to prisons, which were arranged by local activists.

But threaded through the report were a series of testimonials like this one that provided a more visceral witness to the abuse and torture of political prisoners:

> They tied me on top of the table, powerful lights above me. They put cables on my nude body, dampened my skin, and began to apply the current to all parts of my body. The interrogators didn't ask anything, but assured me that "I did it." I denied these monstrosities and they began to hit me in the stomach, abdomen, ribs, chest, testicles, etc. I don't know how long they beat me, but with all the blows to the chest, my throat and lungs filled and I was drowning. I was going to die. They laughed. ... They took us the next day and it was worse. They did things that can't be described ... there were threats of death unless we signed what the interrogators wanted.[38]

These anonymous testimonies were augmented by an appendix to the report that profiled nineteen individual cases, some with photographs, of political repression against former government ministers, academics, doctors, artists, journalists, trade unionists, and students. In these practices of human rights reporting and advocacy, evidence presented in the form of objective data and individual narrative testimony or witness became intertwined. The empirical and the experiential reshaped one another in defining truth about suffering for a global audience.[39]

In dozens of country reports on human rights violations that Amnesty would issue over the decade, the forms of motivated truth that produced the organization's 1974 report on Chile became the interpretive lens for waging its escalating transnational campaigns. In the Chilean case numerous local and transnational human rights advocates joined with Amnesty, resulting in global visibility for the military regime's terror and torture apparatus to the considerable displeasure of the Chilean government. As perhaps the most important of its human rights campaigns in the early 1970s, Amnesty's work in Chile and the alliances that emerged from it also helped build and deepen the broader global human rights movement over the decade. The constellation of actors involved in the making of the Chile report – lawyers, church activists, doctors, journalists, exiles, and the victims themselves – became the face of global non-state human rights politics.[40] At the same time, the motivated truths that structured the report became increasingly believable to the transnational publics who supported these burgeoning global campaigns for human rights.

Yet the insistence on the authenticity of experience that made up the global affect of the 1970s produced its own blind spots. In a classic essay, Joan Scott writes that "the evidence of experience ... precludes critical examination of the working of the ideological system" that produced those experiences and the historically contingent structures of power and authority that gave them shape and form. "It is not individuals who have experience," she argued, "but subjects who are constituted through experience."[41] Frank Newman's recounting of his delegation's mandate in Chile – that Amnesty wanted no exploration of political conditions, revolutionary ideology, or military power – suggests what Scott has in mind. What might be lost through the lens of individual experience was not Amnesty's concern in the 1970s. Amnesty and its supporters worked for the release of individual prisoners of conscience across the world. Full stop. Individual suffering mattered – not the structures of power that produced it. These Amnesty practices recalled the enduring universalism and abstraction of the 1940s human rights imagination in which representations of the Jewishness of Nazi victims were sidelined in favor of discussions of their common humanity.

LOCAL VERNACULARS

If radical transformations in the structure and affect of international order shaped new forms of global social mobilization and the rise of a transnational politics of human rights, its thought and practice remained highly fragmented and uneven. This diverse assemblage of local actors and NGOs did not produce a uniform alternative world order. Instead, the new vocabularies and lexicons of global social mobilization as they were employed and transformed by activists produced a range of sometimes discordant local vernaculars in the 1970s.

Imagined global solidarities were sometimes cross-cut by differences in national perspective. The various national groupings that made up such organizations as MSF, Greenpeace, and Amnesty often differed not only over tactics and strategy but also on fundamental questions of organization and direction. Dutch, Belgian, and French sections of

MSF offered quite different instructions for volunteers engaging in the practice of humanitarian witness. Greenpeace maintained an uneasy alliance between its Canadian, American, and European branches, which held widely divergent views about how confrontational the organization's interventions over whaling and sealing ought to be. Within Amnesty, the German and Scandinavian sections often prioritized what they saw as the most pressing human rights issues very differently than did the International Secretariat based in London.[42] These variances in national points of view were compounded by the structural differences between states, including patterns of volunteerism and charitable giving and their openness to civil society activism. The chasm of financial capacity between an NGO in Cameroon and the Netherlands was easy to see, but real variations in how state and society operated within Western Europe itself also profoundly shaped the fragmented nature of global advocacy in the 1970s.[43]

As Amnesty International expanded its reach in the 1970s, the organization's presence on the ground reflected the fragmentation and partiality of global social movements in this era. By 1979 Amnesty had forty national sections or branches worldwide. The majority of them (61 percent) were based in Western Europe, North America, Australia, New Zealand, and Japan. The remaining groups were scattered across the Global South: Asia (15 percent), Latin American (12 percent), Africa (10 percent), and the Middle East (2 percent). But if its membership was largely Western based, the places in which Amnesty undertook its work against human rights violations were primarily in the Global South. The organization carried out 289 official missions in the 1970s involving negotiating with governments, sending observers to trials and representatives to international conferences and, most commonly, leading fact-finding missions. Of these missions, 206 went to the Global South (77 percent); 54 to Western Europe, North America, and Japan (20 percent); 21 to Eastern Europe (9 percent), and 4 each to Israel and South Africa (4 percent). Reports and publications issued by Amnesty between 1972 and 1979, like the 1974 *Report on Chile*, followed a similar pattern, reinforcing the Global South as the organization's major focus for advocacy. Of the fifty-seven major Amnesty publications from this period, 48 concerned human rights violations in the Global South (86 percent),

6 in Western Europe (12 percent), and 3 in Eastern Europe (4 percent).[44]

In addition to these uneven geographical distributions in advocacy, the new languages of global social movements could be highly charged and were often sharply contested by the activists themselves. The multiple global social mobilizations of the 1970s did not always produce global solidarities. The first United Nations Conference on Women was held in Mexico City in June and July 1975, attended by more than a thousand delegates, to mark what the UN designated International Women's Year. In the meetings of the informal NGO tribune held side by side with the conference, dreams of a "global sisterhood" floundered against competing participants' insistence on the most desirable models for realizing social change, with some arguing for armed revolution while others embraced consciousness raising or state-sponsored projects of modernization. As historian Jocelyn Olcott writes about the event, "Ideological feuds between Marxists and feminists often degenerated into a chicken-or-egg debate over the tired question of whether women's emancipation must precede or follow economic justice – the feminist imaginary of class collaboration to wage the 'battle of the sexes' versus the Marxist paradigm of revolution through class struggle – with fervent partisans in both camps."[45]

At the same time claims to collective economic and social rights by advocates in the Global South offered a powerful alternative construction of what human rights in the decade might mean. The United Nation's General Assembly was at the center of the campaign in the 1970s led by the G-77, or what was then termed the "developing nations" or Third World, for a New International Economic Order, one that called for "the right to development," local control of natural resources, a global regulatory framework for multinational corporations, and the redistribution of financial and technological resources from north to south. Its claims were largely put to the side by most self-styled transnational human rights activists in the West over the decade, who were uncomfortable with the collectivist sensibilities and the privileging of economic over political and civil rights that underlay what was a competing vision of global human rights.[46]

The emergent global human rights imagination of the 1970s, however, never fully crowded out other modes of understanding and speaking about suffering and injustice. At times it sat in an uneasy relationship with religious and other secular expressions of what increasingly came to be called human rights abuses. Recall the crowd that gathered on Moscow's Pushkin Square on December 5, 1965, to protest the arrest of the Soviet writers Sinyavsky and Daniel in a demonstration sometimes termed the "first human rights action" in the Soviet Union. The protestors used Soviet constitutional law or "socialist legality" to claim that the civil liberties of Soviet citizens had been violated by the state. The harsh sentences ultimately imposed on the two writers sparked additional protests, which continued over the next three years in what became a cycle of new arrests of dissidents, trials, and renewed protest by dissident rights defenders.[47]

The failure of the Soviet state to respond to the strategy of socialist legality, so goes the dominant narrative of the emergence of a human rights movement in the Soviet Union, pushed activists toward the global language of human rights and the potential leverage of world opinion to make their case. In the late 1960s a group of activists founded the Initiative Group for the Defense of Human Rights, which sent letters to the United Nation Commission on Human Rights about rights violations in the Soviet Union. Another group began to publish the samizdat periodical *Chronicle of Current Events*, which quoted on each of its cover pages Article 19 of the Universal Declaration promising, "Everyone has the right to freedom of opinion; this right includes freedom of opinion without interference and to seek, receive and impart information and ideas through any media and regardless of frontiers." In November 1970, a group of scientists formed the Committee on Human Rights that encouraged what would become hundreds of letters and petitions from individuals to Soviet authorities about human rights violations. A Moscow section of Amnesty International was formed in 1973, linking Soviet activists to more transnational networks of human rights advocacy.[48]

The most dramatic element of this narrative of the transformational deployment of human rights by dissidents in the Soviet Union is the landmark Helsinki Final Act of 1975. It signators, including the Soviets, promised "respect for human rights and fundamental freedoms" within their borders. The human rights provisions of what was a broader agreement largely came about from pressure from Western European states. Neither the Soviets nor the Americans anticipated their subsequent force and power, but acquiesced to them out of a broader desire to promote détente. Soviet dissidents seized on the Helsinki Accords, becoming part of what became a global nonstate network of Helsinki watch groups that put pressure on the Soviets and Soviet-bloc governments in Eastern European regarding human rights violations. The physicist Andrei Sakharov, a founding member of Moscow Helsinki Watch along with the earlier Committee on Human Rights, who would win the Nobel Peace Prize in 1975 as a spokesperson for what the Nobel committee termed the "conscience of mankind," quickly became the global public face of the new human rights advocacy in the Soviet Union.[49]

But this apparent shift from a local vernacular of socialist civil rights law to the new language of global human rights was more complicated than prevailing narratives of Helsinki and the human rights movement in the Soviet Union acknowledge. The coming of the new human rights lexicon was not so much a rupture as an extension of an already existing dissident repertoire of thought and action. The term "human rights" was often used interchangeably with civil rights by leaders of the new Soviet human rights groups in the 1970s. The influential *Chronicle of Current Events*, for instance, was concerned with both socialist legality and the language of international human rights covenants and conventions. As the Soviet historian Ben Nathans writes, "the local and global dimensions of human rights activism were mutually constitutive." At no point in the Soviet Union, he argues, was "there a repudiation of, or a break with civil rights or citizen-based strategies ... to contain the power of the state." International "human rights became an additional method for achieving the same purpose – from outside as well as below."[50]

Indeed socialist vernaculars mediated how global human rights talk was appropriated and transformed in the Soviet Union. Nathans suggests that the disenchantment of dissidents with the Soviet state, one that began during the period of de-Stalinization in the 1950s, was never accompanied by a full rejection of socialism as a "system of coordinated, equalitarian public welfare." Socialism as an ideology continued to inform the thought and practice of most Soviet dissident human rights activists, and the emphasis on transnational solidarities in Soviet official thought may have shaped the initial inclination of dissidents to embrace a global language of human rights. For example, in setting up the Moscow section of Amnesty International in 1973, its local organizers sent the following message to Amnesty representatives in London:

> Since childhood we have been accustomed to hearing such phrases as "political action of the masses," "the active foreign policy of the government and party," the "struggle for social rights and the social reconstruction of society," "the scientific and technical revolution" – and these are the things we imagined the world was preoccupied with. As for words like "conscience," "dignity," "conviction" – we are accustomed to apply them exclusively to the exertions and strivings of individual human beings. For who can help one to value such words, and to preserve their value, other than one-self and those to whom one is closest? At first we were astonished, and could not grasp, that in fact total strangers can help people who live in the most distant countries in conditions utterly different from one's own, in other cultures. It is this above all that we value in your example and your activity.[51]

The global language of human rights that activists ascribed to Amnesty, Nathans argues, "represented not so much a new morality as a new way of deploying familiar, in fact intimately familiar moral ideas." Human rights did not so much displace socialism for dissident rights advocates in the Soviet Union as become entangled with it.[52]

Again, recall the turn to human rights by Brazil's bishops in 1973, which offers another instance of the complex dynamics of local vernacularization. The decision of the bishops to draw on the language of human rights to witness the growing abuses of the military junta marked a sharp departure from the public statements they had previously made about the regime's indiscriminate use of violence and suspension of civil liberties. As historian Patrick Kelly has argued, their embrace of human rights was a novel one that marked "a chasm in conceptions of human rights by the global Catholic Church in 1960s and what emerged in the 1970s." Progressive church activists had been at the center of the transformations of Catholicism in Vatican II and the rise of liberation theology in Latin

American in the 1960s. The explicit language of human rights, however, was nowhere in the new focus on social justice and on ministering to the needs of the poor, an example, Kelly notes, of "the relative obscurity of human rights language" in 1960s Latin America. When human rights did come to Brazil, it did not so much supplant the more socially transformative vision of liberation theology as become a parallel language to biblical scripture that drew attention to individual rather than collective human suffering. Tellingly, the March 1973 call by the Brazilian bishops to witness the regime's human rights abuses included a booklet with a full list of the thirty rights of the individual contained in the Universal Declaration side by side with passages of clarifying Scripture in what was an intertextual refashioning of the meanings of human rights. Article Three of the Declaration with its promise of the "right to life, liberty and the security of the person," for instance, was paired with "You shall not murder" from the book of Exodus.[53]

Such vernacularization in Brazil was not without its tensions. Along with the church, members of the Brazilian Left, many of whom were victims of the military regime's practices of torture and violence, also discovered the language of human rights in the 1970s. They did so largely through their encounters with emergent human rights NGOs and the growing exile community who had fled the country to avoid further persecution. When the language of human rights came to them, it was reworked by some Brazilian Marxists who, Kelly argues "grafted it on top of Marxist theory and often used both idioms interchangeably." Other leftists dismissed human rights out of hand or ignored it altogether. In debates within the Left over whether to launch a "Human Rights Week" in Brazil to raise awareness of the abuses by the military regime, for example, one hard-line socialist group attacked human rights in good Marxist fashion as a bourgeois fantasy while another more moderate group praised the language from a "tactical" perspective.[54]

It was not only in the Soviet Union and Brazil in the early 1970s that human rights operated as a fluid local vernacular in dialogue with other political and moral languages. In South Korea human rights became bound up in movements for civil rights, social justice, and democracy after the Park Chung Hee government imposed martial law in 1972. As the state began to persecute pro-democracy activists in the Korean labor movement and Christian churches, Korean civil society and church leaders founded a Korean chapter of Amnesty in 1973 and a Human Rights Committee of the Korean National Council of Churches in 1974. Both organizations were as much engaged with political and civil rights as economic welfare. The Korean branch of Amnesty paid little attention to the organization's narrow official mandate to local groups that they only work on human right issues other than their own, and they articulated their concerns through idioms that blurred the lines between secular rights talk and religious faith.[55] In Indonesia and other postcolonial states in Southeast Asia and Africa, the lexicons of social justice and of individual human rights were simultaneously deployed to articulate deeply felt concerns that had animated local politics since the anticolonial movements of the early twentieth century, but had been swept aside with the rise of authoritarian governments after independence. Somewhat later in the decade when the language of human rights came to Czechoslovakia, Poland, and Hungary in the writings of such dissidents as Václav Havel, Adam Michnik, and György Konrád, respectively, it operated alongside an understanding of the world informed by socialism and Eurocommunism, as well as ideas drawn from phenomenology and existentialism.[56]

The 1970s global human rights imagination, like the broader transnational social mobilizations of which it was a part, emerged within new structures of feeling that, in privileging witness and the experiential, began to remake prevailing notions of power and authority. Yet the dynamics that prompted the embrace of human rights were far more intricate than the simple appropriation of a novel transnational language. Instead, what human rights would come to mean over the decade – and those meanings were often unstable and contested – was worked out across a variety of local vernaculars. The sinuous global and local human rights imaginations of the era co-produced one another. When human rights finally came to the United States in the 1970s, its global circulation as a transnational moral vocabulary offered the starting point for the making of an American human rights vernacular.

CHAPTER 6

American Vernaculars I

I N DECEMBER 1973, Jeri Laber opened the latest issue of the *New Republic* and began reading about graphic incidents of state-sponsored torture in the Soviet Union, Poland, Brazil, and Chile. Torture, the article argued, "is everywhere" and had become almost "commonplace."[1] For Laber, it was a revelatory moment. "I had always tended to turn away from upsetting stories, sparing myself the details," Laber wrote later in her memoirs. "Now, however, I had gone too far. Knowing just the little I did about these real-life nightmares, there was no turning back. I was involved."[2] Laber, who became a pioneering American human rights activist and later a founder of Human Rights Watch, was unusual in the depth of her commitment. So too was the author of the article, Rose Styron, a founding member of Amnesty International USA. But in their growing awareness of human rights, Laber and Styron were not alone.

The 1970s explosion of a popular human rights consciousness in the United States was decisively shaped by what Americans learned about victims of human rights abuses in the Soviet Union, Eastern Europe, and Latin America. Headlines such as "Human Rights: Dissidents v. Moscow," "Czechs Expel Human Rights Activists," "Brazil: Terror and Torture," "Human Rights Abuses in Chile," and "Repression in Argentina" became almost routine in the American press over the decade.[3] In daily newspapers, weekly magazines, and reports on the evening television news, Americans encountered stories of Soviet gulags, the suppression of dissent in Czechoslovakia and elsewhere in Eastern Europe, torture chambers in Brazil, executions in Chilean soccer stadiums, and forced disappearances of political opponents in Argentina. Over time human rights abuses in other parts of world also became the subject of stories in the popular press, but American attention to human rights in the 1970s was largely focused on the Soviet East and the Americas. As many as half of the stories that concerned human rights in the *New York Times* and on nightly news broadcasts over the decade focused on the Soviet Union and Eastern Europe. Another third looked to Latin America.[4]

Even more important than the sheer number of news stories about human rights were the meanings Americans began to make of them. Just as it did for the creation of a global human rights imagination elsewhere in the world in the 1970s, the transnational lens of moral witness came to powerfully shape American understandings of what it meant to have, and to lose, human rights. The American human rights vernacular was forged through the transnational flows of writings by nonconforming dissidents such as Alexandr Solzhenitsyn who emerged in the 1970s as global human rights icons. Echoing the significance of visual culture for the making of the 1940s global human rights imagination, American vernaculars were brought into being by the circulation of testimonials about human rights abuses from Latin America in folk art, film, and painting. These testimonials further defined an American human rights imaginary around the practices of torture and disappearance by the military regimes in the region.

Critical to this American receptivity toward moral witness were the ways in which the testimonial turn positioned the individual at the center of an emergent consciousness about human rights. A growing belief in the authenticity of lived experience that brought about the broader shift in global affect during the seventies conditioned how many Americans conceived of themselves and their relationships at home and in the world at large. In a moment that saw the fracturing of the Cold War state, the American human rights vernacular of the era was also pushed along by the growing primacy of the self, a remaking of ethnic politics, and a rising Holocaust consciousness that were all central dimensions of the decade's broader domestic and global landscape. Mediated through these ruptures and new concerns, the testimonials of individual victims about what were increasing called human rights abuses came to define the topography of the human rights imagination in the United States.

INDIVIDUALS, THE BODY, AND MORAL WITNESS

Human rights returned to 1970s America in a structural and affective landscape that its American advocates in the 1940s would not have recognized. The fragmentation of the bipolar superpower-driven Cold War order by the forces of globalization in the late 1960s and 1970s began to create a world of multiple and competing modes of power that were deeply felt in the United States. It was, in the words of the historian Daniel Rodgers, "the age of fracture." Critical to the transformations of the 1970s was a fundamental rethinking of the self. The immediate postwar decades had largely seen individuals as embedded in and governed by social relations and structures, rather than acting on their own free will or autonomous desires. In the Cold War America of the 1950s and 1960s, as Rodgers suggests, prevailing modes of political, economic, and social thought ever more tightly bound individuals into a collective national project. Presidents from Harry Truman to Richard Nixon publicly articulated the pressing sense of communal responsibility to bear the burdens of the Cold War struggle with the Soviet Union. Economic policy reflected the neo-Keynesian consensus of the need for government intervention to manage the workings of the national economy. The era's most influential works of social thought – among them C. Wright Mills's *The White Collar*, Walt Whitman Rostow's *Stages of Economic Growth*, David Riesman's *The Lonely Crowd*, and Robert Dahl's *Who Governs* – helped set an establishmentarian intellectual climate in which the structures, contexts, and institutions of society shaped the individual and lent a collective urgency to Cold War politics.

This all gave way in the 1970s to a more fluid sensibility and grammar of elective identities, free markets, and the thinning of centralized power. Presidential speeches began to focus on individual heroes rather than collective Cold War sacrifice. A new faith in the self-regulated market, deregulation, and supply-side economics shattered the neo-Keynesian economic consensus. The self and contingency rather than big structures now increasingly informed social thought, although often in eclectic ways that were sometimes at odds with one another. Milton Friedman's microeconomic foundations of individual choice or the rise of rational choice among political scientists might seem quite different from the play of meanings in anthropologist Clifford Geertz's thick description and the alternative path to women's moral development that Carol Gilligan charted in her *In a Different Voice*, but they all were a part of the decade's individualist affectual turn. If the immediate postwar era of the Cold War represented "an era of consolidation," as Rodgers argues, the prevailing current of the last quarter of the past century "was toward disaggregation."[5]

Such sweeping characterizations of what came before and after this moment of transformative change inevitably flatten out continuities between both eras and the fissures and contradictions on each side of the divide. The Cold War and the social forms that gave it meaning in the United States did not disappear overnight, even if their larger significance diminished. The individual and the collective did coexist, if uneasily, in both periods, as did oppositional voices to the dominant ethos. More importantly, the global social movements of the 1960s and their iterations in American domestic space through the civil rights, women's, antiwar, environmental, and antinuclear movements marked a critical rupture in how many Americans made sense of the world around them. It is difficult to imagine that the fractured and disaggregated landscape of the 1970s would have emerged in the absence of these wider critiques of the structures of power that activists believed had produced disastrous Cold War policies abroad and had put limits on the exercise of free expression and on who could enjoy rights at home. In fact some of the earliest advocates for human rights came from the movement against the U.S. war in Vietnam and other social protest campaigns. But if the ruptures of the 1960s were necessary to bring into being the conditions of possibility through which Americans rediscovered human rights, they were not sufficient. The receptivity of a growing number of Americans to the new vocabularies that would give human rights shape and meaning was just as deeply embedded in the quotidian particularities of the individualist turn in the 1970s.

With the diminishing of concerns about the social and the collective, an emergent sensibility of individual consciousness and autonomy increasingly framed American thought and practice in what was popularly dubbed the "Me Decade." One revealing indicator of this shift was the prominence throughout the decade of self-help books aimed at building what was variously called "individualization," "self-actualization," or "gaining our authenticity." They circulated widely, with seven self-help books on the *New York Times* best-seller list simultaneously in 1977. *I'm OK, You're OK*, for instance, was first published in 1969, but quickly garnered a readership in the early 1970s, occupying the top spot on the *Times* list in June 1972 and remaining there for another seventy weeks; Gail Sheehy's popular 1976 *Passages*, with its focus on "reaching one's full potential," sat on the list for three years. Although some contemporary observers dismissed these writings as evidence of the narcissism of the Me Decade, their message of individual choice and encouragement of personal growth was built on the redefinition of the self that underlay the new political engagement of 1960s globally inflected social movements in the United States.[6]

The quest for personal meaning and authenticity that began to reshape the political in the 1960s took a broader therapeutic turn in the 1970s as Americans looked to the individual psyche rather than the structures of society to understand their behavior and the nature of social problems. The decade brought a significant widening across socioeconomic and education levels in the numbers of Americans who sought out psychotherapy. Individual and group therapy, according to one leading study, became a "common coin" and were increasingly viewed less as markers of mental abnormality than as a way for people "to explore and expand their personalities." First Lady Betty Ford talked publicly and candidly of her "tell-it-like-it-is conversations" with a psychiatrist who, she reassured her audience, is "nothing more than a sounding board, someone to talk to. I voiced a lot of entrenched feelings that were locked inside. But more important, I got an honest reaction." It is difficult to imagine First Ladies Bess Truman or Mamie Eisenhower saying something similar in the 1940s or 1950s.[7]

Cultivation of self-awareness was an essential starting point in the new therapeutic culture. In Gestalt therapy for instance, whose practice grew exponentially in the 1970s, practitioners started with the premise that their patients could not properly understand themselves or empathize with others without first understanding their own interior psychologies. Patients faced an empty chair and were asked to project a vision of themselves into it, with therapists drawing attention to patients' gestures and spoken emotions to help make them aware of their "true" selves. Consciousness raising or CR groups, another common therapeutic mode of the decade initiated through the women's movement, were rooted in what one scholar calls the conviction that experience is "something we can trust" and emphasized "introspection, emotional self-exposure and the sharing of personal, experiential testimony." But unlike Gestalt therapy, CR groups were just as much about the relationship between the personal and the articulation of a new politics, offering a free space to examine how gender norms and women's subordination were reproduced and maintained.[8]

CR's emphasis on the entanglement of individual cultivation and collective political action sometimes took printed form. Self-help and political empowerment were, for instance, at the heart of the Boston Women's Health Book Collective's *Our Bodies, Ourselves*, first published in the early 1970s and which quickly began to sell millions of copies. First-person narratives by women were quoted throughout the book; indeed they were integral to it and reflected the Health Book Collective's belief that through "sharing our responses we can develop a base on which to be critical of what the experts tell us." *Our Bodies* also reflected the growing centrality of concerns with bodily integrity and personal autonomy throughout the 1970s. Seeking in part to challenge the largely male medical establishment to change and improve the health care women received, its authors argued that the starting point of their project was the assumption that information about one's body was the most essential form of education: "bodies are the physical bases from which we move out in the world."[9] In the therapeutic practices of the decade, individual experience became the embodied watchword. It signaled a heightened awareness that lived experience could produce the ability to discover and solve problems – both one's own and, empathetically, those of others.

The search for an authentic self also manifested itself in the conscious remaking of ethnic identity in the 1970s, a set of processes that indirectly built empathetic connections between individual suffering and human rights. Alex Haley's 1976 best-selling *Roots* was the most dramatic cultural flashpoint in a decade-long preoccupation of many Americans to search for their familial identities. *Roots* told the story of the author's African American family, tracing his enslaved ancestors back to West Africa. Atop best-seller lists for six months and the winner of a National Book Award and a special Pulitzer Prize, Haley's *Roots* attracted an even wider audience as an eight-episode, twelve-hour television miniseries viewed by half of the nation's population in what was then the largest audience in television history. Family genealogy boomed in the aftermath of *Roots*. Books titled *Searching for Your Ancestors* and *Finding Your Roots* found large audiences, while the mass-circulating newsweeklies *Time* and *Newsweek* offered guides to genealogical handbooks and archival collections over headlines such as "Everybody's Search for Roots." *Time* reported that "[a]fter Haley's comet not only blacks but all ethnic groups saw themselves traceable across oceans and centuries to the remotest ancestral village."

Along with the explosion of familial genealogical sleuthing, the phenomenon of "heritage tourism" increased dramatically in the seventies. "Roots: Trace Them to Ireland on Northwest Orient" went one airline advertisement in an era in which jet travel had become increasingly affordable for middle-class Americans. Pan American World Airways created an ethnic quiz and board game called "Heritage Hunt." Tellingly, such tours often had as their destinations places that Americans would come to see as human rights hot spots. Indeed, for some white ethnics and American Jews the search for roots and concerns about human rights became enmeshed. Irish Americans returned to a homeland in which the "Troubles" of Northern Ireland were inescapable. The Chicago-based Poland Travel Agency doubled its charter bookings in 1977 at the same time that Polish American organizations began to express increasing concern about political and labor repression in Poland. Some American Jews who traveled to rediscover their roots in Israel or in Eastern Europe shtetls were increasingly drawn to protest movements at home that sought to raise awareness of the plight of Soviet Jewry.[10]

Who counted as "Americans" in the 1970s also began to shift, with implications for how human rights were perceived in the United States. Almost 70 percent of all immigrants who came to the United States after 1965 were from Latin America, the Caribbean, and Asia in what was part of the global reversal in patterns of migration that in previous decades had centered around Europe. Many of their countries of origin – including Chile, Argentina, South Korea, Philippines, El Salvador, and Guatemala – became subjects of human rights concern in the 1970s.

Although considerably smaller in aggregate numbers, the emigration by
Soviet Jews to the United States in the 1970s and the attention they were
accorded in the American press helped reinforce the growing centrality
of dissent in the Soviet Union as a prime mover of the emergent American human rights imagination. In addition to these quantitative changes
in immigration patterns, the qualitative presence of new immigrant communities in the United States sometimes offered immediate and visceral
instances of what would increasingly be called human rights abuses as
individual victims of torture and political imprisonment in the Americas
and Asia who migrated to the United States or sought asylum there told
their own stories to a variety of American publics.[11]

The decade's preoccupations with the self and the valorization of individual experience were critical to the sympathetic responses of Americans to the kinds of first-person testimonials through which they would
learn about human right abuses in the 1970s. So too was the increasing concern with Holocaust memory as the decade progressed. Outside
the American Jewish community, the Holocaust had been a muted presence in U.S. political culture of the 1950s and 1960s. But the embrace
of moral witness and the authenticity of individual testimony in the wake
of the Eichmann trial came to shape the growing presence of the Holocaust in 1970s America as it did more globally. In the American case,
the airing of the nine-hour television miniseries *The Holocaust* over four
nights in April 1977 marks, as Peter Novick writes in his seminal history
of Holocaust memory, "the most important moment in the entry of the
Holocaust into general American consciousness." Watched by more than
120 million viewers nationwide, *The Holocaust* focused on the experiences
of the fictional Weiss family to tell the story of European Jews under the
Nazi regime. In doing so, it consciously sought to draw out the audience's
emotional responses to the family members' individual stories of persecution, rape, and murder. It was a fictionalized testimonial turn and one
that sparked vigorous national debate, with some critics arguing that *The
Holocaust* trivialized the very event it sought to recover by turning it into
little more than a soap opera. But the miniseries was widely seen by contemporaries as a catalyst for the development of an American Holocaust
memorial culture. In its aftermath, the Holocaust became a household
word, and an avalanche of testimonials by survivors and witnesses began

to appear in print, film, and oral history form. The growing moral authority of survivors such as Nobel Peace Prize winner Elie Wiesel, whose ascendance as a "messenger to all humanity" and "a witness for life" began in the late 1970s, put practices of witness and testimony front and center for Americans as indisputably authentic and persuasive.[12]

As the hyper-individualism and interiority of the 1970s became entangled with the refiguring of ethnic identities and a rising Holocaust consciousness, they helped produce an affinity with global forms of testimonials through which human rights abuses became visible in the United States. Against these transformations in American ways of seeing in the 1970s, a particular conception of human rights began to take shape in the popular imagination in which violations of the body and the traces they left in individual psyches were at the center.

UNDERSTANDING SOLZHENITSYN'S *GULAG*

American self-fashioning of the experiences of dissidents in the Soviet Union and Eastern Europe through the broader prism of the individual and moral witness played a central role in shaping this nascent American human rights imaginary. Figures like Aleksandr Solzhenitsyn, Andrei Sakharov, and Václav Havel assumed an unprecedented prominence on the world stage in the 1970s, becoming readily identifiable figures in the United States. The nonconforming dissident was more broadly lionized for his – and those lifted up in the West tended to be male – "titanic stature," "courage," and "moral grandeur." In a typical representation of the era, an observer wrote in 1973 that "one has an initial duty as a human being to salute them; to salute them for existing, and, by doing that alone, making our world a better and more honourable place."[13] The Cold War was one frame through which the dissident challenge was viewed. But Soviet and Eastern European dissidents also quickly became interwoven in the popular imagination with an emergent human rights consciousness. Here the guest languages of dissent became detached from their Soviet-era contexts to forge the 1970s American human rights vernacular.

Aleksandr Solzhenitsyn was without question the best known of the era's dissidents and, as an emblem of the new global concern with human rights, the most controversial. He first became widely known in and out of the Soviet Union for his novella *A Day in the Life of Ivan Denisovich*, published in the Soviet Union and the West in the early 1960s. The first major imaginative work to critically address the harrowing experiences of imprisonment in the vast network of Stalinist labor camps and prisons that Solzhenitsyn knew intimately from his eight-year sentence to one of them, it was published with Soviet leader Nikita Khrushchev's permission in the cultural thaw that was part of his larger de-Stalinization campaign. Written in a first-person stream of consciousness style, *A Day in the Life* presented an account of surviving the everyday brutalities of prison camp life on a bitterly cold day through the voice of a single inmate, a former bricklayer, who like many of his fellow *zeks* or prisoners was innocent of the charges that had brought him to the camp in the first place. Appreciative Soviet readers also saw the novel's protagonist as a kind of everyman whose harsh life and wily responses to it mirrored the broader contours of daily life under Stalinism. *A Day in the Life* immediately became a worldwide literary sensation, recognized by major American critics as a "flawless classic" akin to Dostoevsky's *House of the Dead* and "one of the most important [books] that has come out of Russia in many years."[14]

With Khrushchev's fall from power, the Soviet state began to look on Solzhenitsyn with disfavor and launched a campaign of escalating repression against him and other dissidents. The manuscripts for his second two books, *First Circle* and *Cancer Ward*, were smuggled to the West and published in the late 1960s. They also focused on the Soviet prison system Solzhenitsyn knew firsthand; as one contemporary American critic wrote, the books "compel the human imagination to participate in the agony and murder of millions that have been the distinguishing feature of our age." *First Circle*, whose title is a deliberate reference to Dante's first circle of hell in his *Divine Comedy*, was set in 1949 in an institute staffed by scientists, engineers, and academicians who had been taken out of labor camps and ordered to produce the technology that would make Stalinist techniques of surveillance and repression more efficient. Like the pre-Christian philosophers who occupy Dante's first circle for eternity, the central characters of *First Circle* come to see their everyday psychological humiliations by the prison authorities as a perpetual way of life. Solzhenitsyn appeared to suggest that their dehumanized condition and stolid acceptance of their fate, along with the absurdities of the projects they were asked to undertake, mirrored the broader conditions of Soviet society. The allegorical *Cancer Ward* was populated by cancer-ridden patients in a 1950s Central Asian hospital, among them former prisoners and guards in Stalinist gulags, whose carefully rendered conversations and interactions offered an even more devastating indictment of post-Stalinist society. As the novel's central character, a former political prisoner, asks at one point, "A man sprouts a tumor and dies – how then can a country live that has sprouted camps and exile?"[15]

Together *First Circle* and *Cancer Ward* solidified Solzhenitsyn's reputation among American and other Western critics as "the greatest living Russian writer." Like *A Day in the Life*, *First Circle* was a Book-of-the-Month Club selection, suggesting the wide circulation of Solzhenitsyn's work among the U.S. reading public throughout the 1960s. He was awarded the Nobel Prize for Literature in 1970. In his Nobel acceptance speech, which he did not deliver in person for fear that the Soviet authorities would prevent him from returning home, Solzhenitsyn did not shy away from a vigorous critique of the Soviet system. He also drew explicit attention to human rights as a parable for understanding the devastating impact of the Soviet system on its individual victims. Lauding the Universal Declaration of Human Rights as the "best document of the last twenty-five years," he nonetheless chastised the United Nations human rights machinery for ignoring the plight of Soviet citizens – what he termed "the groans, screams and beseechings of humble individual PLAIN PEOPLE" – and betraying "those humble people into the will of the governments which they had not chosen." At home Solzhenitsyn was also increasingly outspoken about the ills of the Soviet regime to the displeasure of the Brezhnev Politburo, which banned his writings, had him barred from the Soviet Writer's Union, and ordered the KGB to disrupt his work and family life. Less than two months after the publication of his magna opus *The Gulag Archipelago* in Paris and New York in December 1973, based on microfilm of the manuscript smuggled out of the country by an international network of his supporters, Leonid Brezhnev had him arrested and expelled from the Soviet Union in February 1974.[16]

The American press breathlessly covered Solzhenitsyn's dramatic arrest and deportation, and after he and his family settled in a small

Vermont town, Solzhenitsyn quickly became a significant figure in domestic politics.[17] When President Gerald R. Ford declined to meet him at the White House, his challenger in the 1976 Republican presidential nominating contest, Ronald Reagan, told reporters that Solzhenitsyn "would be welcome to eat dinner anytime at the Reagan White House." Ford and Reagan forces sparred over a "Solzhenitsyn plank" at the Republican convention that turned him into a proxy for the internecine feuds within the Republican Party over the efficacy of détente. Conservative senator Jesse Helms sought to confer honorary citizenship on Solzhenitsyn. Solzhenitsyn's own public speeches in the United States, in which he vehemently denounced what he saw as the tragically wrong-headed policies of détente and encouraged the United States to "intervene" in Soviet domestic affairs, played into a hawkish Cold War reading of his views. Some American liberals took an increasingly skeptical attitude toward Solzhenitsyn's politics, alienated by his "far-fetched" Slavophile nationalism, put off by his "scorn for democracy," and distrustful of "the willful Russian autocrat in him."[18]

But Solzhenitsyn's great imaginative power, even his harshest critics acknowledged, did considerably more than rehash Cold War polemics. In *The Gulag Archipelago*, he offered an entirely original lens through which to apprehend violations of individual human rights far from the United States. To American readers he made an exceptionally compelling claim that human rights ought to matter. In part, the content and reception of *Gulag* are essential to understanding Solzhenitsyn's transformative impact on his readers. Over the course of three volumes, he traced the history of the imprisonment, brutalization, and murder of tens of millions of Soviet citizens by their own government between 1929 and 1953 in "that amazing country of *Gulag* which, though scattered in an Archipelago geographically was, in the psychological sense, fused into a continent – an almost invisible, almost imperceptible, country." The book relied on eyewitness testimony related to him by more than two hundred prisoners, interspersed with his own experiences in the camps and a sweeping account of how he believed Soviet political culture had brought about the destruction of millions of innocent lives.[19]

The reception of *The Gulag Archipelago*, which appeared to rapturous reviews in the United States and elsewhere, was extraordinary

6.1. Alexandr Solzhenitsyn autographs books following an appearance on NBC's "Meet the Press" in Washington, DC, on 13 June 1975. AP Photo/Suzanne Vlamis.

(Figure 6.1). As one American critic claimed, "it is clear that no writer in the world today has been able to explore the compelling experiences of his people as Solzhenitsyn has done or received such an enthusiastic audience." Since its publication in 1973, *Gulag* has sold more than thirty million copies in thirty-five languages. American sales totaled three million by 1985. Although even *Gulag*'s English-language translator admitted that many readers were unlikely to have actually read all eighteen hundred pages of the three-volume work, the sales figures for such an ambitious and demanding work are staggering.[20]

But more important than *Gulag*'s subject and vast circulation for an emergent American human rights consciousness was the impact of its form. Holocaust memory hovered over the reception of *Gulag* and offered a critical frame for American readers of Solzhenitsyn's work. *Gulag*, one reviewer argued, was an account of "the other great Holocaust of our century." Solzhenitsyn, many critics noted, was "a survivor himself" who sought to "sear" the experience of the Soviet gulags "into the collective consciousness" by chronicling its "full horror."[21] *Gulag* made the imprisonment, brutalization, and murder of Soviet citizens visible in the increasingly familiar testimonial mode of Holocaust survivors.

Solzhenitsyn's own subtitle for the project was "An Experiment in Literary Investigation," and his method consciously relied on confronting readers with first-person testimony. He was intent on viscerally pulling his readers into the narrative, insisting on their engagement with the clear intent of altering how they saw and felt about an unfamiliar world. *Gulag* opens in this way:

> Down the long crooked path of our lives we happily rushed or unhappily wandered past a variety of walls and fences – rotten wooden palings, clay embankments, brick and concrete walls, iron railings. It never occurred to us to ask what was behind them, or to look or even think about it. But that was where gulag country began, two yards away. ... All those gates were prepared for us, every last one! And then a fatal door opened and four white hands, unused to work but tenacious, grabbed us by the leg, arm, collar, cap, ear and dragged us like a sack, and slammed the door to our past life shut forever more. "You're under arrest!" And all you can manage to bleat out is, "M-me? What for?"

American readers might have easily pictured the white hands grabbing them as well. Solzhenitsyn uses this direct approach throughout *Gulag*, asking readers to imagine for themselves the harrowing ordeals he describes: "Reader! Just try – sleep like that for one night! It was five degrees Centigrade in the barracks!" Or: "There were tortures, homemade and primitive. They would crush a hand in the door, and it was all in that vein. (Try it, reader!)"[22]

The "I" is omnipresent throughout *Gulag*. For Solzhenitsyn, it was rendered with a mix of indignation and pity to craft a self-styled voice of authenticity that challenged and discredited the prevailing strictures of Soviet official speech. The receptivity of American readers, for whom the language of Soviet socialist realism was largely unknown, to the immediacy of Solzhenitsyn's first-person method was in part conditioned by the increasingly popular style of the New Journalism in 1970s America. Through such works as Truman Capote's *In Cold Blood* and Hunter Thompson's *Fear and Loathing on the Campaign Trail*, the practices of the novel and the journalist were collapsed into a new form that highlighted the subjectivity of the author, who sought to simultaneously engage, inform, and advocate.[23] Solzhenitsyn's *Gulag*, of course, is a

long way from the gonzo journalism of Hunter Thompson. The techniques of the New Journalism played no role in his own experiments
in literary investigation, and his subject matter and moral gravity were
quite different. But the sensibility of Solzhenitsyn's methods and his
desire to so directly involve readers in recovering the world of the gulag
clearly resonated with the spirit of the New Journalism. Even more
importantly, *Gulag*'s first-person voice paralleled the era's concern with
the authenticity of lived experience and moral witness. For his American readers, bringing the "I" into the gulag offered a palpable window
into distant suffering and a visceral sense of the fragility of the human
condition.

MORAL LANGUAGES OF THE SOVIET EAST

Along with Solzhenitsyn, the Soviet physicist Andrei Sakharov and the
Czech playwright Václav Havel shaped the construction of the 1970s
American human rights vernacular. The global circulation of writings by
Sakharov offered a cooler, and for some Americans more satisfying, coun-
terpoint to the emotionality of Solzhenitsyn's rendering of human rights.
Indeed Solzhenitsyn and Sakharov were often seen as mirror opposites
in temperament and affect. An extended 1973 profile of Sakharov by the
chief of the *New York Times* Moscow bureau Hedrick Smith contrasted the
"imposing" and "combative" presence of "the Solzhenitsyn of the barrel
chest, lined and ruddy face, and work-worn hands" who "relished pres-
tige and the limelight" with a "kind of Grant Wood-American Gothic sim-
plicity and modesty" that "permeates Sakharov's life." Noting his "slightly
stooped figure" and "sad compassionate eyes," Smith believed Sakharov
was as "modest in gesture, in manner, in dress, in surroundings" as "an off-
duty night watchman." But behind his lack of pretension, Smith argued,
Sakharov was a "Russian *intelligent*, an intellectual through and through"
whose stature as a theoretical physicist and role in the creation of the
Soviet hydrogen bomb in the 1950s equaled that of Robert Oppenheimer and Edward Teller in the United States. Rooting Sakharov in
this genealogy of self-effacing brilliance, Smith approvingly narrated his
more recent transformation into a human rights activist "sanctified in the
West as a champion of individual rights."[24]

Sakharov's intellectual odyssey in the late 1960s and early 1970s was instrumental in both framing Soviet dissent as part of the emergent vocabulary of human rights and at the same time remaking American sensibilities about what human rights meant and the kinds of political work it could do. Sakharov burst onto the world stage in 1968 with the publication of "Thoughts on Progress, Coexistence, and Intellectual Freedom." The essay appeared in as many as sixty-five editions in seventeen languages around the world. In his memoirs, Sakharov notes that eighteen million copies were published in 1968 and 1969, "in third place after Mao Zedong and Lenin, and ahead of Georges Simenon and Agatha Christie."[25] Variously called by the U.S. press a "thunderbolt," "remarkable," and an "extraordinary" manifesto because of Sakharov's extended critique of the Soviet system and the rise of neo-Stalinism, the essay in part reinforced American Cold War assumptions about the weaknesses of the Soviet Union. But it also argued for what Sakharov termed a "convergence" between the socialist and capitalist worlds that transcended the political and social malaise of the West and the East. Its topical focus moved from thermonuclear extinction to ecological catastrophe, famine, uncontrolled population growth, and a shared spiritual alienation across the Cold War divide. Human rights played a more muted role in Sakharov's argument. He discussed the necessity of intellectual freedom and freedom of expression as among the "rights of man" that were central to political community, raised the plight of political prisoners in the Soviet Union, and argued that "all anticonstitutional laws and decrees violating human rights must be abrogated." But Sakharov did not offer human rights as a primary conceptual means for envisioning a better future both at home and in the wider world.[26]

Seven years later, in a speech titled "Peace, Progress, Human Rights" to mark his being awarded the Nobel Peace Prize in 1975, Sakharov did make that argument. The shift in emphasis in the title from that of his 1968 essay "Progress, Coexistence, and Intellectual Freedom," was telling. In the years in between, Sakharov began to take a growing interest in the rights of Soviet political prisoners and of ethnic and religious minorities as a founding member of the Committee on Human Rights in 1972. He undertook the first of many hunger strikes in 1974 to draw attention to the plight of political prisoners in Soviet labor camps and prisons. That same year a sharp public break with Alexandr Solzhenit-syn, one that was closely followed in the United States, provided Sakharov with an opportunity to articulate human rights as a set of universal moral principles. Sakharov and Solzhenitsyn's personal relations, which were never especially warm, broke down in the spring of 1974 when Sakharov publicly responded to Solzhenitsyn's celebrated *Letter to Brezhnev* that had ultimately provoked the Soviet leader to deport Solzhenitsyn. In his let-ter, Solzhenitsyn had interwoven a sharp critique of the Soviet state with an insistence that Russia also needed to fully break with Western cul-tural and philosophical traditions and embrace its own unique, spiritu-ally inflected, path to national regeneration. In his response to that letter, Sakharov firmly rejected Solzhenitsyn's Russian particularism for a uni-versal pluralism in which guarantees of human rights were foundational. Russians, he argued, were not the only peoples to suffer under commu-nism; so too had other nationalities and ethnic and religious groups. Sakharov's position had been shaped in part by the increasingly expan-sive scope of his work on behalf of Soviet political prisoners. What should ground the state, Sakharov argued, ultimately lay in the supranational realm in what he saw as the common destiny of democratic pluralism through which the human rights of all peoples would flourish.[27]

Sakharov's insistence on the transcendent power of human rights only intensified after this exchange with Solzhenitsyn and ultimately recast his notions of dissent and the place of dissidents in Soviet society. Increas-ingly, the Cold War and détente came to be second-order concerns for Sakharov. Pushing for the centrality of rights, reason, and moral improve-ment in his Nobel address, he said,

> We must today fight for every individual person separately against injustice and the violation of human rights. Much of our future depends on this. In struggling to protect human rights we must, I am convinced, first and foremost act as protectors of the innocent victims of regimes installed in various countries, without demanding the destruction or total condemna-tion of these regimes. We need reform, not revolution. We need a pliant, pluralist, tolerant community, which selectively and tentatively can bring about a free, undogmatic use of the experiences of all social systems.[28]

6.2. Andrei D. Sakharov breaks into a grin after hearing that he was awarded the 1975 Nobel Peace Prize. © Bettmann/Corbis/AP Photo.

As Sakharov argued in *My Country and the World*, published in the United States in 1975 just as his Nobel Prize was announced (Figure 6.2), human rights must be defended everywhere to exist anywhere. And, he added, violations of rights in one country threatened those rights in all other countries.[29]

It was Sakharov's expansive rendering of what human rights could mean, as well as the growing position of global eminence from which he spoke, that helped transform the dissident movement in the Soviet Union and Eastern Europe from a Cold War issue to a human rights cause in the United States. If American readers could begin to better imagine what the visceral particularities of the deprivation of human rights felt like through Solzhenitsyn's imaginative prose, Sakharov acted as a philosopher and guide through whom human rights began to acquire a global moral power. President Jimmy Carter's unprecedented and well-publicized response to a January 1979 letter from Sakharov urging Carter to "raise his voice" in support of human rights activists in the Soviet Union and Eastern Europe points toward Sakharov's transnational moral authority. In his response Carter renewed his "firm commitment to promote respect for human rights not only in our own country but also abroad."[30] For many Americans, Solzhenitsyn and Sakharov together offered an arresting articulation of the moral and global power of human rights.

Like them Václav Havel became a human rights cause célèbre in the 1970s. His plays and political writings helped Americans to recast and deepen the meanings they accorded to human rights. Havel first came to American and global public attention as a coauthor of Charter 77, the Czech manifesto released in January 1977 that criticized the government for failing to implement the Helsinki Accords and UN human rights covenants that it had signed guaranteeing freedom of expression and protections for other political and civil rights. Although the authors of the charter insisted it "did not form the basis for any oppositional political activity," the Czech state responded with severe repression against those who signed it – arresting, trying, and imprisoning Havel and other Charter 77 leaders for subversion against the state. Havel was in prison for three years. After his release, he remained the subject of continual government surveillance and was put under house arrest and in prison for brief periods until, in a dramatic reversal of fortune, Havel became the president of Czechoslovakia in the aftermath of the "Velvet Revolution" that marked the collapse of the communist state in 1989.[31]

Havel began to capture the American imagination in the late 1970s. The Carter administration very publicly protested the Czech state's harassment and imprisonment of Havel and other Charter 77 leaders, and its protestations were lead stories in major American newspapers. Charter 77 was the subject of television evening news broadcasts, which portrayed it as a human rights document.[32] The attention helped raise Havel's profile in the United States. Arthur Miller, as president of PEN International, had visited Czechoslovakia as early as 1969 and met Havel, who later served as the model for the protagonist of Miller's 1977 play *The Archbishop's Ceiling* that explored the complexities of dissent in contemporary Eastern Europe. After Havel's arrest, Miller and other leading American literary figures such as Kurt Vonnegut and Saul Bellow lobbied for his release.[33] But Havel's more enduring impact on the American human rights consciousness flowed from the growing circulation in the United States of his plays and political writings. In them Havel emerged as a figure who shared some of the sensibilities of Soviet dissidents, especially in Charter 77's strategic inclination to publicly contrast the formal

6.3. Vaclav Havel, c. 1976, just before he became part of Charter 77. © Bettman/ Corbis.

promises of the state to protect human rights with the everyday practices of rights violations.[34]

Unlike Sakharov and Solzhenitsyn, however, Havel's iconoclastic artistic and political vision was shaped by his engagement in the global counterculture of the 1960s and the theater of the absurd. Indeed what precipitated Charter 77 was the arrest and trial of the Plastic People of the Universe, a radically unconventional psychedelic Czech rock band whose dark, low-fi music drew inspiration from Frank Zappa and the Velvet Underground. The band was formed after the Soviet invasion of Czechoslovakia in 1968 and immediately attracted a young and enthusiastic cult following. Concerned by what it saw as the band's subversive message, the Czech police broke up their concerts, beating up fans and band members, as part of a growing state campaign in the mid-seventies against freedom of expression. Havel, a Plastic People fan, saw the band's arrest in 1976 as a warning sign of heightened political repression (Figure 6.3). That such concern with the band could act as a spur to the Charter 77 movement points to the palpable presence of a transnationally inflected underground countercultural element in Czech human rights politics that would give Havel a hipster quality in the West quite different from the more austere sensibilities of most Soviet dissidents (Solzhenitsyn did not share Havel's affinity for the Plastic People).[35]

In the wake of Charter 77 and the international notoriety of Havel's imprisonment, his plays, long banned in Czechoslovakia, were increasingly performed in the United States. Influenced by practitioners of the 1960s avant-garde theater of the absurd like Samuel Beckett and Eugène Ionesco, Havel combined satire and subtle word play to lay bare the dehumanization of civil society under the Czech socialist state. American critics called performances of Havel's work in New York City and at regional theater companies "events of artistic and political urgency" and lionized Havel as an "utterly heroic ... fighter for human rights."[36] Most frequently performed were a trilogy of one-act plays whose central character Vanek, a banned playwright whom Havel loosely modeled on himself, served as a public conscience for those who had compromised their morality as collaborators with the state. In *Audience*, Vanek is working in a brewery and is called into the office of the brewmaster who tells him the authorities are asking him to pass on reports each week about Vanek's political activities. Confessing that he is "runnin' outta ideas about what to keep on tellin'em every damn week," the brewmaster asks Vanek if he would write the reports for him. It prompts this exchange:

VANEK: I can't be snitching on myself –

BREWMASTER: What do you mean snitch? Who's talkin' about snitchin' here?

VANEK: It isn't because of me – it couldn't hurt me anymore – but it really is a matter of principle! I just cannot, as a matter of principle, become a part of –

BREWMASTER: A part of what? Go ahead and spell it out! You can't be a part of what?

VANEK: A part of a way of doing things that I don't agree with – *(A short, tense pause.)*

BREWMASTER: And what about me? You're just gonna let me sink, right? You're just gonna say, fuck you! It's okay if I end up being an asshole! Me, I can wallow in this shit, because I don't count. I ain't nothn' but a regular brewery hick – but the VIP here can't have any part of this! Its okay if I get smeared with shit, so long the VIP here stays clean! The VIP is worried about the principle! But he doesn't bother thinkin' about other people! Just as long as he comes out smellin' like a rose! The principle is dearer to him than another human being![37]

If *Audience* conveys sympathy for the working-class brewmaster ensnared in the everyday immoralities of the Czech socialist state, in *Protest*, written just after Charter 77 was issued, Havel turns a withering eye on fellow intellectuals who chose collaboration with the state rather than dissent. Here an old friend, surrounded by the expensive accouterments made possible by his association with the regime, asks the impoverished Vanek to write a petition protesting the arrest of a popular singer while praising him for his courageous "fight for human rights." By chance Vanek has already prepared such a petition and asks his friend to sign it. The friend immediately equivocates. At the end of a lengthy monologue that American critics called "dazzling," the friend explains,

These people [the state] secretly hate the dissidents. They've become their bad conscience, their living reproach! That's how they see the dissidents. At the same time they envy them their honor and their inner freedom, values which they themselves were denied by fate. That is why they never miss an opportunity to smear the dissidents. And precisely this opportunity is going to be offered to them by my signature.

In a monumental act of self-serving moral displacement and convoluted logic, the friend asks if he should think of himself and sign, or think about the dissidents and not sign. He does not, assuring himself as one critic wrote "of the rectitude of moral abdication."[38]

The focus on the individual that made Havel's vision of human rights politics so palpable to American audiences also infused his political writing, which became available in the United States as the seventies came to a close.[39] His best-known essay, "The Power of the Powerless," opened with Havel asking why a greengrocer in Prague might put a placard in his shop window with the slogan, "Workers of the world, unite!" He suggested that few shopkeepers thought much about this practice, one that formed an omnipresent "panorama of everyday life" in socialist Czechoslovakia, nor did passersby really notice the signs. The message did not matter either. It was simply how one got by in a socialist system "thoroughly permeated by hypocrisy and lies" that demanded "conformity, uniformity and discipline." For the system to work, Havel argued, individuals "need not believe" in it, "but they must behave as if they did ... they must live within a lie." In putting his loyalty on display in the shop window, the greengrocer signaled not only his compliance and obedience to the regime but also his complicity in the system. He was "pulled into and ensnared by it, like Faust by Mephistopheles." Everyone, from greengrocers to prime ministers, was "in fact involved and enslaved." If one day the greengrocer "snaps and he stops putting up the slogans," Havel claimed, retribution would be swift – the loss of his position, reduced pay, the loss of special health and education benefits for his family, threats, harassment, and intimidation. For the state, such an action would not have been perceived as an individual or isolated offense. Havel wrote, "He has demonstrated that living a lie is living a lie ... that the emperor is naked ... that it *is* possible to live within the truth ... a truth which might cause incalculable transformations in social consciousness."[40]

Living within the truth, for Havel, was the essence of dissent and what he believed the "struggle for human rights politics" ought to be about. It was an everyday politics, as suspicious of "abstract projects for an ideal political or economic order" in the democratic West as in the socialist East. Havel was also wary of the term "dissident," believing that its prevailing usage in the 1970s too often improperly lifted up prominent leaders and elided the deeper moral politics he believed necessary in a mass movement. Instead Havel reframed its meanings to argue that "the basic job of 'dissident' movements is to serve truth," in part by "defending human rights" but also by developing "parallel structures" where "a different life can be lived, a life that is in harmony with its own aims and which in turn structures itself in harmony with those aims." Through the power of the powerless, Havel argued, the "plurality, diversity, independent self-constitution and self-organization" that is the "essence of the authentic life" could flourish.[41]

Along with Havel's writings, Sakharov's and Solzhenitsyn's positioning of the individual as an authentic voice of moral witness lay at the center of the growing consciousness about human rights in 1970s America. The interiority of feeling that infused the form and content of works by Havel and Solzhenitsyn resonated with broader shifts in how many Americans saw themselves and the world around them. Sakharov's more explicit turn to the language of human rights offered a new vocabulary by which to understand how the suffering of strangers might matter as much as one's own.

Dissidents, and the particular ways in which Americans came to understand them, placed human rights on the mental map of 1970s America. South Africa might seem like another likely geographical space for the making of the American human rights vernacular. The death of anti-apartheid activist Steven Biko in September 1977 attracted global attention. As the leader of South Africa's Black Consciousness Movement, Biko had played a key role in the 1976 Soweto Uprising that offered the decade's strongest challenge to the apartheid state. In the bloody repression that followed, Biko was arrested, tortured, and died under police custody. American commentators talked of "South African gulags," comparing the circumstances of Biko's death to practices in Nazi Germany and the Soviet Union, and foregrounded South African state practices of "institutionalized racism ... maintained by violence."[42] But seldom, if ever, was "human rights" invoked in the United States to explain Biko's politics or to understand the circumstances around his death. Instead, it was the rising tide of torture, extrajudicial killing, and forced disappearances in Latin America throughout the 1970s, along with dissent in the Soviet Union and Eastern Europe, that put human rights front and center in the American imagination.

CHAPTER 7

American Vernaculars II

O N THE MORNING OF SEPTEMBER 30, 1974, Fred Morris, an American United Methodist missionary, met up with a friend on the streets of Recife in northeastern Brazil. Quite suddenly a station wagon roared up, and they were surrounded by three men pointing machine guns and a .45 caliber automatic pistol at their heads. Packed into the back of the car and hooded by brown bags, they were taken to the headquarters of Brazil's 4th Military Region Army. Fifteen minutes after they arrived, Morris was put in an interrogation chamber for the beginning of what became seventeen days of torture and incarceration.

Three months later Morris was in a room at the Rayburn House Office Building in Washington, DC, as the lead witness in a congressional hearing concerning "torture and oppression in Brazil." Morris told the committee:

> The first jolts were quite light, apparently just to let me know that I was wired up, but then the current was increased until I was doubled over and finally fell to the floor. I was immediately ordered to get up, and shocks were given to enforce obedience.... This whole process seemed to be highly entertaining to my questioners, and there was much laughter in the chamber. This phase continued for another 20 minutes or so, when the electrode was removed from my ear and placed on the base of my penis. Again, questions and shocks, the voltage increased successively until it produced muscle spasms in my legs, forcing them to fly out in front of me, causing me to fall, with all my weight on my back.

The procedures continued throughout the day, and although Morris reported that the physical torture ebbed after his fourth day in captivity, "the psychological and emotional torture" continued until his release.

These practices, Morris told the House subcommittee, were the same as those experienced by thousands of Brazilian clergy, trade unionists, lawyers, and political dissidents who had been victims of state torture over the past nine years.[1]

If Soviet and East European dissidents set in motion one crucial dimension of the 1970s American human rights imagination, the experience of victims of human rights abuses in the Americas provided the other. Morris's testimony was given in one of the nearly 150 hearings with more than 500 witnesses convened by the U.S. House Subcommittee on International Organizations and Movements between 1973 and 1979 in what constituted one of the decade's major assertions of congressional interest in U.S. human rights policy. The majority of the hearings dealt with Latin America.[2] But concern with human rights abuses in the region resonated far beyond the confines of the congressional hearing room. Press reports of torture first emerged from Brazil in the late 1960s with that country's tightening of military rule. Civil-military rule in Uruguay beginning in 1973 brought reports of similar human rights abuses. In the wake of the military coup in September 1973 led by Augusto Pinochet against the leftist government of Salvadore Allende, Chile became the major flashpoint, with growing reports of torture and extrajudicial killings there among the most frequently reported regional human rights stories of the 1970s. Events in Chile were brought close to home in 1976 with the assassination of Orlando Letelier, an opponent of the Pinochet regime who had been Allende's ambassador to the United States, by the Chilean secret police on the streets of Washington, DC. A military takeover in Argentina in 1976 marked another sharp uptick in human rights reporting, which focused on the regime's practice of forced disappearance in which the dead bodies of its political opponents were secretly hidden.[3]

The centrality of Latin America for U.S. understandings of human rights in the 1970s was also driven by the long history of U.S. imperialism in the region and by more recent Cold War-inspired overt and clandestine interventions by the U.S. government in support of the military regimes in the Southern Cone. From the Eisenhower to the Nixon administration, the United States offered direct and indirect assistance to the dictatorships in South and Central America, sympathetic to their efforts to crack down on what the military governments termed "leftist subversives." In contrast to the case of the Soviet Union, Americans would come to learn in the 1970s that the United States was itself culpable in the massive violations of human rights in Latin America. This growing awareness further heightened the power of the region for the articulation of the decade's human rights vernacular.[4]

Fred Morris's unstinting testimony before the U.S. Congress of his own torture at the hands of Brazilian authorities foreshadowed how human rights abuses in Latin America were most often conveyed to American and global publics throughout the 1970s. The testimonial turn that made up the broader global human rights imagination of the decade became a central vehicle by which Americans understood the connections between events in Latin America and an emerging human rights consciousness. The impact of Solzhenitsyn's *Gulag* in the United States was in part heightened by its first-person authorial voice of moral witness. In the case of Latin America, testimony and witness became the dominant frames through which Americans came to see human rights abuses as attacks on bodily integrity itself. Like the lexicon of dissent, it too was a guest language in the United States.

In Latin America, testimonial truth or *testimonios* had provided a critical means through which local activists challenged the official erasure of human rights violations by military regimes in the Southern Cone. Operating clandestinely in Latin American countries under the censorship restrictions of the dictatorships, testimony sought to put what historian Steve Stern terms "an authentic voice of suffering ... into the public domain." In Chile, the human rights bulletin of the Santiago Catholic Church's advocacy organization, Vicaría de la Solidaridad, offered one source of testimonial or alternative memory truth. The bulletin circulated in the 1970s as a manuscript rather than a publication, and the testimony contained in it was often conveyed secondhand by word of mouth or rumor. Testimony designed to make visible human rights violations often had a strong religious dimension in the region. As one Chilean priest wrote in 1976, "testimonial actions of solidarity, love, justice ... form part of the voice of the Lord that goes on resonating in this time to announce, through concrete gestures, the good news that today [the Lord] saves, especially the poor, the oppressed, the persecuted."

Testimonios were at the center of campaigns for public awareness among the more than 200,000 Latin Americans who fled into exile beginning in 1973, some of whom later worked to establish solidarity and human rights networks in Europe and North America.[5]

Testimonial truth came to the United States most forcefully through transnational networks based in Latin America and its exile communities. Unlike the dissident case in the Soviet Union and Eastern Europe where the titanic presence of a handful of very male individuals and their written work shaped popular American apprehensions, testimonial flows from Latin America were more diffuse and varied, with women sometimes playing a critical role in their production and dissemination. Cultural forms such as folk art and music, along with first-person written testimonials from the region, were critical in shaping a human rights consciousness in the United States, ultimately bringing into being a distinct American vernacular of moral witness.

TESTIMONIAL TRUTH IN THE AMERICAS

Brazil and its exile community offered Americans one of their first glimpses into what the loss of an individual's human rights might mean. News of political repression and torture in Brazil began to circulate in newspapers and weekly magazines, as well as in religious and progressive periodicals, in the early 1970s. With such titles as *Terror in Brazil: A Dossier* or *Black Book: Terror and Torture in Brazil,* reporting often took testimonial form, with statements from political prisoners and observers smuggled out of Brazil through transnational networks of activists.

Most dramatically at a performance in Madison Square Garden, the Living Theatre Collective, an experimental and politically active Brazilian theater troupe, performed torture for its American audience. The historian James Green writes of the performance:

> Almost imperceptibly, one of the actors, of obvious African heritage, gradually rose and began to look fearfully to the left and right, his dreadlocks whipping in the air as his head moved slowly back and forth in apparent panic. ... The assailants stripped off his clothes and bound his hands to his feet. Sliding a wooden pole between the cruxes of his tightly bound extremities, they lifted him off the floor and perched the pole on

two wooden saw horses, leaving him handing upside down, naked and
exposed. For the next several minutes, the audience witnessed the pan-
tomimed infliction of electric shock to the youth's anus and genital area.
Each surge of imaginary voltage ... sent convulsions through the actor's
body. Howls of pain punctuated each administration of electric current.
After the tenth jolt, the youth's body hung limp and defeated.[6]

This vivid and graphic performance of how torture was experienced by
the human body was not unusual in the 1970s, as the missionary Fred
Morris's congressional testimony in 1974 suggests; neither was its concern
with the interior suffering of the individual.

News reports of the repressive practices of military regimes in Chile,
Uruguay, and Argentina began to crowd out stories about Brazil in the
American press as the decade progressed, but the transnational circulation of Latin American *testimonios* in a variety of cultural forms continued to shape human rights vernaculars in the United States. Chilean
arpilleras or folk tapestries were one especially powerful form of testimonial truth. *Arpilleristras*, largely women who were inhabitants of urban
Chilean shanty towns, used old flour or seed bags made of burlap as
the background for their needlework and appliqués of colorful cloth to
produce tapestries the size of cafeteria trays; these tapestries told family stories of political and social repression under the Chilean military
regime after the coup against the Allende government. Some of their
work also operated in a third dimension, with empty little plates, miniature firearms, or smaller figurines running or crying sometimes attached
to the cloth to depict repression and violations of individual human
rights. Many *arpilleristas* had family members who had been disappeared
or held as political prisoners. As one explained in an oral history interview, "you would do an *arpilleras*, and in it you would show what was happening here. The repression, the protests, when the police arrived and
began hitting people, shooting. We would sew all that."[7] In evoking the
disappeared, some tapestries showed the kidnapping of a disappeared
person or the search by relatives for him or her and its emotional consequences for the family. Others were more allegorical, depicting doves in
cages and hands in chains or illustrating articles of the Universal Declaration of Human Rights.

Many of the *arpilleristas* were organized into workshops at shanty town churches by the Vicariá del la Solidaridad, which became the leading grassroots human rights advocacy organization in post-coup Chile. The workshops were a way to help these unemployed women earn money for their families and provided a safe space for the expression of opposition and resistance to the human rights abuses of the state. Given the hostility of the military regime to any form of public protest, and over time to the work of the *arpilleristas* themselves as they took on a wider global profile, the primary sales market for folk tapestries was in North America and Europe. The Vicariá organized a clandestine network of distributors and sellers, often among Chilean exiles, and at the same time devised strategies for preventing *arpilleras* from being discovered as they were shipped out of the country. The politicized folk tapestries served two other aims of the Vicariá as well: increasing the international awareness of human rights abuses in Chile and cultivating forms of global solidarity. As the sociologist Jacqueline Adams argues, these transnational networks of solidarity enabled "flows of financial and moral support to artists and supporting organizations under the dictatorship, and flows of information about instances of repression, human rights violations … and resistance in the opposite direction, to the outside world.[8] *Arpilleras* operated as a visual testimonial that both raised the human rights consciousness of the buyer and supported the women who made them. Buyers "bought out of solidarity" (*compraron por solidaridad*), as the Vicariá put it. Sellers of *arpilleras* called their buyers *gente solidaria* (solidarity-oriented or supportive people).

Thousands of *arpilleras* were imported to North America, Europe, and Australia in the 1970s. In the United States, they first emerged in mid-decade at Chilean solidarity events organized by exiles and local human rights activists. By the late 1970s, exhibits and sales of *arpilleras* were increasingly common in American galleries and colleges, as well as in nonprofit gift shops associated with peace groups and women's organizations, music festivals, neighborhood fairs and craft shops, and liberal Catholic and Protestant church bazaars.[9] Their ubiquity in the progressive landscape of America was marked in the touring production *Tres Marias y Una Rosa* (*Three Marias and One Rosa*) put on by an experimental Chilean theater group; it was set in a workshop where four women made *arpilleras* in memory of their disappeared relatives for sale in the United States and Europe.[10] As the play made clear, the tactile quality of the folk tapestries and the individual visual expressions of moral witness by the women who made them lent the *arpilleras* an authenticity that resonated for the Americans who encountered or purchased them.

If the visceral materiality of the *arpilleras* drew Americans into a deeper understanding of what violations of human rights might mean, so too did a new 1970s soundscape inflected by Latin American poetry and song. American folk musicians, for instance, helped popularize the poetry of Victor Jara, a prominent leftist Chilean writer and theater director who was tortured and murdered by the Chilean military in the coup that toppled the Allende government. Shortly before Jara was killed, he wrote a poem meditating on the horrific conditions in the soccer stadium in which he and thousands of others were imprisoned after the coup. Later set to music by Pete Seeger, *Estadio Chile* was often performed by Seeger and other folk musicians such as Bob Dylan and Arlo Guthrie before American audiences during concert tours in the mid- and late 1970s:

> We are 5,000 – here in this little part of the sky.
> We are 5,000 – how many more will we be?
> In the whole city, and the country 10,000 hands,
> Which could seed the fields, make run the factories.
> How much humanity now with pain, panic and terror?
>
> We are six of us, lost in space among the stars,
> One dead, one beaten like I never believed a human could be so beaten.
> The other four wanting to leave all the terror,
> One leaping into space, others beating their heads against the wall,
> All with gazes fixed on death.
>
> The military carry out their plans with precision;
> Blood is medals for them,
> Slaughter is the badge of heroism.
> Is this the world you created, O my God?

7.1. In what became weekly marches in the square in front of the presidential palace in Buenos Aires, the Madres del Plaza de Mayo (Mothers of the Plaza de Mayo) protest the disappearances of their children by the Argentine military regime in November 1977. AP Photo.

The Madres del Plaza de Mayo (Mothers of the Plaza de Mayo) were perhaps the most visible presence in the United States of moral witness by Latin American victims of human rights abuses. In 1977, despite the Argentinian government's ban on political organizing, the Madres began to march in the plaza directly in front of the Argentine presidential palace, demanding information about the fate of their children who were among those the regime had disappeared (Figure 7.1). In their weekly marches they wore white cotton headscarves embroidered with the names of their disappeared children. Quite quickly the Madres attracted attention from local human rights groups and Amnesty International, which began to help them establish an international profile; Amnesty soon sent groups of mothers to Western Europe, Canada, and Australia to present their case against the Argentine state. The Madres arrived in Washington, DC, in July 1979, offering the white cotton scarves they wore during their protest marches to the government officials they encountered on Capitol Hill. Moving on to New York City where they hoped to meet representatives of the United Nations, the monolingual Spanish-speaking mothers distributed calling cards that read, "We are the Mothers of the disappeared from Buenos Aires, Argentina, and we are coming to discuss human rights." American press reports of the Madres' visit to the United States sympathetically termed them "merely mothers ... not political players – and all they want to know is what happened to their children."[11]

The experience of imprisonment and torture by the military regime in Argentina emerged with particular power in a widely read memoir by Jacobo Timerman, *Prisoner without a Name, Cell without a Number*. From a prominent European Jewish family that had immigrated to Argentina in the 1920s, Timerman served as the editor and publisher of a leading Buenos Aires daily newspaper critical of the military regime. He publicly demanded accountability on behalf of relatives and families for the wave of disappearances as the regime came to power in the mid-1970s. "Entire families disappeared," Timerman writes in *Prisoner without a Name*. "The bodies were covered with cement and thrown to the bottom of the river." Other corpses were "thrown into old cemeteries under existing graves," "heaved into the middle of the sea from helicopters," or "dismembered and burned."[12] Timerman's memoir weaves together this broader story of political repression with his arrest in the middle of the night in April 1977 by armed gunmen and what became thirty months of imprisonment, torture, and anti-Semitic taunts and threats in one of the clandestine prisons set up by the Argentine military.

Timerman's memoir was on the *New York Times* best-seller list for weeks after its publication and was later selected as one of the "Books of the Century" by the *Times*. Its reception by American readers was shaped by its direct, first-person style of moral witnessing and the links it drew to emergent forms of Holocaust memory. Like Solzhenitsyn's *The Gulag Archipelago*, its opening paragraphs brought readers directly into Timerman's personal ordeal. "The cell is narrow," Timerman writes:

When I stand at the center, facing the steel door, I can't extend my arms. But it is long, and when I lie down, I can stretch out my entire body. ... The floor of the cell is permanently wet. Somewhere there's a leak. The mattress is also wet. I have a blanket, and to prevent that from getting wet I keep it on my shoulders constantly. If I lie down with the blanket on top of me, the part of my body touching the mattress gets soaked. ... I must call the guard to take me to the bathroom. It is a complicated procedure, and they're not always in the mood. ... It amuses them to sometimes tell me that I'm along side the latrine when I am not. Or to guide me – by one hand, or shoving me from behind – so that I stick one foot into the latrine. Eventually they tire of this game and don't respond to my call. I do it on myself.

Along with these everyday humiliations and degradations of solitary confinement, Timerman recounts the varieties of torture he and others endured: the electric shocks from what prisoners called "the machine;" sustained and brutal interrogations; hours sitting blindfolded and handcuffed to a chair, sometimes outside in a cold rain where Timerman says "my pee .... turned icy and the skin on legs, where the urine ran down, hurts." But "nothing can compare," he writes, to the family groups who were tortured in front of each other: "The entire affectual world ... collapses with a kick in the father's genitals ... or the sexual violation of a daughter."[13]

Anti-Semitism and Holocaust memory framed Timerman's self-understanding of the disappearances and his own personal ordeal. For Timerman, the Argentine military regime was like "the German Nazi rulers" and "brought an all-embracing of Nazi ideology as part of its structure." During his imprisonment Timerman was repeatedly challenged in interrogations about his support of Zionism, what the regime called his "leftist Zionism" and the perceived shadowy connections to its political opponents in Argentina.[14] But Timerman is also severely critical of what he terms the "silence" in Argentina's civil society, especially that of Argentine Jews, regarding the crimes of the military regime. Too often, he claims, Argentines looked away. Here Timerman explicitly advances his own framing of Holocaust memory. "The point of reference for Jewish leaders of Buenos Aires, as for Jewish leaders in many parts of the world" in the 1970s, Timerman suggests, "is the horror of the

Holocaust. A gas chamber, a concentration camp, a selection made in front of crematorium ovens, is the point of reference that must determine whether the moment for total and open battle against anti-Semitism has arrived." Equating "Jewish silence of the Hitler years" with that of Argentine Jews in the 1970s, he writes, "I never imagined that there would be Jewish leaders who would utilize the horrors of the Holocaust to maintain that the most advantageous response to certain anti-Semitic aggressions of a much less brutal nature was silence." Reflecting on the arc of his experiences at the close of his memoir, Timerman suggests, "[W]hat obsesses me most is the repetition of silence rather than the possibility of another Holocaust."[15] Cruelty, terror, and persecution short of mass murder, Timerman believed, required the same moral witness as the Holocaust. In *Prisoner without a Name*, he unflinchingly offered such testimonial.

Timerman's memoirs were not without their American critics. Writing in the *Wall Street Journal*, the self-styled neoconservative Irving Kristol argued that Timerman exaggerated the prevalence of anti-Semitism in Argentina and remained mum on his own close connections to leftists who sought to destabilize the government (arguments that coincidently closely followed the regime's own very public efforts to undermine the memoir as it began to receive international acclaim and that were vigorously challenged by many American observers).[16] But the more prevalent response to *Prisoner without a Name* was almost universal admiration for Timerman's "courageous" accounting of human rights violations against himself and others in Argentina. Critics called the memoir "extraordinary" and "the most gripping and the most important book I have read in a long time." Their praise in large measure flowed from an appreciation of the experiential style of the narrative that told of "the total exposure to which Timerman was forced to submit his body, his family, his opinions, his Jewishness" and "gives his book a fierce solemnity that I will not forget." Drawing attention as Timerman did to the silences of the Holocaust, Anthony Lewis wrote in a front-page *New York Times Book Review* essay that his role "is to be a witness – for the rest of us. ... We are blessed as readers and human beings that this witness survived."[17] For many readers Timerman offered an exceptionally compelling moral

7.2. Jack Lemmon and Sissy Spacek on the set of Academy Award-nominated film *Missing* that employed the era's testimonial practices of witness to explore the disappearance and murder of a young American, Charles Horman, in the wake of the military coup in Chile in September 1973. © Christian Simonpierti/Sygma/Corbis.

witness, one that contributed to the making of the 1970s American human rights imagination.

AMERICANS AND THE TESTIMONIAL TURN

As the 1970s came to a close, American writers, filmmakers, and artists began to draw on the testimonial turn in Latin America to offer their own local human rights vernaculars. The story of the young American counterculture journalist Charles Horman who was disappeared in the 1973 Chilean coup – first told in a 1978 book by Thomas Hauser and later circulating more widely in the 1982 Academy Award-nominated film *Missing* with its high-profile stars Jack Lemmon and Sissy Spacek – provided one highly visible vehicle for bringing narratives of human rights abuses back home (Figure 7.2).[18] In this case, it was an American who was the victim. Harvard-educated Charles Horman had gone to Chile while the Allende government was still in power, eager to see the region's first democratically elected socialist in action. When the military coup took place, he was rounded up along with thousands of other Chileans, detained in the Santiago stadium later made famous in Victor Jara's *Estadio Chile* and eventually executed.

Missing focuses on the efforts of Horman's father, Ed, and his wife, Beth, to find their son and husband. Both develop an increasing respect and regard for one another despite Ed's initial suspicions of what he sees as Beth's unconventional radicalism. Ed starts the film as a conservative believer in the sanctity of the American state and is scornful of his son's leftist politics. "If he had just stayed home," Ed says in an exasperated tone at the beginning of the film when he believes Charles is still alive, "this wouldn't have happened." Confused by what he encounters when he visits the stadium where Charles was last seen – the growing political violence and terror in the stadium are at the margins of the frame – Ed issues a passionate appeal over the stadium's sound system: "Charles, I'm here in hopes you can hear me. ... Can you [voice breaking] hear me?" There is silence. In its aftermath, the film traces Ed's growing political consciousness as he comes to believe American diplomatic and military personnel in Chile are hiding more than they reveal about the circumstances of his son's death. In this sense, the film's focus on Horman also speaks to the place of the United States in supporting the bloody Chilean coup. The circumstances of Charles Horman's murder come to stand in for a wider critique of an interventionist American foreign policy in the region and the rights abuses that flowed from it.[19]

The book and the film, which very loudly alleged the culpability of American representatives in Horman's murder, were controversial and prompted a vigorous State Department denial. *Missing*'s director, Costa-Gavras, was no stranger to controversy or political repression. His 1969 film *Z* explored the assassination of a pro-democracy activist by the Greek military junta, and his 1973 film *State of Siege* depicted an official of the U.S. Agency for International Development training the Uruguayan military police in methods of torture. Some critics questioned Costa-Gavras's approach in *Missing*, casting doubt on the veracity of the film's allegations against the U.S. government and the ethics of his choice to make the survival of one American seem more important than the fate of thousands of Chilean victims.[20] More favorable responses to *Missing*, however, were less concerned about its politics than its human dimensions. Many critics emphasized the empathetic resonances evoked by the performances of Lemmon and Spacek. One noted a "stunning scene" in which Beth was unable to get home before the military-imposed curfew, spending the night hiding in an alley hearing ever-closer sounds of gunfire with growing confusion and terror. Another pointed to the focus on Ed's political awakening as helping viewers "palpably" and "undeniably" know "the truth ... of the fascist brutality" in Chile.[21] The words "human rights" are never mentioned in *Missing*, but its raw emotionality reflected the broader individualized frames through which human rights came to have meaning in 1970s American cultural politics.

The Chicago-born realist painter Leon Golub offered another politically charged American human rights vernacular shaped in part by the Latin American testimonial turn. Golub worked in a figurative style for much of his career, often in the shadows of the 1960s art world and its concerns with abstract and Pop art. His work became more politically oriented during the U.S. war in Vietnam, turning in the mid-1970s to what he saw as American responsibility for the sustained violations of human rights carried out by military regimes in Latin America and, later, Central America. The subjects of his work, however, are the everyday perpetrators of political violence and their victims. "If I had to give a description of my work," Golub said in a 1982 interview, "I would say it's a definition of how power is demonstrated through the body and in human actions, and in our time how power and stress and political industrial powers are shown."[22] His paintings of political terror demanded a kind of moral witness from those who encountered them.

Three series of Golub's paintings titled *Mercenaries*, *Interrogation*, and *White Squad* were increasingly shown in American galleries and museums beginning in the late 1970s either in group exhibitions or in one-man shows where they created a sensation. As one prominent critic wrote about *Mercenaries* and *White Squad*, "if a half a dozen pictures were chosen to represent" this era "one of them sure would surely be a Golub." Another said Golub's "pictorial investigation of political terror ... has placed him at the center of present debates about art and politics."[23] Golub consciously took inspiration in his work on political violence from history painting and battle art, including Titian's 1575

The Flaying of Masyas, whose extraordinary image of brutality against the body is Golub's source for the torture victims in the *Interrogation* series, and Goya's 1863 *Disasters of War* etchings that searingly portrayed the atrocities of the Spanish war in Napoleonic France. But Golub's paintings were also informed by conventions of documentary photography, especially situations of danger or threat made visible by the photographic gaze. In all three of these series, he worked from a variety of photographic images, most notably the illustrated magazine *Soldier of Fortune* that depicted scenes of mercenary and covert action, through which he assembled what one critic called an "archive of poses."[24]

The paintings themselves operated on huge canvasses – most were fourteen feet long and ten feet high – that drew viewers into graphic scenes of torture and put them at eye level with the victims of torture. In *Mercenaries I*, for instance, two U.S. soldiers from the Vietnam era carry a charred and tortured body strung from a rope between them. Especially striking are the faces of the soldiers, one who is shirtless and the other chewing on a cigarette. Not only do the soldiers physically tower over the torture victim, himself burned and depicted in an animal-like crouch, but both soldiers also smirk and smile. Golub suspends the act of torture in *Interrogation I and II* (Figures 7.3 and 7.4, see color figures), giving acute visual expression to the tortured body that is often seen as outside of language. The torturer's stick in the first painting is still raised to resume his work, while his compatriot who would likely have directed the violence responds to someone just beyond the painting's frame. In *Interrogation II*, four men have turned to talk and joke seemingly with someone outside the painting in what would be the viewer's space. The shock of the quotidian rendering of the act of torture is heightened by the condition of the torture victims themselves: one is naked, hooded, and roughly tied into a chair, and the other is hanging naked by his heels in what Golub later said was a "situation that has been done in all sorts of societies but is particularly done in Latin America." The flayed chest of the victim in *Interrogation I* and the blood-red oxide that floods the background of *Interrogation II* heightens the contrast between the casual stance of the perpetrators and the tortured body. As one critic noted, "Golub's masked and bound victims are dehumanized, faceless and silent."[25] And yet the composition and the massive scope of the individual paintings offer and invite moral

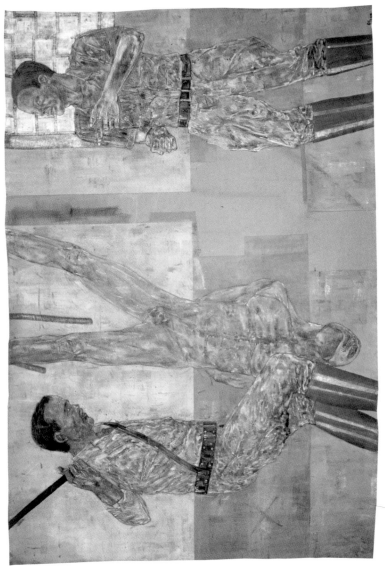

7.3. Leon Golub. *Interrogation I*. 1980–81. Acrylic on linen, 120 × 176 in. (304.8 × 447.04). The Broad Art Foundation. Art © Estate of Leon Golub/Licensed by VAGA, New York, NY.

7.4. Leon Golub. *Interrogation II.* 1981. Acrylic on linen, 305 × 426 cm (120 × 168 in.). Art Institute of Chicago. Art © Leon Golub/Licensed by VAGA, New York, NY. Courtesy Ronald Feldman Fine Arts.

witness, one that makes ethical demands on viewers to see the very interior conditions of violations to bodily integrity.

Not all Americans in the 1970s saw human rights in the same way. Some were not paying attention at all. Still others offered alternative groundings for human rights talk. For some American conservatives, human rights were not so much about a transformation of the self and the new politics of moral witness as an opportunity to recast the ideological battles of the Cold War in new garb. The experiences of dissidents from the East reinforced and reinvigorated their own prevailing conceptions of freedom as the fulcrum that made clear the moral superiority of United States over the Soviet Union. The Solzhenitsyn plank at the 1976 Republication National Convention and the efforts of Senator Helms to accord Solzhenitsyn honorary American citizenship were part of these wider efforts to repurpose emerging notions of human rights in a Cold War frame. For that reason, conservatives greeted public discussion of Latin American human rights abuses skeptically, pointing to the "hypocrisy" of what they saw as a willingness to look away from the human rights violations by America's adversaries while focusing on the behavior of Latin American states who were formal allies of the United States. The Cold War was central to this construction of human rights too, with détente perceived as acting to shield the realities of life in the Soviet Union. Conservatives increasingly put the term "human rights" in scare quotes in the late 1970s, as Irving Kristol did in his review of Jacobo Timerman's memoir. For what Kristol termed "totalitarian regimes" like the Soviet Union, a "staunch and eloquent opposition" to human rights violations "is called for," whereas with what he termed authoritarian regimes, such as those in Latin America, "private criticism and suasion" were "more sensible." Human rights "purists," Kristol argued, were unable to recognize "this key distinction."[26]

But to acknowledge the partiality of the American human rights vernacular of the 1970s is not to deny its larger power. One contemporary political commentator, who sought to capture the influence of human rights across the American landscape, wrote in 1977,

> The good grey liberals on the *New York Times* love it; so do the Friedmanites
> on the *Wall Street Journal.* Senator [Henry M.] Jackson thinks it's made in

heaven, and the hitherto-ignored members of Amnesty International hope that at last it may be coming down to earth. The hawkish neo-conservatives at *Commentary* and the dovish leftists at the *New York Review* have found one issue on which they can agree on – almost. Who could bad mouth human rights? It is beyond partisanship and beyond attack" like "motherhood and apple pie.[27]

The central presence of human rights in late 1970s America was confirmed when they became the subject of Gary Trudeau's Pulitzer-prize-winning comic strip, *Doonesbury*. Trudeau, who in a 1976 poll of American high school seniors edged out Solzhenitsyn as the tenth most admired world figure, made his name by turning the cartoon strip into perhaps the most read commentary on the decade's cultural politics. Offering withering critiques of Nixon-era policy at home and abroad and more gentle satires of the mores of the "Me" generation through a set of increasingly beloved fictional characters, *Doonesbury* captured critical elements of the decade's zeitgeist. One of these characters, Duane Delacourt who was Trudeau's imagined Secretary of Symbolism in the new Carter administration, argued that Carter's embrace of human rights diplomacy would be significantly advanced if the "boss could host a human rights awards banquet."[28] The subsequent gala dinners that Delacourt organizes, rendered in strips that ran in almost all major American newspapers in April 1977 and 1978 (see Figure 7.5), not only poked fun at the ironies and contradictions of the administration's human rights policies but more broadly announced the full arrival of human rights in the American cultural landscape.

Human rights were constructed and given meaning over the seventies in the United States through a process that entangled growing individualist sentiments at home with the transnational rise of moral witness and testimonial truth. Like the broader global human rights imagination of the era, the Cold War was often left to the side. As many Americans refracted what they came to know about the individual experiences of Soviet, Eastern European, and Latin American victims of state imprisonment, torture, disappearance, and political murder, they began to define a particular human rights vernacular rooted in conceptions of bodily integrity and psychic trauma. Its believability and the transformation of

7.5. Garry Trudeau's *Doonesbury* took up human rights in April 1977 and April 1978 in his cartoon strip that ran in almost all major American daily newspapers. DOONESBURY © 1977 and 1978 G. B. Trudeau. Reprinted with permission of UNIVERSAL UCLICK. All rights reserved.

moral sentiments that flowed from it became the motor for what was a fast-growing human rights movement in 1970s America that would shape the thought and practice of human rights politics in the United States for decades to come.

CHAPTER 8

The Movement

ON A WINTRY JANUARY EVENING IN 1973 THE MEMBERS of
Amnesty USA Group 11 gathered on the Upper East Side of New
York City to adopt a new prisoner of conscience, Sutanti Aidit of Indonesia. Aidit, a medical doctor and the wife of the leader of the Indonesian Communist Party, was arrested and imprisoned in the ruthless
campaigns of state repression that followed a failed 1965 coup. At the
order of the Indonesian military regime, killing squads targeted as many
as a half-million suspected leftist sympathizers.[1] Sutanti Aidit was among
the more than 100,000 Indonesians arrested, interrogated, often under
torture, and imprisoned by the state. Half of them remained in custody
for more than a decade housed in prison camps whose sanitation, medical facilities, and food were inadequate at best. They were permitted very
limited contact with the outside world, including family and friends, and
were often harshly mistreated by prison guards. Aidit was incarcerated
in one of the worst of these facilities, Bukit Duri, which had originally
been a brutal Dutch colonial-era prison and was more recently used by
the Indonesian state as a criminal jail for women.[2]

Members of Group 11 worked tirelessly on behalf of Sutanti Aidit for
more than six years. Some wrote letters to Indonesian authorities at the
United Nations and in Jakarta urging her release from prison. Others
sought to develop a direct relationship with Aidit, often sending postcards and small amounts of money to her in prison and making sustained
inquiries into the well-being of her children, sister, and mother. "We have
no way of knowing whether they get through," a member reported at
one of Group 11's monthly meetings; "there is always a possibility. For
prisoners, the cards provide much needed moral support; for officials,

an indication that groups in other countries are concerned about the fate of their prisoners." Group 11's members often looked for personal ways to bridge the distance between them and Aidit. One member, for instance, wrote her a postcard in the summer of 1977 after learning Aidit had been ill. On the front of the card were colorful three-dimensional tropical butterflies with the printed caption – "And think, only hours ago they struggled free from the tight confines of a drab cocoon" – to which the member added on the back: "I want you to know I have been thinking about you and will continue to do so. I hope this card will cheer and perhaps amuse you somewhat. I would like to know whether you need anything. ... Please do let me know." At moments, a kind of compassion fatigue fell over their efforts, with another member suggesting "that we drop this case since we haven't made any progress with it."

But the Group 11 members pressed on with their letter writing throughout the 1970s. Because Aidit was a physician, they also worked to draw the American Women's Medical Association into their campaign. At the same time the group sought to mobilize broader public and government pressure for Aidit's release, conducting petition drives, placing articles in such publications as the *New Yorker* and *Ms. Magazine*, and organizing letter-writing campaigns to congressional representatives, the U.S. State Department, and New York-based corporations doing business in Indonesia.[3]

Amnesty USA Group 11's transnational advocacy for Sutanti Aidit offers a microhistory of what was an explosion in the 1970s of an American human rights movement. In 1970, Amnesty USA had only two local groups. By 1980 there were 203.[4] Like Group 11, they adopted prisoners of conscience assigned to them by Amnesty's international secretariat in London and worked in similar ways to gain their release. They often took on several cases simultaneously. Group 11 was concerned not just with the release of Sutanti Aidit over the course of the decade but also with prisoners in the Soviet Union and Latin America. In addition to the growth in the number of Amnesty's local groups, almost four hundred U.S.-based human rights organizations were established between the mid- to late 1970s. Many were self-styled grassroots and decidedly local operations, whereas others came to be national if not global in scope. At the same time a host of American professional organizations that had previously been unconcerned with global rights questions, along with major philan-thropic institutions, took up the cause of human rights. For the first time doing something about human rights became a part of everyday practice. Doctors, lawyers, journalists, physicists, bankers, accountants, chemists, university and high school teachers, students, senior citizens, social work-ers, ministers, librarians, grants officers at the nation's leading founda-tions, psychologists and psychiatrists, dentists, statisticians, and even civil engineers all found human rights in the 1970s. They never let go.

In its work for Sutanti Aidit's release, Group 11 exemplified what would become standard operating procedure for nonstate human rights advocacy in the United States over the course of the decade. Its mem-bers' concern with a prisoner in Indonesia was a bit of an anomaly, how-ever. More commonly victims of human rights abuses in the Soviet Union, Eastern Europe, and Latin America were the focus of attention for the American human rights movement in this era. In offering moral witness for violations of individual human rights, the singularity of the person and the body was always at the center of 1970s American human rights practice. So too were larger transnational shifts in the framing of moral problems. A few actors in the movement had been present at the cre-ation, experiencing the human rights moment of the 1940s, but most of its leaders were younger than forty years old; for them that earlier decade and its human rights practices were largely forgotten. For these young leaders new forms of witnessing and the telling of motivated truths that reshaped the global meaning of expertise in this era were more cen-tral. Over the decade these new forms became embedded in American professional norms and practices, further deepening and thickening the impact of human rights on the decade's cultural politics.

The movement that emerged in the seventies had lasting significance for the growing belief in human rights as a universal moral language. Arguably human rights became what Americans now almost reflexively call "the idea of our time" less because of the top-down human rights diplomacy of U.S. presidents and legislators than the bottom-up widen-ing of the societal and transnational canvas on which the nonstate prac-tices of human rights played out in 1970s America. Just as importantly the epistemologies and protocols of human rights practice that emerged in this era continue to anchor the forms of human rights politics. If the contemporary believability in human rights is rooted in the 1970s, its enduring limits also emerged in that era. A conscious indifference to the political and social contexts that produced human rights violations in the first place, a sometimes narrow geographic range of attention, and a concern with political and civil rather than social and economic rights inflected the American practice of human rights in the 1970s. So too did a prevailing sense that human rights described problems that happened far from the United States. Only infrequently in the decade were human rights deployed to advance rights at home. For leaders and activists in the emergent human rights movement of the 1970s, many of whom were white middle-class professionals, their campaigns against human rights violations generally began outside the domestic space of the nation.

BUILDING THE MOVEMENT

It is difficult to come by precise numbers of American organizations whose primary concern in the 1970s was with human rights, because smaller groups were sometimes short-lived and larger organizations often had multiple agendas. The most comprehensive accounting in this period puts the number at 403 by the end of the decade, no more than 20 of which were founded before 1970. They included not only Amnesty USA and the American branches of the International Commission of Jurists and the International League for Human Rights but also groups like the American Bar Association, the American Civil Liberties Union, the National Association for the Advancement of Colored Persons, the Japanese American Citizens League, and the National Lawyers Guild whose concern with global human rights issues in the 1940s had ebbed and whose larger missions encompassed a wider brief. The 1970s brought a surge of 383 new American-based groups into the human rights fold. Some of these were established by existing ethnic or religious organizations that turned their attention to human rights in the 1970s, but more than 300 were start-ups.[5]

The geographical focus of their advocacy reinforces the centrality of the Americas, the Soviet Union, and Eastern Europe in the 1970s American human rights imagination. Almost half were organized around rights violations in the Americas, most notably Brazil, Uruguay, Chile, Argentina, El Salvador, Guatemala, and Nicaragua – with the center of gravity shifting from Latin to Central America by the end of the decade. These efforts were often led by church-affiliated and other solidarity groups that came to employ the language of human rights in part through the transnational networks they developed with religious and civil society groups in the region and the growing South and Central American exile diasporas. Such groups ranged from very small ones like the Hartford Chile Solidarity Project and the Pittsburgh Nicaragua Solidarity Committee to the Methodist-based Washington Office on Latin America (WOLA), which was one of the first human rights lobbying groups in Washington, DC, and the 300 chapters of the U.S. Committee in Solidarity with the People of El Salvador.[6]

A quarter of American human rights groups focused on dissidents in the Soviet Union and Eastern Europe and the plight of Soviet Jewry. Many of these campaigns were launched by long-established American ethnic organizations representing Ukrainian, Lithuanian, Estonian, Czech, Hungarian, and Polish interests and such Jewish organizations as the American Jewish Committee and the Jewish World Congress for which the 1970s turn to human rights reinvigorated their advocacy efforts against political and religious persecution. But a variety of newer advocacy groups emerged too, particularly around the rights of immigration and treatment of Soviet Jews. The remaining groups were fragmented in their geographical focus, and their place in the 1970s American human rights movement more subdued. Asia was the most common tertiary target, where concerns about South Korea, the Philippines, Indonesia, Cambodia, Vietnam, and, more gradually, China dominated. A few groups focused on Europe and the Mediterranean, largely Northern Ireland, Turkey, and Cyprus. The anti-apartheid struggle in South Africa and the Arab-Israeli conflict were largely outside the cartographic imagination of most American self-styled human rights activists in the seventies, with only a handful of groups putting attention there.[7]

The locations within the United States of the era's human rights advocacy point toward its broad scope as does its secular and religious orientations. Most of the larger organizations were based in New York City or Washington, DC, and smaller groups tended to be concentrated in

New England, Chicago and the upper Midwest, and in California and the Pacific Northwest. Perhaps unsurprisingly, college towns with traditions of political activism like Berkeley, Ann Arbor, and Madison were overrepresented. Except for a handful of efforts organized in Florida, where a few groups formed around issues relating to Cuba and Haiti, and in university communities in Chapel Hill, Durham, and Nashville, there were very few local human rights groups in the American South. Whereas human rights advocacy in the 1970s was at times avowedly secular, a significant religious dimension was present too. As many as a quarter of American human rights groups in the decade had an exclusive religious orientation, with Catholic organizations predominating followed by mainline Protestant denominational and American Jewish groups. But there was considerable interpenetration between the religious and the secular within many organizations. Networks of information and shared concern often joined secular and religious groups in coalition efforts, especially around rights violations in the Americas.[8]

The tactics and strategies that shaped human rights organizing in 1970s America were directly informed by the larger concern with moral witness and individual testimony that infused the broader global human rights imagination. If human rights was a guest language in the United States – an importation of a transnational affect, rather than the exportation of American values abroad – so too were its practices. Amnesty USA's work exemplified the entanglements of the global and the local in the emergence of the U.S. human rights movement. Amnesty was an organizational import into the United States, with the initially very small Amnesty USA section founded in 1966 long after Amnesty International began its work in Great Britain and Western Europe. Amnesty's London-based International Secretariat set the protocols for what would become American practice. The work of local groups in the United States, such as Group 11 that adopted Sutanti Aidit, was based on the prisoner adoptions Amnesty pioneered earlier in Europe, in which individual groups simultaneously adopted prisoners of conscience from the West, the Soviet bloc, and the Global South to demonstrate the organization's political impartiality.[9]

Collectively, Amnesty offered moral witness on behalf of the suffering of these unjustly incarcerated prisoners as it sought their release.

At the same time the organization encouraged groups to connect with local media, organize public protests, and conduct educational forums to raise public awareness of individual human rights abuses. Amnesty USA was also engaged in Amnesty International's broader public campaigns, most notably its Campaign against Torture beginning in 1973. Informing all of these initiatives and activities were the dozens of country reports that came out of Amnesty's London-based research division. Like the 1974 *Chile: An Amnesty International Report* discussed in Chapter 5, these reports combined carefully compiled accountings of the numbers of human rights abuses and overall conditions of prisons with experiential first-person accounts of detention and torture. In combining more traditional forms of expertise with direct witness and testimonial, they introduced one form of the transnational turn toward motivated truth into the new American human rights advocacy of the 1970s.

Much of the everyday work of local groups revolved around letter writing to the prisoners they had adopted and to various state and international authorities with the potential to secure their release. That Amnesty saw these kinds of transnational epistolary practices as new and unfamiliar for its members is reflected in the painstakingly precise directions the International Secretariat provided to U.S. groups for their execution. Indeed Amnesty's founder Peter Berenson and other London staffers worried that "Americans could not sustain a long enough time span" to write a letter.[10] Along with a more general insistence that "letters to authorities should be worded as courteously as possible," the Secretariat told groups to make an "appeal for," but not "demand the release of" political prisoners. "Demand," it said, could be considered "peremptory and rude." It also offered sample texts of greetings and goodwill in the language of the prisoner when she or he was not a native English speaker. Letters to officials and prisoners were to be sent by registered mail because, Amnesty insisted, officials of foreign governments "have a certain respect for bureaucracy and postal regulations." The broader anxieties underlying these sometimes punctilious directives spoke to the organization's perpetual concern with performing its own impartiality. In the instructions accompanying the case of Aidit to Group 11, for instance, the Secretariat wrote, "There are still many misunderstandings about Amnesty's work; it is regarded by many as being politically left-wing and an 'anti-Indonesian' body. ... Please therefore, always mention the work you do for prisoners in other countries, particularly in the socialist and communist countries."[11]

But Amnesty USA pushed to establish its own set of practices that aimed to broaden who could play a role in American human rights advocacy. In an effort to build its grassroots membership, the canonical adoption groups were augmented in the mid-1970s by the creation of what Amnesty USA termed "Action Groups" that focused on human rights consciousness raising and educational outreach without having to undertake the more time-consuming commitment of prisoner adoptions. House newsletters, the monthly *Amnesty Action* and the quarterly *Matchbox* for U.S. members and contributors, further increased the organization's informational range. In 1976 Amnesty USA opened an office in Washington, DC, to lobby Congress and the executive branch on a variety of human rights issues. In a gradual expansion of its geographical range over the decade, the membership of Amnesty USA's West Coast Branch exceeded that of its New York base by the mid-1970s. Among its West Coast leadership was the celebrity folksinger Joan Baez whose appearance and discussion of Amnesty on the *Tonight Show* in 1973 further raised the organization's profile.[12]

In its work on torture, Amnesty USA also sought to build on the technological changes of the era that enabled faster communication. In 1975, it organized its own version of the Urgent Action Network first established by Amnesty International a few years earlier to intervene in cases where immediate attention might assist prisoners in extreme danger. Several thousand activists became part of the Amnesty USA's "telegram tree" that sought to mobilize activists to contact state public authorities within twenty-four hours after the arrest of a political prisoner, especially those the organization believed were likely to be tortured. "We knew from experience, from research that action for torture had to be really quick," one activist remembered. "Usually torture happens that first week after detention." The grassroots character of the network was reflected by its headquarters in the home of two Amnesty volunteers in the mountains that surround Boulder, Colorado. New forms of overnight mail surmounted their geographical isolation. "UPS was at the heart of the Urgent Action Network," they explained. "The brown UPS truck made its way up a steep mountain road almost daily, bringing news from the Amnesty Secretariat in London of arrests from around the world, and carrying back down the mountain our urgent action instructions to network activists about specific cases."[13]

At the same time Amnesty USA turned to direct mail fundraising to increase the numbers of its individual members and contributors through carefully designed appeals that sought to convey the immediacy of experiences of individual human rights abuses. Direct mail first appeared in the United States after World War II when national charities looked for new ways to expand their donor base. But the introduction of the five-digit zip code by the U.S. Postal Service in 1963 combined with the increasing affordability of compiling and maintaining computer-driven lists of supporters began to ease what had been a tedious and costly process of targeting likely donors. Amnesty began its direct mail efforts in 1974, contracting them out to a burgeoning class of direct mail consultants who purchased lists of donor names and subscribers from nonprofits and periodicals they believed were like-minded fellow travelers. The results, according to an internal 1980 Amnesty memo, were "nothing short of astounding," bringing in almost a half-million dollars in a direct mail campaign the previous fall. Even "cold prospect mail," the term of art for potential donors without any previous ties or knowledge of the organization, "has consistently come in at $225 per thousand or better," the report continued, far exceeding predicted costs. Amnesty USA gained some twenty to thirty thousand members per year through these appeals. Its donations increased from $30,000 in 1972 to $260,000 in 1978.[14]

The letters that arrived in the mailboxes of cold prospects put individuals front and center. Most of Amnesty's fundraising letters told stories of the victims of human rights abuses and let potential donors know how they could help. A letter from the late 1970s, for instance, opened with the story of an "expectant" 24-year-old student Veronica who was imprisoned shortly after the military seizure of power in Argentina:

> During her detention, Veronica was subjected to sexual abuse, beatings and electric shock treatments. Seven months after her arrest, she gave birth to a son in prison. While in labor, she was tied to a stretcher by her

hands and feet and left unattended until the last few minutes. Her new-born baby had to sleep on the floor of her rat-infested cell.

Veronica, the chairman of Amnesty USA's Board wrote in his letter to potential donors, was "one of the lucky ones," unexpectedly released from prison a year after she was arrested. But her case, he continued, was not an isolated phenomenon: "Thousands of men, women and young people in all parts of the world are being tortured or incarcerated for their beliefs today, even as you read this letter." The letter detailed Amnesty's work to release prisoners of conscience and the support it received from "more than 100,000" Americans, concluding, "They are people like you – people who care, who don't want to bury their heads in the sand. ... I invite you to share in our work. ... Prisoners of conscience can be helped. And you are the one who can help them."[15]

Other letters shared the same direct person-to-person style, but asked recipients to imagine that their own human rights were under assault. Typical is this letter from the chair of Amnesty USA's West Coast branch:

> You are walking toward your favorite store, thinking about a wedding gift you plan to buy. An unmarked car pulls up. Two men leap out, drag you into the back seat, plunge a hypodermic needle into your arm. ... Your captors keep beating you with truncheons, kicking you, pushing you up against the wall. They attack you sexually, mocking you and hinting that other members of your family are undergoing the same horror. You don't know why you've been imprisoned. You don't know what your torturers hope to make you say. You don't know where to turn. You've joined the nightmare world of the political prisoner.[16]

Such letters reflected a broader certainty over the decade that first-person immediacy offered a compelling individualistic frame for appre-hending social suffering and human rights abuses. Whether with direct mail donors or members of growing local adoption groups, "conscience" served as the emotive watchword of Amnesty's engagement with human rights. The idea of individual conscience inflected all of its work. Defined by Amnesty USA in a 1977 member newsletter as "a knowledge or feeling of right and wrong, with a compulsion to do right," it captured the global affect that drove American human rights advocacy in the seventies.[17]

HUMAN RIGHTS AS VOCATION

Along with these grassroots and member-based efforts, human rights advocacy also became embedded for the first time into American professional norms and practices in the 1970s. The role of the professions in the making of the Cold War world is well known, particularly the relationships between universities and the rise of the American national security state, the role of the sciences in creating the weapons that shaped the Cold War balance of nuclear terror, and the ways in which the production of knowledge in areas studies informed U.S. political and military engagement abroad.[18] But the place of professionals beginning in the 1970s as nonstate actors who bore witness to what were increasingly seen as transnational concerns about such issues as nuclear weapons, the environment, and human rights is just coming into view. The opposition of scientists and doctors to nuclear weapons offered the earliest iteration of a professional obligation to engage in the political sphere. In the wake of the United States' use of the atomic bomb at Hiroshima and Nagasaki, scientific and medical unease over nuclear proliferation and the radioactive fallout of weapons testing emerged as early as the late 1940s and early 1950s. But these concerns swelled in the following two decades, expanding to include opposition to the peaceful development of nuclear power in a movement that joined some physicists and doctors to a growing grassroots antinuclear campaign. The Federation of American Scientists, established in 1945, intensified its campaign for the international control of nuclear weapons in the 1970s. Similarly Physicians for Social Responsibility, founded in 1961, turned its attention to the medical dangers of nuclear power. The formation of the Boston-based International Physicians for the Prevention of Nuclear War in 1980 reflected the growing willingness of professionals over the decade to combine expertise and advocacy on nuclear issues; this group won the Nobel Peace Prize for its advocacy efforts in 1985.[19]

American professionals – most notably, ecologists, biologists, conservationists, and lawyers – were at the center of the rise of the environmental movement in the 1970s. After the publication of Rachel Carson's 1962 blockbuster *Silent Spring*, which laid out the case for the catastrophic environmental impact of the use of pesticides, ecologists increasingly sought a more public role around environmental problems. Some oceanographers and atmospheric scientists began to take on the problem of climate change and joined with environmentalists in the late 1960s to successfully oppose a cooperative program between government and business to build a commercial passenger aircraft, the SST, that could fly faster than the speed of sound. Stuart Brand's *Whole Earth Catalog*, a ubiquitous countercultural presence in the late 1960s and 1970s, combined a do-it-yourself approach to environmentally sustainable lifestyles with a sharp critique of the centralization and secrecy of corporate- and state-sponsored big science projects. The biologist Barry Commoner, whose best-selling 1971 *The Closing Circle* helped introduce lay audiences to notions of limits to growth, sustainability, and ecological interdependence, became a kind of rock star in the American environmental movement of the 1970s. Traditional and long-established conservation groups such as the National Wildlife Federation, the National Audubon Society, and the Sierra Club remade themselves around environmental advocacy, whereas newly established groups like the Friends of the Earth and Greenpeace undertook even more radical forms of activism. The practice of environmental law boomed during the decade, with litigation seen as an increasingly powerful weapon to advance the movement's agenda. The first American environmental law symposium was held in 1969, and law schools quickly began to offer courses on the subject, soon followed by the establishment of the first environmental law journal. The formation of the Natural Resources Defense Council exemplified this legal turn, bringing scientists and lawyers together for what would become an escalating set of legal interventions in federal and state courts over the decade on cases around air and water pollution and the protection of public lands.[20]

American professional commitments to human rights in the 1970s emerged against this broader domestic landscape, one enmeshed in the deeper global transformation of the very nature of expertise and a new appreciation for lived experience and advocacy that challenged long-standing traditions of professional objectivity and detachment. In their work on human rights over the decade, some American professionals, like their counterparts in Western Europe, began to embrace forms of motivated truth. Its American iterations were shaped by the fracturing of the collectivist structures that had guided U.S. political culture in the postwar era and by the rise of new concerns with the self, individual agency, and contingency. For some, human rights advocacy became a form of professional reenchantment, in part assuaging the guilt they felt about what they increasingly saw as their own culpability in the policies of the American state that contributed to many of the human rights abuses they now worked to address. Across professional communities in the United States, to borrow from Max Weber, human rights became a vocation.[21]

The new engagement by American scientists, health care professionals, foundations, and lawyers in 1970s human rights politics was especially striking. The Federation of American Scientists (FAS), with its traditionally strong organizational focus on nuclear issues, was among the first to become active in human rights, especially around the repression of Andrei Sakharov and other Soviet nuclear scientists; the National Academy of Sciences became similarly involved, forming a Human Rights Committee in 1976. The FAS, like several other scientific organizations, would eventually adopt Sakharov, with its members refusing to participate in scientific exchange with the Soviet Union until he was released from internal exile. The language of adoption had its roots in the work of Amnesty International.[22] Human rights also began to form a part of medical practice and education. As one doctor who had been imprisoned in the Chilean National Stadium after the 1973 military coup argued, "there is a special and significant place for doctors" in campaigns against torture. This "responsibility commits all medical societies and medical associations to condemn the participation of any of their members in any way in the practice of torture."[23] The 1970s brought a significant increase in the teaching of medical ethics not only for doctors but also for nurses, public health workers, and what were sometimes termed nonmedical professionals, including lawyers, clergy, and journalists; in addition the 1970s saw the establishment of major institutes concerned with socioethical issues in medicine. Human rights concerns, particularly around the question of torture, became part of this growing focus on bioethics.[24]

But it was the American Association for the Advancement of Science (AAAS) that was at the center of professional engagement with human rights in the 1970s. It began to take an interest in the human rights of scientists in the Soviet Union and Chile in the early 1970s, offering resolutions in their support and providing U.S.-based jobs for them if they were allowed to emigrate. The eminent Harvard biochemist John T. Erdsall led efforts to establish the AAAS's Committee on Scientific Freedom and Responsibility in 1976, making what was then a novel argument that scientific organizations "have not only a right but a responsibility to concern themselves with the defense of human rights of scientists." Tellingly, to envision the scope and nature of its activities, the committee looked outside the United States to the more developed work undertaken by the British Council for Science and Society on scholarly freedom and human rights.[25]

The AAAS Clearinghouse on Science and Human Rights established in 1977 consciously drew on the practices of Amnesty to review cases of persecuted foreign scientists and refer them to appropriate scientific societies for letter-writing and publicity campaigns. Along with the Soviet Union and Chile, the geographical focus of much of this work was Uruguay and Argentina. These efforts brought in an ever growing number of professional groups to work on global human rights issues in the late 1970s, including the American Chemical Society, American Mathematical Society, American Medical Association, American Psychological Society, American Physical Society, American Public Health Organization, American Statistical Association, the American Society of Civil Engineers, and the National Association of Social Workers. Beginning in the late 1970s, the AAAS and its member organizations augmented publicity and education campaigns with high-level fact-finding missions to investigate the treatment of scientists in Latin America and the Soviet Union and to document the organization's increasing concern with torture and other grave violations of human rights.[26]

The work of the American Statistical Association's (ASA) Committee on Scientific Freedom and Human Rights offers one example of how human rights became embedded in professional practice. Here the quintessential data-driven discipline encountered and was transformed by testimonial witness. It was the story of one individual that first prompted interest by American statisticians in human rights. In the mid-1970s, the ASA began to organize exchange programs with Latin

American statistical societies. A delegation visited Argentina in 1976 and met with Carlos Noriega, who then served as director of the Argentine national statistical office. With the establishment of the new military government Noriega was forced out of office, apparently because he refused military requests to tamper with official data. A few months later Noriega was disappeared. At the same time, the International Statistics Institute announced plans to hold its upcoming biennial meeting in Buenos Aires. The executive director of the ASA successfully persuaded the organization's board of directors to appoint an ad hoc committee on human rights, which recommended a boycott of the Buenos Aires meeting. A majority of the ASA board opposed the boycott, arguing that "science and politics should be kept separate," with some board members so troubled that they sought to dismantle the ad hoc human rights committee altogether. The board did, however, give permission to organize activities before and during the meeting to draw attention to the plight of Noriega and other disappeared Argentine statisticians. In Buenos Aires, the ASA ad hoc committee members met Argentine human rights leaders and families of the disappeared statisticians. They also presented a petition to the acting minister of the interior asking for information about the disappeared, with copies presented to the Argentine press.

Soon protestations about the separation of science and politics began to dissolve. ASA advocacy in Argentina ultimately stimulated the organization's broader engagement in human rights issues. The ad hoc committee was made a permanent fixture in the ASA in the early 1980s, launching pressure campaigns on behalf of statisticians at risk in the Soviet Union and elsewhere in Latin America to, as the organization put it, "defend or promote scientific freedom and human rights." These new forms of advocacy for human rights also inflected their professional practice, with a growing number of American statisticians beginning to collect, analyze, and present qualitative data to measure and monitor the status of human rights around the world.[27] Expertise and advocacy were becoming intertwined with human rights as a variety of professional groups in the United States increasingly saw both as part of their professional responsibilities.

Major American philanthropic organizations first turned their attention to human rights in the seventies, another sign of the coming of age of the human rights movement and the professional turn in human rights advocacy. The year 1975 marked the first instance that "human rights" was listed in the *Foundation Grant Index*, the most comprehensive annual compilation of grants made by major U.S. foundations. That same year a Ford Foundation internal report approvingly termed human rights "the epiphenomena of the times" and called for "a systematic and sustained program in human rights and intellectual freedom," with an initial commitment of $1.5 million in 1976 and 1977.[28] By decade's end, Ford had made thirty major human rights grants, and they became an ever larger portion of the foundation's portfolio. The MacArthur Foundation initiated its own human rights grants program in 1978. Foundation support was often targeted at legal, scientific, medical, and media organizations in and out of the United States to promote continuing education and research initiatives on human rights issues.[29] Ford, for instance, provided funding for the American Statistical Association to undertake a major research project on the role of statistics in the documentation of human rights violations. With foundation support the AAAS sent its first team of forensic and genetic scientists to Argentina to exhume mass graves of Argentine human rights victims and to determine the paternity of children born in detention or abducted from their parents and adopted by supporters of the previous regime. The number of foundation-supported AAAS fact-finding missions around the use of torture and psychiatric abuse grew in the early 1980s in such places as Chile, Uruguay, and the Philippines.[30]

American lawyers were also increasingly drawn into the practice of global human rights in the 1970s. This marked a sharp U-turn for the American Bar Association (ABA), which in the early 1950s had led the successful effort to oppose U.S. ratification of the international human rights conventions drafted in the United Nations in the earlier 1940s moment of global human rights norm making. The ABA's Section on Individual Rights and Responsibilities began publishing a quarterly journal titled *Human Rights* in 1970. Its International Law and Practice Section established a Committee on Human Rights in the mid-1970s. A well-publicized ABA sponsored mock trial in October 1977, one that reflects how deeply concerns with Soviet dissidents made their way into the decade's human rights politics of American professional organizations, ruled on the arrest of dissident and rights activist Anatoly Sharansky for treason by the Soviet authorities. Sharansky was "defended" by Harvard Law Professor Alan Dershowitz before a self-styled "court of world public conscience" that included Idaho Senator Frank Church, ABA President Chesterfield Smith, Columbia University President William J. McGill, and civil rights activists Eleanor Holmes Norton and Bayard Rustin. The ABA court found Sharansky not guilty. In the late 1970s, the ABA formally reversed its opposition to ratification of the Genocide Convention, the American Convention on Human Rights, and the International Covenants on Civil and Political Rights and Economic, Social, and Cultural Rights.[31]

Of more enduring significance was the gradual infusion of human rights into American law school curriculums beginning in the seventies. The leadership of the ABA's Committee on Human Rights was made up of figures, many of them active in human rights politics in the 1940s, who had shaped the emergent field of international human rights law in the United States. Louis Henkin, a drafter of the 1951 Convention of the Status of Refugees, and Louis B. Sohn, who helped produce the American Law Institute's 1944 Statement on Human Rights, offered the first human rights law classes at American universities in 1971 at Columbia and Harvard Law Schools, respectively. Sohn and Thomas Buergenthal, who had survived incarceration as a child in Auschwitz, authored the first casebook in 1973.[32] By decade's end human rights law was becoming institutionalized in and beyond the East Coast. Although Henkin established the Center for the Study of Human Rights at Columbia in 1978, mid-career legal scholars for whom the 1940s were less of a reference point were also involved in many of these efforts. Bert B. Lockwood founded a human rights law center at the University of Cincinnati Law School in 1979 that became the home of *Human Rights Quarterly*, now a leading journal in the field. At the same time Robert Lillich developed a human rights law program at the University of Virginia, and authored an influential casebook.[33] The first law school clinic for human rights was put into place at Berkeley's law school, inspired by the work of Frank C. Newman, who had taken his students to meetings of the United Nations Commission on Human Rights in Geneva in the late 1960s and had worked with Amnesty in the early 1970s as a vocal advocate for Chilean victims of human rights abuses. Human rights legal education programs at private and public law schools continued to grow as the decade came to a close. This growth was fostered in part by the ABA Subcommittee on Human Rights Education, formed in 1979, which promoted human rights education in law schools and political science departments and launched an annual summer institute on human rights education in 1981.[34] So too did the prestigious Aspen Institute, convening meetings and seminars on human rights in the late 1970s that brought together international lawyers, philosophers, and policy makers.[35]

The late 1970s also marked the establishment of new American legal human rights advocacy groups. The New York-based Lawyers Committee for Human Rights (later Human Rights First) was founded in 1978 to encourage young lawyers at major firms to represent applicants for asylum in immigration proceedings; however, it also undertook campaigns on behalf of lawyers outside the United States persecuted for their human rights work and provided legal representation for the families of four American churchwomen killed in El Salvador in 1980. The International Human Rights Law Group (later Global Rights), formed in 1979, offered pro bono representation to groups in and out of the United States filing complaints about human rights violations to international, regional, and domestic bodies; it later worked to train local lawyers and document human rights abuses in Latin America and Africa.[36] American lawyers and other professionals were instrumental in the creation of Human Rights Watch, now among the leading human rights organizations in the world. Although that name and the global mandate it connotes were not adopted until the late 1980s, Human Rights Watch was built out of a series of regional "watch" organizations beginning with the establishment of Helsinki Watch in 1978. Helsinki Watch, part of an emergent transnational network of activists who monitored compliance with the human rights provisions of the 1975 Helsinki Accords, operated largely as a support network for citizen-based human rights groups in the Soviet bloc and to raise global awareness of their concerns. Americas Watch was formed in 1981 (Asia Watch, Africa Watch, and Middle East Watch emerged later in the 1980s) and engaged in the kind of fact finding and reporting common to the genre of country reports pioneered by Amnesty International while also working to foster media coverage of regional human rights abuses and directly engaging with U.S. and international policy makers on human rights questions.[37]

The intersections between the individuals who led these groups, most of them from a generation who came of age long after the 1940s global human rights moment, suggests how tight and cohesive the community of younger human rights professionals became in the 1970s and their lasting importance for the contemporary American human rights movement. Michael H. Posner, who became the founding director of the Lawyer's Committee for Human Rights at twenty-eight, studied with Frank Newman at Berkeley in the mid-1970s, where he worked on documenting human rights atrocities in Uganda. Under Posner's direction, the Lawyer's Committee worked closely with Helsinki Watch and Americas Watch in preparing reports documenting human rights abuses in the Soviet Union and Latin America. Posner led the organization until 2009, when he was appointed Assistant Secretary of State for Democracy, Human Rights and Labor in the Obama administration. When Bruce Kiernan, the initial director of the AAAS Clearinghouse on Science and Human Rights, left in 1980 to take a position with Helsinki Watch he was replaced by Eric Stover who, like Posner, was then twenty-eight. Stover would later lead the Nobel Peace Prize-winning Physicians for Human Rights and serve as director of the University of California-Berkeley's Human Rights Center. Stover remembers his activism in the opposition movement to the Vietnam War as the critical fulcrum that moved him first toward work in the late 1970s as a researcher for Amnesty International in London and then to a concern with U.S. government culpability in human rights abuses in Latin and Central America.[38]

Younger American activists also began to craft new forms of human rights advocacy in the 1970s. Thirty-five-year-old attorney Rhonda Copelon, for instance, led the legal team in the landmark *Filártiga* v. *Peña-Irala* case. In late March 1976, high school student Joelito Filártiga was tortured to death by Americo Peña-Irala, the inspector general of police in the capital city of Paraguay. Joelito was the son of Joel Filártiga, a doctor and long-standing opponent of the regime that had dictatorially ruled Paraguay since 1954. Joel Filártiga unsuccessfully sought redress against Peña and the police in Paraguayan courts for the torture and murder of his son. Several years later Filártiga and his daughter came to the United States seeking permanent political asylum. Learning that Peña was also in the United States and living in Brooklyn, they approached the Center for Constitutional Rights, a New York-based legal advocacy group, to see if a claim could be filed in U.S. courts against Peña for wrongfully causing Joelita's death by torture. The Center had largely been concerned with domestic civil rights questions since its establishment in 1966, but had begun to turn to questions of international human rights law in the late 1970s. Rhonda Copelon, a Yale-trained lawyer who would later found the Women's Human Rights Law Clinic at the City University of New York Law School, had been instrumental in the Center's growing engagement with human rights.[39]

In *Filártiga*, Copelon crafted a creative and original legal strategy. She filed a complaint in U.S. District Court in April 1979 under a then obscure federal statute, the Alien Tort Claims Act of 1789, which gave foreign nationals the right to sue for acts that violate international law if the accused was under the jurisdiction of federal courts. The statute had rarely been evoked since the early nineteenth century, and never before on questions dealing with human rights. In her brief, Copelon argued that state torture violated an emerging norm of customary international law, in part brought into being by the prohibitions against torture in Article 5 of the Universal Declaration of Human Rights, and thus triggered the applicability of the Alien Torts Claim Act to the Filártiga's case. A district court dismissed the complaint, but in a sweeping June 1980 opinion the U.S. Second Circuit Court of Appeals held that deliberate, official torture violated universally accepted norms of international human rights law. Under the 1789 statute, the court ruled, a noncitizen could in fact bring an alleged torturer before federal court even if those actions had not been committed in the United States. "The torturer has become – like the pirate or slave trader before him – *hostis humani generis*, an enemy of all mankind," the presiding judge wrote. With the *Filártiga* precedent in place, U.S. domestic courts began to hear dozens of cases under the Alien Tort Statute around both state and corporate violations of the individual human rights of noncitizen plaintiffs living in the United States.[40]

THE AMBIGUITIES OF PRACTICE

The emergence of what has become today's nonstate human rights establishment in the United States was made possible by the work of well-
intentioned amateurs in the 1970s. There was no real script or established set of protocols for grassroots activists or American professionals
who turned their attention to human rights. Those who undertook the
practice of human rights had Amnesty as a kind of procedural lodestar,
but they often made it up as they went along. These quotidian efforts,
and the kinds of uneasy contradictions their engagement could pose
for those who undertook them, emerge in Harvard Law School Professor David Kennedy's memoir of a human rights fact-finding trip to
Uruguay. Kennedy brought the legal expertise to a three-person team
that also included an investigative journalist and a doctor. The delegation officially represented the American Public Health Association, the
National Academy of Science, the American College of Physicians, and
the American Public Health Association, all of which had established
human rights initiatives in the late 1970s. Its charge was to meet and interview a group of imprisoned male and female medical students who were
believed to have been tortured in prison and to advocate for their release
with Uruguayan officials.[41]

Although the delegation's efforts met with success, Kennedy argues
their apparent victory elided what he terms the "ambiguities and con-
fusions" of the mission itself. The delegation and scientific institutions
that sponsored it, he notes, "were somewhat uncomfortable becoming
involved in human rights work," worried that "it would diminish their
scientific neutrality" and that they would "appear naïve and out of place
in the hurly-burly of human rights work." These doubts, he suggests, were
in part overcome by relying on emergent norms of "professional responsibility and human rights ideology." He writes,

> They give activism a certain structure. The activists will be dispatched pro-
> fessionals, individual advocates deployed upon a foreign context in service
> of human rights. Thinking of ourselves as deployed professionals created a
> double sense of Uruguay as client and abuser, familiar and barbaric. These
> contradictory images of Uruguay could be stabilized, controlled, tamed by

the language of human rights, our professional language. We render the
exotic familiar by scripting the barbarian as "rights abuser" and the victim
as "our client." We now have a role in Uruguay: to "represent" the client
against the abuser. Our mandate channeled our concerns about violence
into a rhetoric of health, our interest in Uruguayan politics into a physical examination of … [a prisoner's body], our outrage into a dispassionate
recounting of rights violated, remedies not provided.[42]

And yet Kennedy contends it was often difficult for the delegation
in Uruguay to know how to disentangle what he calls "our professional
reasonableness from the shocking facts of these particular cases." In nar-
rating the meetings with a prison warden, the prisoners themselves, their
lawyers, and the head of an Uruguayan military court, Kennedy is attentive to the inevitable slippages between his delegation's professionalized
roles and the situations encountered on the ground. How should the
delegation relate to the intimate details of the personal stories of torture
the prisoners told them? Was the experience of listening and recording
their stories best accomplished through solidarity and witness, or did a
lawyerly language of credibility and doubt more effectively translate its
complexities? Did the prisoners see the members of the delegation as
empathetic allies in their own political cause or as detached and distant
strangers? Did the prison warden really believe the delegation was solely
interested in the health of particular prisoners and not in the political
conditions that made torture possible, as it claimed? Why was one of the
Uruguayan lawyers representing the prisoners cynical about the delegation's emphasis on human rights? How best could the delegation make
the case for the release of the prisoners to the senior judge of the military court, who told them before the prisoners had even been tried that
he was certain of their guilt of crimes against the state? Given the unfamiliar complexities of the local situation and the delegation's necessarily
short visit to Uruguay, the answers to these questions were not cut and
dried. "We needed human rights to take us there and bring us back,"
Kennedy concludes, but "for all its promise, for all our need, this discourse keeps congealing, fixing patterns where we felt movement, challenging us, excluding them, and, above all, proliferating itself. As human

rights advocates, our discourse is not our tool, we are its property, and the price of our fealty nags at our conscience."[43]

The simultaneously empowering and constraining language of human rights that emerges in Kennedy's account captures a broader set of tensions embedded in the forms and substance of 1970s global and American human rights practice. Many of the nonstate actors at the forefront of the human rights campaigns of the era were, by conscious choice, indifferent to context. Political repression and its history were presented as moral parable, rather than a causal network of political and social relations.[44] This was especially true for Amnesty International. In the organization's internal and more public articulations of its self-described "impartial" mission, Amnesty continually insisted that "we do not seek to explain the root causes of political repression" and that its work was based on "universally shared values, leaving all other matters to the side."[45] In leaving behind politics as it is conventionally understood, Amnesty drained from many of the cases it publicized the structural forces and local particularities that gave rise to the violations of rights in the first place. Many of the increasingly professionalized American human rights groups established over the decade followed Amnesty International's lead. Substituting the universal for the particular brought victories and gave the movement much of its popular appeal. But it left open, and indeed ignored, the multiple and sometimes conflicting causes that had prompted the rediscovery of global human rights in the seventies.

Moreover, it was the violations of only some rights, often political and civil, and then only in particular geographic spaces that attracted American and other Western human rights activists who became the gatekeepers of transnational human rights talk and practice in the 1970s and beyond. Torture came to matter to American and transnational human rights advocates in some instances and not others. Genocide could sometimes be parsed as a humanitarian rather than human rights problem. For instance, tens of thousands of East Timorese were detained and more than one hundred thousand died in the wake of the Indonesian invasion and occupation of East Timor in 1975. These mass killings were largely greeted with silence by the United States and other Western powers. Efforts by some international NGOs and church groups to raise awareness largely fell on deaf ears. Genocide in East Timor was never a *cause célèbre* for the decade's global human rights community. To the extent that East Timor was on its mental map of the late 1970s, it was as a matter of immediate humanitarian relief rather than the systemic violation of human rights. The willingness to look away from the human rights implications of genocide in East Timor in the mid-1970s reinforces a sense that the seemingly capacious vision of global human rights could at times be distressingly narrow. That Indonesian state torture and political imprisonment required attention, absolutely. How to respond to genocide by the Indonesian state in East Timor was considerably less clear.[46] More generally the 1970s saw a reprise of concern with political and civil rights, but very little attention to the lexicon of economic and social rights that had been considered coeval in the 1940s. Only in the late 1990s, and after years of internal debate of which Amnesty USA was a vocal part, did Amnesty International turn to advocacy for economic and social, as well as women's and LGBTQ, rights.[47]

Some American human rights advocates in the 1970s were attentive to these ambiguities and instabilities. A remarkable eighty-five-page handwritten report by an Amnesty International staffer detailing her visits to some thirty local Amnesty USA groups in late 1977 and early 1978 makes clear that individual members on the ground were keen to interrogate Amnesty's approach to human rights. In almost every local meeting the Amnesty staffer attended, the meaning of the organization's self-professed commitment to impartiality arose. At one meeting a debate around whether or not Amnesty was a political organization produced an especially searching discussion of its underlying principles:

> At least in people's minds, AI [Amnesty International] is being presented as a "non-political" organization. At one of the recent Council Meetings [regional meetings of Amnesty groups] it was agreed that "humanitarian" and "nonpolitical" should really be substituted by terms such as "nonpartisan" or "impartial." This basically came from a feeling that by sticking to the term "non-political" we risked confusing people, not least AI members, since quite clearly this is an organization involved in the political

sphere. By saying non-political, people realized that we merely meant to stress that our involvement is not a partisan political involvement but is entirely impartial.[48]

Sometimes these group conversations had a more specific geographical focus. For instance, one member of the Amnesty USA group in Cambridge, Massachusetts, "had difficulty in accepting that AI should work equally for say prisoners in Nyerere's Tanzania as for prisoners in Argentina: feeling there is a difference between the two kinds of regime and motivations on the one hand are good, on the other hand bad."[49] For this Amnesty member, in contrast to the absolutist position of Amnesty itself, there was a hierarchy of conscience, with the actions of the socialist-leaning Tanzanian state led by Julius Nyerere of less concern than those of the right-wing military junta in Argentina. Other members revealed the kinds of cultural biases that inflected their on-the-ground notions of impartiality. A member of Amnesty group in Cincinnati, for instance, asked, "isn't violence a part of the way of life in the Third World?"[50]

These discussions also threw into sharp relief exactly which Americans were, and were not, a part of the human rights movement in the 1970s. Amnesty kept careful tabs on the demographic profile of its members: some were students or "under 30," but the most common descriptors are "housewives," "secretaries," and the "elderly" or professionals like lawyers, dentists (the reports enumerate a surprising density of Amnesty USA dentists), teachers, ministers, professors, librarians, and social workers, along with a smattering of musicians, artists, and businesspeople. Most members of Amnesty USA were white and middle class, a mix of men and women who fit a classic liberal or left-leaning profile. In her tour of Amnesty groups in the late 1970s, the Amnesty staffer reported that at several group meetings members self-consciously articulated concern about the absence of diversity. The group in Bloomfield, Connecticut, discussed the absence of "working class and black" members. In Belmont, Massachusetts, the group also pointed "to the lack of blacks as AI members" and suggested the organization "buy ... into subscription lists of black magazines/newspapers and not just the *New York Review*

of Books, etc., which perpetuates the white, middle-class, liberal image."
Other groups, like one in Salt Lake City, complained that "the organization was too dominated by interests of the 'sophisticated' groups on the
East and West Coasts."[51] Outside of Amnesty, the human rights movement of the era had very few conservative, nonwhite, or working-class
voices.[52]

One dimension of American human rights practice in the 1970s
did mark a sharp divergence from the broader transnational landscape
of which it was a part. Almost everywhere else in the world the focus
of human rights advocacy was on violations of rights happening at
home. Throughout the Global South, the language of human rights was
employed by hundreds of newly established local human rights NGOs to
combat individual violations of human rights. In Western Europe, human
rights were becoming a resonant regional and domestic political vocabulary, especially as the European Court of Human Rights began to become
operational in the late 1970s, thereby allowing individuals to take their
own states to this transnational court for rights violations.[53] But in the
United States human rights were almost never imagined to have reso-
nance for domestic rights questions in the 1970s. The era's social movements for civil rights, women's rights, and labor rights only infrequently
invoked human rights as a way to frame their causes. And in the rare
instances that they did, it was almost always in a minor key and not without
controversy. Some early gay rights advocates, for instance, urged the use
of human rights rather than gay rights for their public self-presentation.
The Gay Rights National Lobby, which was established in 1978, changed
its name to the Human Rights Campaign Fund in 1980, becoming one
of the major gay and lesbian advocacy groups in the United States. But
others in the movement attacked them as too conservative, of using the
term "human rights" in a way that appeared to consciously signal a desire
to mask or closet their own still socially controversial sexual identities.[54]
Native Americans also turned to human rights in the 1970s, framing challenges to tribal sovereignty by the U.S. government not in the individual vernacular of so much of American rights talk in this era, but in the
language of collective self-determination that was at the center of the
human rights vocabulary of the decolonizing Global South and of other

indigenous peoples elsewhere in the world.[55] These cases, however, were unusual. Most advocacy efforts for domestic rights in the United States throughout the 1970s remained almost completely decoupled from the American human rights imagination. It was the suffering of strangers, rather than one's neighbors, that animated the movement.

The Indonesian government released Sutanti Aidit from prison on December 20, 1979.[56] We do not really know why. It is possible that the Indonesian generals read and were moved by the appeals from Amnesty USA Group 11 or were unnerved by the broader campaign led by Amnesty International and other nonstate human rights actors against Indonesian political repression. They might instead have been pushed by pressures put on them by the U.S. government or other state and international bodies, though arguably that kind of coercion was in turn stimulated by the transnational nonstate campaigns of which Group 11 was a part. It is also quite possible that local politics or the complicated internal dynamics of the military regime ultimately shaped the decision to release Aidit along with thousands of other political prisoners in the late 1970s. The Indonesian archives that might allow us to move beyond speculation remain firmly closed. In this and many other similar cases of advocacy for the victims of human rights abuses, we do not have the empirical evidence to fully understand how their situations were ultimately resolved. But if explanations for the outcome remain murky, what drove the work of Group 11 and its lasting significance are not.

Whether advocating for the release of Sutanti Aidit from an Indonesian prison, raising awareness of the plight of a disappeared Argentine statistician, or bringing Paraguayan torturers to account in U.S. courts, Americans in the 1970s discovered a global human rights imagination that offered them new ways of seeing and being in the world. It was always partial. Some human rights in some places mattered. Other modes and locales did not. It was an American vernacular, but one that took shape and form in a transnational imaginary. Wars hot and cold since the 1960s claimed the lives of millions. The violence and terror they unleashed and the practices of authoritarian regimes on the Left and the Right that emerged in their wake devastated local societies across the globe.

In the almost unfathomable suffering that was so palpably a part of the late twentieth-century world, the American human rights movement and the forms of advocacy that flowed from it came to order perceptions of the past and present and to offer a believable, if imperfect, hope for a different future.

The Sense of an Ending

WE LIVE IN AN AGE OF HUMAN RIGHTS, one whose scale would astonish the makers of the 1940s global human rights imagination and that even the fiercest advocates of human rights in the 1970s could not have fully anticipated. International legal guarantees have grown exponentially since the adoption of the Universal Declaration Human of Rights in 1948. Six of what the United Nations terms the ten "core" international human rights instruments became part of international law after 1980, offering protections against torture and forced disappearance and for the rights of children, migrant workers, and persons with disabilities. A wider range of United Nations declarations, principles, and standards speak to indigenous rights, antiracism, violence against women, protections for the imprisoned, sexual rights, respect for cultural diversity, and the right to development. New human rights declarations and conventions in Africa, Asia, and the Middle East offer regional guarantees for a variety of political, civil, economic, and social rights.

The commitment to transnational juridical accountability for abuses of individual human rights that first emerged in the Nuremberg trials of the 1940s is now institutionalized. Since 2002 an International Criminal Court has operated in The Hague with the power to prosecute individuals for what are understood to be international crimes of genocide, crimes against humanity, and war crimes. At the same time the crush of litigation before the European Court of Human Rights shows no sign of abating. The caseload of the Inter-American Court for Human Rights is increasing, and an African Court of Justice is in the process of being established to hear petitions from victims of human rights violations.

This vast United Nations and regional machinery is paralleled by an even larger number of international, regional, national, and local nongovernmental human rights organizations. Human Rights Watch's 400-person staff and its $69 million budget in 2014 are of a quite different order of magnitude than the skeletal workforce and comparatively modest funding that fueled the activities of Amnesty International or Helsinki Watch in the 1970s.[1] Beyond the behemoths of nonstate human rights politics, there are literally tens of thousands of small grassroots advocacy groups, many of them increasingly virtual and operating on social media, which see the moral authority of human rights as critical to advancing their political projects.

In all this the United States is an ambiguous presence. Viewed against the history of the 1940s and 1970s, that should not come as a surprise. Human rights have become more and more embedded in everyday American professional practices since the 1970s, as has the believability of truth claims that draw on individual moral witness and testimony. But if the place of the United States in the making of a global human rights order was always less central than Americans often acknowledged in these two decades, it has further diminished in the early twenty-first century.

One arresting indication of the marginality of the United States in the contemporary global human rights imagination is the sharp decline of the use of the U.S. Constitution and its Bill of Rights as the model for drafters of written charters in new states. As late as 1987, *Time* magazine reported that of the 170 countries then in existence as many as 160 used the American model for their constitutions. By the beginning of the twenty-first century, however, the use of the U.S. constitution had gone into what one legal scholar terms a "free fall." No single document has replaced it. Instead contemporary constitution making is shaped by a pluralist sensibility drawn from newer national constitutions like the 1982 Canadian Charter of Rights and Freedoms and 1996 South African Constitution, along with international and regional human rights instruments such as the International Covenant on Civil and Political Rights and the European Convention on Human Rights. Associate Justice of the

U.S. Supreme Court Ruth Bader Ginsberg has said, "I would not look to the American Constitution if I were drafting a constitution in the year 2012." Similarly judges around the world, who had habitually gone first to the decisions of the U.S. Supreme Court to craft their own judgments during much of the second half of the twentieth century, no longer do so. Now they more frequently cite decisions by the European Court of Human Rights.[2]

As much of the world is turning away from the United States for its human rights inspiration, the continuing reluctance of the American state to engage in the global human rights order is also striking. The United States has always been slow to embrace international human rights treaties and norms. The U.S. Senate only ratified the Genocide Convention in 1988, some forty years after it was adopted by the United Nations. In 2016, it remained the only country in the world that had not signed the Convention on the Rights of the Child. It is among only seven countries that have failed to ratify the Convention on the Elimination of All Forms of Discrimination against Women. The United States is not a participant in the International Criminal Court. It signed the Rome Statute that established the court, but there has been vigorous opposition to bringing the statute forward in the Senate for ratification. The United States was the twenty-second country to legalize gay marriage.

American courts also use international and regional human rights law in their jurisprudence far less often than other national courts. In the rare instances that they do, such as the U.S. Supreme Court's 2003 *Lawrence* v. *Texas* decision striking down that state's sodomy laws that drew on similar decisions by the European Court for Human Rights, their invocation stirred a political tempest. In his dissent to *Lawrence* Justice Antonin Scalia called the majority's use of foreign law a "[d]angerous dicta." This court, he wrote, "should not impose foreign moods, modes, or fashions on Americans." Other Supreme Court justices have viewed foreign law more generously, but their actual use of it remains parsimonious.[3] The broader American political climate has not been encouraging. Since the *Lawrence* decision, a resolution circulates annually in the U.S. House of Representatives calling for a constitutional amendment that would prohibit U.S. courts from basing opinion on international law.[4] This American allergy to international human rights law, so different from practices elsewhere in the world, suggests that the ghost of the Bricker challenge in the 1950s to the use of the human rights provisions in the UN Charter for cases of domestic racial discrimination – a challenge that also stopped U.S. ratification of the International Covenant on Political and Civil Rights and the Genocide Convention in its tracks – continues to cast a long shadow. The robust human rights jurisprudence in the wake of the landmark use of the Alien Torts Statute in the 1979 *Filártiga* case, for instance, that allowed foreign nationals to sue in U.S. courts for rights abuses committed in other nations largely came to an end with the Supreme Court's 2013 decision in *Kiobel* v. *Royal Dutch Petroleum.* In that case a majority of the court claimed the statute could not be invoked for misconduct that took place outside the United States, seeming to align with critics who saw the use of statute as an example "judicial imperialism."[5]

At the same time human rights have never come home again as a fully believable language at the grassroots level to address domestic rights issues. An NAACP delegation did travel to Geneva in 2012 to bring the question of voting rights in the United States to the attention of the United Nations Human Rights Commission. In what was a conscious reprise of the organization's 1947 *An Appeal to the World* led by W. E. B. Du Bois that sought to make visible racial discrimination in the United States at the United Nations, the NAACP presented its report, *Defending Democracy: Confronting Modern Barriers to Voting Rights in the United States,* to draw global attention to state legislation that threatened the voting rights of millions of persons of color.[6] American gay rights and Native American rights activists also continued to employ global human rights vocabularies as they had beginning in the 1970s. These efforts were, however, largely the exceptions that proved the rule, and even there the presence of human rights was muted.

Most of the major American social movements at the beginning of the twenty-first century – among them the Occupy Protests, the Fair Immigration Movement, the Fight for $15, the Marriage Equality Movement, and Black Lives Matter – took primary inspiration from alternative political and moral lexicons. In their challenges to the mounting chasm in wealth and income between the top 1 percent of Americans and the rest, to the mass incarceration of African Americans, to escalating detentions and deportations of immigrants, and to growing racial disparities in policing, education, and income, these movements might have turned to the language of the Universal Declaration of Human Rights and its promises of universal guarantees to economic and social rights, to free movement, and to live without racial and gender discrimination. At times all of these movements made rhetorical gestures to the lexicon of human rights, but their energies and tactics on the ground operated largely around a domestic space in which the global human rights imagination remained in a minor key. With the number of families in the United States living at the $2-a-day poverty level more than doubling since 1996, the human rights lexicon is losing some of its moral power to instruct in an era when structural arguments about economics and race are displacing other kinds of oppositional political discourses.

But perhaps most dramatically for Americans, the contemporary age of human rights collided with the U.S.-led global war on terror launched in the aftermath of the attacks by Al-Qaeda on the World Trade Center in New York City and the Pentagon in Washington, DC, on September 11, 2001. "The United States does not torture," President George W. Bush told the American people in 2006. "It is against our laws. And it's against our values." But in fact it did. In what Vice President Dick Cheney ominously termed a willingness to work the "dark side," torture became a key instrument of American state power after September 11. The evidence surfaced first in chilling images from the Abu Ghraib prison in Iraq. A U.S. Army Reserve soldier holding a leash attached to a groveling inmate made to crawl and bark like a dog. A pyramid of naked prisoners, stacked like cordwood one on top of the other. Another reservist, taking a selfie, smiled and gave a thumbs up next to a brutalized and bloody corpse. And most famously, an image of a hooded prisoner standing on a box with electrical wires dangling from his outstretched arms.[7]

Reports by journalists, human rights groups, and humanitarian organizations soon told a wider and even more unsettling story of the culpability of the U.S. Central Intelligence Service (CIA) in torture. Hundreds of terrorist suspects held in American military bases like Guantanamo

Bay and at secret rendition sites around the globe were subjected to waterboarding, sleep deprivation, beatings, forced nudity in ice-cold cells, prolonged shackling of hands and feet, and sustained confinement in coffin like-boxes. As one prisoner explained to representatives of the International Committee of the Red Cross, CIA agents in Afghanistan subjected him to five incidents of waterboarding during a single week of interrogation in 2002:

> I was put on what looked like a hospital bed, and strapped down very tightly with belts. A black cloth was then placed over my face and the interrogators used a mineral water bottle on the cloth so that I could not breathe. After a few minutes, the cloth was removed and the bed was rotated into an upright position. The pressure of the straps on my wounds caused severe pain. I vomited. The bed was then again lowered to a horizontal position and the same torture carried out. ... I struggled without success to breathe. I thought I was going to die.[8]

Stripped of its context the report could easily have been mistaken for one of Amnesty's country reports on torture in Latin American that circulated so widely in the 1970s. But now violations of human rights were no longer only happening somewhere else out in the world as many Americans in the seventies had believed. Although torture had been part of the arsenal of weapons through which the United States had fought the Cold War, American culpability in it was largely invisible to the general public.[9] The photographs from Abu Ghraib put torture front and center, both to Americans and the wider world. And Americans were clearly the perpetrators.

It was an uncomfortable moment. The Bush administration turned somersaults to demonstrate the legality of what it preferred to call "enhanced interrogation techniques" rather than torture. "These are enemy combatants who are waging war on our nation," President Bush argued. "We have a right under the laws of war, and an obligation to the American people, to detain these enemies and stop them from rejoining the battle."[10] From the American human rights community came a vigorous rebuttal and strong condemnations of these claims. Torture, they argued, was simply wrong, as immoral as it was illegal. One needed to look no further than the Convention against Torture, ratified by the

United States and that came into force in 1987, or to the Third Geneva Convention of 1949 on the humanitarian treatment of prisoners of war, largely authored by Americans in the human rights moment of the 1940s. "Fighting terrorism is central to the human rights cause," wrote Kenneth Roth, executive of Human Rights Watch in 2006. "But the willingness to flout human rights to fight terrorism is not only illegal and wrong; it is counterproductive."[11]

In the shock of an attack on U.S. soil, many Americans were not so sure. Some political theorists and legal scholars, even those sympathetic to the global rights order, argued that political leaders in dire circumstances might need to "dirty their hands" by turning to torture and offered what one called "torture warrants" to provide some degree of accountability.[12] American public opinion was initially skeptical about the turn to torture. In a 2004 Pew Research Center poll, the majority of respondents said torture could never be justified. But over the next seven years, public opinion began a slow reversal, with a majority in 2011 saying that torture can often or sometimes be justified. Tough talk about torture by the Republican candidates in the 2016 presidential election cycle was "a guaranteed applause line."[13] In the wake of September 11, the absolutist disavowals of torture and attacks on bodily integrity so commonly felt in the 1970s were starting to come unmoored. And with this recalibration came a new uncertainty about what human rights meant to being in the world.

As it did, the efficacy of the international legal scaffolding around human rights and the work of the nonstate human rights movement itself became the subjects of severe criticism. "Human rights law," writes the legal scholar Eric Posner in one particularly sharp attack, "has failed to accomplish its objectives." It is not just that the United States tortures, he points out, but also that human rights violations by states continue unabated around the globe irrespective of whether they are liberal democracies or authoritarian countries. There "is little evidence," Posner argues, "that human rights treaties, on the whole, have improved the well-being of people, or even resulted in respect for the rights in those treaties." Critics also claim that the human rights movement has lost its bearings. The political scientist Stephen Hopgood juxtaposes "Human Rights, capitalized" to "human rights, with lowercase initials" to locate what he sees as a growing and disturbing divergence between professional and grassroots human rights activists. In the former arena, he scornfully suggests, an inflexible set of staff-driven top-down organizations with bloated budgets "raise money, write reports, run international campaigns, and claim to speak with singular authority in the name of humanity as a whole." By contrast, Hopgood celebrates human rights in lower case as a "spontaneous and diverse" network of local and transnational activists who seek to bring the human rights abuses they face to a global audience.[14]

In what is an admittedly uncertain if not sometimes hostile domestic climate for human rights, the declension narrative offered by critics of human rights such as Posner and Hopgood nevertheless fails to help us understand the enduring presence of human rights in the American cultural landscape. The use of human rights as a form of moral reasoning has seemed to wane in recent years, but to say it is in absolute decline or that the human rights movement is bifurcated between villains and heroes is too simplistic. Human rights remain deeply imprinted on the ways Americans think about how to be in the world. One can read the workings of international human rights law in more measured ways than does Posner. The political scientist Beth Simmons undertook a quantitative examination of the impact of thirteen human rights treaties on national human rights practices. In seven of these treaties she observes a statistically significant improvement in human rights. In countries that ratified the Convention on Children, for instance, Simmons reports a decrease in the rate of child labor and an increase in child immunization. Her work, however, suggests that ratification of the Convention against Torture has not prevented the state use of torture, as the American case after 9/11 troublingly confirms. Even here, however, the painstaking denials that its practices were not torture in what was a blizzard of internal legal memos produced by the Bush administration require comment. Why, as political scientist Kathryn Sikkink asks, leave a paper trail? She sees what have been colloquially been termed the "torture memos" as a response to the quickening of international human rights prosecutions at the turn of the millennium. Global human rights law did not protect the victims of torture. But the repeated insistence by American field operatives and their superiors for legal assurances that would shield them from prosecution suggests these new norms of individual criminal accountability for human rights violations were acutely felt.[15]

Similarly, to see the contemporary American human rights movement, as Hopgood does, as divided into a unbridgeable chasm between on-the-ground activists and high-handed professionals obscures more than it reveals. The transnational circulation of moral witness, individual testimony, and motivated truth that gave human rights practice in the seventies shape and form drove both grassroots advocates and would-be human rights professionals. The very notion of human rights as an American professional vocation that emerged over the decade closely followed broader social trends in the United States since the 1960s in which civic associations and nonprofits have become increasingly professionalized. Although some decry narrowing opportunities for citizen engagement, professionalization does not inevitably produce a zero-sum game at the expense of grassroots movement activists.[16] Without question there can be tensions, but their practices are interwoven. To take one example, the New York City-based Witness has trained some six thousand people in ninety-seven countries since 1992 in how to use video to expose human rights violations in ways that will be credible in court. The protocols they have developed are complex, the product of expertise by filmmakers and documentary photographers, along with a professional staff that provides volunteer training and helps facilitate local advocacy.[17] Other new practices of human rights advocacy that some pejoratively dismiss as "slacktivism," like pushing a button on a cell phone to text your support for an individual victim of human rights abuses in Bahrain or Berlin, are more accurately understood as a reinscription in new media form of what were among the classic practices of 1970s human rights activism embraced by the grassroots and professionals alike.[18]

The genre of the human rights country report pioneered in the 1970s and its reworking of the relationship between fact and experience in making truth claims have become fully institutionalized. Human Rights Watch and the U.S. State Department annually release *World Report* and *Country Reports on Human Rights Practice*, respectively, that catalog human rights advances and abuses on a state-by-state basis, and the release of these reports generally brings considerable press fanfare.[19] American professionals continue to play a leading role in human rights advocacy in ways that reflect the interplay between expertise and testimonial that shaped notions of motivated truth in the 1970s. The International Forensics Program at Physicians for Human Rights, for instance, brings together forensic pathologists and anthropologists whose exhumations of mass graves have provided key evidence at a variety of international human rights courts and tribunals in Argentina, Yugoslavia, Rwanda, and Sierra Leone. Even in what would appear to be a quintessentially scientific enterprise, testimonial sensibilities infuse professional practice as researchers look for ways of "making the bones speak."[20] In fact one sign of the continuing prevalence of witness are critiques of the International Criminal Tribunals for the former Yugoslavia and Rwanda for their over reliance on witness testimony.[21]

The contemporary American human rights movement pushes ever deeper into everyday practice. If the 1970s marked the beginning of human rights as a vocation in which doctors, lawyers, scientists, and a range of other American professionals came to embrace human rights as part of their professional practices, the turn has only intensified in our contemporary age of human rights and shows no signs of diminishing. This growing professional engagement in international human rights has recovered some of the cosmopolitan diversity of the 1940s human rights moment in the United States. Women of color have played an especially important role in the legal realm, among them Catherine Powell, who served on the White House National Security Council staff as director for human rights in the Obama administration, and Gabrelle Kirk McDonald, who was the presiding justice in the International Criminal Tribunal for the Former Yugoslavia.[22]

Human rights are now deeply embedded in the curriculums of most professional schools, from schools of medicine and law to business. There are a proliferation of undergraduate and graduate programs in human rights at U.S. colleges and universities, with many of their graduates going to work in what is now considered "the human rights field" at nonprofits or in government and business.[23] The quotidian spread of human rights into the fabric of contemporary American society can be quite remarkable. It is not just New York state fifth graders who spend as much time reading the Universal Declaration of Human Rights as they do Mark Twain's *Tom Sawyer*; a middle school shop teacher switched out his usual cuckoo clock project and instead had his students build birdhouses to illustrate the Universal Declaration's Article 25 guarantee of the right to shelter. The simple acts of buying coffee or a piece of fish are now mediated through human rights concerns with fair trade and slavers.[24]

Like the human rights moments of the 1940s and 1970s, there are limits to these individual commitments, to the rights activists seek to protect, and to the places the human rights movement turns its attention. But now, as then, they offer a set of vocabularies and practices that can mobilize Americans to make human rights their own.

On Thanksgiving Sunday in November 2001, the thirty-one-year-old photographer Zoe Strauss turned the space underneath Interstate Highway 95 in south central Philadelphia into an outdoor gallery. The construction of an expressway through the center of Philadelphia in the 1960s and 1970s had dramatically reshaped the city's topography. Its route divided affluent largely white neighborhoods in the city center from predominantly black neighborhoods in the south, solidifying new economic and racial barriers within the city. The site beneath I-95 at the intersection of Front Street and Washington Avenue that Strauss had chosen for her installation was more commonly the scene of drug sales or a refuge for the homeless. Throughout four blocks on each side of the dozens of concrete columns that held up the expressway, Strauss pasted single color prints, 11 by 17 inches, of the photographs she had made of this blighted urban neighborhood. The crowds for the one-day exhibition were sparse. Family and a few friends attended. Nine years later, what became an annual event called *Under I-95* drew thousands of visitors who viewed 231 of Strauss's photographs. As one observer noted in 2010, the crowds moving slowly from column to column with maps that matched numbers and titles to pictures gave a "processional, almost solemn quality to the experience." Some visitors lingered for the day, sitting and chatting in lawn chairs they had brought with them about what they had seen.[25]

Among the photographs visitors encountered was one of two young African American boys (Figure Coda 1), one flipped upside down, having used a bed of abandoned mattresses as an urban trampoline, while his

Coda 1. Zoe Strauss. South Philly (*Mattress Flip Front*). 2001 (negative); 2003 (print). Chromogenic print, 6 ⅞ × 10 ⅛ in. (17.5 × 25.7 cm). Philadelphia Museum of Art. Purchased with funds contributed by Theodore T. Newbold and Helen Cunningham, 2003. Courtesy of Zoe Strauss.

friend looks on. At one level *Mattress Flip Front* is a visual catalog of the failures to secure human rights for everyone in the United States. The shredded mattresses on a littered streetscape, bricked-up and graffiti-filled red walls with a paint line that looks like the high-water mark of a recent flood, that they are black children whose lives are led on the bleak streets the expressway had helped create around them – all convey too familiar aspects of the structural racial and economic inequalities of contemporary American life. Outside the frame of the photograph itself, the urge to read it in this way is even stronger. Six years after it was made the boy in the background was dead, killed by random street gunfire.[26]

In the moment of the photograph itself, however, Strauss captures something quite different: a creative explosion of unalloyed youthful joy, what she calls the "heroic act" of simply "navigating the world and being live in one's skin."[27] In mid-air, upside down, arms deftly swung out to the side for balance and with a smile of elation on his face, the dangling boy is untethered, set free from the ground below him. The delighted expression of his friend, fist in front of his face in partial disbelief, reinforces the sheer chutzpah of the daredevil flip and its sense of infinite possibilities. The harsh urban environment that frames the photograph is not beside the point. But neither is it the point.

Our contemporary era of human rights is shaped in part by the empathetic visual connections that photographers such as Dorothea Lange and Walker Evans sought to make with the subjects and viewers of their photographs in the 1930s. Like the public display of *Mattress Flip Front* underneath an expressway, now ionic photographs like *Migrant Mother* were often initially encountered through intimate traveling exhibitions held in libraries, schools, and department stores. In capturing the lives of the disadvantaged and oppressed, Depression-era photographers hoped those who saw the social suffering they made visible would make it their own. The work of Zoe Strauss is not a simple reinscription of these photographs, although she is influenced by them. But the lightness of being that *Mattress Flip Front* depicts, perhaps all that much more arresting in its emotional impact because of its context, demands a similar kind of empathy. In juxtaposing racialized poverty with young promise, it also leaves open what might come. As it did for those who made and viewed the documentary photographs in the 1930s, the sense of an ending remains just out of view. Human rights might, or might not, give them meaning and power.

This book has argued that the entangled history of the United States in the making of the global human rights imagination is best understood as a contrapuntal one. Its concern has not been with offering a conventional narrative of human rights history around an invented origins story and its triumph or declension. Rather the book has sought to expose how the transformational moments of the 1940s and the 1970s gave human rights particular meanings for Americans, helping shape the ways it felt to be both in and out of the world after the mid-twentieth century. The language of human rights is still there for the taking today, but its continuing believability and the kind of work that human rights might do at home and in the world are less clear. *Mattress Flip Front* suspends us between the feeling of freedom that the now familiar aspirational language of the Universal Declaration of Human Rights promised to bring into being and the enduring reality of a world in which human rights are too often ignored in the breach. In that liminal space, with or without the global human rights imaginary and its American vernaculars, the moral politics of the twenty-first century will unfold.

Notes

INTRODUCTION: HOW IT FEELS TO BE FREE

1. Elie Wiesel, "A Tribute to Human Rights," in *The Universal Declaration of Human Rights: Fifty Years and Beyond*, Yael Danieli et al., eds. (Amityville, NY: Baywood, 1999): 3; and Kofi Annan, "Forward," in ibid.: xii; quoted in Michael Ignatieff, *Human Rights as Politics and Idolatry* (Princeton: Princeton University Press, 2001): 53.

2. George W. Bush, "Rights and Aspirations of the People of Afghanistan" (georgew bush-whitehouse.archives.gov/infocus/afghanistan/20040708.html); "Blair's Address to a Joint Session of Congress," *New York Times*, July 17, 2003; "Pussy Riot Pair Sue Russia over Imprisonment," July 29, 2014, BBC News (www.bbc.com/news/entertainment-arts-28541656); "English Class in the Common Core Era," *New York Times*, June 19, 2015: 1; David Rieff, "The Precarious Triumph of Human Rights," *New York Times Magazine*, August 8, 1999: 37.

3. "Universal Rights: UNESCO Exhibition Open in Paris," *UNESCO Courier*, 2.9 (October 1, 1949): 5, 7. The exhibition traveled to other sites in Western Europe and the Americas in the early 1950s, but to extend its circulation UNESCO organizers packaged a kind of pop-up exhibition for public distribution, reproducing photographs of key parts of the exhibition and their captions in book form as a series of detachable plates to encourage local organizations throughout the world to mount their own mini-didactic exhibits; see *A Short History of Human Rights* (Paris: UNESCO, 1950).

4. The diffuse rather than direct connections between the Enlightenment age of rights and twentieth-century global human rights emerge most clearly in Dan Edelstein, "Enlightenment Rights Talk," *Journal of Modern History* 86.3 (September 2014): 1–36; Peter de Bolla, *The Architecture of Concepts: The Historical Formation of Human Rights* (New York: Fordham University Press, 2013); and Laurent Dubois, "Fire in the Cane," in his *Avengers of the New World: The Story of the Haitian Revolution* (Cambridge, MA: Harvard University Press, 2004): 91–114.

5. For the antislavery movement, Thomas Haskell, "Capitalism and the Origins of Humanitarian Sensibility, Parts 1 and 2," *American Historical Review* 90.2 (April 1985): 339–61 and 90.3 (June 1985): 547–66; and Robin Blackburn, *The American Crucible: Slavery, Emancipation and Human Rights* (London: Verso, 2012) are useful starting points in what is

a vast literature. On the rise of nineteenth-century practices of humanitarianism, see Michael Barnett, *Empire of Humanity: A History of Humanitarianism* (Ithaca: Cornell University Press, 2013).

6. See Kevin Grant, "The Limits of Exposure: Atrocity Photographs in the Congo Reform Campaign," and Peter Balakian, "Photography, Visual Culture, and the Armenian Genocide," in *Humanitarian Photography: A History*, Heide Fehrenbach and Davide Rodogno, eds. (Cambridge: Cambridge University Press, 2015): 64–114.

7. On international concerns with collective rights for minority groups, see Eric D. Weitz, "From the Vienna to the Paris System: International Politics and the Entangled Histories of Human Rights, Forced Deportations and Civilizing Missions," *American Historical Review* 113.5 (December 2008): 1313–43; and Carole Fink, *Defending the Rights of Others: The Great Powers, the Jews, and International Minority Protection, 1878–1938* (Cambridge: Cambridge University Press, 2004).

8. See, for instance, George Kennan, *American Diplomacy, 1900–1950* (Chicago: University of Chicago Press, 1951); John Lewis Gaddis, *Strategies of Containment* (New York: Oxford University Press, 1982); and Melvyn Leffler, *A Preponderance of Power* (Stanford: Stanford University Press, 1992).

9. An exception is the work of Carol Anderson, which has been centrally concerned with the relationship between human rights and civil rights in the United States. See her *Eyes off the Prize: The United Nations and the African American Struggle for Human Rights, 1944–55* (Cambridge: Cambridge University Press, 2003); and *Bourgeois Radicals: The NAACP and the Struggle for Colonial Liberation, 1941–1960* (Cambridge: Cambridge University Press, 2014). I offer a more sustained discussion of these fraught connections in Chapter 4 and the introduction to Part Two.

10. Linda K. Kerber, "We Are All Historians of Human Rights," *Perspectives on History* (October 2006): 3. For excellent introductions to the new human rights history, see Akira Iriye, Petra Goedde, and William I. Hitchcock, eds., *The Human Rights Revolution: An International History* (New York: Oxford University Press, 2012); Stefan-Ludwig Hoffmann, ed., *Human Rights in the Twentieth Century* (Cambridge: Cambridge University Press, 2010); and William I. Hitchcock, "The Rise and Fall of Human Rights?: Searching for a Narrative from the Cold War to the 9/11 Era," *Human Rights Quarterly*, 37.1 (February 2015): 80–106.

11. Samuel Moyn, *The Last Utopia: Human Rights in History* (Cambridge, MA: Harvard University Press, 2011): 7.

12. On the 1940s compare Jay Winter and Antoine Prost, *René Cassin and Human Rights: From the Great War to the Universal Declaration* (Cambridge: Cambridge University Press, 2013) or Elizabeth Borgwardt, *A New Deal for the World: America's Vision for Human Rights* (Cambridge, MA: Harvard University Press, 2005) to Samuel Moyn's skepticism in his *Last Utopia*: ch. 2. On the 1970s, see Moyn, *Last Utopia*: ch. 4; Jan Eckel and Samuel Moyn, eds., *The Breakthrough: Human Rights in the 1970s* (Philadelphia: University of Pennsylvania Press, 2013); and Barbara J. Keys, *Reclaiming American Virtue: The Human Rights Revolution of the 1970s* (Cambridge, MA: Harvard University Press, 2013).

13. Frank Kermode, *The Sense of an Ending: Studies in the Theory of Fiction* (Oxford: Oxford University Press, 1967): 44–46; and Kermode, "The Man in the Macintosh, the Boy in the Shirt," in his *The Genesis of Secrecy* (Cambridge, MA: Harvard University Press, 1979): 44–73. My thinking about the instabilities of historical time is also influenced by Stefan Tanaka, *New Times in Modern Japan* (Princeton: Princeton University Press, 2006); Moishe Postone, *Time, Labor and Social Domination: A Reinterpretation of Marx's Critical Theory* (Cambridge: Cambridge University Press, 1996); Heonik Kwon, *The Other Cold War* (New York: Columbia University Press, 2010); and Vanessa Ogle, *The Global Transformation of Time, 1870–1950* (Cambridge, MA: Harvard University Press, 2015).

14. On the richness of friction as a metaphor for rethinking how the encounters between local and global processes work in practice, see Anna Lowenhaupt Tsing, *Friction: An Ethnography of Global Connections* (Princeton: Princeton University Press, 2004).

15. Lauren Berlant, *Cruel Optimism* (Durham: Duke University Press, 2011): 4, 6. My thinking on the importance of affect for the writing of human rights history is also shaped by Brian Massumi, *The Power at the End of the Economy* (Durham: Duke University Press, 2014); Kathleen Stewart, *Ordinary Affects* (Durham: Duke University Press, 2007); and the classic formulation of "structures of feeling" by Raymond Williams in his *Marxism and Literature* (Oxford: Oxford University Press, 1977).

16. On the enduring problems of exceptionalist historiographies, see Daniel T. Rodgers, "Exceptionalism," in *Imagined Histories: American Historians Interpret the Past*, Anthony Molho and Gordon S. Wood, eds. (Princeton: Princeton University Press, 1998): 21–40; Charles Bright and Michael Geyer, "Where in the World Is America? The History of the United States in the Global Age," in *Rethinking American History in the Global Age*, Thomas Bender, ed. (Berkeley: University of California Press, 2002): 63–100; and Dipesh Chakrabarty, *Provincializing Europe: Postcolonial Thought and Historical Difference* (Princeton: Princeton University Press, 2007). See also Michael Ignatieff, ed. *American Exceptionalism and Human Rights* (Princeton: Princeton University Press, 2005).

17. The broader contours of the transnational turn in the writing of American history since the late 1990s are best captured in Bender, *Rethinking American History in the Global Age;* Ian Tyrell, "Reflections on the Transnational Turn in United States History: Theory and Practice," *Journal of Global History* 4.3 (November 2009): 453–74; Paul Kramer, "Power and Connection: Imperial Histories of the United States in the World," *American Historical Review* 116.5 (2011): 1348–91; and Brooke L. Blower and Mark Philip Bradley, eds., *The Familiar Made Strange: American Icons after the Transnational Turn* (Ithaca: Cornell University Press, 2015). On the perils of potentially reinscribing the centrality of the United States in these new histories of America and the world, see Louis A. Pérez, "We Are the World: Internationalizing the National, Nationalizing the International," *Journal of American History* 89.2 (September 2002): 558–66.

18. Walter F. LaFeber, "Responses to Charles S. Maier, 'Marking Time: The Historiography of International Relations,'" *Diplomatic History* 5.4 (October 1981): 362; and Fredrik Logevall, "Politics and Foreign Relations," *Journal of American History* 95.4 (March 2009): 1076. More generally see Leffler, *Preponderance of Power;* and Campbell Craig and Fredrik

Logevall, *America's Cold War: The Politics of Domestic Insecurity* (Cambridge, MA: Harvard University Press, 2009).

19. Daniel T. Rodgers, *Atlantic Crossings: Social Politics in a Progressive Era* (Cambridge, MA: Harvard University Press, 1998): 488, 487, 508.

20. Billy Taylor, "I Wish I Knew How It Would Feel to Be Free," Manuscript Score, 19(107C), Music Division, Library of Congress, Washington, DC. On the relationship between Simone and Taylor's song, see Ruth Feldstein, *How It Feels to Be Free: Black Women Entertainers and the Civil Rights Movement* (New York: Oxford University Press, 2013): ch. 3.

PART ONE: THE 1940S

1. "UN Code of Rights Hailed on 1st Year," *New York Times*, December 11, 1949.

2. Preamble, United Nations Charter, June 26, 1945 (www.un.org/en/documents/charter/preamble.shtml).

3. Aaron Copland and Vivian Perlis, *Copland, since 1943* (New York: St. Martin's Press, 1989): 148–49; and Howard Pollack, *Aaron Copland: The Life and Work of an Uncommon Man* (New York: Henry Holt and Company, 1999): 438–39.

4. Article 2, United Nations Universal Declaration of Human Rights, December 10, 1948 (www.un.org/en/documents/udhr/).

5. Preamble and Articles 1, 13, 55, 56, 60, 62, 68, Charter of the United Nations (www.un.org/en/documents/charter/).

6. Article 23 of *The Covenant of the League of Nations* mentions labor and trafficking (http://avalon.law.yale.edu/20th_century/leagcov.asp).

7. See Paul Gordon Lawrence, *The Evolution of International Human Rights: Visions Seen*, 2nd ed. (Philadelphia: University of Pennsylvania Press, 2011): 139–204; Elizabeth Borgwardt, *A New Deal for the World: America's Vision for Human Rights* (Cambridge, MA: Harvard University Press, 2005); and Borgwardt, "FDR's Four Freedoms and Wartime Transformations in America's Discourse of Rights," in *Bringing Human Rights Home: A History of Human Rights in the United States*, Cynthia Soohoo and Catherine Albisa, eds. (Philadelphia: University of Pennsylvania Press, 2009): 40–67. In this more heroic mode, see also Mary Ann Glendon, *A World Made New: Eleanor Roosevelt and the Universal Declaration of Human Rights* (New York: Random House, 2001); and Jay Winter and Antoine Prost, *René Cassin and Human Rights: From the Great War to the Universal Declaration* (Cambridge: Cambridge University Press, 2013).

8. More measured accounts have recently begun to emerge in Rowland Brucken, *A Most Uncertain Crusade: The United States, the United Nations, and Human Rights, 1941–1953* (DeKalb: Northern Illinois University Press, 2014); Glenn Mitoma, *Human Rights and the Negotiation of American Power* (Philadelphia: University of Pennsylvania Press, 2013); and Christopher N. J. Roberts, *The Contentious History of the International Bill of Human Rights* (Cambridge: Cambridge University Press, 2015).

9. See Samuel Moyn, *The Last Utopia: Human Rights in History* (Cambridge, MA: Harvard University Press, ch. 2); Mark Mazower, "The Strange Triumph of Human Rights, 1933–1950," *Historical Journal* 47.2 (2004): 379–98; and Mazower, *No Enchanted Palace: The End*

of Empire and the Ideological Origins of the United Nations (Princeton: Princeton University Press, 2009): 28–65.

10. Churchill offered this piece of rhetorical excess in an October 1942 speech before the World Jewish Congress in London, one that was picked up by various wartime advocates for human rights language in the United Nations. See *Times* (London), October 30, 1942; and Hersch Lauterpacht, *An International Bill of Rights of Man* (New York: Columbia University Press, 1945): 6, 69, 86.

11. *New York Times*, December 11, 1949: 1; readers of the *Times* would have had to wait until p. 30 to learn of the Carnegie Hall anniversary event in an article itself almost overwhelmed by a three-quarter page advertisement on the same page featuring women's rhinestone-studded "cutaway" shirts and "umbrella-pleated" dresses.

CHAPTER 1: AT HOME IN THE WORLD

1. Dorothea Lange, "The Assignment I'll Never Forget," *Popular Photography*, February 1960: 42–43; Linda Gordon helps set this scene in her luminous biography, *Dorothea Lange: A Life beyond Limits* (New York: Norton, 2009): 235–36.

2. Franklin D. Roosevelt, "Annual Message to the Congress," January 6, 1941, in *War and Peace Aims of the United Nations*, Louise W. Holborn and Hajo Holborn, eds. (Boston: World Peace Foundation, 1943): 33–34; *Atlantic Charter*, August 14, 1941 (http://avalon .law.yale.edu/wwii/atlantic.asp); Sumner Welles, "Requirements for the Four Freedoms: Address before the New York Herald-Tribune Forum, New York City, November 17, 1942," in *Vital Speeches of the Day*, vol. 9: 114–16; *Declaration by the United Nations*, January 1, 1942, *Department of State Bulletin*, vol. 5 (1942): 3; Cordell Hull, "Address on the War and Human Freedom (broadcast over all national radio networks)," July 23, 1942 in *War and Peace Aims*: 103.

3. "This Is Our War," Reel 2, 0298 Exhibits, 1942–43, *Information Control and Propaganda: Records of the Office of War Information, Part I: The Director's Central Files, 1942–1945* (Microfilm, University Publications of America). The OWI exhibit was part of a massive wartime effort to build morale around what one author calls the imaginary of freedom. On making the Four Freedoms legible visually, see Eric Foner, *The Story of American Freedom* (New York: Norton, 1998): 221–34; and Robert B. Westbrook, "Fighting for the American Family: Private Interests and Political Obligation in World War II," in *The Power of Culture: Critical Essays in American History*, Richard Wightman Fox and T. J. Jackson Lears, eds. (Chicago: University of Chicago Press, 1993): 195–221. But see also Benjamin L. Alpers, *Dictators, Democracy and American Public Culture: Envisioning the Totalitarian Enemy, 1920s–1950s* (Chapel Hill: University of North Carolina Press, 2003): 157–87; Wendy L. Wall, *Inventing the "American Way": The Politics of Consensus from the New Deal to the Civil Rights Movement* (Oxford: Oxford University Press, 2008): 103–59; James T. Sparrow, *Warfare State: World War II American and the Age of Big Government* (New York: Oxford University Press, 2011): 65–77; and John Morton Blum, *V Was for Victory: Politics and American Culture during World War II* (New York: Harcourt Brace, 1976): 15–52.

4. *Public Opinion, 1935–46*, edited by Hadley Cantril (Princeton: Princeton University Press, 1951): 1083. See also Sparrow, *Warfare State*: 45; and Blum, *V Was for Victory*: 46.

5. A search of the *New York Times* electronic database for the term "human rights" indicates an uptick in wartime usage, as does a Google Ngram graphing of its use between 1900 and 1945. See also Borgwardt, "FDR's Four Freedoms and Wartime Transformations in America's Discourse of Rights": 53–54.

6. Richard Rorty, "Human Rights, Rationality and Sentimentality," in *On Human Rights: The Oxford Amnesty Lectures 1993*, Stephen Shute and Susan Hurley, eds. (Oxford: Oxford University Press, 1993): 113–34. See also Annette C. Baier, *A Progress of Sentiments: Reflections on Hume's Treatise* (Cambridge, MA: Harvard University Press, 1991).

7. Martha Nussbaum, *Love's Knowledge* (New York: Oxford University Press, 1990): 3.

8. Lynn Hunt, *Inventing Human Rights: A History* (New York: Norton, 2007): 34. But see also Thomas L. Haskell, "Capitalism and the Origins of Humanitarian Sensibility, Parts I and II," *American Historical Review* 90.2 (April 1995): 339–61 and 90.3 (June 1995): 547–66; Thomas Laqueur, "Bodies, Details and the Humanitarian Narrative," in *The New Cultural History*, Lynn Hunt, ed. (Berkeley: University of California Press, 1989): 176–201; and Samuel Moyn, "Empathy in History, Empathizing with Humanity," *History and Theory* 45 (2006): 397–415.

9. "Orbis Pictus," *The Nation*, October 16, 1935: 426.

10. Joshua Brown, *Beyond the Lines: Pictorial Reporting, Everyday Life and the Crisis of Gilded Age America* (Berkeley: University of California Press, 2002); Bonnie Yochelson and Daniel Czitrom, *Rediscovering Jacob Riis: Exposure Journalism and Photography in Turn-of-the-Century New York* (New York: New Press, 2007); Kate Sampsell-Willmann, *Lewis Hine as Social Critic* (Jackson: University of Mississippi Press, 2009); Alan Trachtenberg, "Camera Work, Social Work," in his *Reading American Photographs* (New York: Hill and Wang, 1990): 169–230; and Mary Ting Yi Lui, "Saving Young Girls from Chinatown: White Slavery and Woman Suffrage, 1910–1920," *Journal of the History of Sexuality* 18.3 (September 2009): 393–417. See also the contributors to *Humanitarian Photography: A History*, Heide Fehrenbach and Davide Rodogno, eds. (Cambridge: Cambridge University Press, 2015).

11. Matthew S. Witkovsky, *Foto: Modernity in Central Europe, 1918–1945* (New York: Thames and Hudson, 2007): 58–59; and Cara A. Finnegan, *Picturing Poverty: Print Culture and FSA Photographs* (Washington, DC: Smithsonian Books, 2003): 170–79.

12. Bodo von Dewitz, ed., *Kiosk: A History of Photojournalism* (Göttingen: Steidl, 2008).

13. On the emergence of *reportage* in multiple national contexts, see David Midgley, *Writing Weimar: Critical Realism in German Literature 1918–1933* (Oxford: Oxford University Press, 2000); Saros Cowasjee, *So Many Freedoms: A Study of the Major Fiction of Mulk Raj Anand* (Delhi: Oxford University Press, 1977); Charles A. Laughlin, *Chinese Reportage: The Aesthetics of Historical Experience* (Durham: Duke University Press, 2002); Greg Lockhart, "Introduction," in his *The Light of the Capital* (Singapore: Oxford University Press, 1996): 1–49; and Anna Indych-Lopez, *Muralism without Walls: Rivera, Orozco and Siqueiros in the United States, 1927–1940* (Pittsburgh: University of Pittsburgh Press, 2009). Although they accord minimal attention to the global context shaping

American forms, the starting point on *reportage* in the United States remains these works: William Stott, *Documentary Expression and Thirties America*, 2nd ed. (Chicago: University of Chicago Press, 1986); essays by Lawrence Levine and Alan Trachtenberg in *Documenting America, 1935–43*, Carl Fleischhauer and Beverly W. Brannan, eds. (Berkeley: University of California Press, 1988); and Trachtenberg, "A Book Nearly Anonymous," in his *Reading American Photographs*: 231–85. See also Michael Denning, *The Cultural Front: The Laboring of American Culture in the Twentieth Century* (London: Verso, 1977).

14. Witkovsky, *Foto: Modernity in Central Europe:* 141–57; Takeba Joe, "The Age of Modernism: From Visualization to Socialization," and Kaneko Ryuichi, "Realism and Propaganda: The Photographer's Eye Trained on Society," in *The History of Japanese Photography*, Anne Wilkes Tucket et al. eds. (New Haven: Yale University Press, 2003): 144–57, 186–93.

15. Margaret Bourke-White, *Eyes on Russia* (New York: Simon and Schuster, 1931). The Soviet photographs of individuals appear in a series of *New York Times* pieces dated February 14; March 6, 13, and 27; May 22; and September 11, 1932. On Bourke-White's visit to Moscow, see Sharon Corwin, "Constructed Documentary: Margaret Bourke-White from the Steel Mill to the South," in *American Modern: Documentary Photography by Abbott, Evans, and Bourke-White*, Sharon Corwin, Jessica May, and Terri Weissman, eds. (Berkeley: University of California Press, 2010): 120–21.

16. Margaret Bourke-White, *Portrait of Myself* (New York: Simon and Schuster, 1963): 410; Corwin, "Constructed Documentary": 121, 124.

17. Letter from Modotti to Anita Breener, October 9, 1929, cited in Sarah M. Lowe, *Tina Modotti: Photographs* (New York: Harry N. Abrams, Inc., 1995): 36. My discussion of Modotti's work and background draws on ibid: 32–39; Margaret Hodes, *Tina Modotti: Photographer and Revolutionary* (New York: Harper Collins, 1993): chs. 12 and 13; and Letizia Argenteri, *Tina Modotti: Between Art and Revolution* (New Haven: Yale University Press, 2003): chs. 6 and 8. Modotti was forced to leave Mexico in 1930 after a short period of imprisonment for her political views; she then worked for international leftist and socialist causes in Germany, France, the Soviet Union, and Spain in the 1930s before returning to Mexico in 1939. She died in Mexico City in 1942.

18. For discussions of some of these works, see Patrick Iber, *Neither Peace nor Freedom: The Cultural Cold War in Latin America* (Cambridge, MA: Harvard University Press, 2015): 19–48; Ana Lopez, "Crossing Nations and Genres: Traveling Filmmakers," in *Visible Nations: Latin American Cinema and Video*, Chon Noriega, ed. (Minneapolis: University of Minnesota Press, 2000): 33–50; and Carl J. Mora, *Mexican Cinema: Reflections of a Society* (Berkeley: University of California Press, 1989).

19. Carleton Beals, *The Crime of Cuba* (Philadelphia: J. B. Lippincott, 1933) includes thirty-one of Evans's photographs. On his involvement with Diego Rivera and the controversy over the Rockefeller Center mural, see James R. Mellow, *Walker Evans* (New York: Basic Books, 1999): 202–06, 224–25. My discussion of Evans's experiences in Cuba draws on Andrei Codrescu, "Walker Evans: The Cuba Photographs," in *Walker Evans: Cuba* (Los Angeles: J. Paul Getty Museum, 2001): 11–32.

20. Margaret Bourke-White and Erskine Caldwell, *You Have Seen Their Faces* (New York: Modern Age Books, 1937); Archibald MacLeish, *Land of the Free* (New York: Harcourt, Brace

and Co., 1938); Dorothea Lange and Paul Taylor, *American Exodus* (New York: Reynal & Hitchcock, 1939); James Agee and Walker Evans, *Let Us Now Praise Famous Men* (Boston: Houghton Mifflin, 1941); and Richard Wright, *12 Million Black Voices* (New York: Viking Press, 1941).

21. On these circulatory forms that documentary photographs took in the 1930s, see Cara A. Finnegan, *Picturing Poverty: Print Culture and FSA Photographs* (Washington, DC: Smithsonian Books, 2003); John Raeburn, *A Staggering Revolution: A Cultural History of Thirties Photography* (Urbana: University of Illinois Press, 2006): 183–93; Stott, *Documentary Expression and Thirties America*: 211–37; Anne Whiston Spirn, *Daring to Look: Dorothea Lange's Photographs and Reports from the Field* (Chicago: University of Chicago Press, 2008): 36–50; and Gordon, *Dorothea Lange: A Life beyond Limits*: 279–86. On Steinbeck and Lorentz, respectively, see Denning, *The Cultural Front: The Laboring of American Culture in the Twentieth Century*: 259–82; and Finis Dunaway, *Natural Visions: The Power of Images in American Environmental Reform* (Chicago: University of Chicago Press, 2005): 60–86.

22. See, for instance, James Curtis, *Mind's Eye, Mind's Truth: FSA Photography Reconsidered* (Philadelphia: Temple University Press, 1989); John Tagg, *The Burden of Representation: Essays on Photographies and Histories* (Minneapolis: University of Minnesota Press, 1988); and Maren Stange, *Symbols of Idea Life: Social Documentary Photography in America, 1890–1950* (New York: Oxford University Press, 1989).

23. Curtis, *Mind's Eye, Mind's Truth*: 5. Such critiques were more deeply rooted in a broader interrogation of photography's political and ethical potency advanced in such influential works as Susan Sontag, *On Photography* (New York: Farrar, Straus and Giroux, 1977); Roland Barthes, *Camera Lucida* (New York: Hill and Wang, 1981); Alan Sekula, "Dismantling Modernism, Reinventing Documentary (Notes on the Politics of Representation)," in his *Photography against the Grain: Essays and Photo Works, 1973–1983* (Halifax: Nova Scotia College of Art and Design, 1984: 53–76; and Sontag, *Regarding the Pain of Others* (New York: Farrar, Straus and Giroux, 2003).

24. See John A. Walker, "Reflections on a Photograph by Margaret Bourke-White," *Creative Camera* 167 (May 1978): 148–49; and James Guimond, *American Photography and the American Dream* (Chapel Hill: University of North Carolina Press, 1991): 112–16.

25. Caldwell and Bourke-White, *You Have Seen Their Faces*: 51. For a critical discussion of Bourke-White's work, see Carol Schloss, *Invisible Light: Photography and the American Writer: 1840–1940* (New York: Oxford University Press, 1987): ch. 5; Stott, *Documentary Expression and Thirties America*: 213–23; and Gordon, *Dorothea Lange: A Life beyond Limits*: 280–81. Critiques of Evans's rearrangements of his subjects and their settings are somewhat more subdued; see, for instance, Curtis, *Mind's Eye, Mind's Truth*: 23–44.

26. Raeburn, *A Staggering Revolution*: 215–18. See also Lawrence Levine, "The Historian and the Icon: Photography and the History of the American People in the 1930s and 1940s," in his *The Unpredictable Past: Explorations in American Cultural History* (New York: Oxford University Press, 1993): 256–90.

27. Norman Cousins review quoted in *Book Review Digest, 1937*, cited in Corwin, "Constructed Documentary": 125.

28. Sarah M. Miller, *"Inventing 'Documentary' in American Photography, 1930–1945"* (Ph.D. dissertation, University of Chicago, 2009): 277.

29. Transcription of selected "Response Cards of People Attending First International Photographic Exposition at the Grand Central Palace, New York, April 1938" appears in ibid.: 311–12; originals in "Security Administration Exhibitions, 1936–62," Roy Stryker Papers, Photographic Archive, University of Louisville; and "Exhibits," Box 3, Office Files, 1935–44, Records of the Farm Security Administration, Library of Congress, Washington, DC.

30. The most detailed critique of these manipulations appears in Curtis, *Mind's Eye, Mind's Truth*: 47–67. The subject of *Migrant Mother*, Florence Thompson, made herself known to Lange decades after the photograph was taken, upset that it was in widespread circulation without her permission and threatening a lawsuit over royalties. Because the photograph was produced for the FSA, Lange herself did not control its use, nor had she earned royalties from it. See Gordon, *Dorothea Lange: A Life beyond Limits*: 240–43; and Robert Hariman and John Louis Lucaites, *No Caption Needed: Iconic Photographs, Public Culture and Liberal Democracy* (Chicago: University of Chicago Press, 2007): 61–64.

31. Gordon, *Dorothea Lange: A Life beyond Limits*: 236–40; and Wendy Kozol, "Madonnas of the Field: Photography, Gender, and 1930's Farm Relief," *Genders* 2 (Summer 1988): 1–23.

32. Hannah Arendt, "Understanding Politics (The Difficulties of Understanding)," in *Essays in Understanding: 1930–1945*, Jerome Kohn. ed. (New York: Schocken Books): 307–8. I am indebted to Sharon Sliwinski for bringing this work by Arendt to my attention in her *Human Rights in Camera* (Chicago: University of Chicago Press, 2011): 14. The primacy Sliwinski places on the aesthetic judgments of viewers of atrocity images has informed my broader reading of 1930s American documentary photography, as does Susie Linfield's insistence that photographs can bring us closest to an empathetic understanding of social suffering and human rights in her *Cruel Radiance: Photography and Political Violence* (Chicago: University of Chicago Press, 2010).

CHAPTER 2: THE WARTIME RIGHTS IMAGINATION

1. *The World's Destiny and the United States* (Chicago: World Citizens Association, 1941): 102–3. On the organization of the conference, see World Citizens Association Central Committee Records, Box 6, Folders 2–4; and Quincy Wright Papers, Box 14, Folder 9 in Special Collections Research Center, University of Chicago Library.

2. Ibid.: 105, 110, 111.

3. Ibid.: 113.

4. Ibid.: 137.

5. H. G. Wells's 1941 *Rights of Man* was another early iteration of wartime rights talk, but its influence appears to have been stronger in Great Britain than in the United States.

6. Hersch Lauterpacht, *An International Bill of Rights of Man* (New York: Columbia University Press, 1945): 7.

7. The "Statement," widely circulated in pamphlet form beginning in February 1944, is reprinted in *Annals of the American Academy of Political and Social Sciences* 243 (January 1946): 18–26. See also William Draper Lewis, "An International Bill of Rights," *Proceedings of the American Philosophical Society* 85.5 (September 30, 1942): 445–47, and "The State of Essential Human Rights by Representatives of the Principal Cultures of the World," *Proceedings of the American Philosophical Society* 89.3 (October 1945): 489–94. Louis B. Sohn provides a first-person account in his "How American International Lawyers Prepared for San Francisco," *American Journal of International Law* 89.3 (July 1995): 540–53. An archivally informed account of the American Law Institute's efforts emerges in Hanne Hagtvedt Vik, "Taming the States: The American Law Institute and the 'Statement of Essential Human Rights,'" *Journal of Global History* 7.3 (November 2012): 461–82.

8. Lauterpacht, *International Bill of Rights of Man*. On the American Jewish Committee's invitation and Lauterpacht's work on this project, see Elihu Lauterpacht, *The Life of Hersch Lauterpacht* (Cambridge: Cambridge University Press, 2010): 251–57. Drafted in 1943 but not published until June 1945, the conceptual underpinnings of the book emerged in Hersch Lauterpacht, "The Law of Nations, the Law of Nature and the Rights of Man," *Transactions of the Grotius Society* 29 (1943): 1–33. On the relationship between human rights and Lauterpacht's Zionism, see James Loeffler, "The 'Natural Rights of the Jewish People': Zionism, International Law, and the Paradox of Hersch Lauterpacht" in *The Law of Strangers: Critical Perspectives on Jewish Lawyering and International Legal Thought*, James Loeffler and Moria Paz, eds. (Cambridge: Cambridge University Press, forthcoming).

9. U.S. Department of State Special Subcommittee on Legal Problems, "Bill of Rights," December 3, 1942, in Harley Notter, *Postwar Foreign Policy Preparation, 1939–1945* (Washington, DC: U.S. Government Printing Office, 1949): 483–85; "Article 9, Human Rights, Draft Charter of the United Nations," August 14, 1943 in ibid.: 530. On these State Department efforts, see Roland Brucken, *A Most Uncertain Crusade: The United States, the United Nations and Human Rights, 1941–53* (DeKalb: Northern Illinois University Press, 2014): 28–37.

10. Mexican Ministry of Foreign Affairs, "International Protection of the Essential Rights of Man," and Cuban Ministry of Foreign Affairs, "Declaration of the International Duties and Rights of the Individual," in *Report of the Delegation of the United States of America to the Inter-American Conference on Problems of War and Peace, Mexico City, 27 February to 8 March 1954* (Washington, DC: U.S. Department of State, 1945): 141–44, 156–60; Inter-American Juridical Committee, "Draft Declaration of the International Rights and Duties of Man" and "Accompanying Report," December 31, 1945 (Washington, DC: Pan-American Union, 1946). On the contributions of Latin American states to human rights thought and practice in the 1940s, see Kathryn Sikkink, "Latin American Countries as Norm Protagonists of the Idea of International Human Rights," *Global Governance* 20.3 (July–September 2014): 389–404.

11. The Commission to Study the Organization of the Peace issued a series of broadly disseminated annual reports between 1941 and 1944 along with occasional papers and

radio broadcasts. Those dealing with the centrality of human rights to the postwar peace include (1941) *Preliminary Report, Treatment of Minorities, Social Justice within and among Nations, Fundamental Problems of World Organization, Peaceful Change, Judicial Settlement in World Affairs*; (1942) *Second Report, Political Conditions of the Period of Transition*; (1943) *Third Report, Human Rights and World Order, Protection of Human Rights, Justice and World Order*; NBC Radio Broadcast *Justice and Human Rights*; and (1944) *Fourth Report, Security and World Organization, International Safeguard of Human Rights*. For a helpful discussion of the Commission's human rights work, see Glenn Tatsuya Mitoma, "Civil Society and International Human Rights: The Commission to Study the Organization of the Peace and the Origins of the UN Human Rights Regime," *Human Rights Quarterly* 30.3 (August 2008): 607–30; and his *Human Rights and the Negotiation of American Power* (Philadelphia: University of Pennsylvania Press, 2013): ch. 1.

12. On the American Jewish community and wartime human rights talk, see James Loeffler, "'The Conscience of America': Human Rights, Jewish Politics and American Foreign Policy at the 1945 United Nations San Francisco Conference," *Journal of American History* (September 2013): 405–12. See also Jerold S. Auerbach, "Human Rights at San Francisco," *American Jewish Archives* 16.1 (April 1964): 51–70.

13. These linkages emerge in the minutes on the discussions of the State Department's draft bill in the Subcommittee on Legal Problems between October and December 1942 in Box 72, Records of Harley A. Notter, 1939–1945, Record Group 59, National Archives, Washington, DC; Inter-American Juridical Committee, "Draft Declaration": 19–20; Auerbach, "Human Rights at San Francisco": 55–60.

14. On social and economic rights in the prewar Latin American context, see Greg Grandin, "The Liberal Traditions in the Americas: Rights, Sovereignty, and the Origins of Liberal Multilateralism," *American Historical Review* 117.1 (February 2012): 68–91.

15. Although the starting point for understanding American attitudes toward national organization during the World War II remains Robert A. Divine, *Second Chance: The Triumph of Internationalism in American during World War II* (New York: Atheneum, 1967), Borgwardt's *New Deal for the World* and James T. Sparrow's *Warfare State: World War II American and the Age of Government* (New York: Oxford University Press, 2011) are also essential. For a brilliant rethinking of isolationism, see Brooke L. Blower, "From Isolationism to Neutrality: A New Framework for Understanding American Political Culture, 1919–1941," *Diplomatic History* 38.2 (April 2014): 345–76.

16. Quincy Wright, *Human Rights and World Order* (New York: Commission to Study the Organization of the Peace, 1943): 6. See also L Minutes 6, November 12, 1942, Box 72, Notter Files: 3; Lauterpacht, *International Bill of Rights of Man*: 6, 84–87; Draper, "International Bill of Rights": 445; Inter-American Juridical Committee, "Draft Declaration": 15; and "Third Report of the Commission to Study the Organization of the Peace: The United Nations and the Organization of the Peace," *International Conciliation* (April 1943): 211.

17. See Benjamin L. Alpers, *Dictatorships, Democracy and American Public Culture: Envisioning the Totalitarian Enemy, 1920s–1950s* (Chapel Hill: University of North Carolina Press, 2003): 129–56; Alan Brinkley, *The End of Reform* (New York: Alfred A. Knopf, 1995):

154–74; and Abbott Gleason, *Totalitarianism: The Inner History of the Cold War* (New York: Oxford University Press, 1995): 31–61.

18. On these broader campaigns, see Alpers, *Dictatorships, Democracy and American Public Culture*: 188–219; Sparrow, *Warfare State*: 19–77; Allan M. Winkler, *The Politics of Propaganda: The Office of War Information, 1942–45* (New Haven: Yale University Press, 1978): 38–72; and Divine, *Second Chance*.

19. "Tableaux to Show 'Hitler Platform,'" *New York Times*, May 11, 1943: 23; and "Many See Exhibit of War's Horrors," *New York Times*, May 18, 1943: 19.

20. Commission to Study the Organization of the Peace, *Fourth Report: Part III, International Safeguard of Human Rights* (May 1944): 6; "Preliminary Report of the Commission to Study the Organization of the Peace," *International Conciliation* (April 1941): 5, 9. 11.

21. Lauterpacht, *International Bill of Rights of Man.*: 88; Commission to Study the Organization of the Peace, *Fourth Report:* 6.

22. Mexican Ministry of Foreign Affairs, "International Protection of the Essential Rights of Man": 156; American Jewish Committee's Committee on Peace Problems, *Protection of Human Rights* (December 1944): 5. See also Inter-American Juridical Committee, "Draft Declaration": 14.

23. Quincy Wright, "Protection of Human Rights, Proceedings of the February 27, 1943 Conference of the Commission to Study the Organization of the Peace," *Bulletin of the Commission to Study the Organization of the Peace*, 3.3–4 (March–April 1943): 6–7.

24. Woodrow Wilson, "Make This League a Vital Thing (1919)," reprinted in *International Organization* 10.4 (1956): 525, 526; *World's Destiny*: 104. On Wilson's insistence on the significance of world public opinion, see Thomas J. Knock, *To End All Wars: Woodrow Wilson and the Quest for a New World Order* (Princeton: Princeton University Press, 1995).

25. Wright, "Protection of Human Rights": 7.

26. Robert E. Park and Ernest W. Burgess, *Introduction to the Science of Sociology* (Chicago: University of Chicago Press, 1921): 67, 489 quoted in Wright, *Human Rights and the World Order*: 21.

27. Lauterpacht, *International Bill of Rights of Man*: 3, 86, 87, 53. These ideas are worked out in even more detail in his 1943 essay, "The Law of Nations, the Law of Nature and the Rights of Man."

28. "Agenda, Conference of Advisors to the American Law Institute, 5–7 November 1942": 5–7; and "Report of the Session of the American Law Institute for the Discussion of the International Bill of Rights Project," November 12, 1942, Box 72, Notter Files. See also "Draft Outline," Commission for the Study of the Peace, September 1942, Folder 14, Box 5, Quincy Wright Papers.

29. Lauterpacht, *International Bill of Rights of Man.*: 106; Inter-American Juridical Committee, "International Bill": 27.

30. Inter-American Juridical Committee: 26; Quincy Wright, "Protection of Human Rights": 6. On the concerns of postcolonial states, see Kenneth Cmeil, "Human Rights, Freedom of Information and the Origins of Third-World Solidarity," in *Truth Claims: Representation and Human Rights*, Mark Philip Bradley and Patrice Petro, eds. (New Brunswick:

Rutgers University Press, 2002): 107–30; and Samuel Lebovic, "*Fighting for Free Informa-tion: American Democracy and the Problem of Press Freedom in the Totalitarian Age, 1920–1950*" (Ph.D. dissertation, University of Chicago, 2010).

31. Daniel T. Rodgers, *Atlantic Crossings: Social Politics in a Progressive Age* (Cambridge, MA: Harvard University Press, 1988): 488–98.

32. National Resources Planning Board, "Our Freedoms and Rights," in *Post-War Planning – Full Employment, Security, Building America* (Washington, DC: U.S. Government Printing Office, 1942): 32 and "A New Bill of Rights," January 1942, in *National Resources Devel-opment Report for 1943, Part I, Post-War Plan and Program* (Washington, DC: U.S. Gov-ernment Printing Office, 1943): 3. On the wider context of the plan, see Patrick D. Reagan, *Designing a New America: The Origins of New Deal Planning* (Amherst: University of Massachusetts Press, 2000); and Rodgers, *Atlantic Crossings*: 497–98.

33. Bruce Bliven, Max Lerner, and George Soule, "Charter for America," *New Republic*, April 19, 1943): 523–24; "A New Bill of Rights," *Nation*, March 20, 1943: 401.

34. Franklin D. Roosevelt, State of the Union Message to Congress, January 11, 1944. See Cass Sunstein, *The Second Bill of Rights: FDR's Unfinished Revolution* (New York: Basic Books, 2004); and Sparrow, *Warfare State*: 197–98.

35. "Philadelphia Charter of the ILO," *New York Times*, May 11, 1944: 14; "Roosevelt Hails ILO Declaration," *New York Times*, May 18, 1944: 13. The conference deliberations over the charter were closely followed by the State Department; see "Summary of Report on International Labor Conference, 26th Session, April 20–May 12, 1944, Philadelphia," in Box 175, Notter Files.

36. The drafting records of the American Law Institute Project are full of constitutions col-lected from around the world; see Box 1, Statement of Essential Human Rights Project Records, American Law Institute Archives, ALI.04.006, Biddle Law Library, University of Pennsylvania Law School, Philadelphia, Pennsylvania. But more generally the "go to" guide for these comparative efforts was the door-stopper 755-page *Constitutional Provisions Concerning Social and Economic Policy* (Montreal: International Labour Office, 1944).

37. "Report of the Session of the Annual Meeting of the American Law Institute on its International Bill of Rights Project," May 13, 1943: 4; and "Reports (Preliminary) of the Subcommittees of Advisors," February 1943: 17, 25–45 passim in Box 72, Notter Files. See also Lauterpacht, *International Bill of Rights of Man*: 157–59; Inter-American Juridical Commission: 8, 10; and U.S. Department of State, "Bill of Rights": 483. On the 1917 Mexican constitution, see Grandin, "The Liberal Traditions in the Americas": 75–76; and Patrick Iber, *Neither Peace nor Freedom: The Cultural Cold War in Latin America* (Cambridge, MA: Harvard University Press, 2015): 23–24.

38. *World's Destiny*: 116–18.

39. "Summary of Proceedings," World Citizens Association Central Committee Records, Box 6, Folder 1; and *World's Destiny*: 119–21.

40. "Report of the Session of the Annual Meeting of the American Law Institute": 4; *Amer-ican Law Institute Proceedings* (1943): 184–204; Lauterpacht, *International Bill of Rights of Man*: 160; L Minutes 5, November 5, 1942, and L Minutes 7, November 9, 1942, in

Box 72, Notter Papers: 8. See also Inter-American Juridical Commission: 49–51; "Draft Declaration"; and the French legal sociologist Georges Gurvitch's *The Bill of Social Rights* (New York: International Universities Press, 1945).

41. Letter from Hudson to Lewis, January 12, 1943, in "Reports (Preliminary)": 22–23; and "Report of the Session": 5 in Box 72, Notter Files.

42. "Resolutions Adopted at the National Manufacturers Association," *New York Times*, December 8, 1944: 16. See also contemporary critiques of the National Resources Planning Board's bill of rights and Roosevelt's second bill of rights proposals in Brinkley, *End of Reform*: 254–64. Philip W. Warken, "A History of the National Resources Planning Board, 1933–1943" (Ph.D. dissertation, Ohio State University, 1969): 230–37; and John Blum, *V is for Victory: Politics and American Culture During World War II* (New York: Harcourt Brace, 1977): 245–54.

43. Draper, *Essential Human Rights* (1946): 491; Lauterpacht, *International Bill of Rights of Man*: 160–62.

44. L Minutes 8, December 3, 1942, Box 72, Notter Files: 8–9; Lauterpacht, *International Bill of Rights of Man*: 126–28; Inter-American Juridical Commission, "Draft Declaration," 37, 38. The American Jewish Committee's concern about statelessness emerged in two extensive wartime reports as well as the broader proposals it put forward for a postwar human rights order: see Committee on Peace Problems, *Statelessness* (American Jewish Committee, December 1944); Marc Vishniak, *The Legal Status of Stateless Persons* (American Jewish Committee Research Institute on Postwar Peace and Problems, 1945); and American Jewish Committee, *To the Counsellors of Peace*: 89–100.

45. On the minority treaty system and its more recent historiography, see Eric D. Weitz, "From the Vienna to the Paris System: International Politics and the Entangled Histories of Human Rights, Forced Deportations and Civilizing Missions," *American Historical Review* 113.5 (December 2008): 1313–43; Susan Pedersen, "Review Essay: Back to the League of Nations," *American Historical Review* 112.4 (October 2007): 1099–1103; and Simpson, *Human Rights and the End of Empire*: 121–45.

46. Lauterpacht, *International Bill of the Rights of Man*: 216, 215, 219, and more generally 151–55, 215–224.

47. Oscar I. Janowsky, "The Treatment of Minorities," *International Conciliation* (April 1941): 91, 92, 93. See also his *International Aspects of German Racial Policies* (New York: Oxford University Press, 1937), which frames German policy as a violation of human rather than minority rights; *Nationalities and National Minorities* (New York: Macmillan, 1945); and *Jews and Minority Rights* (New York: Columbia University Press, 1933). Susan Pederson's *The Guardians: The League of Nations and the Crisis of Empire* (New York: Oxford University Press, 2015) argues that the colonial mandates supervised by the League of Nations did not work in quite the effective or disinterested ways that Janowsky suggests.

48. Jacob Robinson et al., *Were the Minority Treaties a Failure?* (New York: Institute of Jewish Affairs of the American Jewish Congress and World Jewish Congress, 1943). Along with Janowsky, other influential works in framing wartime perceptions of the minorities treaty system included Pablo de Azcárate, *League of Nations and National Minorities: An Experiment* (Washington, DC: Carnegie Endowment for International Peace, 1945); and

Georges Kaeckenbeeck, *The International Experience of Upper Silesia* (New York: Oxford University Press, 1942). More recent scholarship on the minority treaty regime supports 1940s-era critiques, but offer differing, and often competing, explanations to account for them: see Carole Fink, *Defending the Rights of Others: The Great Powers, the Jews, and International Minority Protection, 1878–1938* (Cambridge: Cambridge University Press, 2004); and Christian Raitz von Frentz, *A Lesson Forgotten: Minority Protection under the League of Nations, the Case of the German Minority in Poland, 1920–1934* (New York: St. Martin Press, 1999).

49. Raphael Lemkin, *Axis Rule in Occupied Europe* (Washington, DC: Carnegie Edowment for the International Peace, 1944): xiv; Lauterpacht, *International Bill of Rights of Man*: vii, 220.

50. American Jewish Committee, *Protection of Human Rights*: 8, 18. The Committee did call for special provisions in the immediate postwar period to protect Jews and other minorities who had lived in Axis-controlled territory; see Simon Segal, "Problems of Minorities Regarding an International Bill of Rights," *Journal of Educational Sociology* 18.5 (January 1945): 301–310; and *To the Counsellors of Peace*: 25–66. On Lemkin, see John Cooper, *Raphael Lemkin and the Struggle for the Genocide Convention* (Basinstoke: Palgrave Macmillan, 2008).

51. Lauterpacht, *International Bill of Rights of Man*: 137–38; 140.

52. L Minutes 3, October 22, 1942: 6 and L Minutes 5, November 5, 1942: 9 in Box 72, Notter Files.

53. Commission to Study the Organization of the Peace, *Fourth Report, Part III: International Safeguard of Human Rights* (May 1944): 21.

54. "Address by Walter White Closing the NAACP Conference in Chicago," July 16, 1944, Reel 19, *The Papers of Eleanor Roosevelt, 1933–1945*.

55. On the NAACP's wartime concern with human rights, see Carol Anderson, *Eyes off the Prize: The United Nations and the African American Struggle for Human Rights, 1944–1955* (Cambridge: Cambridge University Press, 2003): 8–57.

56. Lauterpacht, *International Bill of Rights of Man*: 119, 120; L Minutes 5, November 5, 1942, Box 72, Notter Files: 6. Katherine M. Marino has begun to recover the connections between transnational feminism and international protections for women's rights in this period in her "Transnational Pan-American Feminism: The Friendship of Bertha Lutz and Mary Wilhelmine Williams, 1926–1944," *Journal of Women's History* 26.2 (Summer 2014): 63–87 and "Marta Vergara, Popular-Front Pan-American Feminism and the Transnational Struggle for Working Women's Rights in the 1930s," *Gender & History* 26.3 (November 2014): 642–60.

57. George A. Finch, "The International Rights of Man," *American Journal of International Law* 35.4 (October 1941): 663–64; Sohn, "American International Lawyers": 541–46; and Jan Herman Burgers, "The Road to San Francisco: The Revival of the Human Rights Idea in the Twentieth Century," *Human Rights Quarterly* 14 (1992): 450–54.

58. Lauterpacht, *International Bill of Rights of Man*: vi, 82.

59. Wright, *Human Rights and World Order*: 14; American Jewish Committee, *Protection of Human Rights*: 7.

60. Jessup quote in Committee to Study the Organization of the Peace, *International Safe-guard of Human Rights* (1944): 16; Hans Kelsen, *Peace through Law* (Chapel Hill: University of North Carolina Press, 1944): 41–42. See also Beryl Levy, "Justice and Human Rights," *Bulletin of the Committee to Study the Organization of the Peace* (December 1943): 14–16.

61. Nicolas Politis, *New Aspects of International Law* (Washington, DC: Carnegie Endowment for International Peace, 1928): 31. The growing interwar consensus about the legal personality of the individual under international law also emerges in Hersch Lauterpacht, *Private Law Sources and Analogies of International Law* (New York: Longmans, 1927), Quincy Wright, *Research in International Law since the War* (Washington, DC: Carnegie Endowment for International Peace, 1930), John Fischer Williams, *Aspects of Modern International Law* (New York: Oxford University Press, 1939); and Han Aufricht, "Personality in International Law," *American Political Science Review* 37.2 (April 1944): 217–43.

62. "Principles for the International Law of the Future," *American Journal of International Law* 38.2, Supplement: Office Documents (April 1944): 74, 76.

63. U.S. Department of State Subcommittee on Postwar Legal Problems, "Bill of Rights: International Implementations," L Document 30, November 4, 1942; and L Minutes 3, October 22, 1942: 8–10 in Box 72, Notter Files.

64. Quincy Wright, "Protection of Human Rights": 8.

65. The wartime consensus is most fully articulated in Quincy Wright, "Human Rights: Protections for the Individual, Address given March 9, 1944, at the New School for Social Research, New York City," Folder: "Human Rights," Box 83, Addenda 1, Quincy Wright Papers.

66. Lauterpacht, *International Bill of Rights of Man*: 9, 170. American Jewish Committee, *Protection of Human Rights*: 18.

67. Committee to Study the Organization of the Peace, *International Safeguards on Human Rights* (1944): 20.

68. The marginal place of human rights at Dumbarton Oak has been explained as the result of Soviet and British pressures or as evidence of a broader American official caution against human rights issues. On the former, see Robert C. Hilderbrand, *Dumbarton Oaks: The Origins of the United Nations and the Search for Postwar Security* (Chapel Hill: University of North Carolina Press, 1990): 86–93; Borgwardt, *New Deal for the World*: 262. For the latter see, Brucken, *A Most Uncertain Crusade*: 59–70.

CHAPTER 3: BEYOND BELIEF

1. I borrow this phrase from Deborah E. Lipstadt, *Beyond Belief: The American Press and the Coming of the Holocaust, 1933–1945* (New York: Free Press, 1986). My broader thinking about Holocaust photography and human rights in this chapter is influenced by Barbie Zelizer, *Remembering to Forget: Holocaust Memory through the Camera Eye* (Chicago: University of Chicago Press, 1998); Janina Struk, *Photographing the Holocaust: Interpretations of*

the Evidence (London: I. B. Tauris, 2004): 124–49; and Sharon Sliwinski, *Human Rights in Camera* (Chicago: University of Chicago Press, 2011): 83–110.

2. *New York Times*, December 15, 1944: 10.

3. *New York Times*, April 23, 1944: 11; *New York Times*, March 19, 1943: 1; Ronald W. Pruessen, *John Foster Dulles: The Road to Power* (New York: Free Press, 1982): 190–217; and Roland Brucken, *A Most Uncertain Crusade: The United States, the United Nations and Human Rights, 1941–53* (DeKalb: Northern Illinois University Press, 2014): 66–67. For a useful framing of the broader Protestant engagement in wartime internationalism, see David A. Hollinger, "The Realist-Pacifist Summit Meeting of March 1942 and the Political Reorientation of Ecumenical Protestantism in the United States," in his *After Cloven Tongues of Fire: Protestant Liberalism in Modern American History* (Princeton: Princeton University Press, 2013): 56–81.

4. "Catholic Association for International Peace: Report of Several Committees, Washington, 1941" in *War and Peace Aims of the United Nations* (September 1, 1939–December 31, 1942), Louise W. Holborn and Hajo Holborn, eds. (Boston: World Peace Foundation, 1943): 631, 633; Jacques Maritain, *The Natural Law and Human Rights* (Windsor: Christian Culture Press, 1942); *New York Times*, April 15, 1945: 7; and more broadly Samuel Moyn, *Christian Human Rights* (Philadelphia: University of Pennsylvania Press, 2015).

5. James Loeffler, "'Conscience of America': Human Rights, Jewish Politics, and the American Policy at the 1945 San Francisco Conference," *Journal of American History* 100. 2 (September 2013): 403, 405–12; and Loeffler, "The Particularist Pursuit of American Universalism: The American Jewish Committee's 1944 'Declaration of Human Rights,'" *Journal of Contemporary History* 50.2 (October 2014): 274–95. American Jewish Committee staffer Morris Waldman's November 19, 1944, article in the *New York Times Magazine*, "A Bill of Rights for All Nations," conveys the burden of the organization's arguments for an international bill of human rights.

6. On the larger patterns of these interfaith efforts, see Wendy L. Wall, *Inventing the "American Way": The Politics of Consensus from the New Deal to the Civil Rights Movement* (New York: Oxford University Press, 2008): 133–48.

7. *Report of the American Delegation of the United States of America to the Inter-American Conference on the Problems of War and Peace* (U.S. Department of State Publication Number 2497, 1946): 141, 14–15, 142–44; Political Memorandum No. 4, February 7, 1945, in *Foreign Relations of the United States 1945, Vol. 9, The American Republics* (Washington, DC: U.S. Government Printing Office: 1969): 92; Harley Notter, *Postwar Foreign Policy Preparation, 1939–1945* (Washington, DC: U.S. Government Printing Office, 1949): 398–407. See also Brucken, *A Most Uncertain Crusade:* 71–72.

8. Clark M. Eichelberger, *Organizing for Peace: A Personal History of the Founding of the United Nations* (New York: Harper & Row, 1977): 253; Dorothy B. Robins, *Experiment in Democracy: The Story of U.S. Citizen Organizations in Forging the Charter of the United Nations* (New York: Parkside Press, 1971): 63–64; "American Jewish Committee Leaders Present Postwar Program to President Roosevelt," War and Peace File, AJC Subject File, Correspondence and Memoranda on AJC's Post-War Program, American Jewish Committee Internet Archives.

9. *Chicago Tribune*, April 18, 1945: 7 and April 23, 1945: 4; *Los Angeles Times*, April 15, 1945: 4; and *Washington Post*, April 19, 1945: 2.

10. *Chicago Tribune*, April 25, 1945: 1.

11. Zelizer, *Remembering to Forget*: 86–140.

12. New York Times, May 2, 1945: 3.

13. *St. Louis Post-Dispatch*, May 31, June 20, and June 24, 1945; Library of Congress, *Lest We Forget* (Washington, DC: U.S. Government Printing Office, 1945).

14. "Interview with John Henry Baker Jr. on Ohrdurf," February 27, 1980, Fred R. Crawford Witness to the Holocaust Project, Emory University cited in Zelizer, *Remembering to Forget*: 133. The Crawford Witness Project contains numerous oral histories with soldiers involved in the liberation as well as copies of some of their photographs (http://sage .library.emory.edu/data1/findaids/0608_fa.html#case).

15. See, for instance, Paul Gordon Lauren, *The Evolution of International Human Rights: Visions Seen* (Philadelphia: University of Pennsylvania Press 1998): 291; and Michael Ignatieff, *Human Rights as Politics and Idolatry* (Princeton: Princeton University Press, 2001): 5. For especially thoughtful considerations of connections between 1940s-era human rights talk and the Holocaust, see G. Daniel Cohen, "The Holocaust and the 'Human Rights Revolution': A Reassessment," in *The Human Rights Revolution: An International History*, Akira Iriye, Petra Goedde, and William I. Hitchcock, eds. (New York: Oxford University Press, 2011: 53–72; and Marco Duranti, "The Holocaust, the Legacy of 1789 and the Birth of International Human Rights Law: Revisiting the Foundational Myth," *Journal of Genocide Research* 14.2 (June 2012): 159–86. As Hasia Diner makes clear, American Jewish memory has a quite different history; see her *We Remember with Reverence and Love: American Jews and the Myth of Silence after the Holocaust, 1945–1962* (New York: NYU Press, 2010).

16. The *New York Times* was especially reluctant to contextual the Jewish dimensions of the atrocity photographs, as Laurel Leff makes clear in her *Buried by the* Times*: The Holocaust and America's Most Important Newspaper* (Cambridge: Cambridge University Press, 2005): 294–318.

17. Zelizer, *Remembering to Forget*: 93, 98, 49–85.

18. *Baltimore Sun*, April 9, 1945: 1; *New York Times*, April 20, 1945: 3; Edward R. Morrow, "For Most of It I Have No Words," Buchenwald, April 15, 1945, in *Reporting World War II, Part Two: American Journalism 1944–46* (New York: Library of America, 1995): 681–85.

19. Zelizer, *Remembering to Forget*: 64.

20. *St. Louis Post-Dispatch*, May 31, 1945.

21. *Time*, April 30, 1945: 38–46; *Life*, May 7, 1945: 32–37. See also Harold Denny, "The World Must Not Forget," *New York Times Magazine*, May 6, 1945. In my survey of the coverage by four newspapers (*Chicago Tribune, Los Angeles Tribune, New York Times*, and *Washington Post*) between April and June 1945, at least 60 percent of their stories and photographs on the Nazi camps appeared during this two-week period.

22. On the presence of the consultants at the conference and State Department concerns about public opinion, see Robert A. Divine, *Second Chance: The Triumph of Internationalism in American during World War II* (New York: Atheneum, 1967): 279–98; Lukas Haynes and Michael Ignatieff, *Mobilizing Public Support for the United Nations* (Harvard

University Center for Public Leadership Working Paper, 2003); and Andrew Johnstone, "Creating a 'Democratic Foreign Policy': The State Department's Division of Public Liaison and Public Opinion, 1944–1953," *Diplomatic History* 35.3 (June 2011): 483–503.

23. "Letter submitted to Secretary of Stettinius by Consultants Regarding Human Rights," May 2, 1945, in Robins, *Experiment in Democracy*: 218–21.

24. Joseph M. Proskauer, *A Segment of My Time* (New York: Farrar, Straus and Giroux 1950): 224–25. For a careful parsing of Proskauer's speech, see Loefller, "The Conscience of America": 416–17.

25. "Minutes of the Twenty-Sixth Meeting of the United States Delegation, San Francisco, May 2, 1945," *Foreign Relations of the United States 1945: General, United Nations* (Washington, DC: U.S. Government Printing Office, 1967): 532, 534.

26. Compare William Korey, *NGOS and the Universal Declaration of Human Rights: "A Curious Grapevine"* (New York: St. Martin's Press, 1998): 29–42 and Lauren, *The Evolution of International Human Rights*: 179–80 to Kristen Sellars, *The Rise and Rise of Human Rights* (Stroud: Sutton Publishing, 2002): 4–5 and Elizabeth Borgwardt, *A New Deal for the World: America's Vision for Human Rights* (Cambridge, MA: Harvard University Press, 2005): 189–91.

27. See discussion at Fifth Meeting of the U.S. Delegation, Washington, DC, April 9, 1945, *FRUS, UN 1945*: 220, 251.

28. On the critical importance of the domestic political context in understanding the motivations of the American Jewish Committee at this meeting, see Loeffler, "The Conscience of America": 422–23, 427–28.

29. Lauren, *The Evolution of International Human Rights*: 187–88, 190.

30. *FRUS 1945 United Nations*: 533.

31. Secretary of State Stettinius, "Provisions on Human Rights," May 15, 1945, in *Department of State Bulletin* (May 20, 1945): 928.

32. Oscar Cox, "United Nations Conference Forum," ABC Radio, June 1945, transcript reprinted in *Free World* 10.1 (July 1945): 32.

33. *The Committee Reporter* (AJC), 2.7 (July 1945): 5; "Harry S. Truman Address at the Closing Session of the United Nations Conference," June 26, 1945, in *Public Papers of the Presidents of the United States: Harry S. Truman*, Vol. 1 (Washington, DC: U.S. Government Printing Office, 1961): 142. See also Edward R. Stettinius Jr., "Human Rights in the United Nations Charter," and Henri Bonnet, "Human Rights are Basic to the Success of the United Nations," *Annals of the American Academy of Political and Social Science* 243 (January 1946): 1–3, 6–7.

34. Fifth Meeting of the U.S. Delegation, Washington, DC, April 9, 1945, in *Foreign Relations of the United States, United Nations 1945*: 220, 251; Arthur Vandenberg, *The Private Papers of Senator Vandenberg* (Boston: Houghton Mifflin, 1952): 185.

35. Minutes of the Third Four-Power Consultative Meeting on Charter Proposals, San Francisco, May 3, 1945, in *FRUS, United Nations 1945*: 581; and *The Rotarian* (May 1945): 10. For the national United Nations Charter Week in November 1945, Rotary International prepared a booklet *From Here On!* for its members that highlighted the critical role of human rights in the Charter.

36. *The Charter of the United Nations: Hearings before the Committee on Foreign Relations, United States Senate*: 462, 511, 520, 561, 572.

37. Standard Oil Company of New Jersey, *Annual Report for 1946*: 3, quoted in Arthur N. Holcombe, *Human Rights in the Modern World* (New York: New York University Press, 1948): 1. For a critical history of global corporate social responsibility see the contributors to *Corporate Social Responsibility? Human Rights in the New Global Economy*, Charlotte Walker-Said and John D. Kelly, eds. (Chicago: University of Chicago Press, 2015).

38. Han Kelsen, "The Preamble of the Charter – A Critical Analysis," *Journal of Politics* 8.2 (May 1946): 148; Kelsen, "Limits and Function of the United Nations," *Yale Law Journal* 55.5 (August 1946): 1007; and Philip C. Jessup, "Review of *An International Bill of Rights* by H. Lauterpacht," *American Journal of International Law* 39.4 (October 1945): 847.

39. Articles 2.7 and 56, *United Nations Charter* (www.un.org/en/documents/charter/).

40. On the lynching postcards and their uses, see John Lewis et al., *Without Sanctuary: Lynching Photography in America* (Santa Fe: Twin Palms Publishers, 2004); and Jacqueline Goldsby, *A Spectacular Secret: Lynching in American Life and Literature* (Chicago: University of Chicago Press, 2006): 214–81. The August 1930 lynching in Marion, Indiana, is dissected in James H. Madison, *A Lynching in the Heartland: Race and Memory in America* (New York: Palgrave Macmillan, 2003).

41. Thomas J. Sugrue, *The Origins of the Urban Crisis: Race and Inequality in Postwar Detroit* (Princeton: Princeton University Press, 1997); and Martha Biondi, *To Stand and Fight: The Struggle for Civil Rights in Postwar New York City* (Cambridge, MA: Harvard University Press, 2006).

42. On Harrington's cartoon and its broader context, see M. Thomas Inge, ed., *Dark Laughter: The Satiric Art of Oliver W. Harrington* (Jackson: University Press of Mississippi, 1993): xxiii–xxiv.

43. Jasmine Alinder, *Moving Images: Photography and the Japanese American Incarceration* (Urbana: University of Illinois Press, 2009): 15. See also Linda Gordon and Gary Y. Okihiro, eds., *Impounded: Dorothea Lange and the Censored Images of Japanese American Interment* (New York: Norton: 2006). On the internment see Greg Robinson, *By the Order of the President: FDR and the Internment of Japanese Americans* (Cambridge, MA: Harvard University Press, 2001); and Roger Daniels, *Prisoners without Trial: Japanese Americans in World War II* (New York: Hill and Wang, 1993).

44. Article 1, *United Nations Charter* (www.un.org/en/documents/charter/). On the possibilities of interracial alliances between African Americans and Japanese Americans in the wartime and immediate postwar periods, see Matthew M. Briones, *Jim and Jap Crow: A Cultural History of 1940s Interracial America* (Princeton: Princeton University Press, 2012).

CHAPTER 4: CONDITIONS OF POSSIBILITY

1. My discussion of the particulars of the McGhee case relies on *Sipes* v. *McGhee*, 316 Mich. 614, 25 N.W.2d 638; and Clement E. Vose, *Caucasians Only: The Supreme Court, the*

NAACP, and the Restrictive Covenant Cases (Berkeley: University of California Press, 1959): ch. 6.

2. "Brief for the Appellants, *Sipes* v. *McGhee*," which reproduces the decision of the Ontario High Court *In Re Drummond Wren* (4 D.L.R. 1945) in Appendix B; "Brief for National Association for Advancement of Colored Peoples as *amicus curiae, Sipes* v. *McGhee*"; "Brief for Wolverine Bar Association as *amicus curiae, Sipes* v. *McGhee*"; State of Michigan Archives, Lansing, Michigan.

3. My consideration of the particulars of the Oyama case is informed by *Oyama* v. *California*, 29 Cal.2d 164, 173 P.2d 794; *Oyama* v. *California*, 332 U.S. 633; and Frank F. Chuman, *The Bamboo People: The Law and Japanese Americans* (Del Mar, CA: Publishers Inc., 1976): ch. 12.

4. "Brief for the Petitioners, *Oyama* v. *California*," California State Archives, Sacramento, California.

5. "Brief for the Japanese American Citizens League as *amicus curiae, Oyama* v. *California*"; Folder 2, Box 539, Frank F. Chuman Papers, Special Collections, Young Research Library, University of California at Los Angeles. Brief for ACLU as *amicus curiae, Oyama* v. *California*, California State Archives.

6. In addition to *Sipes* and *Oyama*, among them are *Barrows* v. *Jackson*, 346 U.S. 249 (1953), *Bob-Lo Excursion Co.* v. *Michigan*, 333 U.S. 28 (1948), *Bolling* v. *Sharpe*, 347 U.S. 497 (1954), *Henderson* v. *United States*, 339 U.S. 816 (1950), *Hurd* v. *Hodge*, 82 U.S. App. DC 180, 162 F.2d 233, *Namba* v. *McCourt*, 185 Ore. 579, 204 P.2d 569, *Sei Fujii* v. *California*, Superior Court of Los Angeles County, 24 April 1950, *Shelley* v. *Kraemer*, 355 Mo. 814, 198 S.W.2d 679, *Stainback* v. *Mo Hock Ke Lok Po*, 336 U.S. 368 (1949), *Sweatt* v. *Painter*, 339 U.S. 629 (1950), and *Takahashi* v. *Fish & Game Commission*, 334 U.S. 410 (1948). These cases were first examined in Bert J. Lockwood Jr., "The United Nations Charter and United States Civil Rights Litigation: 1946–1955," *Iowa Law Review* 69 (1983–84): 901–56, whose essay is foundational for my own thinking about them.

7. On postwar internationalism outside a Cold War frame, see James T. Sparrow, *Warfare State: World War II Americans and the Age of Big Government* (New York: Oxford University Press, 2011); Elizabeth Borgwardt, *A New Deal for the World: America's Vision for Human Rights* (Cambridge, MA: Harvard University Press, 2005); and Robert Latham, *The Liberal Moment: Modernity, Security and the Making of Postwar International Order* (New York: Columbia University Press, 1997).

8. More canonical accounts of this period, despite differing interpretative emphases, that read it against a long *durée* history of cold war, include John Lewis Gaddis, *The Cold War: A New History* (New York: Penguin Press, 2005); Melvyn Leffler, *Preponderance of Power: National Security, the Truman Administration, and the Cold War* (Stanford: Stanford University Press, 1992); and Odd Arne Westad, *The Global Cold War: Third World Interventions and the Making of Our Times* (New York: Cambridge University Press, 2005).

9. My emphasis on a contingent and decentered understanding of the Cold War in this period is influenced by Masuda Hajimu, *Cold War Crucible: The Korean Conflict and the Postwar World* (Cambridge, MA: Harvard University Press, 2014); and Heonik Kwon, *The Other Cold War* (New York: Columbia University Press, 2010).

10. On the making of the Universal Declaration, see Mary Ann Glendon, *A World Made New: Eleanor Roosevelt and the Universal Declaration of Human Rights* (New York: Random House, 2002); and Johannes Morsink, *The Universal Declaration of Human Rights: Origins, Drafting and Intent* (Philadelphia: University of Pennsylvania Press, 2000). Malek cited in Glendon, *A World Made New.* 164.

11. For the American Declaration, which has not yet received sustained attention by historians, see *Project of the International Rights and Duties of Man* (Washington, DC: Pan American Union, 1948); and *Ninth International Conference of American States, Bogota, Columbia March 30–May 2, 1948: Report of the American Delegation* (Washington, DC: U.S. Department of State Office of Public Affairs, 1948). For two contrasting approaches to the making of the European Convention on Human Rights, see A. W. Brian Simpson, *Human Rights and the End of Empire: Britain and the Genesis of the European Convention* (Oxford: Oxford University Press, 2001); and Marco Duranti, *Human Rights and Conservative Politics in Postwar Europe* (New York: Oxford University Press, 2015).

12. On the genocide convention, see Samantha Power, *A Problem from Hell: America and the Age of Genocide* (New York: Basic Books, 2002): chs. 2–4; and John Cooper, *Raphael Lemkin and the Struggle for the Genocide Convention* (London: Palgrave Macmillan, 2008). On the freedom of information covenant, see Kenneth Cmeil, "Human Rights, Freedom of Information, and the Origins of Third-World Solidarity," in *Truth Claims: Representation and Human Rights,* Mark Philip Bradley and Patrice Petro, eds. (New Brunswick: Rutgers University Press, 2002): 107–30. On refugees and statelessness, see Gerald Daniel Cohen, *In War's Wake: Europe's Displaced Persons in the Postwar World* (New York: Oxford University Press, 2012); and Linda K. Kerber, "Statelessness as the Citizen's Other: A View from the United States," *American Historical Review* 112.1 (February 2007): 1–34.

13. Jean S. Pictet, *Commentary on the Geneva Convention Relative to the Protection of Civilian Person in Time of War* (Geneva: International Committee of the Red Cross, 1958): 12, 26; cited in William A. Hitchcock, "Human Rights and the Laws of War: The Geneva Conventions of 1949," in *The Human Rights Revolution,* Akira Iriye et al., eds. (Oxford: Oxford University Press, 2012): 97, 103. My discussion here is informed by Hitchcock's analysis.

14. International Military Tribunal, *Trial of Major War Criminals before the International Military Tribunal, Nuremberg, 14 November 1945 – October 1946 [TWC]* (Buffalo: Hein &Co., 2001), 1: 57.

15. Ibid., 11: 941.

16. On the Nuremberg trial, Elizabeth Borgwardt's much anticipated book, *The Nuremberg Idea,* will be transformative, but Telford Taylor's first-person account, *The Anatomy of the Nuremberg Trials* (New York: Alfred A. Knopf, 1992), remains important, as does Geoffrey Robinson's *Crimes against Humanity: The Struggle for Global Justice* (New York: New Press, 2000); and Arieh Kochavi, *Prelude to Nuremberg: Allied War Crimes Policy and the Questions of Punishment* (Chapel Hill: University of North Carolina Press, 1998). On the Soviet dimension see Francine Hirsch, "The Soviets at Nuremberg: International Law,

Propaganda and Postwar Order," *American Historical Review* 113.3 (June 2008): 701–30.

17. On the Tokyo trials, see Yuma Totani, *The Tokyo War Crimes Trial: The Pursuit of Justice in the Wake of World War II* (Cambridge, MA: Harvard University Press, 2008); and Timothy Brook, "The Tokyo Judgment and the Rape of Nanking," *Journal of Asian Studies* 60.3 (August 2001): 673–700.

18. Jacquelyn Dowd Hall, "The Long Civil Rights Movement and the Political Uses of the Past," *Journal of American History* 91.4 (March 2005): 1233–63; and Risa Goluboff, *The Lost Origins of Civil Rights* (Cambridge, MA: Harvard University Press, 2007). See also Mary Dudziak, *Cold War Civil Rights: Race and the Image of American Democracy* (Princeton: Princeton University Press, 2010); Thomas Borstelmann, *The Cold War and the Color Line: American Race Relations in the Global Arena* (Cambridge, MA: Harvard University Press, 2002); Penny Von Eschen, *Race against Empire: Black Americans and Anticolonialism, 1937–1957* (Ithaca: Cornell University Press, 1997); and Zaragosa Vargas, *Labor Rights Are Civil Rights: Mexican American Workers in Twentieth-Century America* (Princeton: Princeton University Press, 2005).

19. Minutes of Meeting, "NAACP Lawyers and Consultants on Methods of Attacking Restrictive Covenants," Chicago, July, 9–10, 1945, Papers of the NAACP. On these broader conversations, see Minutes, "Conference on Restrictive Covenants hold at Howard University," January 26, 1946, Reel 21, Part 5: The Campaign Against Residential Segregation, 1914–1955, Papers of the NAACP; Minutes, Joint Committee of American Agencies on Human Rights, January 15, 1947, Folder 2, Box 1149, Papers of the American Civil Liberties Union, Mudd Manuscript Library, Princeton University.

20. Among them see Harold I. Kahen, "Validity of Anti-Negro Restrictive Covenants: A Reconsideration of the Problem," *University of Chicago Law Review* 12.2 (February 1945): 198–213; D.O. McGovney, "Racial Residential Segregation by State Court Enforcement of Restrictive Agreements, Covenants or Conditions in Deeds Is Unconstitutional," *California Law Review* 33 (March 1945): 5–39; Charles Abrams, "Homes for Aryans Only," *Commentary* (May 1947): 421–27; "Note: Anti-Discrimination Legislation and International Declarations as Evidence of Public Policy against Racial Restrictive Covenants," *University of Chicago Law Review* 13.4 (June 1946): 477–86; Sidney A. Jones Jr., "Legality of Race Restrictive Covenants," *National Bar Journal* 4 (March 1946): 14; Robert S. Hunt, "The Alien Land Laws: A Reappraisal," *Yale Law Journal* (June 1947): 1017, 1033–34 Paul Sayre, "*Shelley* v. *Kraemer* and United Nations Law," *Iowa Law Review* 34 (November 1948): 1–11; and Milton R. Konvitz, *The Alien and the Asiatic in American Law* (Ithaca: Cornell University Press, 1946): ch. 1 and passim.

21. On *In Re Drummond Wren* (4 D.L.R. 1945) as "landmark," see Paul Sayre, "United Nations Law," *Canadian Bar Review* 25.8 (October 1947): 821; and Canadian Jewish Congress, *A Victory for Democracy: The Crucial Decision of Mr. Justice Mackey in Supreme Court of Ontario Declaring Void a Restrictive Land Covenant* (Toronto: Canadian Jewish Committee, 1945). On this period in Canadian human rights history, see Dominique Clément, *Canada's Rights Revolution: Social Movements and Social Change, 1937–82* (Vancouver: University of British Columbia Press, 2008): ch. 3.

22. Nonstate organizations filed briefs with UN Charter claims in the following cases: *Bob-Lo Excursion Co. v. Michigan* (NAACP, ACLU, National Lawyers Guild); *Henderson* v. *United States* (American Veterans Committee); *Hurd* v. *Hodge* (NAACP, Japanese American Citizens League); *Oyama* v. *California* (ACLU, National Lawyer's Guild); *Shelley* v. *Kraemer* (NAACP, Civil Liberties Department of the Grand Lodge of Elks, National Lawyers Guild, B'nai B'rith, American Indian Citizens League of California, ACLU, American Association for the United Nations, American Unitarian Association, Congress of Industrial Organizations); *Sweatt* v. *Painter* (American Jewish Committee, B'nai B'rith); and *Takahashi* v. *Fish and Game Commission* (NAACP, American Veterans Committee, American Jewish Congress, National Lawyers Guild, ACLU).

23. Nanette Dembtiz to Osmond K. Fraenkel, February 15, 1947, Folder 18, Box 558, ACLU Papers. The coordination between the ALCU, NAACP, National Lawyer's Guild, the American Jewish Committee, and the Japanese American Citizens League emerges in correspondence on the African American and Japanese American rights cases in Folder 19, Box 558; Folder 11, Box 559; Folder 21, Box 563; Folder 1, Box 565; Folder 4, Box 1055; and Folder 8, Box 1099, ACLU Archives.

24. "Brief for the National Association for the Advancement of Colored People as *amicus curiae, Bob–Lo Excursion Company* v. *Michigan*": 12–13; and "Brief for the American Civil Liberties Union as *amicus curiae, Oyama* v. *California*": 13–14 in Folder 19, Box 558, ACLU Papers.

25. *To Secure These Rights: The Report of the President's Committee on Civil Rights* (New York: Simon and Schuster, 1947): 110–12. See also Proceedings of the Committee-Transcripts, Boxes 14–16, Records of the President's Committee on Civil Rights, Record Group 220, Harry S. Truman Library.

26. Brief for the United States as *Amicus Curiae, Shelley* v. *Kraemer, et al*, December 1947, in Tom Campbell Clark et al., *Prejudice and Property: An Historic Brief against Racial Covenants* (Washington, DC: Public Affairs Press, 1948): 70–74.

27. Gross to Clark, November 4, 1947, Box 89, Office of the Legal Advisor, Division of United Nations Affairs, 1945–59, U.S. Department of State, Lot File 62D204, National Archives, Washington, DC. On the broader sensitivities of the postwar American state to international opinion on domestic racial questions and its impact on policy making, see Dudziak, *Cold War Civil Rights*; and Borstelmann, *The Cold War and the Color Line*: 45–135.

28. National Association for the Advancement of Colored People, *An Appeal to the World!: A Statement on the Denial of Human Rights to Minorities in the Case of Citizens of Negro Descent in the United States of America and an Appeal to the United Nations for Redress* (New York: NAACP, 1947): 12, 13. On this NAACP effort see Carol Anderson, *Eyes off the Prize: The United Nations and the African American Struggle for Human Rights, 1944–1955* (Cambridge: Cambridge University Press, 2003): 92–96, 101–12, 146–49.

29. Carol Solberg, *Hubert Humphrey: A Biography* (New York: W. W. Norton & Company, 1984): 17–18; Hubert H. Humphrey, *The Education of a Public Man: My Life and Politics* (New York: Doubleday & Company, 1976): 110–117; Robert Caro, *Master of the Senate* (New York: Alfred A. Knopf, 2002): 439–43.

30. My approach to these opinions is shaped in part by Ronald Dworkin's contention that "legal reasoning is an exercise in constructive interpretation." See his *Law's Empire* (Cambridge, MA: Harvard University Press, 1986).

31. *Sipes* v. *McGhee*, Supreme Court of Michigan, May 3, 1948, 316 Mich. 614, 25 N.W.2d 638.

32. *Hurd* v. *Hodge*, Edgerton dissenting, 82 U.S. App. D.C. 180 (May 26, 1947). Similar arguments were put forward in a concurring opinion by Judge Jesse W. Carter that overturned California's anti-miscegenation law in October 1940; *Perez* v. *Sharp*, Carter concurring, 32 Cal. 2d 77, 198 P. 2d 17 (Cal. 1948). For a lucid discussion of the place of UN Charter human rights language in cases dealing with race and marriage, see Jane Dailey, *Sex and Civil Rights* (Chicago: University of Chicago Press, forthcoming).

33. Frances Levenson to Charles Huston, June 17, 1947, Folder 11, Box 559, ACLU Papers. The Supreme Court commonly granted certiorari, or judicial review, in cases where Edgerton dissented; of the twenty-three dissents it reviewed, the Court made seventeen reversals of decisions he voted against. See Simon Rosensweig, "The Opinions of Judge Edgerton: A Study in the Judicial Process," *Cornell Law Quarterly* 37 (Winter 1952): 149–78. In the event, the Court did overturn *Hurd* in its *Shelley* decision outlawing racial covenants, but it did not take up Edgerton's UN charter arguments; see *Shelley* v. *Kraemer*, 334, U.S. 1 (1948).

34. *Namba* v. *McCourt*, Supreme Court of Oregon, March 29, 1949, 185 Ore. 579, 204 P.2d 569; Oregon State Archives, Salem, Oregon.

35. *Oyama* v. *California*, Black concurring, 332 U.S. 650 (1948).

36. *Oyama* v. *California*, Murphy concurring, 332 U.S. 673 (1948). The draft memorandums of Murphy's concurrence, which changed substantially over time, all reveal the presence, and intensification, of Charter-based human rights arguments; see Folder: "Oyama vs. California (#44)," Subseries: "1947 Term," Supreme Court Case Files, 1939–1948, Roll 138, Frank Murphy Papers, Bentley Historical Library, University of Michigan.

37. *Sei Fujii* v. *California*, Superior Court of Los Angles County, April 24, 1950, pp. 9, 13, 20, 21; California State Archives.

38. *Sei Fujii* v. *California*, on respondent's petition for rehearing, May 22, 1950, pp. 2, 1; California State Archives.

39. Lockwood, "United Nations Charter": 924.

40. U.S. Congress, House of Representatives, 81st Cong., 2nd sess., April 24, 1950, *Congressional Record*, 96: A3108; U.S. Congress, Senate, 81st Cong., 2nd sess., April 28, 1950, *Congressional Record*, 96: 5996.

41. Frank Holman, "Treaty-Law Making: A Blank Check for Writing a New Constitution," *American Bar Association Journal* 36 (September 1950): 788, 787.

42. Manley O. Hudson to Fred N. Howser, April 28, 1950 in *Sei Fujii* v. *California*, State of California Attorney General Petition for Rehearing, May 9, 1950: 5; California State Archives. See also Manley O. Hudson, "Charter Provisions on Human Rights in American Law," *American Journal of International Law* 44 (July 1950): 543–48.

43. Hans Kelsen, *Law of the United Nations* (London: Stevens and Sons, 1951): 100. *New York Times*, May 16, 1950: 27. See also *New York Times*, April 26, 1950: 16 and May 23, 1950: 27; *Washington Post*, April 26, 1950; *Los Angeles Daily Journal*, April 25, 1950; *Newsweek*, May 8, 1950: 31.

44. Frank E. Holman, "An 'International Bill of Rights': Proposals Have Dangerous Implications for U.S." *American Bar Association Journal* 34 (November 1948): 984, 986; and his "Human Rights on Pink Paper," *American Affairs* 11 (January 1949): 18–24; *Documents for Study in the 1949 Series of Regional Group Conferences of the American Bar Association*, February 1949, Folder 6, Box 1150, ACLU Papers; *Report of Special Committee on Peace and Law through the United Nations*, American Bar Association, September 1, 1949; and *Resolutions of the American Bar Association House of Delegates on the Human Rights Covenant and Genocide Convention*, September 8, 1949. See also Holman, "Proposals Affecting So-Called Human Rights," *Contemporary Problems* 14.3 (Summer 1949): 479–89; and his "Treaty Law-Making": 707–10, 787–90; and Carl B. Rix, "Human Rights and International Law: Effect of the Covenant under Our Constitution," *American Bar Association Journal* 35 (July 1949): 551–54, 618–21.

45. For official ABA testimony in opposition to the Genocide Convention, see U.S. Congress, Senate, Subcommittee of the Committee on Foreign Relations, *Genocide Convention Hearings*, 81st Cong., 2nd Sess, 1950: 155–221. For the New York Bar Association and ABA members offering private testimony in support of the convention, see *Genocide Convention Hearings*: 77–79, 230–255. On the ABA Section of International and Comparative Law recommendations favoring the Genocide Convention and the draft Covenant on Human Rights, see their *Report and Recommendations*, September 5, 1949.

46. "Brief Submitted for the United States Committee for the Genocide Convention in Support of Ratification," January 1950, Folder 3, Box 1152, ACLU Papers; E. H. C., "The Declaration of Human Rights, the United Nations Charter and their Effects on the Domestic Law of Human Rights," *Virginia Law Review* 36.8 (December 1950): 1059–1084, quotes on 1084, 1082; Zechariah Chafee Jr., "Some Problems of the Draft International Covenant on Human Rights," *Proceedings of the American Philosophical Society*, 95.3 (October 1951): 471–89, quote on 487; Quincy Wright, "National Courts and Human Rights – The Fujii Case," *American Journal of International Law* 45 (January 1951): 62–82. See also Moses Moskowitz, "Is the UN's Bill of Human Rights Dangerous? A Reply to President Holman," *American Bar Association Journal* 35 (April 1949): 283–88, 358–62; and Chafee Jr., "Federal and State Powers under the UN Covenant on Human Rights," *Wisconsin Law Review* 3 and 4 (1951) 389–473, 400–12.

47. *Congressional Record*, Senate, 1951: 8255, 8261–8262.

48. U.S. Congress, Senate, Committee on the Judiciary, Treaties and Executive Agreements, *Hearings*, 82nd Congress, 2nd session, 1952. See also U.S. Congress, Senate, Committee on the Judiciary, Treaties and Executive Agreements, *Hearings*, 83rd Congress, 1st session, 1953.

49. On the very large literature concerning the Bricker Amendment controversy, see especially Natalie Hevener Kaufman, *Human Rights Treaties and the Senate: A History of Opposition* (Chapel Hill: University of North Carolina Press, 1990): ch. 4; Christopher N. J.

Roberts), *The Contentious History of the International Bill of Human Rights* (Cambridge: Cambridge University Press, 2015): ch. 3; Glenn Mitoma, *Human Rights and the Negotiations of American Power* (Philadelphia: University of Pennsylvania Press, 2013): ch. 5; Roland Brucken, *A Most Uncertain Crusade: The United States, the United Nations and Human Rights, 1941–1953* (DeKalb: Northern Illinois University Press, 2014): chs. 4 and 6; and Duane Tananbaum, *The Bricker Amendment Controversy* (Ithaca: Cornell University Press, 1988). For an important broader discussion of conservative visions of the state and the problematics of American liberal responses to them in the immediate postwar period, see Jonathan Bell, *The Liberal State on Trial: The Cold War and American Politics in the Truman Years* (New York: Columbia University Press, 2004). On the perceived dangers that the UN presented to policies of Jim Crow segregation, see Anderson, *Eyes off the Prize.*

50. Thomas Blom Hansen and Finn Stepputat, *Sovereign Bodies: Citizens, Migrants, and States in the Postcolonial World* (Princeton: Princeton University Press, 2005): 3. See also Giorgio Agamben, *Homo Sacer: Sovereign Power and Bare Life* (Stanford: Stanford University Press, 1988); Judith Butler, *Gender Trouble: Feminism and the Subversion of Identity*, 2nd ed. (New York: Routledge, 2006); and the contributors to *Sovereign Bodies.*

51. The conservative campaign against the Genocide Convention in the Senate hearings on ratification held in 1950 exhibits a similar performance of sovereignty. See U.S. Congress, Senate, Committee on Foreign Relations, *The Genocide Convention: Hearings*, 81st Cong., 2d session, 1950.

52. On Bricker himself, see Richard O. Davies, *Defender of the Old Guard: John Bricker and American Politics* (Columbus: Ohio State University Press, 1993).

53. U.S. Congress, Senate, Committee on the Judiciary, Treaties and Executive Agreements, *Hearings*, 82nd Congress, 2nd session, 1952: 445, 443.

54. Ibid.: 242.

55. U.S. Congress, Senate, Committee on the Judiciary, Treaties and Executive Agreements, *Hearings*, 83rd Congress, 1st session, 1953: 124. On Eisenhower's and Dulles's antipathy to Bricker and the administration's opposition to the Bricker Amendment, see *Foreign Relations of the United States 1952–1954, Vol 1: General, Economic and Political Matters, Part 2* (Washington, DC: U.S. Government Printing Office, 1983): 1768–1858.

56. On this retreat, see Anderson, *Eyes off the Prize*: ch. 5 and Von Eschen, *Race against Empire*: 167–89.

57. *First United Nations General Assembly*, 2nd Part, No. 75: 831. On the Indian case more generally, see Official Records of the General Assembly, *Plenary Meeting of the General Assembly Verbatim Records, 23 October–16 December 1946*: 1006–1061; Official Records of the General Assembly, *Jt. Committee of the First and Sixth Committees Summary Record of Meetings, 21–30 November 1946*; Lorna Lloyd, "'A Most Auspicious Beginning': The 1946 United Nations General Assembly and the Question of the Treatment of Indians in South Africa," *Review of International Studies* 16 (1990): 131–53; and Mark Mazower, *No Enchanted Palace: The End of Empire and the Ideological Origins of the United Nations* (Princeton: Princeton University Press, 2009): ch. 4.

58. Hersch Lauterpacht, "Human Rights, the Charter of the United Nations, and the International Bill of the Rights of Man: A Preliminary Report for the Human Rights

Committee, International Law Association Brussels Conference, 1948": 5, 8, 11, 14, 16, 20, Folder 3, Box 1150, ACLU Papers. Lauterpacht's unpublished report was circulated by the State Department to domestic organizations with human rights interests, including all of those that filed amicus briefs in the various global rights cases; State Department Memo to ACLU, March 25, 1948, Folder 3, Box 1150, ACLU Papers. Lauterpacht's arguments about the elasticity of the domestic jurisdiction clause in practice also emerged in more muted form in Leland M. Goodrich, "The United Nations and Domestic Jurisdiction," *International Organization* 3.1 (February 1949): 14–28; and Goodrich and Edvard Hambro, *Charter of the United Nations: Commentary and Documents* (Boston: World Peace Foundation, 1949): 110–21.

59. Lora Wildenthal, *The Language of Human Rights in West Germany* (Philadelphia: University of Pennsylvania Press, 2012); and Pertti Ahonen, *After the Expulsion: West Germany and Eastern Europe 1945–1990* (New York: Oxford University Press, 2004).

60. Samuel Moyn, *The Last Utopia: Human Rights in History* (Cambridge, MA: Harvard University Press, 2010): 54, 76, 79. See also Duranti, *Human Rights and Conservative Politics*; and Moyn, *Christian Human Rights* (Philadelphia: University of Pennsylvania Press, 2015).

61. Gerald Daniel Cohen, *In War's Wake: Europe's Displaced Persons in the Postwar Order* (New York: Oxford University Press, 2012): 79–99, quote at 83. See also Atina Grossman, *Jews, Germans and Allies: Close Encounters in Occupied Germany* (Princeton: Princeton University Press, 2007).

62. B. V. A. Rölling and C. F. Ruter, eds., *The Tokyo Judgment, The International Military Tribunal for the Far East: 29 April 1946–12 November 1948* (Amsterdam: APA-University Press, 1977): 1232.

63. *TWC*, 3: 970, 4: 467; and Telford Taylor, *Final Report to the Secretary of the Army on the Nuremberg War Crimes Trials* (Buffalo: Hein & Co, 1997): 65 cited in Totani, *Tokyo War Crimes Trial*: 251, 252.

64. Tony Kushner, "'I Want to Go on Living after My Death': The Memory of Anne Frank," in *War and Memory in the Twentieth Century*, Martin Evans and Ken Lunn, eds. (Oxford: Berg, 1997): 17. See also Allen H. Rosenfeld, "Popularization and Memory: The Case of Anne Frank," in *Lessons and Legacies: The Meanings of the Holocaust in a Changing World*, Peter Hayes, ed. (Evanston: Northwestern University Press, 1991): 243–78; and Aniel Levy and Nathan Sznadier, *Holocaust and Memory in the Global Era* (Philadelphia: Temple University Press, 2006): 57–63. For a more general discussion of the universalizing climate that shaped Holocaust memory in the early Cold War period, and one that reads the Frank diary somewhat differently, see Peter Novick, *The Holocaust in American Life* (Boston: Houghton Mifflin, 2000): 85–123.

65. Executive Board, American Anthropological Association, "Statement on Human Rights," *American Anthropologist* 49.4 (Oct.–Dec. 1947): 539–43. See Karen Engle, "From Skepticism to Embrace: Human Rights and the American Anthropological Association," *Human Rights Quarterly* 23.3 (August 2001): 533–47.

66. Mahatma Gandhi, "Letter to Director-General of UNESCO," in *Human Rights: Comments and Interpretations* (New York: Columbia University Press, 1949): 18. The shape

of the broader UNESCO project emerges in Records of the Comité sur le principes philosophiques des droits d'home, 1947–52, Secretariat, UNESCO.

67. For an exceptionally strong critique that sees 1940s UN rights talk as a dangerous extension of Western imperialism, see Roger Normand and Sarah Zaidi, *Human Rights at the United Nations: The Political History of Universal Justice* (Bloomington: Indiana University Press, 2007): chs. 3–6. Thoughtful discussions of the problems of universalism for writing the human rights history of this period emerge in Glenda Sluga, *Internationalism in the Age of Nationalism* (Philadelphia: University of Pennsylvania Press, 2013); Sunil Amrith and Glenda Sluga, "New Histories of the United Nations," *Journal of World History* 19.3 (September 2008): 251–74; and Samuel Moyn, "The First Historian of Human Rights," *American Historical Review* 116.1 (February 2011): 58–79.

68. For a useful discussion of the strategic Cold War deployment of human rights talk by the Soviet Union, see Jennifer Amos, "Embracing and Contesting: The Soviet Union and the Universal Declaration of Human Rights, 1948–1958," in *Human Rights in the Twentieth Century*, Stefan-Ludwig Hoffmann, ed. (Cambridge: Cambridge University Press, 2011): 147–65.

69. Hajimu, *Cold War Crucible*: 7, 200.

70. For concerns over implications of human rights protections for British imperial policy, see Simpson, *Human Rights and the End of Empire.*

71. For the range of competing interpretative perspectives on the relationship between decolonization and global human rights politics within the Global South, see Bradley Simpson, *The First Right: Self-Determination and the Transformation of Post-1941 International Relations* (New York: Oxford University Press, forthcoming); Roland Burke, *Decolonization and the Evolution of International Human Rights* (Philadelphia: University of Pennsylvania Press, 2010); Jan Eckel "Human Rights and Decolonization: New Perspectives and Open Questions," *Humanity* 1.1 (Fall 2010): 111–35; Manu Bhagavan, "A New Hope: India, the United Nations and the Making of the Universal Declaration of Human Rights," *Modern Asian Studies* 44.2 (March 2010): 311–47; Cmiel, "Human Rights, Freedom and the Origins of Third-World Solidarity;" and Moyn, *Last Utopia*: ch. 3.

72. *Rice v. Sioux City Memorial Park Cemetery, Inc.*, 60 N.W. 2d 116–17 (1953). For the particulars of the extralegal dimensions of the case, see Dean J. Kotlowski, "Burying Sergeant Rice: Racial Justice and Native American Rights in the Truman Era," *Journal of American Studies* 38.23 (2004): 199–225.

73. Brief in support of petition for writ of certiorari to the United States Supreme Court at 18–19. The U.S. Supreme Court, after initially suggesting otherwise, declined to hear the case, and it was dismissed in 1955.

74. Daniel M. Cobb, *Native Activism in Cold War America: The Struggle for Sovereignty* (Lawrence: University of Kansas Press, 2010): 30–57; and his "Taking the Language of the Larger World: Politics in Cold War (Native) America," in *Beyond Red Power: American Indian Politics and Activism since 1900*, Daniel M. Cobb and Loretta Fowler, eds. (Santa Fe: School for Advanced Research, 2007): 161–77. On similar concerns with self-determination and collective rights among African Americans and Puerto Ricans, see Anderson, *Eyes off the Prize*; and Lorrin Thomas, *Puerto Rican Citizen: History and Political*

Identity in Twentieth Century New York City (Chicago: University of Chicago Press, 2010).

PART TWO: THE 1970S

1. "Inaugural Address of President Jimmy Carter," January 20, 1977, in *Public Papers of the Presidents, Jimmy Carter 1977, Book 1* (Washington, DC: U.S. Government Printing Office, 1978): 2–3; "Address at Commencement Exercises at the University of Notre Dame, 22 May 1977"; *Public Papers of the Presidents, Jimmy Carter, Book 1*: 958; Joe Aragon to Hamilton Jordan, White House Memorandum, July 7, 1978, in National Security Archive Electronic Briefing Book No. 391 (www.gwu.edu/~nsarchiv/NSAEBB/NSAEBB391/).

2. Barbara Keys, "Kissinger, Congress and the Origins of Human Rights Diplomacy," *Diplomatic History* 34.5 (November 2010): 823–51: and Jussi Hanhimäki, "'They Can Write It in Swahili': Kissinger, the Soviets, and the Helsinki Accords, 1973–75," *Journal of Transatlantic Studies* 1.1 (2003): 37–58. For an alternative perspective arguing that human rights mattered in 1960s America, see Sarah Snyder, "The Rise of Human Rights during the Johnson Years," in *Beyond the Cold War: Lyndon Johnson and the New Global Challenges of the 1960s*, Francis J. Gavin and Mark Atwood Lawrence, eds. (New York: Oxford University Press, 2014): 237–60.

3. On the NAACP retreat, see Carol Anderson, *Eyes off the Prize: The United Nations and the African American Struggle for Human Rights, 1944–1955* (Cambridge: Cambridge University Press, 2003): 254–70, 276.

4. Malcolm X, "The Ballot or the Bullet," April 3, 1964, in *Malcolm X Speaks* (New York: Grove Weidenfeld, 1965): 35; and Thomas F. Jackson, *From Civil Rights to Human Rights: Martin Luther King, Jr. and the Struggle for Economic Justice* (Philadelphia: University of Pennsylvania Press, 2006). African-American civil rights practice in the 1960s was far from monolithic, with dimensions of global human rights thought important especially in the Black Power movement; see J. Timothy Lovelace, "International Legal History from Below: The Civil Rights Movement and the U.S. Origins of the International Convention on the Elimination of All Forms of Racial Discrimination, 1960–1965" (Ph.D. dissertation, University of Virginia, 2012); and Peniel E. Joseph, *Waiting 'til the Midnight Hour: A Narrative History of Black Power in America* (New York: Henry Holt, 2006).

5. Samuel Moyn, "From Antiwar Politics to Anti-Torture Politics," in *Law and War*, Austin Sarat, Douglas Lawrence, and Martha Umphrey, eds. (Stanford: Stanford Law Books, 2014): 154–97; Keys, "Kissinger, Congress and the Origins of Human Rights Diplomacy": 58. By contrast, the U.S. military turned to the language and practices of humanitarianism as a way of remaking itself in the post-Vietnam era; see Jana K. Lipman, "'A Precedent Worth Setting … ' Military Humanitarianism: The U.S. Military and the 1975 Vietnamese Evacuation," *Journal of Military History* 79.1 (January 2015): 151–79.

6. Mark Philip Bradley, "President Jimmy Carter's Inaugural Address," in *The Familiar Made Strange: American Icons and Artifacts after the Transnational Turn*, Brooke L. Blower and Mark Philip Bradley, eds. (Ithaca: Cornell University Press, 2015): 143–44.

7. Jeri Laber, *The Courage of Strangers: Coming of Age with the Human Rights Movement* (New York: PublicAffairs, 2002): 74.

8. Barbara J. Keys, *Reclaiming American Virtue: The Human Rights Revolution of the 1970s* (Cambridge, MA: Harvard University Press, 2014): 14, 8. Along with Keys, perspectives on the Carter era's turn to human rights that emphasize the domestic emerge in Sandy Vogelsang, *American Dream, Global Nightmare: The Dilemma of U.S. Human Rights Politics* (New York: W. W. Norton, 1980); Gaddis Smith, *Morality, Reason and Power: American Diplomacy in the Carter Years* (New York: Hill and Wang, 1986); Joshua Muravchik, *Uncertain Crusade: Jimmy Carter and the Dilemmas of Human Rights Policy* (Lanham, MD: Hamilton Press, 1986); David P. Forsythe, "Human Rights in U.S. Foreign Policy: Retrospect and Prospect," *Political Science Quarterly* 105.3 (Autumn 1990): 435–54; Burton I. Kaufman, *The Presidency of James Earl Carter* (Lawrence: University of Kansas Press, 1993); Scott Kaufman, *Plans Unraveled: The Foreign Policy of the Carter Administration* (DeKalb: Northern Illinois University Press, 2008): 27–46; and Julian E. Zelizer, *Jimmy Carter* (New York: Times Books, 2010): 61–62.

9. My thinking about human rights as a guest language is influenced by Lydia Liu, *Translingual Practice: Literature, National Culture, and Translated Modernity – China, 1900–1937* (Stanford: Stanford University Press, 1995); Carol Gluck and Ann Lowenhaupt Tsing, eds., *Words in Motion: Toward a Global Lexicon* (Durham: Duke University Press, 2009); and Sally Engle Merry, *Human Rights and Gender Violence: Translating International Law into Local Justice* (Chicago: University of Chicago Press, 2005).

10. American historians are only now turning to the seventies as a historical subject. The most useful conceptual overviews of the decade, some of which I build on in these chapters, are Daniel T. Rodgers, *The Age of Fracture* (Cambridge, MA: Harvard University Press, 2011); Daniel J. Sargent, *A Superpower Transformed: The Remaking of American Foreign Relations in the 1970s* (Oxford: Oxford University Press, 2015); Thomas Borstelmann, *The 1970s: A New Global History from Civil Rights to Economic Inequality* (Princeton: Princeton University Press, 2012); and Jefferson Cowie, *Stayin' Alive: The 1970s and the Last Days of the Working Class* (New York: New Press, 2010). On the new histories of the 1970s, see also Judith Stein, *Pivotal Decade: How the United States Traded Factories for Finance in the Seventies* (New Haven: Yale University Press, 2011); Laura Kalman, *Right Star Rising: A New Politics, 1974–1980* (New York: Norton, 2010); and Rick Perlstein, *The Invisible Bridge: The Fall of Nixon and the Rise of Reagan* (New York: Simon & Shuster, 2014).

11. See, for example, Kathryn Sikkink, *Mixed Signals: U.S. Human Rights Policy and Latin America* (Ithaca: Cornell University Press, 2004); William Michael Schmidli, *The Fate of Freedom Elsewhere: Human Rights and U.S. Cold War Policy toward Argentina* (Ithaca: Cornell University Press, 2013); Christian Philip Peterson, "The Carter Administration and the Promotion of Human Rights in the Soviet Union," *Diplomatic History* 38.3 (June 2014): 628–56; Sarah B. Snyder, *Human Rights Activism and the End of the Cold War: A Transnational History of the Helsinki Network* (Cambridge: Cambridge University Press, 2011); Jason M. Colby, "'A Chasm of Values and Outlook': The Carter Administration's Human Rights Policy in Guatemala," *Peace & Change* 35.4 (October 2010): 561–93; and

Kenton Clymer, "Jimmy Carter, Human Rights and Cambodia," *Diplomatic History* 27.1 (April 2003): 245–78.

CHAPTER 5: CIRCULATIONS

1. *Daily Mirror*, December 11, 1961: 1; "Peter Berenson, Typescript Memoir, August 1983," Folder 982, International Secretariat Archives, Amnesty International, International Institute of Social History, Amsterdam, Netherlands; Peter Berenson, "The Forgotten Prisoners," *The Observer* (London), May 28, 1961: 20.
2. Benjamin Nathans, "The Dictatorship of Reason: Alekandr Vol'pin and the Idea of Rights under 'Developed Socialism,'" *Slavic Review* 66.4 (Winter 2007): 653–58; Joshua Rubenstein, *Soviet Dissidents: Their Struggle for Human Rights* (Boston: Beacon Press, 1985): 30–42; Ludmilla Alexeyeva, *Soviet Dissent: Contemporary Movements for National, Religious, and Human Rights* (Middletown, CT: Wesleyan University Press, 1985: 274–77; quotes on 275, 276.
3. "Universal Declaration of Human Rights – Proposals approved at the XIIIth General Assembly of the National Conference of the Bishops of Brazil, 15 March 1973," in *International Protection of Human Rights: Hearings*, Subcommittee on International Organizations and Movements, U.S. House of Representatives, 93rd Cong., 1st Sess. (Washington, DC: U.S. Government Printing Office, 1974): 675–80; Scott Mainwaring, *The Catholic Church and Politics in Brazil, 1916–1985* (Stanford: Stanford University Press, 1986): 99.
4. Amnesty International membership numbers from *Amnesty International Annual Report 1972–73* (London: AI Publications, 1973): 90; and *Amnesty International Annual Report 1980* (London: AI Publications, 1980): 408. On the increase in international local human rights NGOs, see Margaret Keck and Kathryn Sikkink, *Activists without Borders: Advocacy Networks in International Politics* (Ithaca: Cornell University Press, 1998): 11; Human Rights Internet, *Human Rights Directory: Latin America, Asia and Africa* (Washington, DC, 1981) and *Human Rights Directory: Western Europe* (1982).
5. Hakan Thörn, *Anti-Apartheid and the Emergence of a Global Civil Society* (New York: Palgrave Macmillan, 2006); Ryan M. Irwin, *Gordian Knot: Apartheid and the Unmaking of Liberal World Order* (New York: Oxford University Press, 2012); Joshua P. Howe, *Behind the Curve: Science and the Politics of Global Warming* (Seattle: University of Washington Press, 2014): 67–92; and Jean Quataert, *Advocating Dignity: Human Rights Mobilizations in Global Politics* (Philadelphia: University of Pennsylvania Press, 2009): 156–161. On the entanglement of environmental activism with other global social movements, see Christoff Mauch, Nathan Stoltzfus, and Douglas R. Weiner, eds., *Shades of Green: Environmental Activism around the Globe* (Lanham, MD: Rowman & Littlefield, 2006); and Ramachandra Guha, *Environmentalism: A Global History* (New York: Longman Publishing Group, 1999).
6. Akira Iriye, *Global Community: The Role of International Organizations in the Making of the Contemporary World* (Berkeley: University of California Press, 2002): 129. More generally see Iriye, "The Making of a Transnational World," in *Global Interdependence: The World after 1945*, Akira Iriye, ed. (Cambridge, MA: Harvard University Press, 2014): 679–847; and Keck and Sikkink, *Activists without Borders*.

7. See, for instance, John Lewis Gaddis, *The Cold War: A New History* (New York: Penguin Press, 2005).

8. On the intensification of the Cold War in the Global South in the 1970s, see Odd Arne Westad, *The Global Cold War* (Cambridge: Cambridge University Press, 2005).

9. Saskia Sassen, *Territory, Authority, Rights: From Medieval to Global Assemblages* (Princeton: Princeton University Press, 2006): 9, and chs. 4 and 5 passim.

10. My discussion here relies on Daniel J. Sargent: *A Superpower Transformed: The Remaking of American Foreign Relations in the 1970s* (Oxford: Oxford University Press, 2015): 5, 9, 12–13; and chs 1 and 4. On the global dimensions of these transformations, see also Charles Maier, "Consigning the Twentieth Century to History: Alternative Narrative for the Modern Era," *American Historical Review* 105.3 (June 2000): 807–31; and the contributors to Akira Iriye, ed., *Global Interdependence: The World after 1945* (Cambridge, MA: Harvard University Press, 2014).

11. Sassen, *Territory, Authority, Rights*: 17; Anne-Marie Slaughter, *A New World Order* (Princeton: Princeton University Press, 2004); pp. 12–15; Karen J. Alter, "Jurist Advocacy Movements in Europe: The Role of Euro-Law Associations in European Integration (1953–1975)," in her *The European Court's Political Power* (Oxford: Oxford University Press, 2009): 63–91. See also Keck and Sikkink: *Activists without Borders* and Iriye, *Global Interdependence*.

12. Stephen Castles et al., *The Age of Migration: International Population Movements in the Modern World*, 5th ed. (New York: Guilford Press, 2013): 104, 132, 148–53; David Held et al., *Global Transformations: Politics, Economics and Culture* (Stanford: Stanford University Press, 1999): 297–302.

13. My discussion of the broader structural impact of the end of empire draws on John Kelly and Martha Kaplan, *Represented Communities: Fiji and World Decolonization* (Chicago: University of Chicago Press, 2001).

14. On the Indian-Pakistan war that produced the state of Bangladesh and its broader impact, see Srinath Raghavan, *1971: A Global History of the Creation of Bangladesh* (Cambridge, MA: Harvard University Press, 2013); and Gary J. Bass, *The Blood Telegram: Nixon, Kissinger and a Forgotten Genocide* (New York: Alfred A. Knopf, 2013).

15. Astri Suhrke, "Uncertain Globalization: Refugee Movements in the Second Half of the Twentieth Century," in *Global History and Migrations*, Wang Gungwu, ed. (Boulder: Westview Press, 1997): 217–37; Iriye, "Making of a Transnational World": 739–40.

16. On the relationship between empire and the European Convention, see A. W. Brian Simpson, *Human Rights and the End of Empire: Britain and the Genesis of the European Convention* (Oxford: Oxford University Press, 2001).

17. *Global Transformations*: 343, 358, 361; Institute of International Education, *International Students: Enrollment Trends* (www.iie.org/Research-and-Publications/Open-Doors/Data/International-Students/Enrollment-Trends/1948-2012).

18. Marc Levinson, *The Box: How the Shipping Container Made the World Smaller and the World Economy Bigger* (Princeton: Princeton University Press, 2006); Daniel Bernhofen, Zouheir El-Sahli, and Richard Kneller, *Estimating the Effects of the Container Revolution on World Trade*, Lund University Working Paper (February 2013); Jaos Ribas et al., FAX

(New York: Independent Curators International, 2009); Greg Niemann, *Big Brown: The Untold UPS Story* (New York: Jossey-Bass, 2007); Rodger Frock, *Changing How the World Does Business: Fedex's Incredible Journey to Success* (San Francisco: Berrett-Keohler, 2006); and Marshall McLuhan, *Understanding Media: The Extensions of Man* (New York: New American Library, 1964): 6.

19. On this earlier moment of globalization, see the contributors to *A World Connecting: 1879–1945*, edited by Emily Rosenberg (Cambridge, MA: Harvard University Press, 2012).

20. Thomas Piketty, *Capital in the Twenty-First Century* (Cambridge, MA: Harvard University Press, 2014): chs. 7–10 passim; David Harvey, *A Brief History of Neoliberalism* (New York: Oxford University Press, 2007).

21. Sidney Tarrow, *The New Transnational Activism* (Cambridge: Cambridge University Press, 2005): 28–29; Ben Lazier, "Earthrise; or, The Globalization of the World Picture," *American Historical Review* 116.3 (June 2011): 606. See also Robert Poole, *Earthrise: How Man First Saw Earth* (New Haven: Yale University Press, 2008); and Joshua J. Yates, "Mapping the Good World: The New Cosmopolitans and Our Changing World Picture," *Hedgehog Review* 11.3 (Fall 2009): 7–27.

22. Iriye, "Making of a Transnational World": 730. On the range of sensibilities around global social protest in the 1960s, see Philip Gassert and Martin Klimke, eds., *1968: Memories and Legacies of a Global Revolt* (Washington, DC: German Historical Institute, 2009); Jeremi Suri, *Power and Protest: Global Revolution and the Rise of Détente* (Cambridge, MA: Harvard University Press, 2003); Martin Klimke, *The Other Alliance: Student Protest in West Germany and the United States in the Global 1960s* (Princeton: Princeton University Press, 2011); and Richard Ivan Jobs, "AHR Forum: The International 1968, Part I, Japan 1968: The Performance of Violence and the Theater of Protest," *American Historical Review* 114.1 (2009): 97–135.

23. Annette Wieviorka, *The Era of Witness* (Ithaca: Cornell University Press, 2006). On the Eichmann trial, the classic account is Hannah Arendt, *Eichmann in Jerusalem* (New York: Viking Press, 1963), which marshals the emotionality of witness testimony to sustain her critique of it as a show trial. On the Eichmann and other Holocaust trials in this period, see also Deborah Lipstadt, *The Eichmann Trial* (New York: Schocken, 2011); Devin O. Pendas, *The Frankfurt Auschwitz Trial, 1963–1965: Genocide, History, and the Limits of the Law* (Cambridge: Cambridge University Press, 2006); and Daniel Levy and Nathan Sznaider, *Holocaust and Memory in a Global Age* (Philadelphia: Temple University Press, 2005).

24. Lawrence Douglas, *The Memory of Judgment: Making Law and History in the Trials of the Holocaust* (New Haven: Yale University Press, 2005): 103.

25. Wieviorka, *The Era of Witness*: 77, 87. See also Shoshana Felman and Dori Laudb, *Testimony: Crises of Witnessing in Literature, Psychoanalysis, and History* (New York: Routledge, 1992). For a suggestive approach to the imbrications between Holocaust consciousness and expressions of anticolonial claims in the era of decolonization, see Michael Rothberg, *Multidirectional Memory: Remembering the Holocaust in the Age of Decolonization* (Stanford: Stanford University Press, 2009).

26. Didier Fassin, "The Humanitarian Politics of Testimony: Subjectification through Trauma in the Israeli-Palestinian Conflict," *Cultural Anthropology* 23.3 (2008): 532, 539. On the makings of a new humanitarian sensibility, see also Fassin and Richard Rechtman, *The Empire of Trauma: An Inquiry into the Condition of Victimhood* (Princeton: Princeton University Press, 2009); Fassin, *Humanitarian Reason: A Moral History of the Present* (Berkeley: University of California Press, 2011); Ilana Feldman, "The Quaker Way: Ethical Labor and Humanitarian Relief," *American Ethnologist* 34.4 (2007): 689–705; and James Dawes, *That the World May Know: Bearing Witness to Atrocity* (Cambridge, MA: Harvard University Press, 2007).

27. On the Biafran War, see Michael Gould, *The Biafran War: The Struggle for Modern Nigeria* (New York: I. B. Tauris, 2013). On Biafra and human rights, see Lasse Heerten, "The Dystopia of Postcolonial Catastrophe: Self-Determination, the Biafran War of Secession and the 1970s Human Rights Moment," in *The Breakthrough: Human Rights in the 1970s,* Jan Eckel and Samuel Moyn, eds. (Philadelphia: University of Pennsylvania Press, 2014): 14–32; and his "'A' as in Auschwitz, 'B' is in Biafra: The Nigerian Civil War, Visual Narratives of Genocide, the Fragmented Universalism of the Holocaust," in *Humanitarian Photography: A History,* Heide Fehrenbach and Davide Rodogno, eds. (Cambridge: Cambridge University Press: 2015): 249–74.

28. Peter Redfield, *Life in Crisis: The Ethical Journey of Doctors without Borders* (Berkeley: University of California Press, 2013): chs. 2 and 4.

29. Michal Givoni, "Humanitarian Governance and Ethical Cultivation: Médecins sans frontières and Advent of the Expert-Witness," *Millennium* 40.1 (2011): 55 and passim.

30. Frank Zelko, *Make it a Green Peace!: The Rise of Countercultural Environmentalism* (New York: Oxford University Press, 2013): 4, 20–31, 322; and Paul Watson, *Sea Shepherd: My Fight for Whales and Seals* (New York: W. W. Norton, 1982): 93–94 cited in Zelko: 255. The practices of Quaker witness are nicely unpacked in Feldman's "The Quaker Way."

31. Berenson, "The Forgotten Prisoners," *The Observer* (London), 28 May 1961: 20. The best account of Amnesty's early history and practices remains Tom Buchanan, "'The Truth Will Set you Free': The Making of Amnesty International," *Journal of Contemporary History* 37.4 (October 2002): 575–97.

32. "Interview with Peter Berenson," Folder 983, Oral History Project, International Secretariat Archives, Amnesty International; Buchanan: 582. See also Edy Kaufman, "Prisoners of Conscience: The Shaping of a New Human Rights Concept," *Human Rights Quarterly* 13.3 (August 1991): 339–67; and Stephen Hopgood, *Keepers of the Flame: Understanding Amnesty International* (Ithaca: Cornell University Press, 2006): 60–65. The starting point on Amnesty's Campaign against Torture remains Ann Marie Clark, *Diplomacy of Conscience: Amnesty International and Changing Human Rights Norms* (Princeton: Princeton University Press, 2001).

33. Peter Redfield, "A Less Modest Witness: Collective Advocacy and Motivated Truth in a Medical Humanitarian Movement," *American Ethnologist* 33.1 (2006): 5, 17, and passim. See also Michal Givoni, "Beyond the Humanitarian/Political Divide: Witnessing and the Making of Humanitarian Ethics," *Journal of Human Rights* 10 (2011): 55–75.

On the enduring problems of scientific and professional "objectivity," see Loraine Daston and Peter Galison, *Objectivity* (New York: Zone Books, 2007); and Andrew Porter, *Trust in Numbers: The Pursuit of Objectivity in Science and Public Life* (Princeton: Princeton University Press, 1995).

34. Fassin, "Humanitarian Politics": 539.

35. Frank C. Newman, Oral History Interview, Conducted 1989 and 1991 by Carole Hicke, Regional Oral History Office, University of California at Berkeley, for the California State Archives State Government Oral History Program: 283.

36. Ibid.: 285–86, 288–97.

37. *Chile: An Amnesty International Report* (London: Amnesty International, 1974): 7.

38. Ibid.: 57–58.

39. Ibid.: 70–78; Redfield: 13, 18–19.

40. On the broader impact of the Chile campaigns, see Jan Eckel, "'Under a Magnifying Glass': The International Human Rights Crusade against Chile in the Seventies," in *Human Rights in the Twentieth-Century*, Stefan-Ludwig Hoffmann, ed. (Cambridge: Cambridge University Press, 2011): 312–42; and Patrick Kelly, "'Magic Words': The Advent of Human Rights Activism in Latin America's Southern Cone in the 1970s," in Eckel and Moyn, *The Breakthrough*: 88–106.

41. Joan W. Scott, "The Evidence of Experience," *Critical Inquiry* 17 (Summer 1991): 778, 779.

42. Redfield, "Less Modest Witness": 9–10; and Zelko, *Make it a Green Peace!*: 294–315. The tensions between national sections within in Amnesty emerge in "Amnesty International Five Years Hence: Report and Recommendations of the Long Range Planning Committee," May 31, 1972, Folder 438, International Secretariat Archives, Amnesty International, International Institute of Social History, Amsterdam, Netherlands.

43. On the ways in which national environments shaped global activism, see Sarah S. Stroup, *Borders among Activists: International NGOs in the United States, Britain and France* (Ithaca: Cornell University Press, 2012).

44. These figures are based on data gathered from Amnesty International's published annual reports issued from 1970 to 1979.

45. Jocelyn Olcott, "Globalizing Sisterhood: International Women's Year and the Politics of Representation" in *The Shock of the Global: The 1970s in Perspective*, Niall Ferguson et al., eds. (Cambridge, MA: Harvard University Press, 2010): 282–83; and her "Cold War Conflicts and Cheap Cabarets: Sexual Politics at the 1975 United Nations International Women's Year Conference," *Gender & History* 22.3 (November 2010): 733–54.

46. On the articulation of the New International Economic Order and the longer fraught history of the relationship between global rights talk and the postcolonial world, see "Special Issue: Toward a History of the New International Economic Order," *Humanity* 6.1 (Spring 2015); Stephen L. Jensen, *The Making of International Human Rights: The 1960s, Decolonization and the Reconstruction of Global Values* (Cambridge: Cambridge University Press, 2016); Roland Burke, *Decolonization and the Evolution of Human Rights* (Philadelphia: University of Pennsylvania Press, 2010); and Samuel Moyn, *The Last*

Utopia: Human Rights in History (Cambridge, MA: Harvard University Press, 2010): ch. 3.

47. Alexeyeva, *Soviet Dissent*: quote at 274; Nathans, "Dictatorship of Reason": 658–60.

48. For these more conventional narratives, see Rubenstein, *Soviet Dissidents*; Ludmilla Alexeyeva, *Soviet Dissent*; and, more broadly, Marshal Shafts, *Soviet Dissent in Historical Perspective* (Cambridge: Cambridge University Press, 1980).

49. On the Helsinki Accords see Sarah B. Snyder, *Human Rights Activism and the End of the Cold War: A Transnational History of the Helsinki Network* (Cambridge: Cambridge University Press, 2011); and Daniel C. Thomas, *The Helsinki Effect: International Norms, Human Rights and the Demise of Communism*(Princeton: Princeton University Press, 2001).

50. Nathans, "Soviet Dissidents, Human Rights and the New Global Morality," in Eckel and Moyn, *The Breakthrough*: 42, 43.

51. Groupa-73, Moscow to Amnesty International 6th International Council, Vienna, 15 September 1973 cited and translated in Nathans, "Soviet Dissidents": 41.

52. Nathans, "Soviet Dissidents": 41–42.

53. Patrick William Kelly, "Sovereignty and Salvation: Transnational Human Rights Activism in the Long 1970s" (Ph.D. dissertation, University of Chicago, 2015): 40, 43, 57.

54. Ibid.: 45. The complexities of student activism in Brazil more broadly in this period emerge in Victoria Langland, *Speaking of Flowers: Student Movements and the Making and Remembering of 1968 in Military Brazil* (Durham: Duke University Press, 2013).

55. Ingu Hwang, "Making Human Rights Politics in South Korea in the 1970s" (Ph.D. dissertation, University of Chicago, 2015): ch. 2.

56. Brad Simpson, "'Human Rights Are like Coca-Cola': Contested Human Rights Discourses in Suharto's Indonesia, 1968–1980," in Eckel and Moyn, *The Breakthrough*: 186–203; Gregory Mann, *From Empires to NGOs in the West African Sahel* (Cambridge: Cambridge University Press, 2015); Jonathan Bolton, *Worlds of Dissent: Charter 77, the Plastic People of the Universe and Czech Culture under Communism* (Cambridge, MA: Harvard University Press, 2012).

CHAPTER 6: AMERICAN VERNACULARS I

1. Rose Styron, "In Political Prisons: Torture," *New Republic*, December 8, 1973: 21, 17.

2. Jeri Laber, *The Courage of Strangers: Coming of Age with the Human Rights Movement* (New York: PublicAffairs, 2002): 70.

3. *Time*, February 21, 1971: 1; *CBS Evening News*, February 13, 1974, Vanderbilt Television and News Archive; *Washington Post*, November 5, 1973: 28; *Los Angeles Times*, May 26, 1976: 26.

4. These estimates draw on an electronic database search by country of the use of the term "human rights" from 1970 to 1979 in the *New York Times Index* and the Vanderbilt Television News Archive.

5. Daniel Rodgers, *Age of Fracture* (Cambridge, MA: Belknap Press, 2012): 5, and passim.

6. Tom Wolfe, "The 'Me' Decade and the Third Great Awakening," *New York*, August 23, 1976: 26–40. My discussion of authenticity and the therapeutic turn is informed by

Ellen Herman, *The Romance of American Psychology: Political Culture in the Age of Experts* (Berkeley: University of California Press, 1995); Douglas Rossinow, *The Politics of Authenticity: Liberalism, Christianity, and the New Left in America* (New York: Columbia University Press, 1998): 335–46; and Elizabeth Lunbeck, *The Americanization of Narcissism* (Cambridge, MA: Harvard University Press, 2014). The decade's most famous jeremiad against the culture of self-awareness is Christopher Lasch, *The Culture of Narcissism: American Life in an Age of Diminishing Expectations* (New York: Warner Books, 1979).

7. Joseph Veroff et al., *Mental Health in America: Patterns of Help-seeking from 1957–1976* (New York: Basic Books, 1981): 96, 271; Rick Perlstein, *The Invisible Bridge: The Fall of Nixon and the Rise of Reagan* (New York: Simon & Shuster, 2014): 279.

8. Frank Zelko, *Make it a Green Peace!: The Rise of Counterculture Environmentalism* (New York: Oxford University Press, 2013): 45, Frederick S. Perls, *Gestalt Therapy Verbatim* (Lafayette: Real People Press, 1969); and Herman, *The Romance of American Psychology*: 298.

9. Boston Women's Health Collective, *Our Bodies, Ourselves* (New York: Simon and Schuster, 1973): 4. On the history of the book and its growing transnational influence, see Kathy Davis, *The Making of Our Bodies, Ourselves: How Feminism Travels across Borders* (Durham: Duke University Press, 2007).

10. My discussion in this and the previous paragraph is informed by Matthew Frye Jacobson, *Roots Too* (Cambridge, MA: Harvard University Press, 2006): especially 26, 42–46. Jacobson's own analysis of these developments, it should be said, downplays the individual remaking of identities I foreground here, arguing it was a broader project of white political and social backlash in the aftermath of the civil rights movement. On *Roots*, see also Robert J. Norrell, *Alex Haley and the Books that Changed a Nation* (New York: St. Martin's Press, 2015): 141–58.

11. Jesse Hoffnung-Garskof, "The Immigration Reform Act of 1965," in *The Familiar Made Strange: American Icons after the Transnational Turn*, Mark Philip Bradley and Brooke L. Blower, eds. (Ithaca: Cornell University Press, 2015): 128–29; Maria Cristina Garcia, *Seeking Refuge: Central American Immigration to Mexico, the United States, and Canada* (Berkeley: University of California Press, 2006); Gal Beckerman, *When They Come for Us, We'll Be Gone: The Epic Struggle to Save Soviet Jewry* (Boston: Houghton Mifflin, 2010).

12. Peter Novick, *The Holocaust in American Life* (New York: Houghton Mifflin, 2009): 209; Jeffrey Shandler, *While America Watches: Televising the Holocaust* (New York: Oxford University Press, 2000): 179, 203.

13. Bernard Levin, "We Must Not Leave It to That Nice Mr. Brezhnev," *London Times*, October 2, 1973: 16, cited in Robert Horvath, "'The Solzhenitsyn Effect': East European Dissidents and the Demise of Revolutionary Privilege," *Human Rights Quarterly* 29.4 (November 2007): 880. Ludmilla Alexeyeva's *Soviet Dissent: Contemporary Movements for National, Religious and Human Rights* (Middletown, CT: Wesleyan University Press, 1985) and Joshua Rubenstein's *Soviet Dissidents: Their Struggle for Human Rights* (Boston: Beacon Press 1980) were widely read activist accounts (Alexeyeva was a founding member of Moscow Helsinki Watch and later emigrated to the United States, whereas Rubenstein was a regional director for Amnesty USA in the 1970s) whose work reinforced the prevailing heroic American perspectives of the Soviet dissident movement. Although

their studies remain foundational, Benjamin Nathan's forthcoming work on Soviet dissidents promises to offer a more critical historical perspective.

14. Aleksandr Solzhenitsyn, *One Day in the Life of Ivan Denisovich* (New York: Dutton, 1963); Harrison Salisbury, "Books of the Times," *New York Times*, January 22, 1963: 7; Philip Rahv, "House of the Dead," *New York Review of Books*, February 1, 1963. See also laudatory reviews in *Time*, February 8, 1963: 8; *Newsweek*, February 4, 1963: 81; *Saturday Review*, February 9, 1963: 27; *New Yorker*, April 27, 1963: 168; and *New Republic*, May 11, 1963: 19.

15. Aleksandr Solzhenitsyn, *The First Circle* (New York: Harper and Row, 1968); Solzhenitsyn, *Cancer Ward* (New York: Dial Press, 1968): 601; Patricia Blake, "A Diseased Body Politic," *New York Times*, October 27, 1978: BR2; *Saturday Review*, November 9, 1968: 42.

16. Nobel Lecture, www.nobelprize.org/nobel_prizes/literature/laureates/1970/solzhen itsyn-lecture.html. On Solzhenitsyn and the Soviet state, see Michael Scammel, introduction to *The Solzhenitsyn Files* (Chicago: Edition Q, 1995): xvii–xxxix.

17. On the avalanche of U.S. press coverage of Solzhenitsyn's exile from the Soviet Union, see "7 Russians Make Forcible Arrest of Solzhenitsyn" and "Solzhenitsyn Exiled to West Germany," *New York Times*, February 13 and 14, 1974: 1. *The Washington Post, Boston Globe, Chicago Tribune*, and *Los Angeles Times* ran similar front-page stories on February 14 and 15, 1974. ABC, NBC, and CBS Evening News broadcasts devoted major coverage to Solzhenitsyn's arrest and deportation on February 12, 13, and 14, 1974; Vanderbilt Television News Archive.

18. *New York Post*, April 12, 1976; Jesse Helms, "Honorary Citizenship for Solzhenitsyn," *East Europe* (July 1974): 5; "Reagan's Plank Criticizes Ford-Kissinger Policies," *New York Times*, August 17, 1976: 1; 48; Arthur Schlesinger Jr., "The Solzhenitsyn We Refuse to See," *Washington Post*, June 25, 1978: D1. The best short survey of Solzhenitsyn's place in the American Cold War political imagination remains John D. Dunlop, "Solzhenitsyn's Reception in the United States," in *Solzhenitsyn in Exile*, John B. Dunlop et al., eds. (Stanford: Hoover Institution Press, 1985): 24–55; see also Kathleen Parthé, "The Politics of Détente-Era Cultural Texts, 1969–76," *Diplomatic History* 33.4 (September 2009): 723–33.

19. Aleksandr Solzhenitsyn, *The Gulag Archipelago: An Experiment in Literary Investigation* (New York: Harper & Row, 1973): x, 4–5, 587.

20. Joshua Rubenstein, "The Gulag Archipelago 1918–1956," *New Republic*, June 22, 1974: 22. *Gulag*'s sales are chronicled in Edward E. Ericson, Jr., "Introduction," in Alexsandr I. Solzhenitsyn, *The Gulag Archipelago*, abridged edition (New York: Harper & Row, 1985): xi–xii. The initial visibility of *Gulag* was heightened by a series of excerpts that in the *New York Times* beginning on December 30, 1973. Among the featured reviews of Volume 1 of *Gulag* that hailed it as a major political and cultural event were ones in the *New York Times Book Review*, June 16, 1974: 1; *Time*, July 15, 1974: 90; *Newsweek*, July 1, 1974: 65; *Saturday Review*, April 20, 1974: 22; and *New York Review of Books*, March 12, 1974: 3.

21. *New York Times Book Review*, June 16, 1974: 1.

22. Solzhenitsyn, *Gulag*: 4–5; Solzhenitsyn, *The Gulag Archipelago Two* (New York: Harper & Row, 1974): 383, 385. My reading of *Gulag* in this and the following paragraph is

informed by Susan Richards, "The Gulag Archipelago as 'Literary Document,'" in Dunlop et al., *Solzhenitsyn in Exile*: 145–163.

23. The classic formulation of the New Journalism appears in Wolfe, "The Birth of the New Journalism," *New York Magazine*, February 14, 1972.

24. Hedrick Smith, "The Intolerable Andrei Sakharov: Ideological Bombshells from an Atomic Scientist," *New York Times Magazine*, November 4, 1973. Smith's characterizations of Sakharov were common throughout the 1970s. See for instance "Sakharov/Soviet Dissidents," *ABC Evening News*, July 3, 1974; "Sakharov," *CBS Evening News*, November 19, 1975; and *Time* magazine's February 21, 1977, cover story on the "painfully modest" Sakharov titled "Human Rights: Dissidents v. Moscow" that called him the "Pilgrim of Conscience."

25. On the essay's reception see Jay Bergman, *Meeting the Demands of Reason: The Life and Thought of Andrei Sakharov* (Ithaca: Cornell University Press, 2009): 135; Joshua Rubenstein and Alexander Bribanov, eds., *The KGB File of Andrei Sakharov* (New Haven: Yale University Press, 2005): 1–2; and Andrei Sakharov, *Memoirs* (New York: Alfred A. Knopf, 1990): 288.

26. "Thoughts on Progress, Peaceful Coexistence, and Intellectual Freedom," *New York Times*, July 22, 1968: 14.

27. Andrei Sakharov, "On Aleksandr Solzhenitsyn's Letter to the Soviet Leaders," April 1974, reprinted in Michael Meerson-Aksenov and Boris Shragin, eds., *The Political, Social and Religious Thought of Russian 'Samizdat': An Anthology* (Belmont: Nordland Publishing Company, 1977): 291–301. My discussion here draws on Jay Bergman, *Meeting the Demands of Reason*: 211–17; and Sakharov's *Memoirs*. See also Aleksandr I. Solzhenitsyn, *Letter to the Soviet Leaders* (New York: Harper & Row, 1974).

28. Andrei Sakharov, "Peace, Progress, Human Rights," Nobel Lecture, December 11, 1975; www.nobelprize.org/nobel_prizes/peace/laureates/1975/sakharov-lecture.html.

29. Andrei Sakharov, *My Country and the World* (New York: Alfred A. Knopf, 1975): iv, 108.

30. Sakharov to Carter, January 21, 1977, *New York Times*, January 29, 1977: 2; Carter to Sakharov, February 5, 1977, *New York Times*, January 18, 1977: 3. See also Rubenstein and Gribanov, *KGB File of Andrei Sakharov*: 222–24; and Sakharov, *Memoir*: 462–70.

31. "The Charter 77 Declaration," *New York Times*, January 27, 1977: 16. On Havel, see John Keane, *Václav Havel, A Political Tragedy in Six Acts* (New York: Basic Books, 2000); and Eda Kriseová, *Václav Havel* (New York: St. Martin's Press, 1993). For a thoughtful and sustained discussion of the local vernaculars of Czech dissidence that is skeptical of its indigenous human rights frame, see Jonathan Bolton's *Worlds of Dissent: Charter 77, the Plastic People of the Universe, and Czech Culture under Communism* (Cambridge, MA: Harvard University Press, 2012).

32. "Department Comments on Subject of Human Rights in Czechoslovakia," *Department of State Bulletin* (January 26, 1977): 154; "US Asserts Prague Violates Covenants about Human Rights," *New York Times*, January 27, 1977: 1; "Prague's War of Nerves," *Washington Post*, January 22, 1977: A1; "Czechoslovakia/Human Rights Movement," *CBS Evening News*, January 10, 1977, Vanderbilt Television News Archive. See also "Man in the

News: A Thoroughly Politicized Czech Playwright," *New York Times*, October 25, 1979; "Portrait of a Playwright as an Enemy of the State," *New York Times*, March 23, 1986: H1; and Department of State Bureau of Research and Intelligence, "The Human Rights Movement in Czechoslovakia," October 11, 1979, http://nsarchive.gwu.edu/NSAEBB/NSAEBB213/usdocs/USDoc9.pdf.

33. On the relationship between Havel and various American literati, see Brian K. Goodman, "Philip Roth's Other Europe: Counter-Realism and the Late Cold War," *American Literary History* 27.4 (2015): 717–40.

34. Havel provides an extended discussion of the concern with "legality" in his essay, "The Power of the Powerless," originally written in 1977 and circulated in *samizdat* form; see Václav Havel, "The Power of the Powerless," in his *Open Letters: Selected Writings, 1965–1990* (New York: Vintage Books, 1992): 181–92. For a more critical perspective, see Bolton, *Worlds of Dissent*, 220–38.

35. The Plastic People and their significance for Charter 77 are best approached through Bolton, *Worlds of Dissent*: ch. 4. See also Václav Havel, "The Trial (October 1976)," in *Open Letters*: 102–8; *The Plastic People of the Universe* (Jana Chytilová, dir.; 2001); Richie Unterberger, *Underground Legends of Rock 'n' Roll* (San Francisco: Miller Freeman, 1998): 190–96; and Tom Stoppard, *Rock 'n' Roll* (London: Farber and Farber, 2007). On the broader rise and significance of a global counterculture in the 1960s, see contributors to the "AHR Forum: The International 1968," Parts I and II, *American Historical Review* 114.1 (February 2009): 42–135 and 114.2 (April 2009): 329–404; and Timothy Brown and Lorena Anton eds., *Between the Avant-Garde and the Everyday: Subversive Politics in Europe from 1957 to the Present* (Oxford: Berghahn Books, 2012).

36. "Stage: Havel's *Private View* Opens," *New York Times*, November 21, 1983: C16; John Simon, "Farcical Worlds," *New York Magazine* (December 5, 1983): 149–50. See also *New Yorker* (December 5, 1983): 183; *New Leader* (December 26, 1983): 16–17; and *New Republic* (March 12, 1984): 27–29. The most complete production histories of Havel's plays are in Helena Albertová's "A List of Theatrical Productions of the Plays of Václav Havel," in her *Václav Havel: A Citizen and a Playwright* (Prague: Divadelní ústav, 1999). On theater of the absurd and Havel, see Martin Esslin, *The Theatre of the Absurd*, 3rd ed. (New York: Vintage Books, 2004); and Carol Rocamora, *Acts of Courage: Václav Havel's Life in the Theater* (Hanover, NH: Smith and Kraus, 2004).

37. Václav Havel, "Audience," in *The Vanek Plays: Four Authors, One Character*, Marketa Goetz-Stankiewicz, ed. (Vancouver: University of British Columbia, 1987): 22, 23–24.

38. Václav Havel, "Protest" in *The Garden Party and Other Plays* (New York: Grove Press, 1993): 262; *New York Times*, November 21, 1983: C16.

39. Daily newspapers including the *New York Times, Boston Globe, Washington Post, Chicago Tribune, Los Angeles Times*, and *Christian Science Monitor* featured reviews of collections of Havel's political writings beginning in the late 1970s and early 1980s, as did periodicals such as the *Economist*, the *National Review*, the *New York Review of Books*, the *New York Times Book Review*, and the *Times Literary Supplement*. My discussion here is informed by a penetrating, and rare, analysis of Havel's work that explores the overlapping

concerns of his plays and political writing: D. Christopher Brooks, "The Art of the Political: Havel's Dramatic Literature as Political Theory," *East European Quarterly* 39.4 (Winter 2005): 491–521.

40. Havel, "Power of the Powerless": 132, 134, 135, 136, 143, 146, 147, 150.

41. Ibid.: 166, 161, 192, 194, 134.

42. Anthony Lewis, "South Africa's Gulag," *New York Times*, November 24, 1977: 19. See also "Death in South Africa," *Boston Globe*, September 17, 1977: 4; Roy Wilkins, "Left Cold by Leader's Death," *The Afro-American*, October 4, 1977: 4; "Something to be Answered For," *Los Angeles Times*, October 12, 1977: E6; Daniel Marolent, "Biko's Death a Great Tragedy," *New York Amsterdam News*, November 5, 1977: 9; "Steve Biko is Dead," *Nation*, October 15, 1977: 356–57; "Biko's Friend," *New Yorker*, May 29, 1978: 21–23; and Connor Cruise O'Brien, "Martyr," *New York Review of Books*, June 15, 1978 (www.nybooks.com/articles/archives/1978/jun/15/martyr/).

CHAPTER 7: AMERICAN VERNACULARS II

1. "Statement of Rev. Fred Morris," in *Torture and Oppression in Brazil: Hearing Before the Subcommittee on International Organizations and Movements of the Committee on Foreign Affairs, House of Representatives, 93rd Congress, 2nd Session, December 11, 1974* (Washington, DC: U.S. Government Printing Office, 1975): 6. A shorter version of Morris's testimony had appeared as "Torture, Brazilian Style," in *Time*, November 18, 1974.

2. On the congressional hearings, see Barbara J. Keys, *Reclaiming American Virtue: The Human Rights Revolution of the 1970s* (Cambridge, MA: Harvard University Press, 2014): 142–48; and Sarah Snyder, "'A Call for U.S. Leadership': Congressional Activism on Human Rights," *Diplomatic History* 37.2 (March 2013): 372–97.

3. On the growing global presence in the 1970s of human rights abuses in Latin America, see James N. Green, *We Cannot Remain Silent: Opposition to the Brazilian Military Dictatorship in the United States* (Durham: Duke University Press, 2010); Patrick William Kelly, "The 1973 Chilean Coup and the Origins of Transnational Human Rights Activism," *Journal of Global History*, 8.1 (March 2013): 165–186; and Kelly "'Magic Words': The Advent of Transnational Human Rights Activism in Latin America's Southern Cone in the Long 1970s," in *The Breakthrough: Human Rights in the 1970s*, Jan Eckel and Samuel Moyn, eds. (Philadelphia: University of Pennsylvania Press, 2013): 88–106. On the Letelier assassination, see Vanessa Walker, "At the End of Influence: The Letelier Assassination, Human Rights, and Rethinking Intervention in US-Latin American Relations," *Journal of Contemporary History*, 46.1 (2011): 109–35.

4. On United States policy toward Chile in the 1970s, see Peter Kornbluh, *The Pinochet File*, 2nd ed. (New York: New Press, 2013); and John Dinges, *The Condor Years* (New York: New Press, 2005). On the Latin American Cold War and the longer history of American empire in Latin America, see Tanya Harmer, *Allende's Chile and the Inter-American Cold War* (Chapel Hill: University of North Carolina Press, 2014); Walter LaFeber, *Inevitable Resolutions: The United States and Central America*, 2nd ed. (New York: W. W. Norton, 1993); and Greg Grandin, *Empire's Workshop: Latin America, the United States and the Rise of the New Imperialism* (New York: Metropolitan Books, 2006).

5. Steve J. Stern, *Battling for Hearts and Minds: Memory Struggles in Pinochet's Chile, 1973–1988* (Durham: Duke University Press, 2006): 97, 121, 93–100. On the central place of exiles in the emergence of Latin American human rights politics, see Patrick Kelly, "Sovereignty and Salvation: Transnational Human Rights Activism in Americas in the Long 1970s" (Ph.D. dissertation, University of Chicago, 2014); Mario Sznajder and Luis Roniger, *The Politics of Exile in Latin America* (Cambridge: Cambridge University Press, 2009); and Vania Markarian, *The Left in Transformation: Uruguayan Exiles and Latin American Human Rights Networks 1967–1984* (New York: Routledge, 2005).

6. Green, *We Cannot Remain Silent*: 4–5, passim.

7. Jacqueline Adams, *Art against Dictatorship: Making and Exporting Arpilleras under Pinochet* (Austin: University of Texas Press, 2013): 2.

8. Ibid.: 12, 260. My broader discussion of *arpilleras* is informed by Adams and by Stern, *Battling for Hearts and Minds*: 84–89.

9. The circulation of *arpilleras* in the United States emerges in *Los Angeles Times*, September 10, 1978: H4 *Chicago Tribune*, June 5, 1980: W4; January 23, 1983: NA2; *Washington Post*, September 20, 1979: B1; and *New York Times*, November 14, 1984: C13.

10. *Washington Post*, March 29, 1981: K3.

11. "Missing Persons, Anguished Mothers," *Washington Post*, July 18, 1979: E1. On the Madres, see Marguerite Guzman Bouvard, *Revolutionizing Motherhood: The Mothers of the Plaza de Mayo* (Lanham, MD: SR Books, 1994); Jo Fisher, *Mothers of the Disappeared* (Boston: South End Press, 1989); and Jean H. Quataert, *Advocating Dignity: Human Rights Mobilizations in Global Politics* (Philadelphia: University of Pennsylvania Press, 2009): ch. 3.

12. Jacobo Timerman, *Prisoner without a Name, Cell without a Number* (New York: Alfred A. Knopf, 1981: 50. The book was also excerpted at great length and widely circulated as "No Name, No Number" in the *New Yorker*, April 20, 1981.

13. Ibid.: 3, 4, 40, 148.

14. Ibid.: 72–77, 112–113, 116–17.

15. Ibid.: 140–41. On silences in Argentine civil society, see Sebastián Carassai, *The Argentine Silent Majority: Middle Classes, Politics, Violence, and Memory in the Seventies* (Durham: Duke University Press, 2014).

16. Irving Kristol, "The Timerman Affair," *Wall Street Journal*, May 29, 1981: 24. See also Mark Falcoff, "The Timerman Case," *Commentary* 42 (July 1981): 15–23. On the efforts of the Argentine government to discredit Timerman, see *New York Times*, January 3, 1979: A4; and Michael Walzer, "Timerman and His Enemies," *New York Review of Books*, September 24, 1981: 10–18.

17. *Newsweek*, May 18, 1981: 108; *New Republic*, June 20, 1981: 33; *New York Times Book Review*, May 10, 1981: 1, 30, 32. See also *Nation*, June 13, 1981: 733; *Time*, June 15, 1981: 79; and *The Economist*, June 13, 1981: 93.

18. Thomas Hauser, *The Execution of Charles Horman* (New York: Harcourt, Brace Jovanovich, 1978); *Missing* (dir., Costa-Gavras, 1982).

19. On U.S. culpability in the Chilean coup, see Harmer, *Allende's Chile and the Inter-American Cold War*; and Joaquín Fermandois, "The Persistence of a Myth: Chile in the Eye of the Cold War Hurricane," *World Affairs* 167.3 (Winter 2005): 101–12.

20. *New Republic*, March 10, 1982: 25–26; *Village Voice*, February 23, 1982: 45; and *National Review*, March 5, 1982: 209–10. See also Flora Lewis, "New Film by Costa-Gavras Examines the Chilean Coup," *New York Times*, February 7, 1982: 26.

21. *New York Times*, February 12, 1982: C14; *Commonweal*, April 9, 1982: 212. See also *Saturday Review*, February 1982: 48; *New York*, February 22, 1982: 67; *Nation*, April 17, 1982: 466–69; *National Review*, March 19, 1982: 308–9; and *Christian Science Monitor*, February 25, 1982: 14.

22. Kate Horsfield and Lyn Blumenthal, "Interview with Leon Golub," *Profile* 2.2 (March 1982): 22.

23. Thomas McEvilley, "Frontal Attack: The Word of Leon Golub," in *Leon Golub* (Malmö: Konsthall an Kulturhuset, 1993): 7; and *New York Times*, September 28, 1984: C29. For a full list of Golub's exhibitions in the United States during this period, see Jon Bird, *Leon Golub: Echoes of the Real* (London: Reaktion Books, 2000): 208–9, 215–16.

24. Bird, *Leon Golub: Echoes of the Real*: 101.

25. Ibid.: 111. On the tortured body as beyond language, see Elaine Scarry, *The Body in Pain: The Making and Unmaking of the World* (New York: Oxford University Press, 1985).

26. *Wall Street Journal*, May 29, 1981: 24. For a thoughtful discussions of conservative apprehensions of human rights in the 1970s see Keys, *Reclaiming American Virtue*: ch. 5; and Carl J. Bon Tempo, "Human Rights and the U.S. Republican Party in the Late 1970s," in *The Breakthrough*: 146–65.

27. Ronald Steel, "Where the Old Left Meets the New Left: Motherhood, Apple Pie and Human Rights," *New Republic*, June 4, 1977: 14.

28. G. B. Trudeau, *Doonesbury*, April 8, 1977; High School Seniors Poll, March 22, 1976, http://doonesbury.washingtonpost.com/strip/archive/timeline/1970.

CHAPTER 8: THE MOVEMENT

1. On the adoption of Sutanti Aidit, see Minutes of Amnesty USA Group 11, January 10, 1973, Folder 2, Box 15, Yadja Zeltman Papers 1972–1985, Amnesty International USA (AIUSA) Archives, University of Colorado Library. On the 1965 coup and the extrajudicial killings, see Benedict O'G. Anderson and Ruth McVey, *A Preliminary Analysis of the October 1, 1965 Coup in Indonesia* (Ithaca: Cornell Southeast Asia Program, 1971); John Roosa, *Pretext for Mass Murder: The September 30th Movement and Suharto's Coup d'État in Indonesia* (Madison: University of Wisconsin Press, 2006); Robert Cribb, "Genocide in Indonesia, 1965–66," *Journal of Genocide Research* 3.2 (2001): 219–31; Douglas Kammen and Katharine McGregor, eds., *The Contours of Mass Violence in Indonesia* (Honolulu: University of Hawaii Press, 2012); and two remarkable films on the perpetrators and victims of extrajudicial killings by Joshua Oppenheimer, *Act of Killing* (2012) and *The Look of Silence* (2015).

2. Amnesty International Secretariat "Dr. Sutanti Aidit Case Sheet," July 17, 1975, Folder 9, Box 17, Yadja Zeltman Papers, AIUSA Archives. On the experiences of imprisonment, see Greg Fealy, *The Release of Indonesia's Political Prisoners: Domestic versus Foreign Policy, 1975–1979* (Clayton: Monash University Centre of Southeast Asian Studies

Working Paper, 1995): 2–9; Carmel Budiardjo, *Surviving Indonesia's Gulag* (London: Cassell, 1996): 150–60; Baskara T. Wardaya, ed., *Truth Will Out: Indonesian Accounts of the 1965 Mass Violence* (Clayton: Monash University Publishing (2013).

3. Minutes of Amnesty USA Group 11, October 15, 1973, April 11, 1974, September 12, 1974, Folder 2, Box 15; Minutes, April 21, 1976, April 27, 1977, and January 4, 1978, Folder 3, Box 15; and Minutes, 11 April 1978, November 30, 1978, and April 26, 1979, Folder 4, Box 15, Yadja Zeltman Papers, AIUSA Archive.

4. "Amnesty International Group Development," September 25, 1970, Folder 1, Box 33, New York Office Papers, AIUSA Archive; and "Amnesty International Member Statistics," AI Index ORG 40/02–96, cited in Stephen Hopgood, *Keeper of the Flame: Understanding Amnesty International* (Ithaca: Cornell University Press, 2006): 109.

5. Human Rights Internet, *Human Rights Directory: North America* (Washington, DC, 1984). On the challenges of compiling such directories and the likelihood that some smaller local committees and groups were not included, see *Human Rights Directory: North America*: 5. By contrast to the American movement, Human Rights Internet put the numbers of human rights groups at 1,401 in Western Europe and 667 in the Global South in this same period, reinforcing a sense of the United States as a part (and not always the dominant part) of a larger global movement. See Human Rights Internet, *Human Rights Directory: Western Europe* (Washington, DC, 1982) and *Human Rights Directory: Latin America, Africa, Asia* (Washington, DC 1981).

6. The synoptic overview the 1970s American grassroots human rights movement in this and the following two paragraphs is informed by the data in *Human Rights Directory: North America*, which combines aggregate numbers with self-reporting for each individual organization on its activities and membership. On WOLA's significance, see Patrick William Kelly, "Sovereignty and Salvation: Transnational Human Rights Activism in the Long 1970s" (Ph.D. dissertation, University of Chicago, 2015): ch. 5. There are very few densely textured histories of the work of local American groups. Along with Kelly, important exceptions are James Green, *We Cannot Remain Silent: Opposition to the Brazilian Military Dictatorship in the United States* (Durham: Duke University Press, 2010); Gal Beckman, *When They Come for Us We'll Be Gone: The Epic Struggle to Save Soviet Jewry* (Boston: Houghton Mifflin, 2010): 211–410; and Ingu Hwang, "Making Human Rights Politics in South Korea in the 1970s" (Ph.D. dissertation, University of Chicago, 2014): chs. 1–3.

7. The American anti-apartheid movement gathered momentum in the 1970s with the formation of TransAfrica in July 1977 and more local campaigns for divestment, but the movement's real period of growth and its intersection with the broader human rights movement came after 1980. See Donald R. Culverson, "The Politics of the Anti-Apartheid Movement in the United States," *Political Science Quarterly* 111.1 (Spring 1996): 127–49. On China, see Rosemary Foot, *Rights Beyond Borders: the Global Community and the Struggle over Human Rights in China* (Oxford: Oxford University Press, 2000).

8. The engagement of American evangelicals in global human rights politics was largely a post-1970 phenomenon. The rough outlines emerge in Allen D. Hertzke, *Freeing God's Children: The Unlikely Alliance for Global Human Rights* (New York: Rowman & Littlefield,

2004). Melani McAlister's ongoing work promises to provide the definitive treatment; see, for instance, her "US Evangelicals and the Politics of Slave Redemption as Religious Freedom," *Southern Atlantic Quarterly* (Winter 2014): 87–108.

9. For a penetrating account of how Amnesty International's organizational structure simultaneously centralized the control of information and agenda setting while decentralizing through local member groups how its campaigns were implemented, see Wendy H. Wong, *Internal Affairs: How the Structure of NGOs Transforms Human Rights* (Ithaca: Cornell University Press, 2012): ch. 3. See also Hopgood, *Keeper of the Flame:* ch. 4.

10. "Interview with Peter Benensen," November 12, 1983, Folder 393 and "Interview with Keith Siviter," June 5, 1984, Folder 992, Amnesty International Research Department (London), International Secretariat Archives, Amnesty International, International Institute of Social History, Amsterdam, Netherlands.

11. "Amnesty International Handbook for Groups," c. 1973, Folder 442, International Secretariat Archives Amnesty International; "Indonesia: Instructions and Address List for Groups (Confidential)," July 1974, Folder 9, Box 17, Yadja Zeltman Papers, AISUA Archives. On the early history of tensions between Amnesty International and Amnesty USA stemming from differences over human rights practice, see Sarah B. Snyder, "Exporting Amnesty International to the United States: Transatlantic Human Rights Activism in the 1960s," *Human Rights Quarterly* 34.3 (August 2012): 779–99.

12. "Handbook for Action Groups," c. 1974, Folder 11, Box 134; David Hawk, "Report to the Membership and Board of Directors," 1976–77, Folder 7, Box 280; "Meeting of the Board of Directors," August 1, 1973, Folder 10, Box 2, New York Office Papers, AIUSA Archives. "Three Year Report on the Activities of the San Francisco Branch," 1976, Box 2, Folder 10, Papers of Ginetta Sagan, AIUSA Archives. Amnesty USA's internal history over the 1970s and the persisting tensions with the London International Secretariat are detailed in Keys, *Reclaiming American Virtue:* 184–205. See too Kenneth Cmiel, "The Emergence of Human Rights Politics in the United States," *Journal of American History* 86.3 (December 1999): 1237–38, 1240–44, 1246–48.

13. Testimony of Michael McClintock, "Court Reporter's Transcript of Testimony and Proceedings," *Romagoza Arce el al* v. *Garcia and Vides Casanova,* July 2, 2002, United States District Court, Southern District of Florida: 735. Interview with Ellen Moore and Scott Harrison, December 15, 2005.

14. "Direct Mail Fundraising," July 2, 1974, Folder 11, Box 134; A. Witney Ellsworth to AIUSA Board and Staff, March 14, 1980, Folder 9, Box 135; and "Report of the Fundraising Committee," June 1979, Folder 6, Box 3, New York Office Papers, AIUSA Archives.

15. "Cold Mail Control" attached to "Sample Direct Mail Letters," Folder 9, Box 135, New York Office Papers, AIUSA Archives.

16. "Sample Direct Mail Letters," Folder 9, Box 135, New York Office Papers, AIUSA Archives; for a very different reading of this letter, see Keys, *Reclaiming American Virtue:* 203.

17. "Amnesty International 1977: Prisoner of Conscience Year," Folder 9, Box 344, New York Office Papers, AIUSA Archives.

18. For a useful introduction to what is a massive literature on the relationship between knowledge production and the Cold War state, see David C. Engerman, "American Knowledge and Global Power," *Diplomatic History* 31.4 (September 2007): 599–622. One important starting point on the depolitization of American science after 1950 is Jessica Wang, *American Science in the Age of Anxiety: Scientists, Anti-Communism, and the Cold War* (Chapel Hill: University of North Carolina Press, 1999). Histories that consider the relationship between professions later drawn into human rights advocacy and the postwar American state include Daniel Kevles, "The Cold War and Hot Physics: Science, Security and the American State, 1945–1956," *Historical Studies in the Physical Sciences* 20 (1990): 239–64; Stuart A. Leslie, *The Cold War and American Science: The Military-Industrial-Academic Complex at MIT and Stanford* (New York: Columbia University Press, 1994); Bruce Cumings, "Boundary Displacement: The State, the Foundations, and International and Area Studies during and after the Cold War," in his *Parallax Visions* (Durham: Duke University Press, 1999): 173–204; and Frederick Cooper and Randall M. Packer, eds., *International Development and the Social Sciences: Essays on the History and Production of Knowledge* (Berkeley: University of California Press, 1998).

19. Lawrence S. Wittner, *Confronting the Bomb: A Short History of the World Disarmament Movement* (Stanford: Stanford University Press, 2009); and Kyle Harvey, *American Anti-Nuclear Activism, 1975–1990: The Challenge of Peace* (London: Palgrave Macmillan, 2014).

20. Linda J. Lear, *Rachel Carson: Witness for Nature* (New York: Henry Holt, 1997): 375–453; Joshua P. Howe, *Behind the Curve: Science and the Politics of Global Warming* (Seattle: University of Washington Press, 2014): ch. 2; Michael Egan, *Barry Commoner and the Science of Survival: The Remaking of American Environmentalism* (Cambridge, MA: MIT Press, 2007); Adam Rome, *The Genius of Earth Day: How a 1970s Teach-In Unexpectedly Made the First Green Generation* (New York: Hill and Wang, 2013): ch. 1; David Zelko, *Make It A Greenpeace!: The Rise of Counterculture Environmentalism* (New York: Oxford University Press, 2013); and Richard J. Lazarus, *The Making of Environmental Law* (Chicago: University of Chicago Press, 2004): ch 5. On the rise of the American environmental movement more generally see, Samuel B. Hays, *Beauty, Health, and Permanence: Environmental Politics in the United States, 1955–1985* (New York: Cambridge University Press, 1987); and Philip Shabecoff, *The Fierce Green Fire: The American Environmental Movement*, rev. ed. (Washington, DC: Island Press, 2003). On the global dimensions of the American environmental movement in the 1970s, see Stephen Macekura, *Of Limits and Growth: Global Environmentalism and 'Sustainable Development' in the Twentieth Century* (Cambridge: Cambridge University Press, 2015).

21. My discussion of professional reenchantment builds on Michal Givoni, "Humanitarian Governance and Ethical Cultivation: Médecins sans frontières and Advent of the Expert-Witness," *Millennium* 40.1 (2011): 43–63.

22. Federation of American Scientist human rights concerns emerge in issues of its newsletter, *FAS Public Interest Report*, devoted to Sakharov and other Soviet scientists in issues dated October 1973, December 1975, March 1976, March 1980 (reporting on their adoption of Sakharov), and January 1982. On the work of the National Academy of

Sciences Human Rights Committee, see Robert W. Kates, "Human Issues in Human Rights," *Science* 201.4355 (11 August 1978): 502–6.

23. Alfredo Jadresic, "Doctors and Torture: An Experience as a Prisoner," *Journal of Medical Ethics* 6.3 (September 1980): 124–27.

24. Robert M. Veatch and Diane Fenner, "The Teaching of Medical Ethics in the United States of America," *Journal of Medical Ethics* 1.2 (July 1975): 99–103; and Eric Stover, *The Open Secret: Torture and the Medical Profession in Chile* (Washington, DC: AAAS Committee on Scientific Freedom and Responsibility, 1987).

25. Early AAAS human rights resolutions include "Freedom for Soviet Scientists, March 1, 1974," "Assisting Chilean Scholars, March 1, 1974," "Position of Scholars in Chile, January 31, 1975" (http://archives.aaas.org/docs/resolutions.php?t_id=56); John T. Edsall, *Scientific Freedom and Responsibility* (Washington, DC: American Association for the Advancement of Science, December 1974). Reliance of the AAAS committee on the 1977 British Council for Science and Society's report, *Scholarly Freedom and Human Rights: The Problem of Persecution and Oppression of Science and Scientists*, emerges in John Edsall and Joel Primack, "Human Rights," *Science* 195.4275 (January 21, 1977): 245–46.

26. The newsletter of the AAAS Committee on Scientific Freedom and Responsibility, *Clearinghouse Report on Science and Human Rights*, offers detailed coverage of this work beginning in 1979; issues in Mif 936, Human Rights Documents Micromaterial Collection, Florida State University Law School. On the AAAS fact-finding missions, see Eric Stover, *Scientists and Human Rights in Argentina since 1976* (Washington, DC: American Association for the Advancement of Science, 1981); Christopher Joyce and Eric Stover, *Witnesses from the Grave: The Stories Bones Tell* (Boston: Little, Brown & Company, 1991): 215–305; and Richard Goldstein et al., *Human Rights and the Medical Profession in Uruguay since 1972* (Washington, DC: American Association for the Advancement of Science, 1982).

27. Thomas B. Jabine and Douglas A. Samuelson, "Human Rights of Statisticians and Statistics of Human Rights: Early History of the American Statistical Association's Committee on Scientific Freedom and Human Rights," in *Statistical Methods for Human Rights*, J. Asher et al., eds. (2008): 183, 185 and 181–193 and passim; Richard P. Claude and Thomas B. Jabine, eds., "Symposium: Statistical Issues in the Field of Human Rights," *Human Rights Quarterly* 8.4 (November 1986): 551–699.

28. Cmiel, "The Emergence of Human Rights Politics in the United States": 1244; David Heaps, "Draft Report on Human Rights," August 1975, #005643 and International Division Conference, Session III-1, "Human Rights and Intellectual Freedom," September 20, 1975, #009959, Ford Foundation Archives cited in Patrick Kelly, *Sovereignty and Salvation*: 122, 125.

29. Shepard Forman and Kojo Bentsi-Enchill, "International Human Rights Efforts: Human Rights and Governance Programs," June 1983, #006622, Ford Foundation Archives; Ford Foundation, *Annual Report* (1979); MacArthur Foundation, *Advancing Human Rights and International Justice* (2009).

30. Stover, *The Open Secret*; Richard P. Claude et al., *Health Professionals and Human Rights in the Philippines* (Washington, DC: American Association for the Advancement of Science, 1987).

31. "Proceedings of the Ad Hoc Commission on Justice for Anatoly Sharansky," *Human Rights* 6.3 (Spring 1977): 245–300. The case for reversing the ABA position was made forcefully in "Ratification Now," *Human Rights* 7.2 (September 1978): 36–39, 51–52.

32. Louis B. Sohn and Thomas Buergenthal, eds., *International Protection of Human Rights* (Indianapolis: Bobbs-Merrill Company, Inc., 1973) and *Basic Documents on International Protection of Human Rights* (Indianapolis: Bobbs-Merrill Company, Inc., 1973). See also Buergenthal's memoir of his time in Auschwitz and its impact on his work in human rights law, *A Lucky Child* (Boston: Back Bay Books, 2015).

33. Richard B. Lillich and Frank C. Newman, *International Human Rights: Problems of Law and Politics* (Boston: Little, Brown, and Company, 1979).

34. On the heightened attention given to human rights in law schools in the 1970s, see Samuel Moyn, *The Last Utopia: Human Rights in History* (Cambridge, MA: Harvard University Press, 2012): 201–11. On Newman and ABA efforts, see "Transcript of Oral History Interview with Frank C. Newman," California State Archives State Government Oral History Program (www.sos.ca.gov/archives/oral-history/pdf/newman.pdf): 261–309; and "A Plan for Promoting the Teaching of International Human Rights in the United States" (ABA Subcommittee on Human Rights, 1980); and "Report on the Proceedings of the first International Human Rights Teaching Institute held July 28 through August 1, 1980" (ABA Subcommittee on Human Rights Education, 1980) in Mif 936.

35. Alice H. Henkin, *Human Dignity: The Internationalization of Human Rights* (New York: Aspen Institute for Humanistic Studies, 1979); and *The Road to Madrid: Developing a Western Consensus on Human Rights* (New York: Aspen Institute for Humanistic Studies, 1980).

36. The work of the Lawyer's Committee emerges in the *Lawyer's Committee Bulletin* and *Justice in El Salvador: A Case Study* (1982) in Mif 936. Similarly, activities of the International Human Rights Law Group are detailed in its newsletter titled *The Law Group Docket* and its quarterly "Activities Reports" also in Mif 936.

37. The early history of Human Rights Watch emerges in the memoirs by Aryeh Neier and Jeri Laber along with Neier's *The International Human Rights Movement: A History* (Princeton University Press, 2012): ch. 9. See Neier, *Taking Liberties: Four Decades in the Struggle for Rights* (New York: PublicAffairs, 2005); and Jeri Laber, *The Courage of Strangers: Coming of Age with the Human Rights Movement* (New York: PublicAffairs, 2005). Archivally based histories of Human Rights Watch are only starting to be written. One early promising effort is Peter Slezkine, "From Helsinki to Human Rights Watch: How an American Cold War Monitoring Group Became an International Human Rights Organization," *Humanity* (Winter 2014): 345–70. On the global networks of which Helsinki Watch was a part, see Sarah B. Snyder, *Human Rights Activism and the End of the Cold War: A Transnational History of the Helsinki Network* (Cambridge: Cambridge University Press, 2011).

38. "Statement of Michael H. Posner, Nominee for Assistant Secretary of State Bureau of Democracy, Human Rights and Labor before the Senate Foreign Relations Committee," July 28, 2009, www.foreign.senate.gov/imo/media/doc/PosnerTestimony090728a.pdf; interview with Eric Stover, October 28, 2014.

39. "Rhonda Copelon, Lawyer in Groundbreaking Human Rights Cases, Dies at 65," *New York Times*, May 8, 2010.

40. *Filártiga* v. *Peña-Irala*, 630 F.2d 876 (2d Cir. 1980), 878. The fullest discussion of the events that gave rise to the *Filártiga* case can be found in Richard Allan White, *Breaking Silence: The Case That Changed the Face of Human Rights* (Washington, DC: Georgetown University Press, 2004). On the jurisprudence under the Alien Torts Statute after the *Filártiga* decision, see George P. Fletcher, *Tort Liability for Human Rights Abuses* (Portland: Hart Publishing, 2008); and Elizabeth Borgwardt, "Commerce and Complicity: Corporate Accountability for Human Rights Abuses as a Legacy of Nuremberg," *Diplomatic History* 34.4 (September 2010): 627–40.

41. David Kennedy, "Spring Break," *Texas Law Review* 63.5 (May 1985): 1377–1423; a revised version appeared as *The Rights of Spring: A Memoir of Innocence Abroad* (Princeton: Princeton University Press, 2009). Citations here are from the 1985 version.

42. Ibid.: 1380, 1386–87.

43. Ibid.: 1396, 1415. The complex dynamics of human rights talk and practice also emerge with probing clarity in Geoffrey Robinson, "'*If You Leave Us Here We Will Die*': How Genocide was Stopped in East Timor* (Princeton: Princeton University Press, 2009); and in James Dawes, *That the World May Know: Bearing Witness to Atrocity* (Cambridge, MA: Harvard University Press, 2007).

44. I build here on Greg Grandin's arguments about the somewhat different but related work of truth and reconciliation commissions in the 1990s, "The Instruction of Great Catastrophe: Truth Commissions, National History and State Formation in Argentina, Chile and Guatemala," *American Historical Review* 110.1 (February 2005): 46–67.

45. *Amnesty International Report 1980* (London, Amnesty International Publications, 1980): 2, 4, 7. See also Jan Eckel, "'Under a Magnifying Glass': The International Human Rights Crusade against Chile in the Seventies," in *Human Rights in the Twentieth-Century*, ed. Stefan-Ludwig Hoffmann (Cambridge: Cambridge University Press, 2011): 312–42.

46. See East Timor and Indonesia, see Robinson, "*If You Leave Us Here We Will Die*": chs. 2–4 Bradley R. Simpson, "Denying the 'First Right': The United States, Indonesia and the Ranking of Human Rights by the Carter Administration," *International History Review* 31.4 (December 2009): 798–826; and Simpson, "'Illegally and Beautifully': The United States, the Indonesian Invasion of East Timor, and the International Community, 1974–1976," *Cold War History* 5.3 (August 2005): 281–315. On unevenness more generally see, Barbara Keys, "Anti-Torture Politics: Amnesty International, the Greek Junta and the Origins of the Human Rights 'Boom' in the United States," in *Human Rights Revolution: An International History*, Akira Iriye et al., eds. (New York: Oxford University Press, 2012): 201–22.

47. On the opening up of Amnesty's mandate in the 1990s, see Hopgood, *Keeper of the Flame*: 32–33, 118–120.

48. Boston Meeting, November 4, 1977 in "Notes by Maggie [Magaret Bierne]," February 1977, Folder 18, Box 233, New York Office, AIUSA Archives.

49. USA 69, November 9, 1977, "Notes by Maggie," Folder 18, Box 233, New York Office, AIUSA Archives.

50. USA 86, December 1, 1977, "Notes by Maggie," Folder 18, Box 233, New York Office, AIUSA Archives.

51. "Notes by Maggie," February 1977. USA 98 Notes, November 20, 1977; USA 24 Notes, November 10, 1977, Salt Lake City Notes, February 2, 1978, Folder 18, Box 233, New York Office, AIUSA Archives.

52. The place of human rights in conservative American politics of the 1970s is addressed in Keys, *Reclaiming American Virtue*. ch. 5; and Carl Bon Tempo, "Human Rights and the U.S. Republican Party in the Late 1970s," in *The Breakthrough: Human Rights in the 1970s*, Jan Eckel and Samuel Moyn, eds. (Philadelphia: University of Pennsylvania Press, 2014): 147–65. Bon Tempo's ongoing work promises to offer the authoritative history of the American conservative turn to human rights in the 1980s.

53. On the European Court, see Jonas Christoffersen and Mikael Madsen, eds., *The European Court of Human Rights between Law and Politics* (Oxford: Oxford University Press, 2011). For a journalistic account, see Michael Goldhaber, *A People's History of the European Court of Human Rights* (New Brunswick: Rutgers University Press, 2007).

54. "Battle over Gay Rights," *Newsweek*, June 6, 1977. Human rights language had a secondary place in 1970s African American civil rights advocacy, but one of its local iterations is traced in Winston A. Grady-Willis, *Challenging U.S. Apartheid: Atlanta and Black Struggles for Human Rights, 1960–1977* (Durham: Duke University Press, 2006).

55. On the employment of human rights language by Native Americans in the 1970s, see Bradley Simpson, "The United States and the Curious History of Self-Determination," *Diplomatic History* 36.4 (2012): 691–93; and Daniel Cobb, *Native Activism in Cold War America: The Struggle for Sovereignty* (Lawrence: University of Kansas Press, 2010).

56. Amnesty International USA, "Release of Indonesian Political Prisoners," December 1979, Folder 9, Box 17, Yadja Zelman Papers, AIUSA Archive.

CODA: THE SENSE OF AN ENDING

1. See www.hrw.org/sites/default/files/related_material/financial-statements-2014.pdf.

2. *Time*, July 6, 1987: 92; "'We the People' Loses Appeal with People around the World," *New York Times*, February 6, 2012: A1; "U.S. Supreme Court Justice Ruth Bader Ginsberg to Egyptians: Look to the Constitutions of South Africa or Canada, Not to the U.S. Constitution," Middle East Media Research Institute TV Monitor Project, January 30, 2012 (www.memritv.org/clip/en/3295.htm); and "U.S. Court, a Long Time Beacon, Is Now Guiding Fewer Nations," *New York Times*, September 18, 2008: A1. On these processes more generally, see David S. Law and Mila Versteeg, "The Declining Influence of the U.S. Constitution," *New York University Law Review* 87 (June 2012): 762–858; and Hanne Hagtvedt Vik, "How Constitutionalism Concerns Framed the US Contribution to the International Human Rights Regime from its Inception, 1947–53," *International History Review* 34.4 (December 2012): 887–909.

3. *Lawrence v. Texas*, 539 U.S. 558, 598 (2003) (Scalia, J., dissenting). By contrast, Associate Justice Stephen G. Breyer offers a robust defense of the use of international law by U.S.

courts in his *The Court and the World: American Law and the New Global Realities* (New York: Alfred Knopf, 2015).

4. See, for instance, www.congress.gov/bill/113th-congress/house-joint-resolution/54.

5. *Kiobel* v. *Royal Dutch Petroleum Co*, 133 S.Ct. 1359 (2013). On concerns with "judicial imperialism," see José Cabranes, "Withholding Judgment: Why US Courts Shouldn't Make Foreign Policy," *Foreign Affairs*, September/October 2015 (www.foreignaffairs .com/articles/2015-08-18/withholding-judgment). For a sharp critique of the *Kiobel* decision and a sustained defense of the use of the Alien Torts Statute for human rights purposes, see Breyer, *The Court and the World*: ch. 6.

6. See www.naacp.org/news/entry/naacp-brings-u.s.-voting-rights-problems-before-un-human-rights-commission.

7. President George W. Bush, "Address from the East Room: President Discusses Creation of Military Commission to Try Suspected Terrorists," September 6, 2006, www.georgewbush-whitehouse.archives.gov/news/releases/2006/09/20060906-3 .html. On Abu Ghraib, see Seymour M. Hersh, "Torture at Abu Ghraib," *New Yorker*, May 10, 2004 (www.newyorker.com/magazine/2004/05/10/torture-at-abu-ghraib); and Philip Gourevitch and Errol Morris, *Standard Operating Procedure* (New York: Penguin Press, 2008.

8. *ICRC Report on the Treatment of Fourteen "High Value Detainees" in CIA Custody*, February 2007: 10.

9. On the longer history of American state practices of torture, see Alfred W. McCoy, *The Question of Torture: CIA Interrogation from the Cold War to the War on Terror* (New York: Henry Holt & Company, 2006).

10. Bush, "Address from the East Room." For a careful dissection of Bush policy, see Mark Daner, *Torture and Truth: American, Abu Ghraib and the War on Terror* (New York: New York Review Books, 2004); Jane Mayer, *The Dark Side: The Inside Story of How the War on Terror Turned into a War on American Ideals* (New York: Doubleday, 2008); and Karen J. Greenberg and Joshua L. Dratel, eds., *The Torture Papers: The Road to Abu Ghraib* (New York: Cambridge University Press, 2005).

11. *Human Rights Watch World Report 2006* (New York: Seven Stories Press, 2006): 2.

12. See, for instance, Michael Walzer, "Political Action: The Problem of Dirty Hands," and Alan Dershowitz, "Tortured Reasoning," in *Torture: A Collection*, Sanford Levinson, ed. (Oxford: Oxford University Press, 2004): 61–76 and 257–80.

13. Pew Research Center, "About Half See CIA Interrogation Methods as Justified," December 2014 (www.people-press.org/files/2014/12/12-15-14-CIA-Interrogation-Release .pdf); "Can They Do That?: Trump Favors Torture That's Illegal," *New York Times*, 29 February 2016.

14. Eric A. Posner, *The Twilight of Human Rights Law* (New York: Oxford University Press, 2014): 7 and passim; Stephen Hopgood, *The Endtimes for Human Rights* (Ithaca: Cornell University Press, 2013): vii–x and ch. 5. The larger tensions and partialities in contemporary global human rights talk are usefully sketched in Susan Marks, "Four Human Rights Myths," in *Human Rights: Old Problems, New Possibilities*, David Kinley, Wojciech Sadurski, and Kevin Walton, eds. (London: Edward Elgar, 2013): 217–35.

15. Beth A. Simmons, *Mobilizing for Human Rights: International Law in Domestic Politics* (Cambridge: Cambridge University Press, 2009): 236–53; and Kathryn Sikkink, *The Justice Cascade: How Human Rights Prosecutions Are Changing the World* (New York: Norton, 2011): 191. More measured appraisals of the impact of human rights treaties on national practice also emerge in Oona Hathaway, "Do Human Rights Treaties Make a Difference?" *Yale Law Journal* 111 (2002): 1935–2042; and Eric Neumayer, "Do International Human Rights Treaties Improve Respect for Human Rights?" *Journal of Conflict Resolution* 49.6 (December 2005): 925–53.

16. Compare, for instance, Robert Putnam's lament in his *Bowling Alone* (New York: Simon and Schuster, 2000) to Sidney G. Tarrow, *Power in Movement: Social Movements and Contentious Politics*, 3rd ed. (Cambridge: Cambridge University Press, 2011). For nuanced appraisals of the relationship between the grassroots and professionalism in the American environmental movement, see Christopher J. Bosso, *Environment Inc.: From Grassroots to Beltway* (Lawrence: University of Kansas Press, 2005) and David Zelko, *Make It a Greenpeace! The Rise of Countercultural Environmentalism* (New York: Oxford University Press, 2013).

17. On Witness, see Matthew Shaer, "'The Media Doesn't Care What Happens Here': Can Amateur Journalism Bring Justice to Rio's Favelas?," *New York Times Magazine*, February 18, 2015 (www.nytimes.com/2015/02/22/magazine/the-media-doesnt-care-what-happens-here.html?_r=0); and https://witness.org. For a thoughtful discussion of the structural and ideational complexities embedded in the work of contemporary human rights fieldworkers that moves productively beyond a framework that puts grassroots and professional human rights concerns in opposition to one another, see John Shifton, *Violence All Around* (Cambridge, MA: Harvard University Press, 2015).

18. On slacktivism, see Evgeny Morozov, *The Net Delusion: The Dark Side of Internet Freedom* (New York: PublicAffairs, 2011); and Hopgood, *The Endtimes for Human Rights*: 106–9.

19. For examples of the country reports, see *Human Rights Watch World Report 2015* (www.hrw.org/sites/default/files/wr2015_web.pdf); and U.S. Department of State Bureau of Democracy, Human Rights, and Labor, *Country Reports on Human Rights Practices for 2014* (www.state.gov/j/drl/rls/hrrpt/humanrightsreport/index.htm#wrapper).

20. On forensic science and human rights advocacy, see http://physiciansforhumanrights.org/justice-forensic-science/ifp/; Christopher Joyce and Eric Stover, *Witnesses from the Grave: The Stories Bones Tell* (Boston: Little Brown, 1986); and Sonali Thakkar, "Human Rights, Human Remains: Forensic Anthropology and the Personhood of the Dead" (unpublished paper in the possession of the author).

21. See, for instance, Nancy Coombs, *Fact Finding Without Facts: The Uncertain Evidentiary Foundation of International Criminal Tribunals* (Cambridge U Press, 2010). For a very different argument that emphasizes how forensic evidence now trumps testimonials, see Thomas Keenan and Eyal Weizman, *Mengel's Skull: The Advent of a Forensics Aesthetics* (Berlin: Sternberg Press, 2012).

22. Stanlie James's work in progress explores the engagements of a variety of African American women in the public and private practices of global human rights law.

23. In the spirit of full disclosure, I direct one of those programs at the University of Chicago.

24. Interview with Lauren Stokes, November 2010; Laura T. Raynolds, Douglas Murray and John Wilkinson, eds., *Fair Trade: The Challenge of Transforming Globalization* (New York: Routledge, 2007); "Slavery and the Shrimp on Your Plate," *New York Times*, June 21, 2014.

25. Pierre Barberie, "Zoe Strauss under I-95," in *Zoe Strauss: 10 Years*, Pierre Barberie, ed. (Philadelphia: Philadelphia Museum of Art, 2012): 121 and passim.

26. Tara Murtha, "Photographer Zoe Strauss Took This Photograph 10 Years Ago: Here Is the Story of Mattress Flip," *Philadelphia Weekly*, January 10, 2012 (www.philadelphia weekly.com/news-and-opinion/Zoe-Strauss-Mattress-Flip-Laurence-Boo-Rose-Philadelphia-Museum-of-Art.html).

27. Barberie, "Zoe Strauss under I-95": 120.

Index